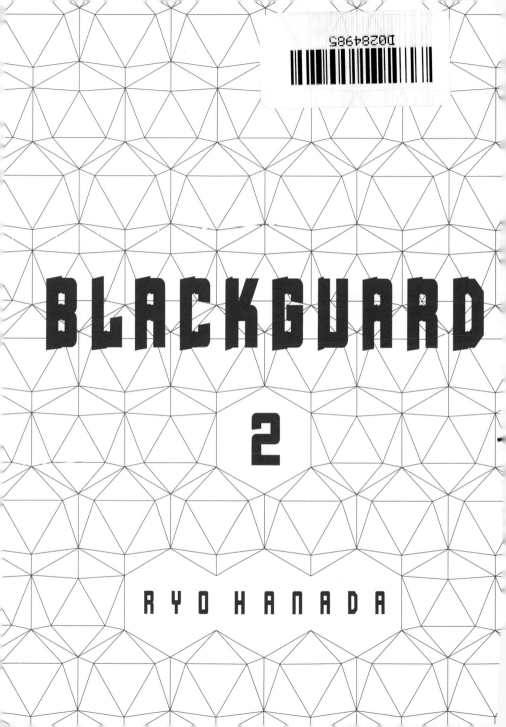

BLACKGUARD

2

RYO HANADA

CONTENTS

WARNING: This volume contains references to suicide. If you or someone you know has suicidal thoughts or feelings, you are not alone, and there is free, 24/7 help.

National Suicide Prevention Lifeline offers confidential support for those in crisis or emotional distress. You can call 1-800-273-TALK (8255) or go to SuicidePreventionLifeline.org for free, 24/7 help.

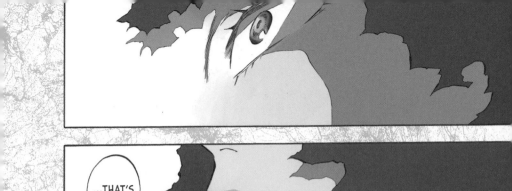

...THAT'S HIM.

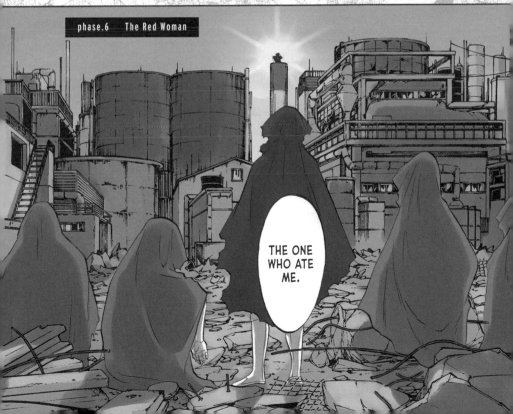

phase.6   The Red Woman

THE ONE WHO ATE ME.

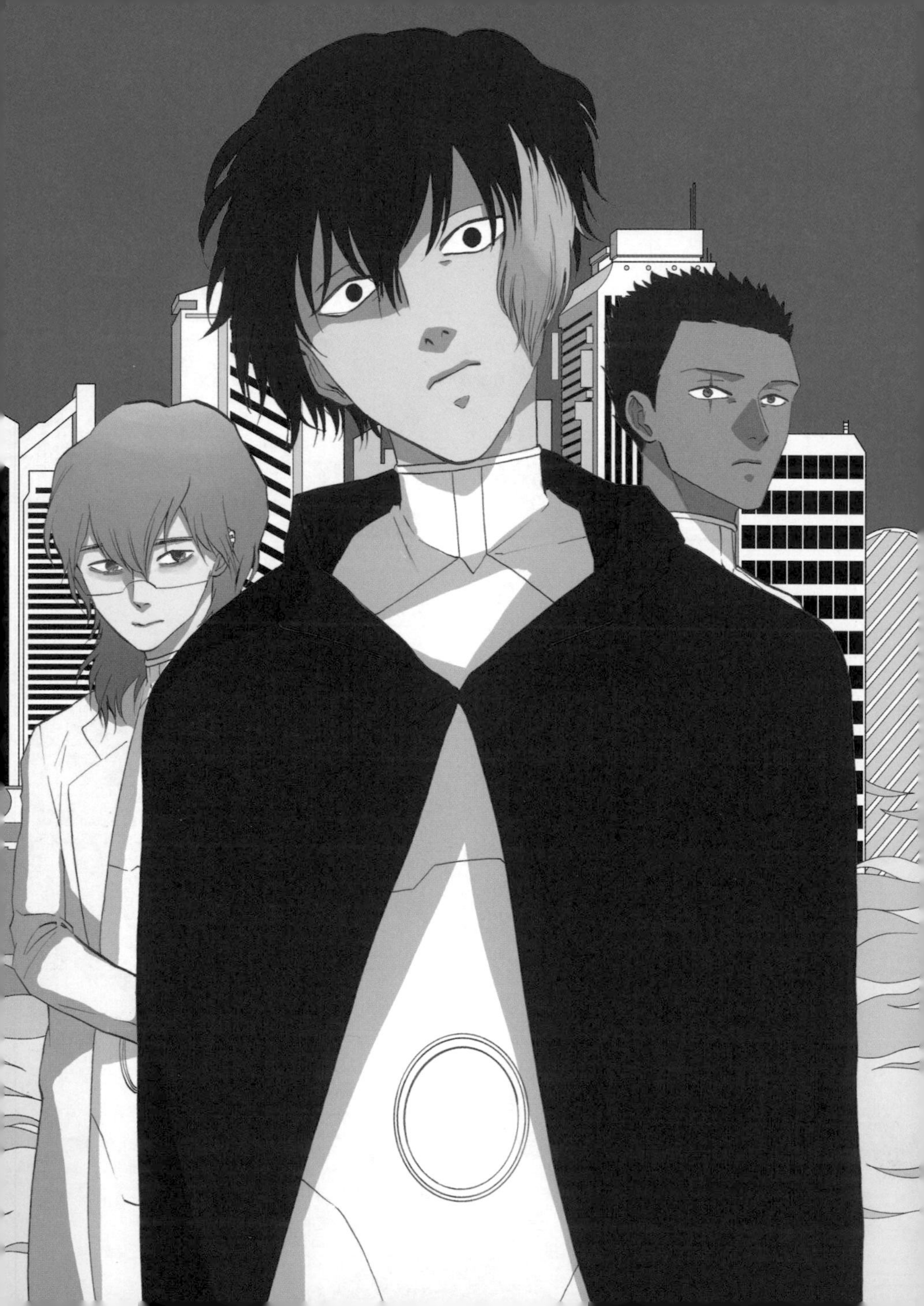

phase.6 The Red Woman

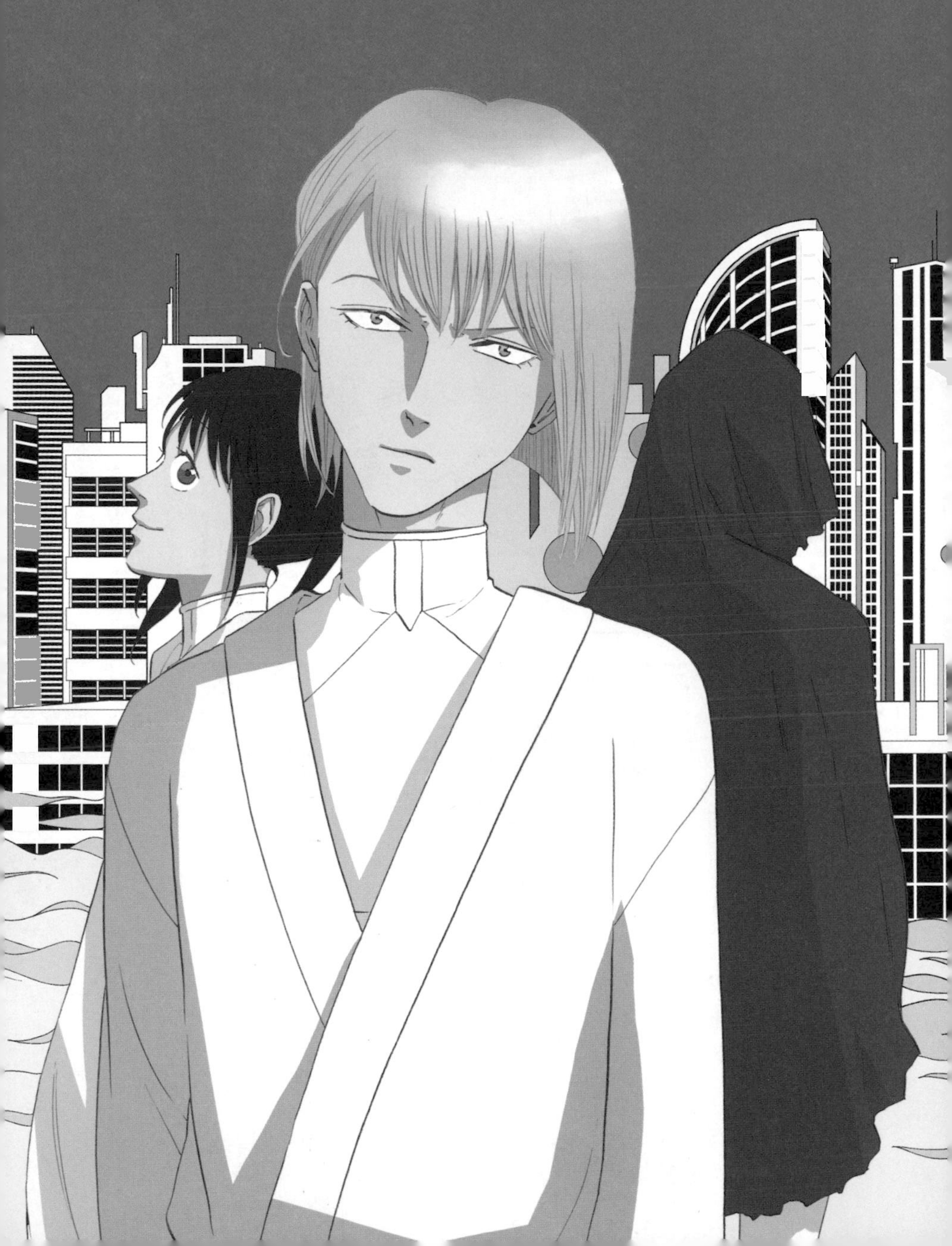

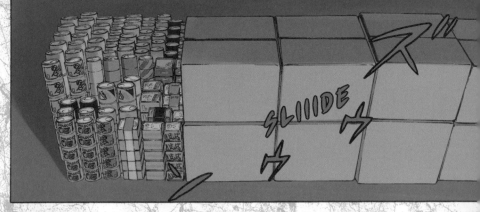

SLIIIDE

WELL...

...WHAT THE HELL ARE THESE CANS AND POUCHES?!

FOO

BOOM

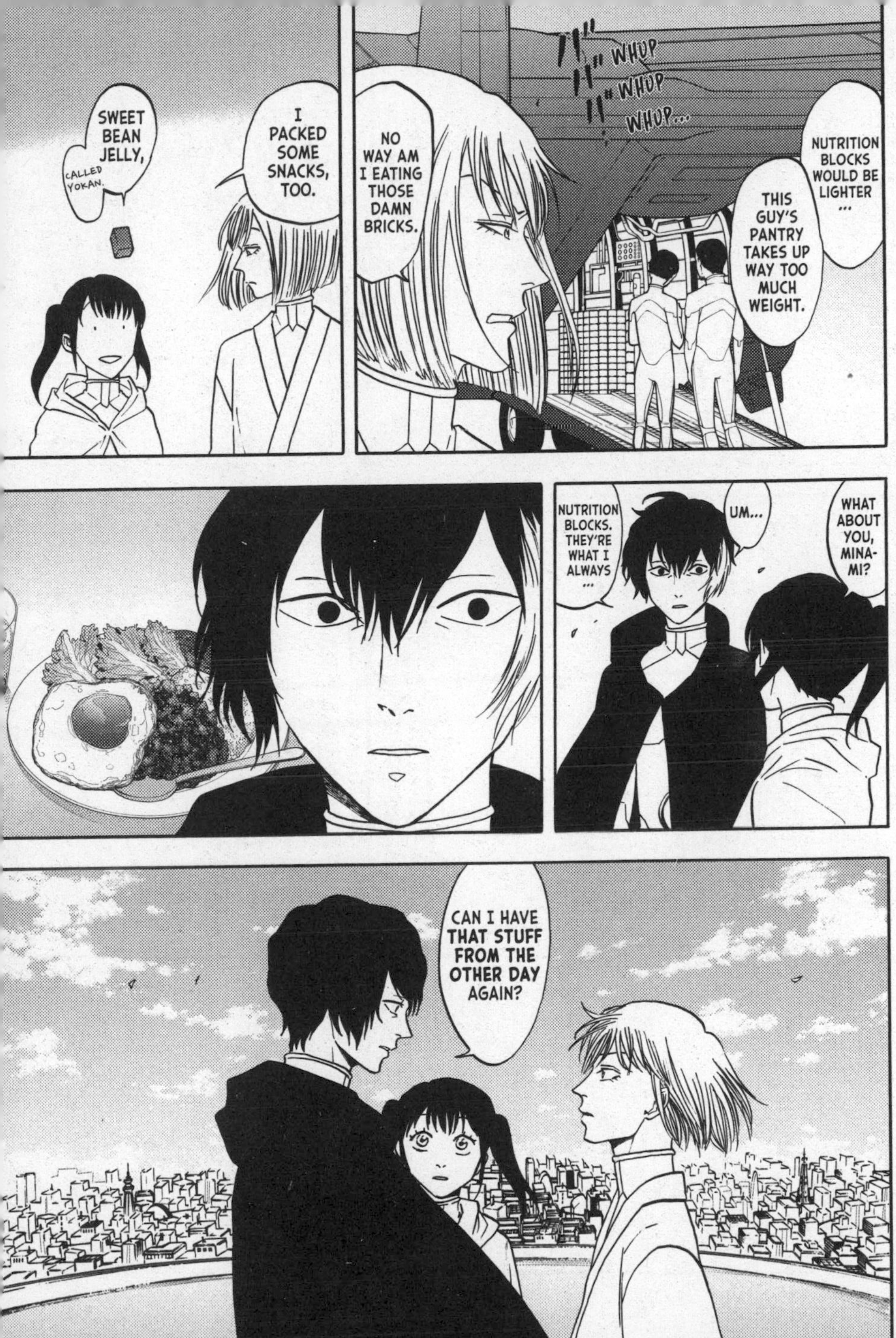
WHUP WHUP WHUP...
NUTRITION BLOCKS WOULD BE LIGHTER...
THIS GUY'S PANTRY TAKES UP WAY TOO MUCH WEIGHT.
NO WAY AM I EATING THOSE DAMN BRICKS.
I PACKED SOME SNACKS, TOO.
SWEET BEAN JELLY,
CALLED YOKAN.
WHAT ABOUT YOU, MINAMI?
UM...
NUTRITION BLOCKS. THEY'RE WHAT I ALWAYS...
CAN I HAVE THAT STUFF FROM THE OTHER DAY AGAIN?

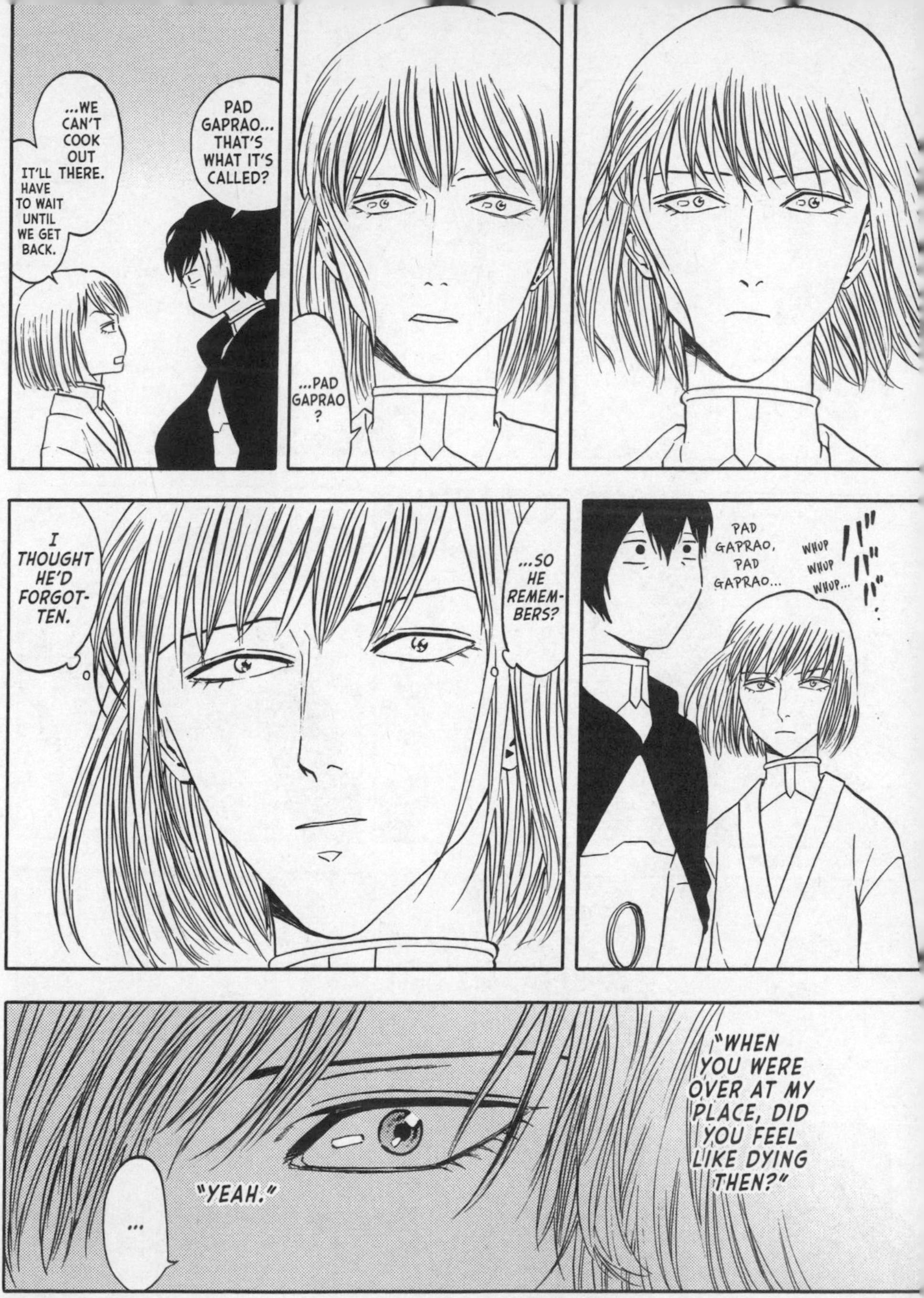
...PAD GAPRAO?
PAD GAPRAO... THAT'S WHAT IT'S CALLED?
...WE CAN'T COOK OUT THERE. IT'LL HAVE TO WAIT UNTIL WE GET BACK.
PAD GAPRAO, PAD GAPRAO...
WHUP WHUP WHUP...
...SO HE REMEMBERS?
I THOUGHT HE'D FORGOT-TEN.
"WHEN YOU WERE OVER AT MY PLACE, DID YOU FEEL LIKE DYING THEN?"
"YEAH."
...

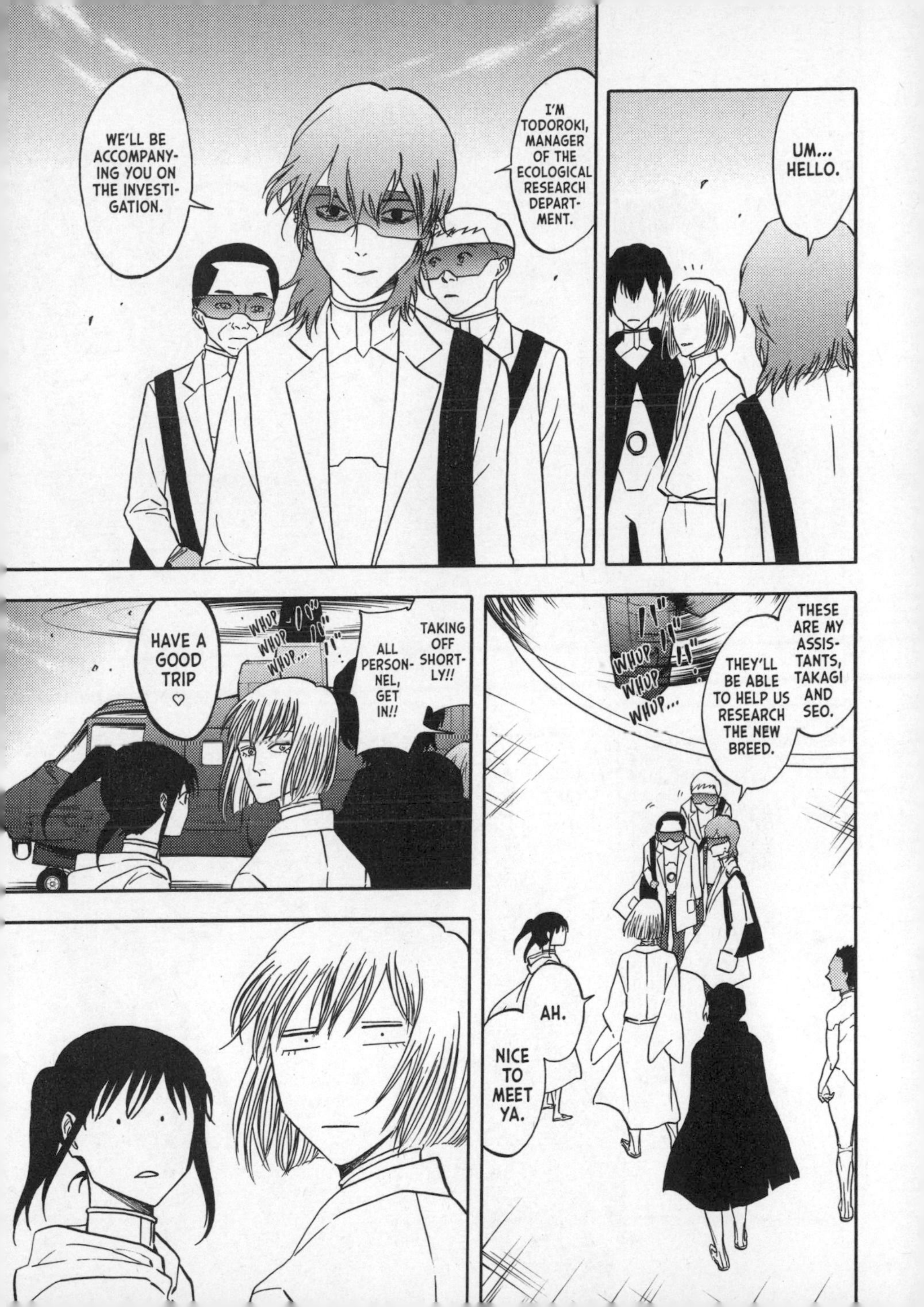
UM... HELLO.
I'M TODOROKI, MANAGER OF THE ECOLOGICAL RESEARCH DEPARTMENT.
WE'LL BE ACCOMPANYING YOU ON THE INVESTIGATION.
THESE ARE MY ASSISTANTS, TAKAGI AND SEO.
THEY'LL BE ABLE TO HELP US RESEARCH THE NEW BREED.
WHUP WHUP WHUP...
AH.
NICE TO MEET YA.
TAKING OFF SHORTLY!!
ALL PERSONNEL, GET IN!!
WHUP WHUP WHUP...
HAVE A GOOD TRIP ♡

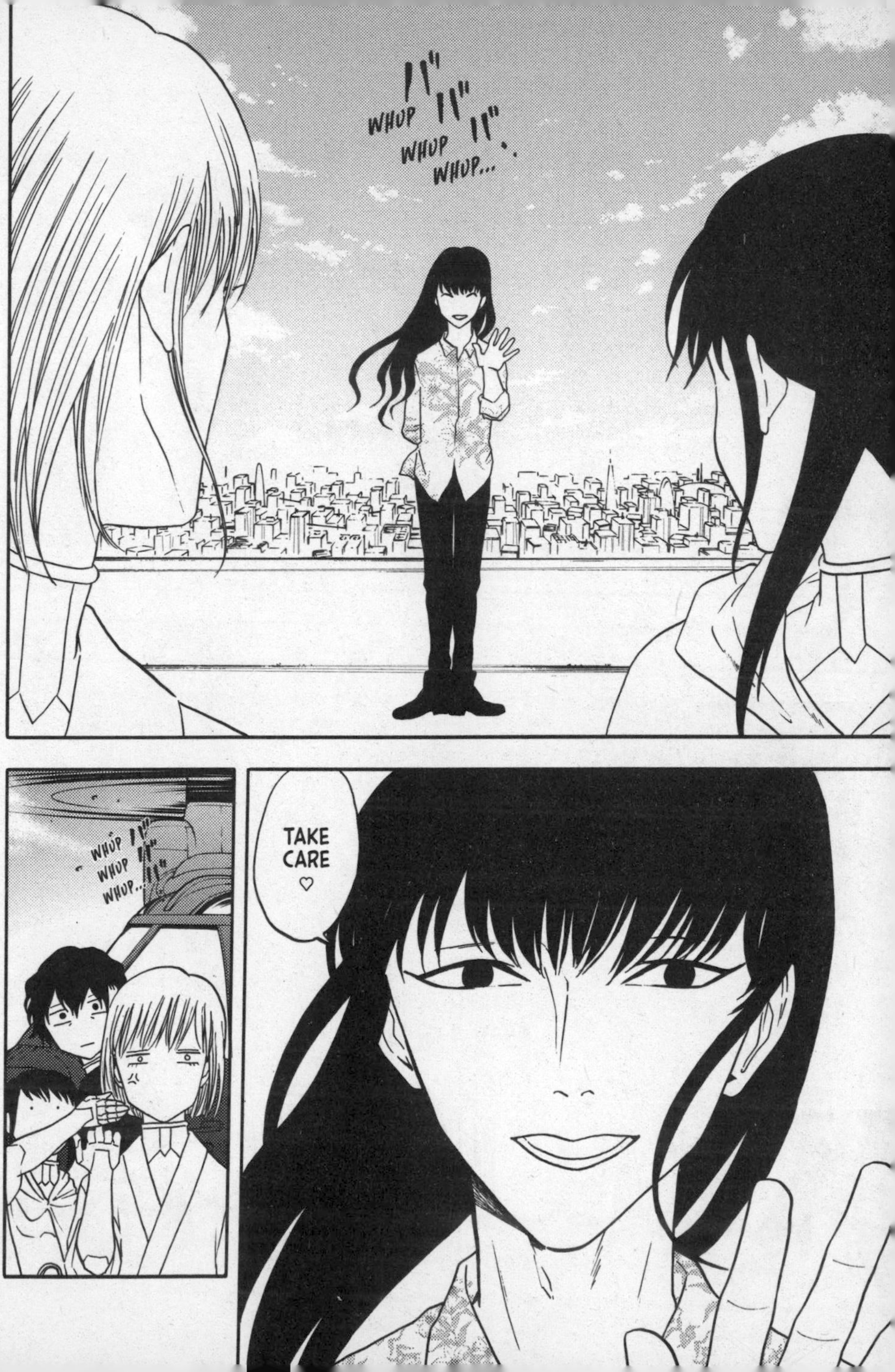
バ
WHUP
バ
WHUP
バ
WHUP...
TAKE CARE ♡
WHUP バ
WHUP バ
WHUP... バ

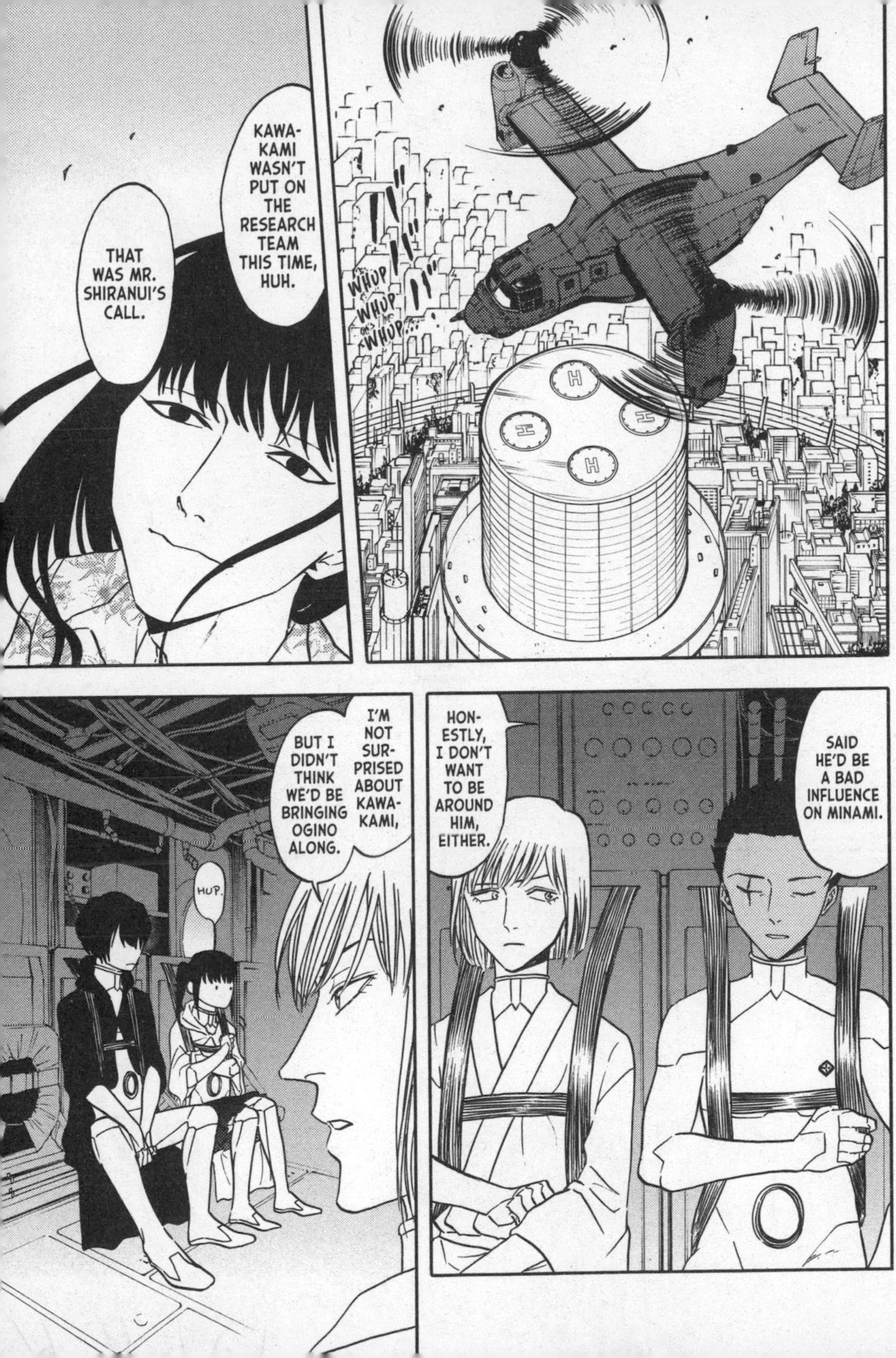
WHUP WHUP WHUP...
KAWA-KAMI WASN'T PUT ON THE RESEARCH TEAM THIS TIME, HUH.
THAT WAS MR. SHIRANUI'S CALL.
SAID HE'D BE A BAD INFLUENCE ON MINAMI.
HON-ESTLY, I DON'T WANT TO BE AROUND HIM, EITHER.
I'M NOT SUR-PRISED ABOUT KAWA-KAMI,
BUT I DIDN'T THINK WE'D BE BRINGING OGINO ALONG.
HUP.

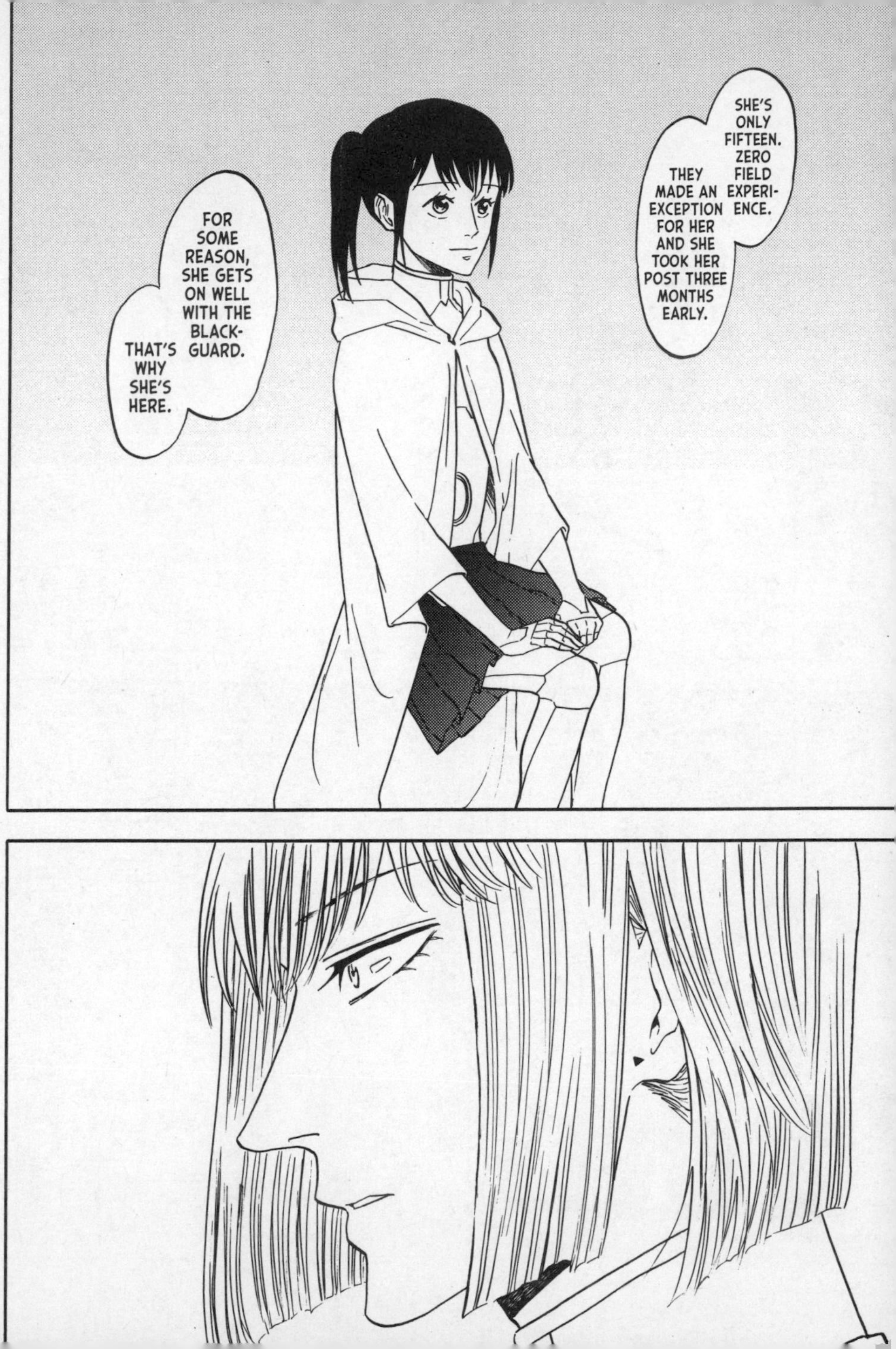
SHE'S ONLY FIFTEEN. ZERO FIELD EXPERIENCE.
THEY MADE AN EXCEPTION FOR HER AND SHE TOOK HER POST THREE MONTHS EARLY.
FOR SOME REASON, SHE GETS ON WELL WITH THE BLACK-GUARD.
THAT'S WHY SHE'S HERE.

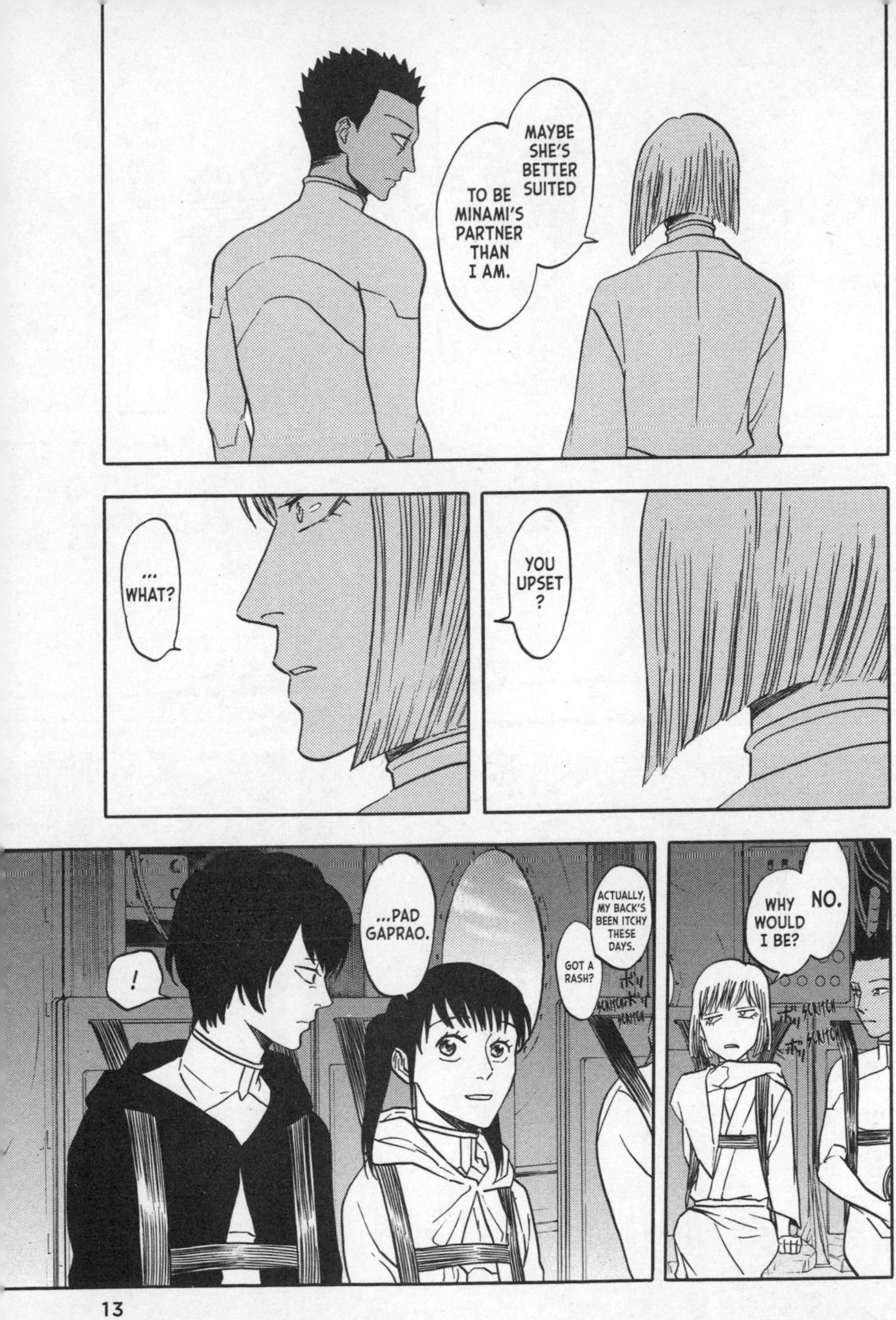
MAYBE SHE'S BETTER SUITED
TO BE MINAMI'S PARTNER THAN I AM.
YOU UPSET?
... WHAT?
NO.
WHY WOULD I BE?
SCRATCH SCRATCH
ACTUALLY, MY BACK'S BEEN ITCHY THESE DAYS.
GOT A RASH?
SCRATCH SCRATCH
...PAD GAPRAO.
!

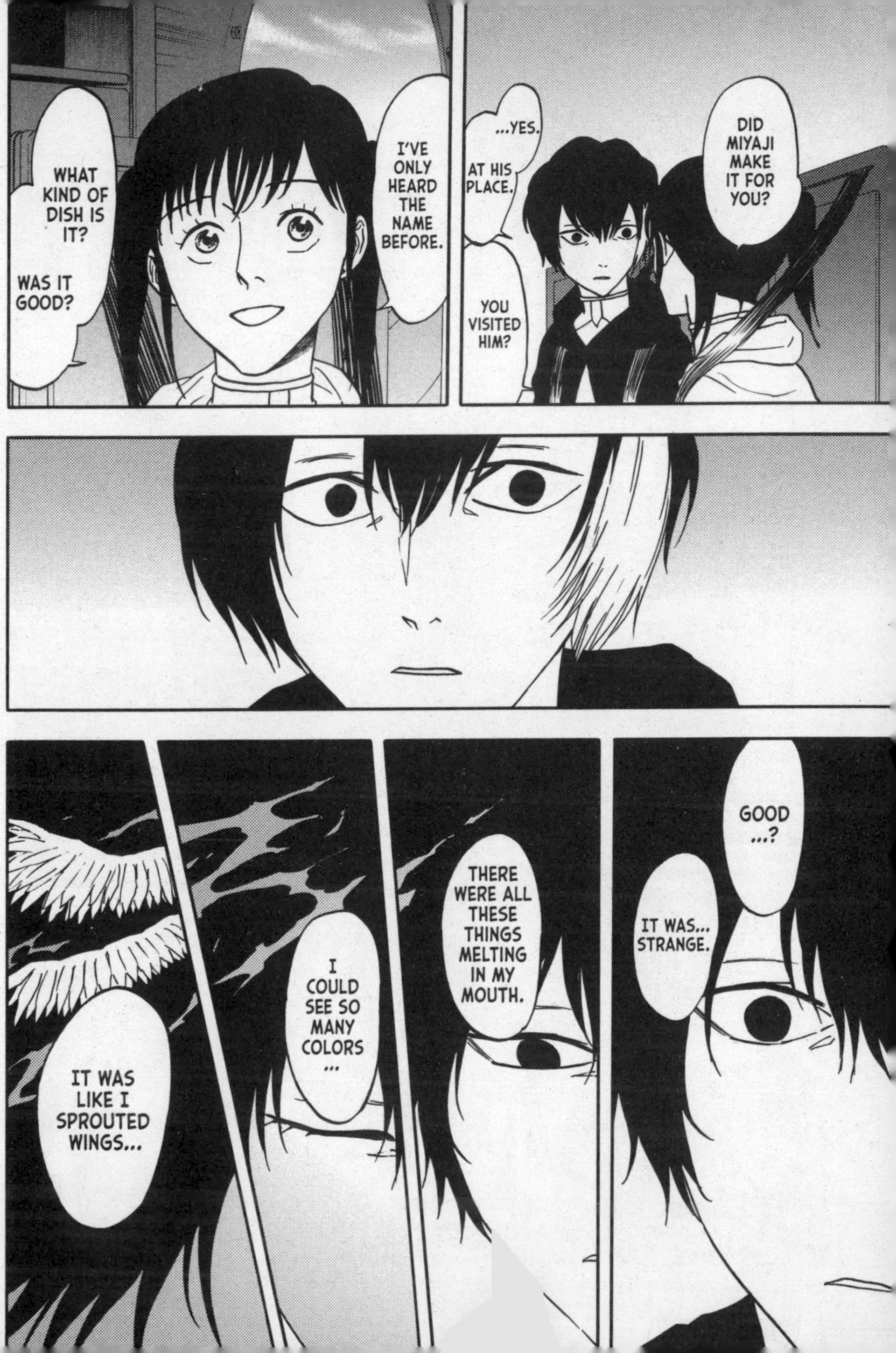
DID MIYAJI MAKE IT FOR YOU?
...YES.
AT HIS PLACE.
YOU VISITED HIM?
I'VE ONLY HEARD THE NAME BEFORE.
WHAT KIND OF DISH IS IT?
WAS IT GOOD?
GOOD ...?
IT WAS... STRANGE.
THERE WERE ALL THESE THINGS MELTING IN MY MOUTH.
I COULD SEE SO MANY COLORS ...
IT WAS LIKE I SPROUTED WINGS...

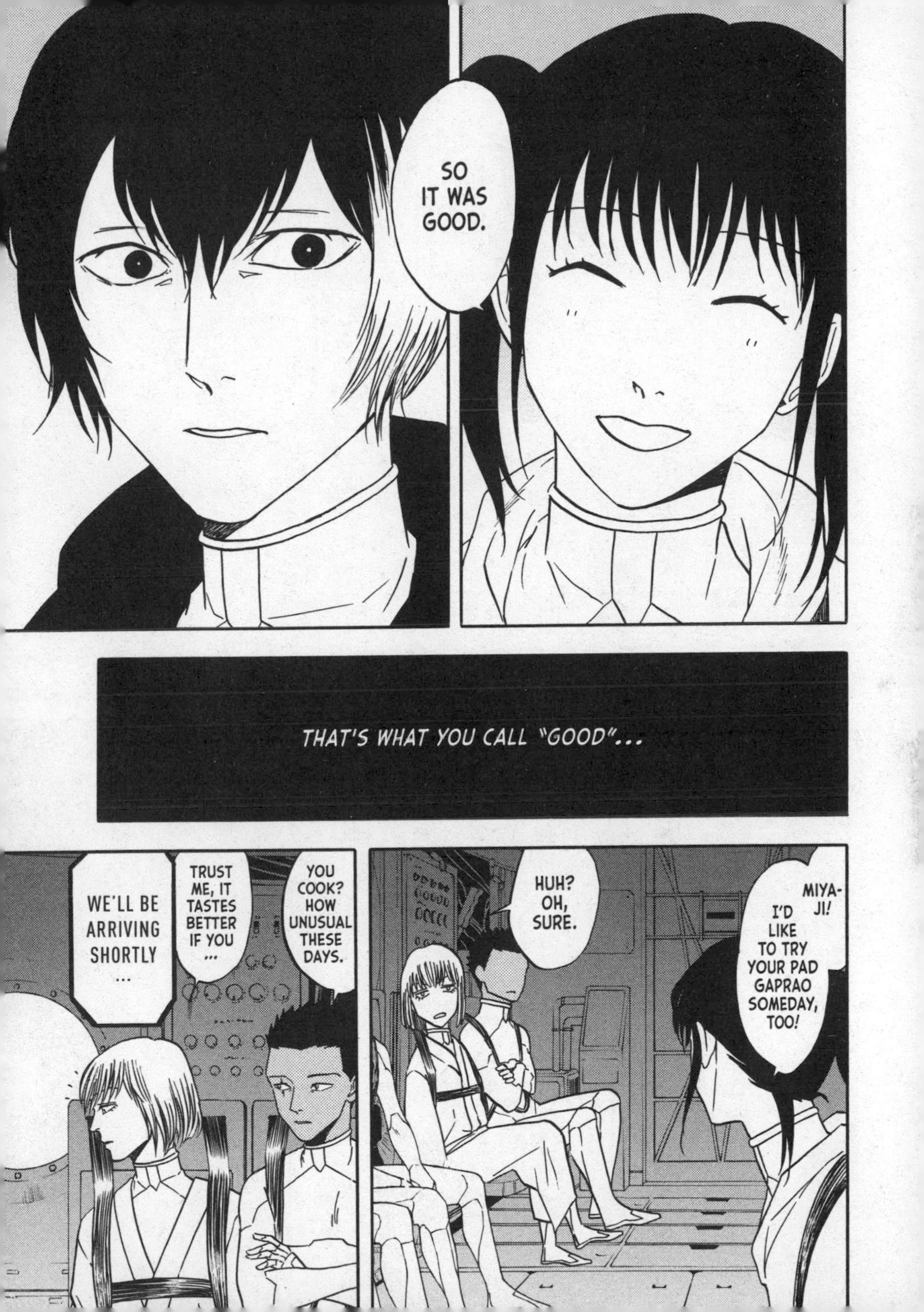
SO IT WAS GOOD.
THAT'S WHAT YOU CALL "GOOD"...
MIYA-JI! I'D LIKE TO TRY YOUR PAD GAPRAO SOMEDAY, TOO!
HUH? OH, SURE.
YOU COOK? HOW UNUSUAL THESE DAYS.
TRUST ME, IT TASTES BETTER IF YOU ...
WE'LL BE ARRIVING SHORTLY ...

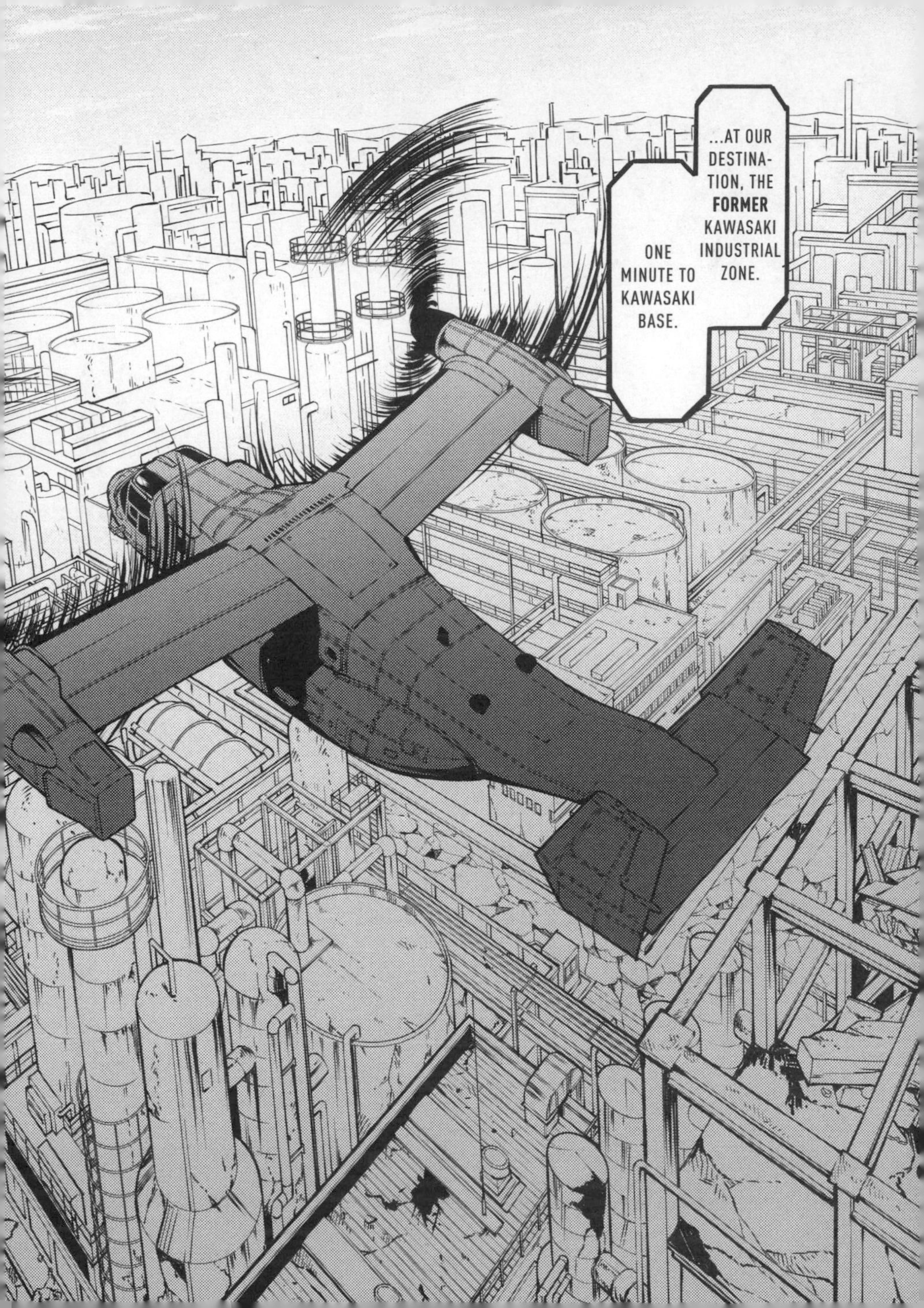
ONE MINUTE TO KAWASAKI BASE.
...AT OUR DESTINATION, THE **FORMER** KAWASAKI INDUSTRIAL ZONE.

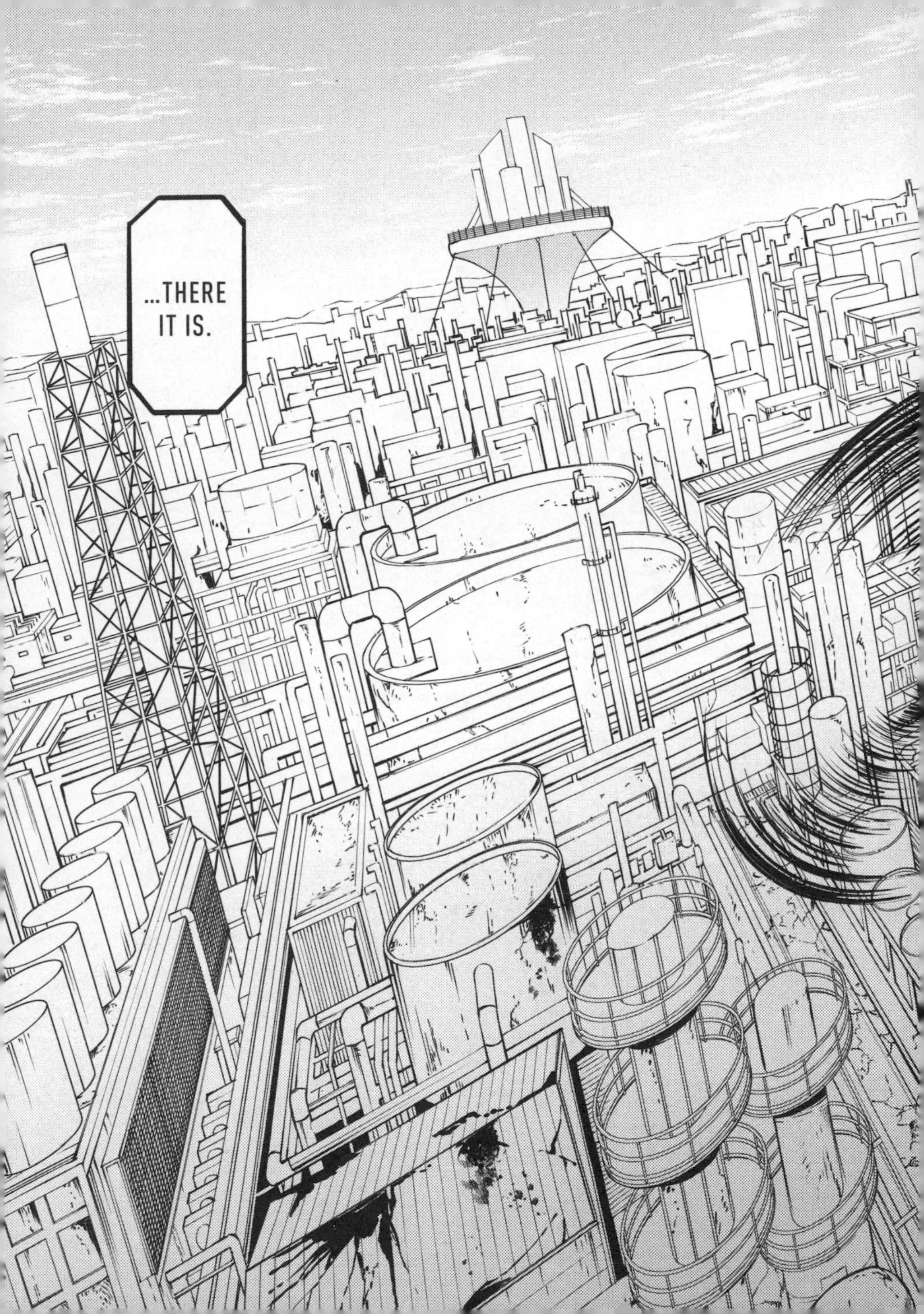
...THERE IT IS.

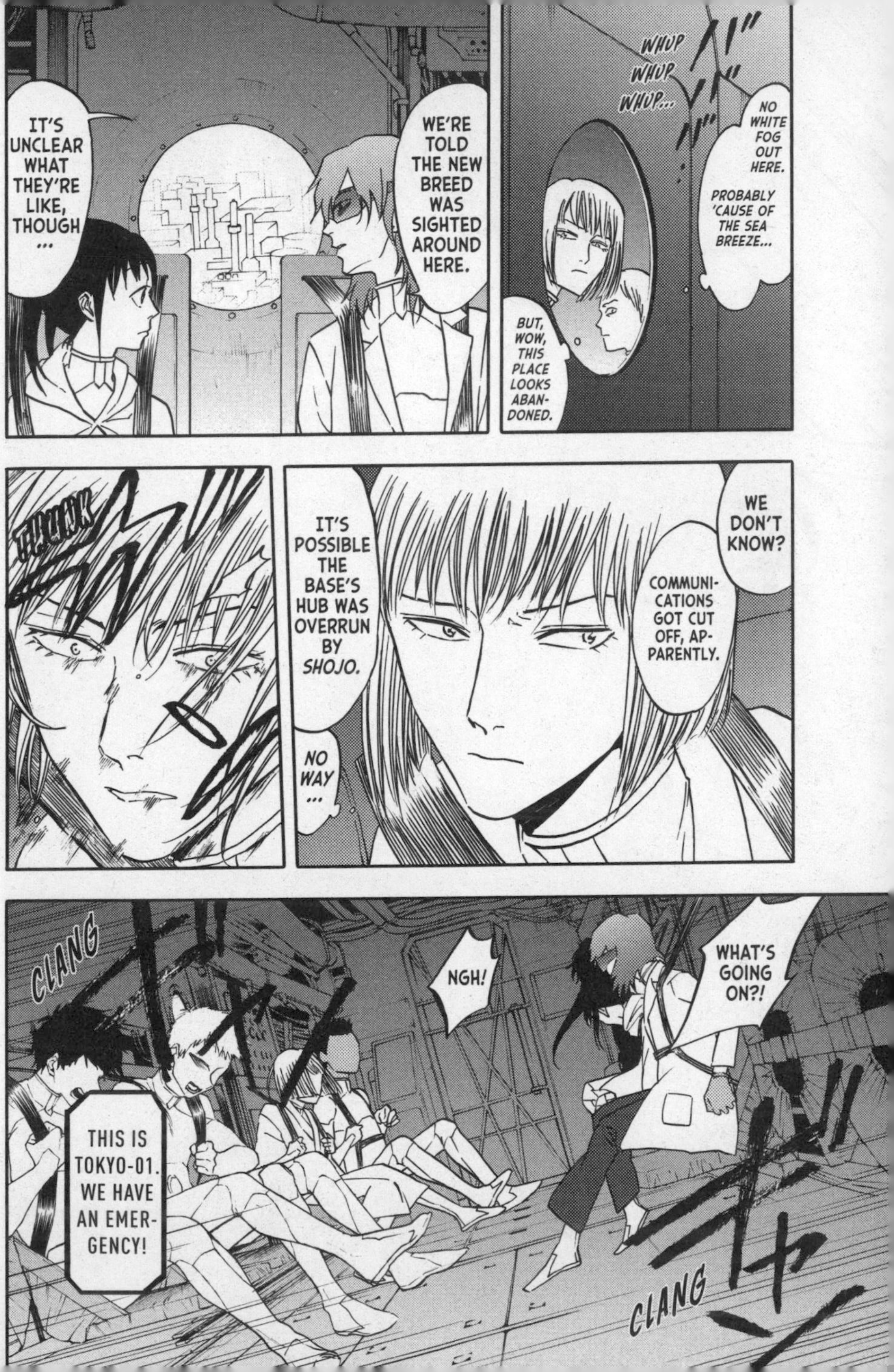
WHUP WHUP WHUP...
NO WHITE FOG OUT HERE.
PROBABLY 'CAUSE OF THE SEA BREEZE...
BUT, WOW, THIS PLACE LOOKS ABAN-DONED.
WE'RE TOLD THE NEW BREED WAS SIGHTED AROUND HERE.
IT'S UNCLEAR WHAT THEY'RE LIKE, THOUGH...
WE DON'T KNOW?
COMMUNI-CATIONS GOT CUT OFF, AP-PARENTLY.
IT'S POSSIBLE THE BASE'S HUB WAS OVERRUN BY SHOJO.
NO WAY...
WHAT'S GOING ON?!
NGH!
CLANG
THIS IS TOKYO-01. WE HAVE AN EMER-GENCY!
CLANG

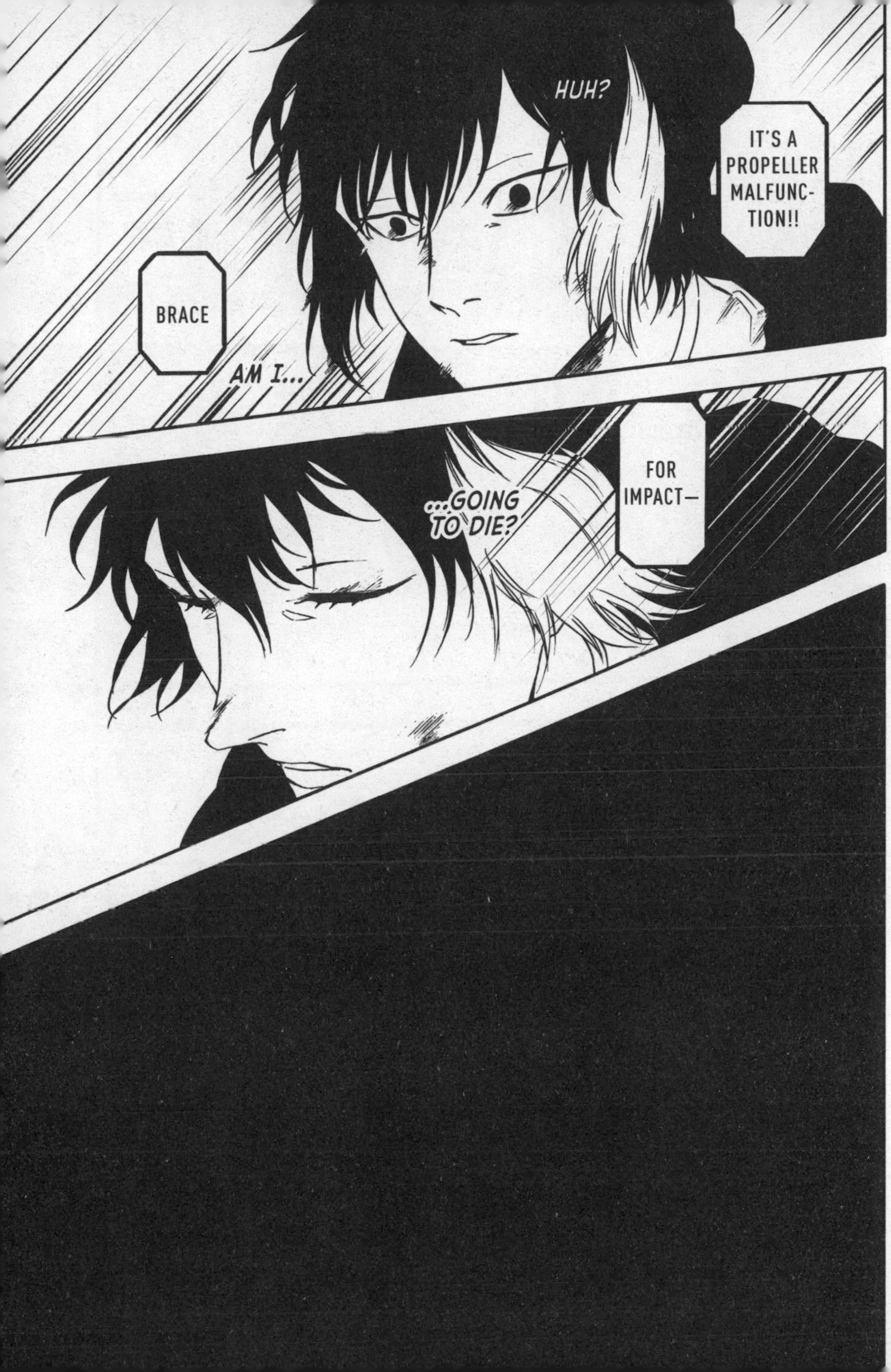
HUH?
IT'S A PROPELLER MALFUNC-TION!!
BRACE
AM I...
FOR IMPACT—
...GOING TO DIE?

ビーッ BEEEP
ビーッ BEEEP
ビーッ BEEEP
ビーッ BEEEP
ビーッ BEEEP
ビーッ BEEEP
ビーッ BEEEP

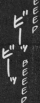

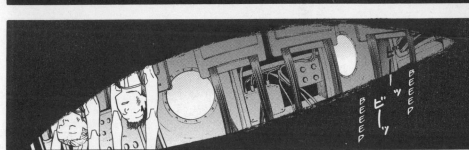

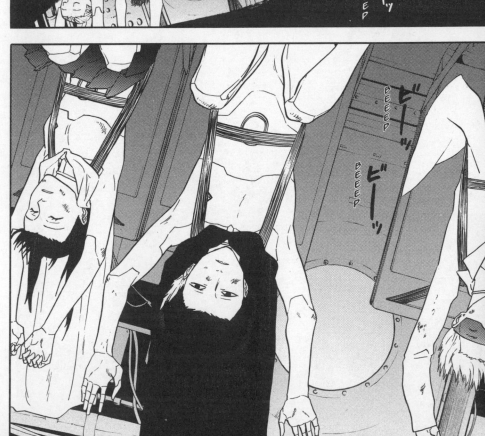

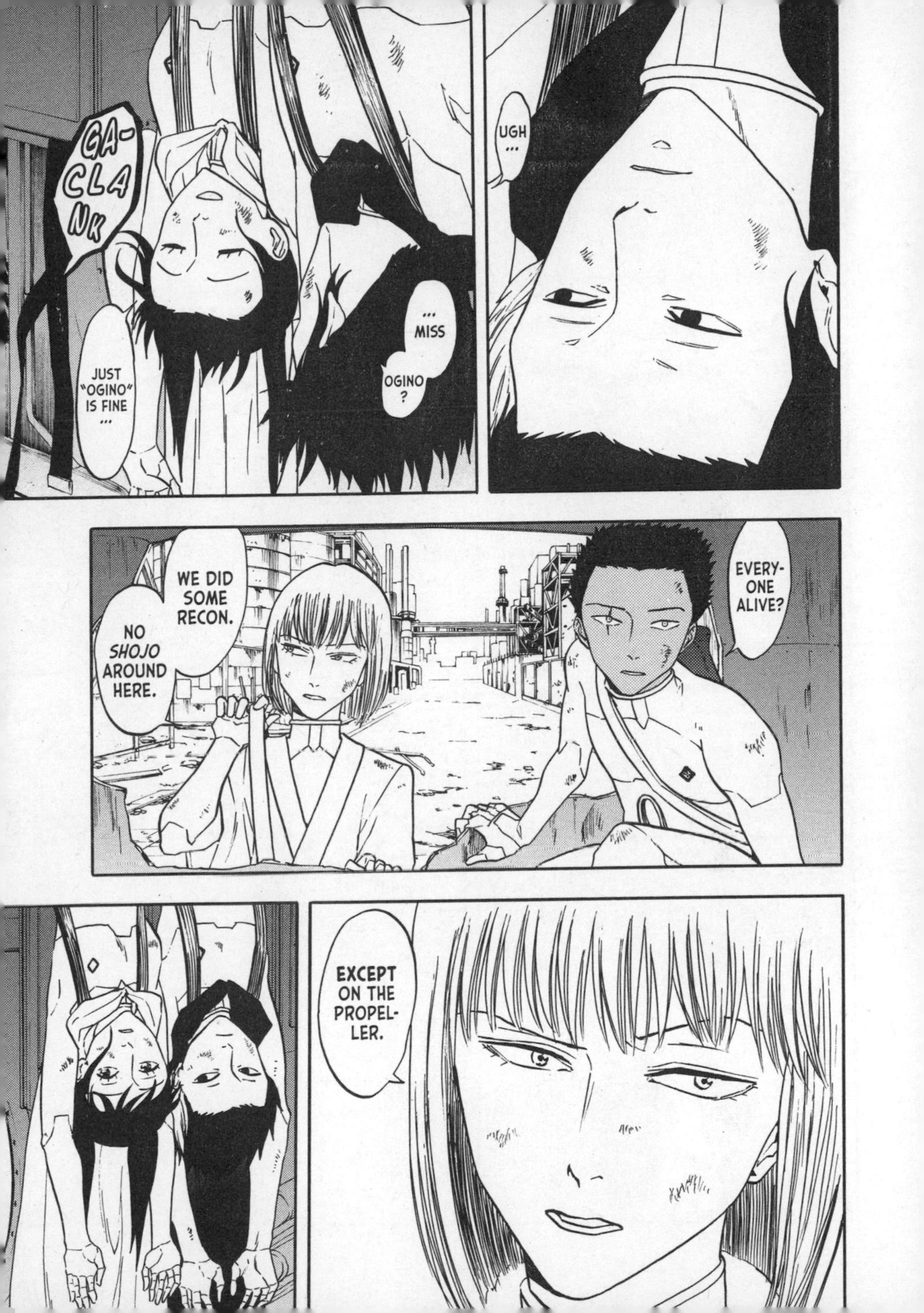
UGH ...
... MISS OGINO ?
GA-CLANK
JUST "OGINO" IS FINE ...
EVERY-ONE ALIVE?
WE DID SOME RECON.
NO *SHOJO* AROUND HERE.
EXCEPT ON THE PROPEL-LER.

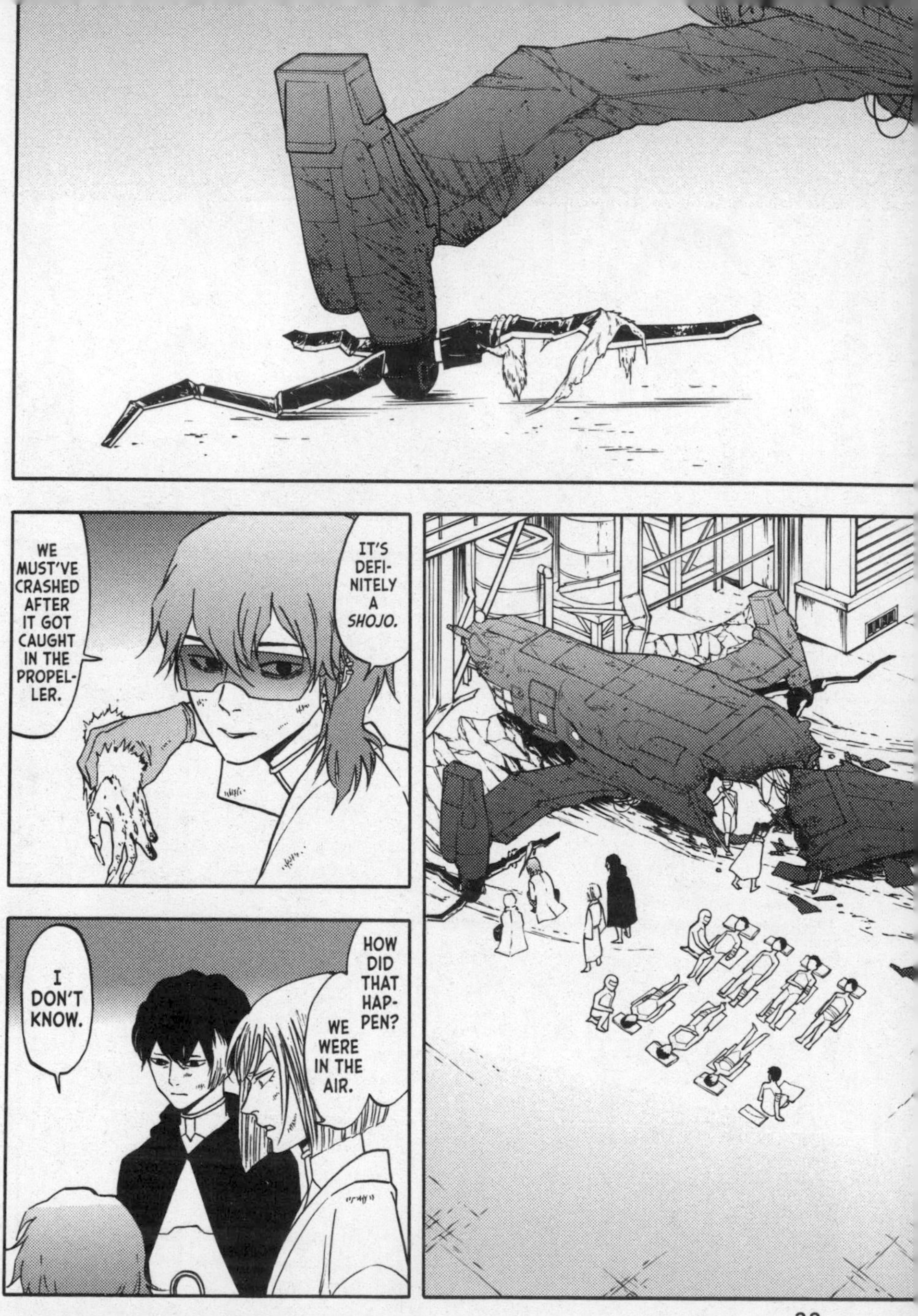
IT'S DEFINITELY A *SHOJO.*
WE MUST'VE CRASHED AFTER IT GOT CAUGHT IN THE PROPELLER.
HOW DID THAT HAPPEN?
WE WERE IN THE AIR.
I DON'T KNOW.

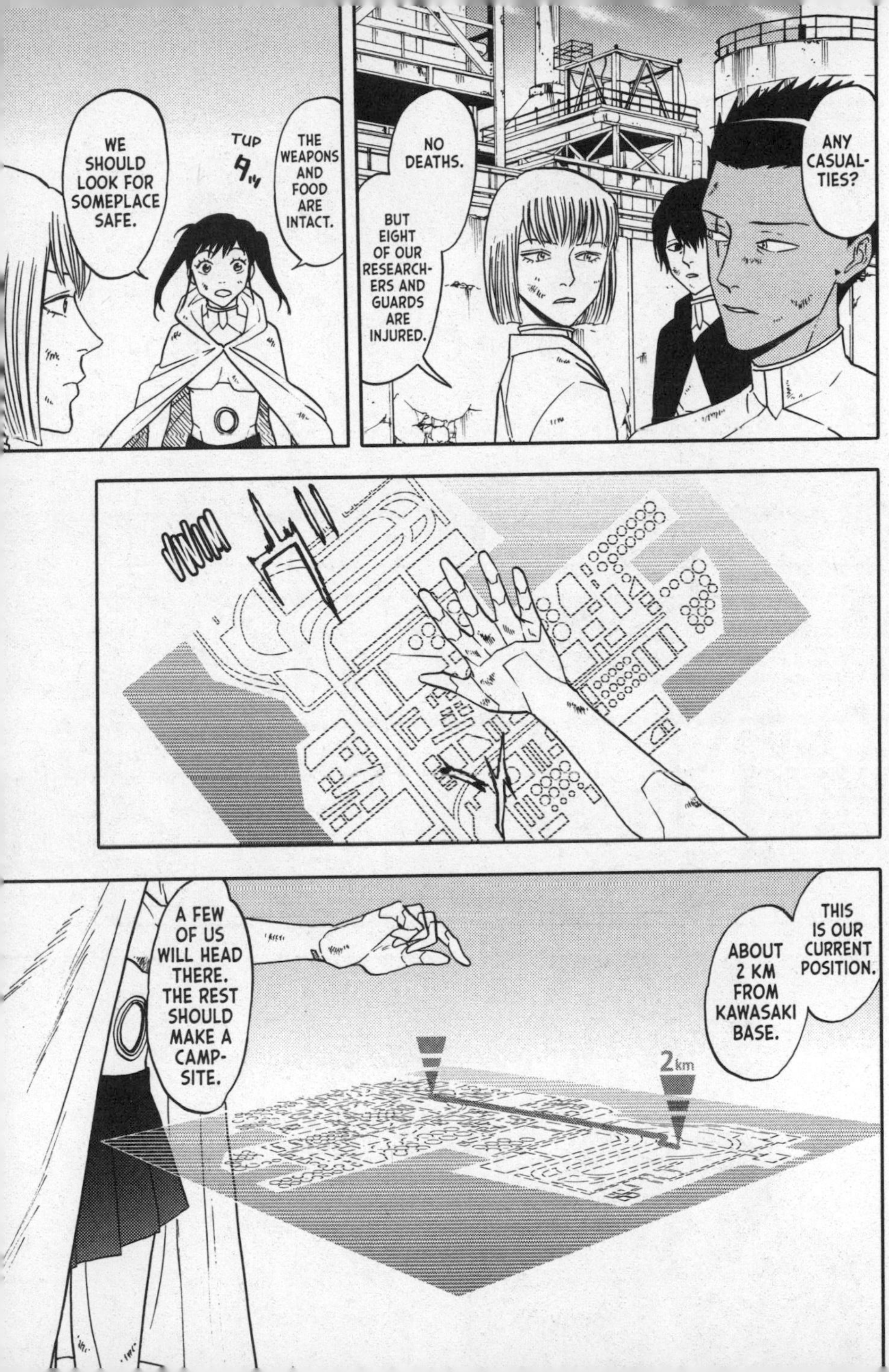
ANY CASUAL-TIES?
NO DEATHS.
BUT EIGHT OF OUR RESEARCHERS AND GUARDS ARE INJURED.
THE WEAPONS AND FOOD ARE INTACT.
TUP
タッ
WE SHOULD LOOK FOR SOMEPLACE SAFE.
THIS IS OUR CURRENT POSITION.
ABOUT 2 KM FROM KAWASAKI BASE.
2km
A FEW OF US WILL HEAD THERE. THE REST SHOULD MAKE A CAMP-SITE.

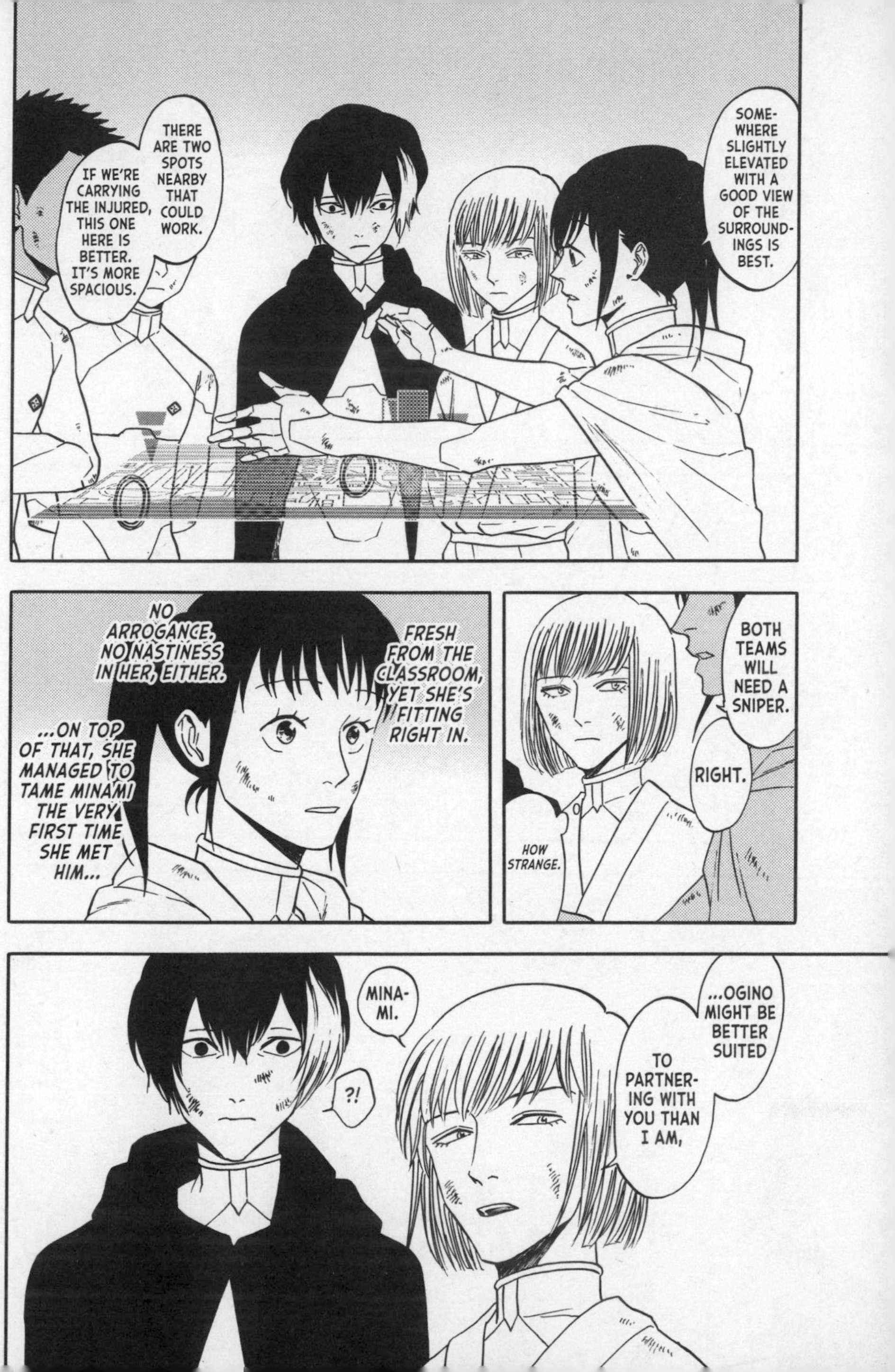
SOME-WHERE SLIGHTLY ELEVATED WITH A GOOD VIEW OF THE SURROUNDINGS IS BEST.
THERE ARE TWO SPOTS NEARBY THAT COULD WORK.
IF WE'RE CARRYING THE INJURED, THIS ONE HERE IS BETTER. IT'S MORE SPACIOUS.
BOTH TEAMS WILL NEED A SNIPER.
RIGHT.
HOW STRANGE.
FRESH FROM THE CLASSROOM, YET SHE'S FITTING RIGHT IN.
NO ARROGANCE. NO NASTINESS IN HER, EITHER.
...ON TOP OF THAT, SHE MANAGED TO TAME MINAMI THE VERY FIRST TIME SHE MET HIM...
...OGINO MIGHT BE BETTER SUITED
TO PARTNER-ING WITH YOU THAN I AM,
MINA-MI.
?!

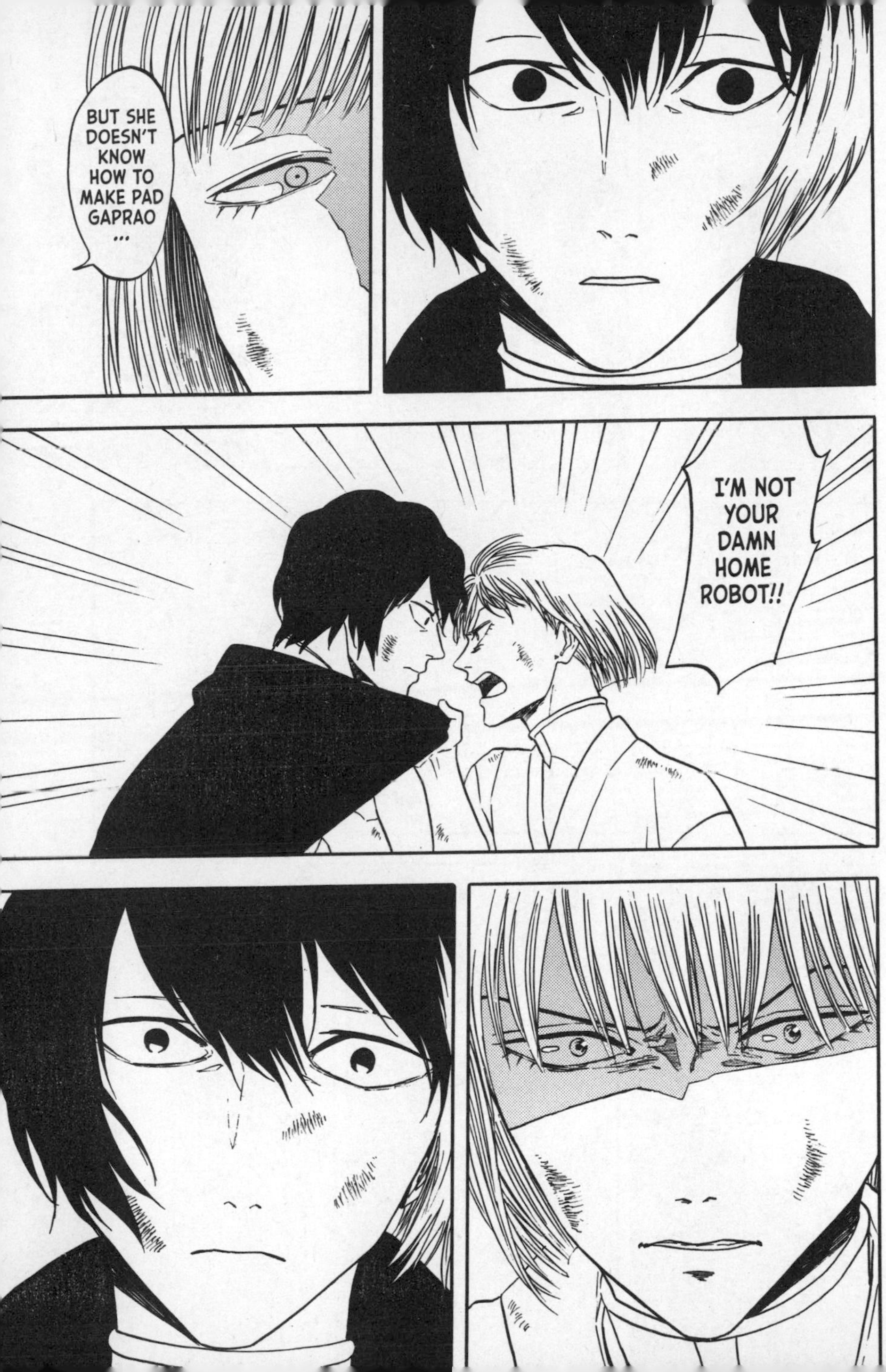
BUT SHE DOESN'T KNOW HOW TO MAKE PAD GAPRAO ...
I'M NOT YOUR DAMN HOME ROBOT!!

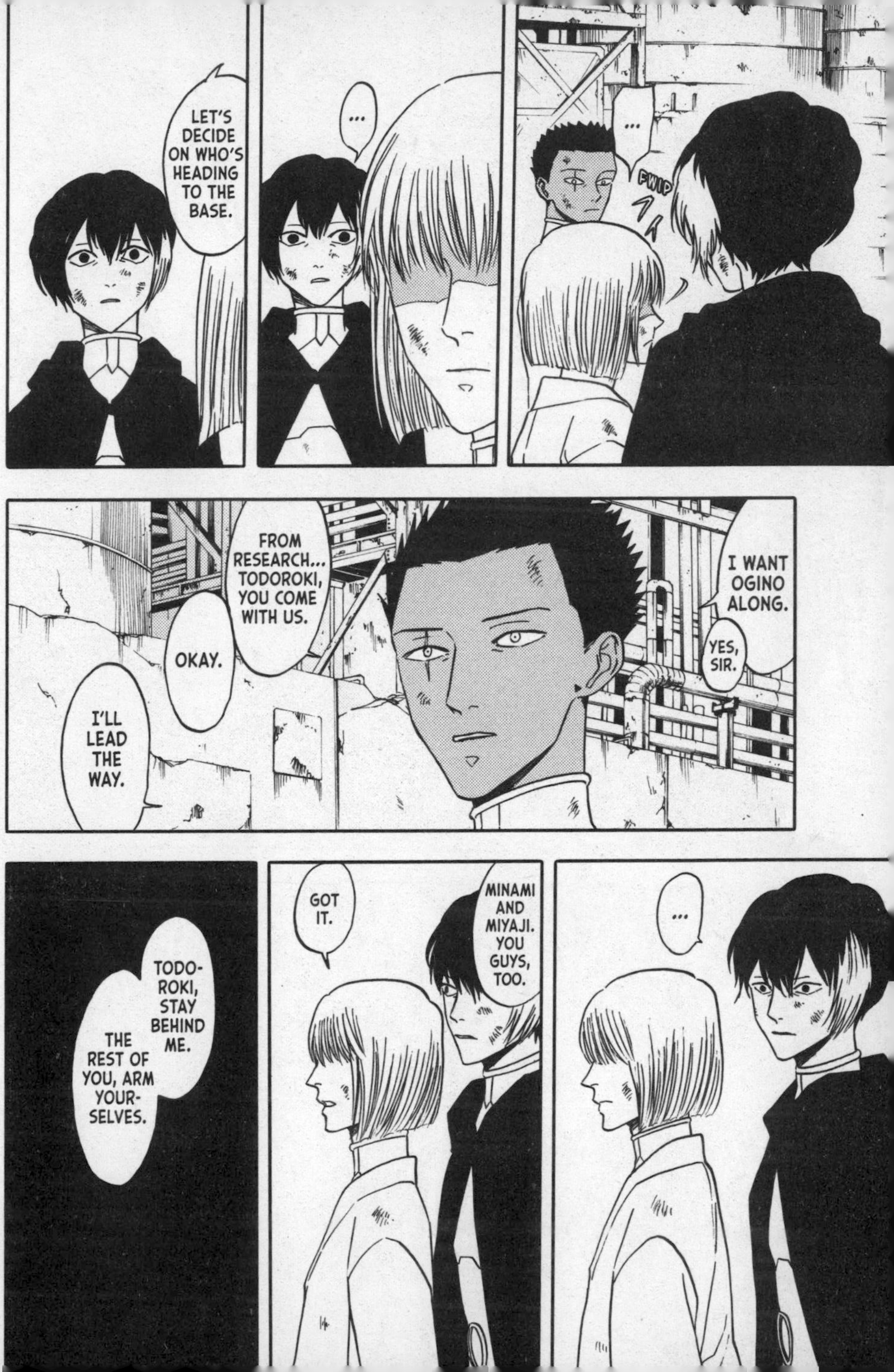
...
FWIP
...
LET'S DECIDE ON WHO'S HEADING TO THE BASE.
I WANT OGINO ALONG.
YES, SIR.
FROM RESEARCH... TODOROKI, YOU COME WITH US.
OKAY.
I'LL LEAD THE WAY.
...
MINAMI AND MIYAJI. YOU GUYS, TOO.
GOT IT.
TODO-ROKI, STAY BEHIND ME.
THE REST OF YOU, ARM YOUR-SELVES.

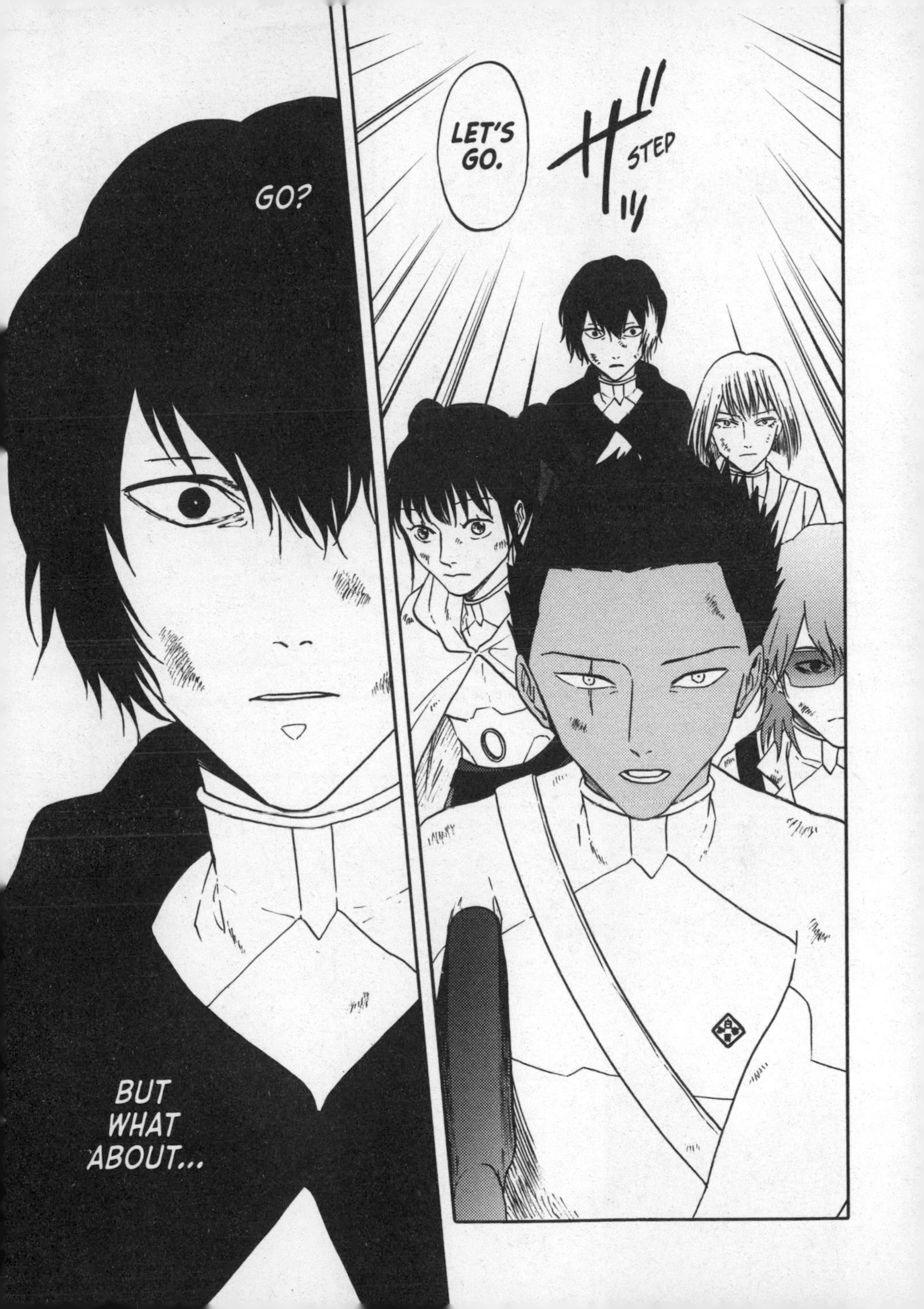
LET'S GO.
STEP
GO?
BUT WHAT ABOUT...

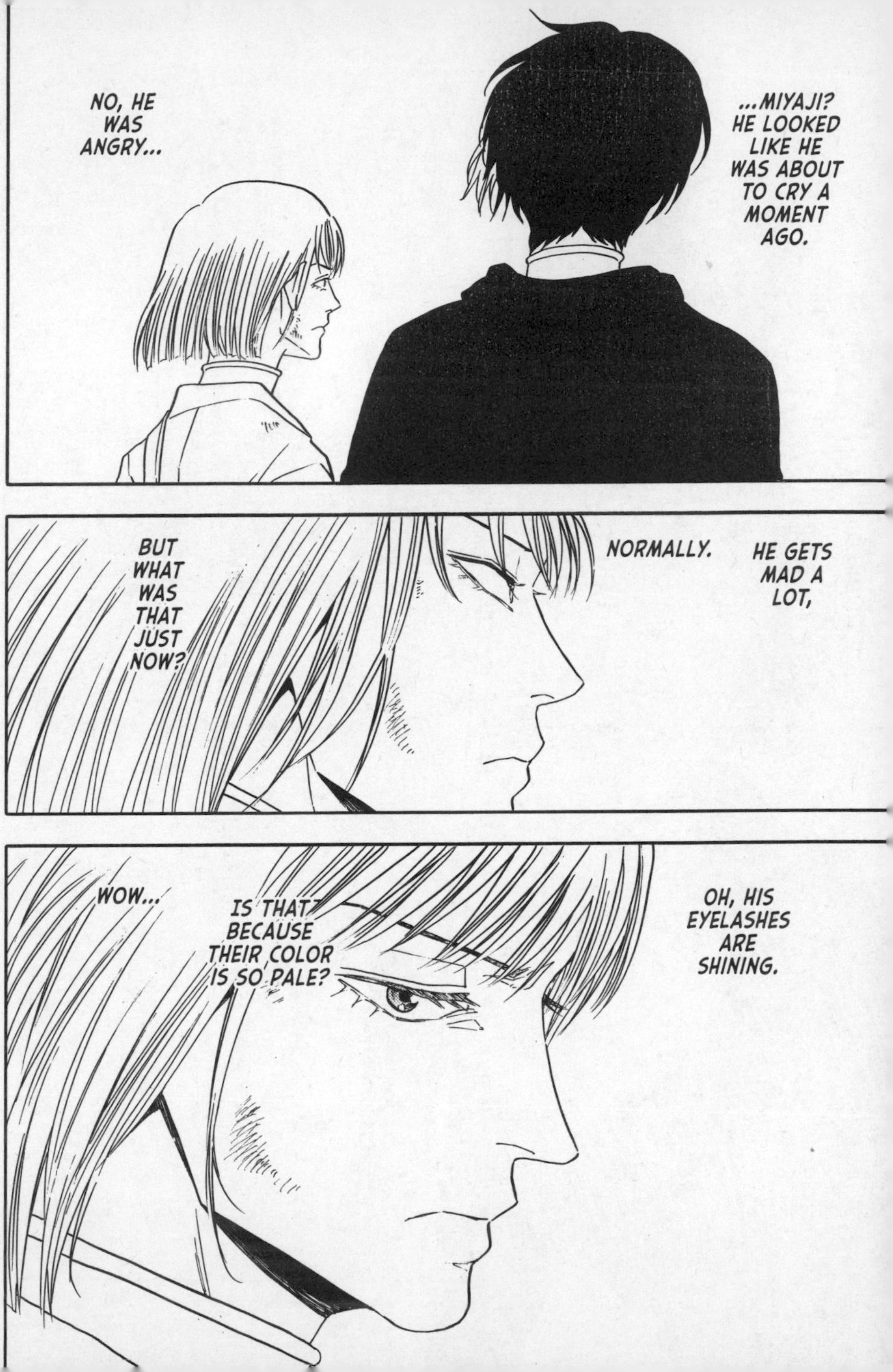
...MIYAJI? HE LOOKED LIKE HE WAS ABOUT TO CRY A MOMENT AGO.
NO, HE WAS ANGRY...
HE GETS MAD A LOT,
NORMALLY.
BUT WHAT WAS THAT JUST NOW?
OH, HIS EYELASHES ARE SHINING.
IS THAT BECAUSE THEIR COLOR IS SO PALE?
WOW...

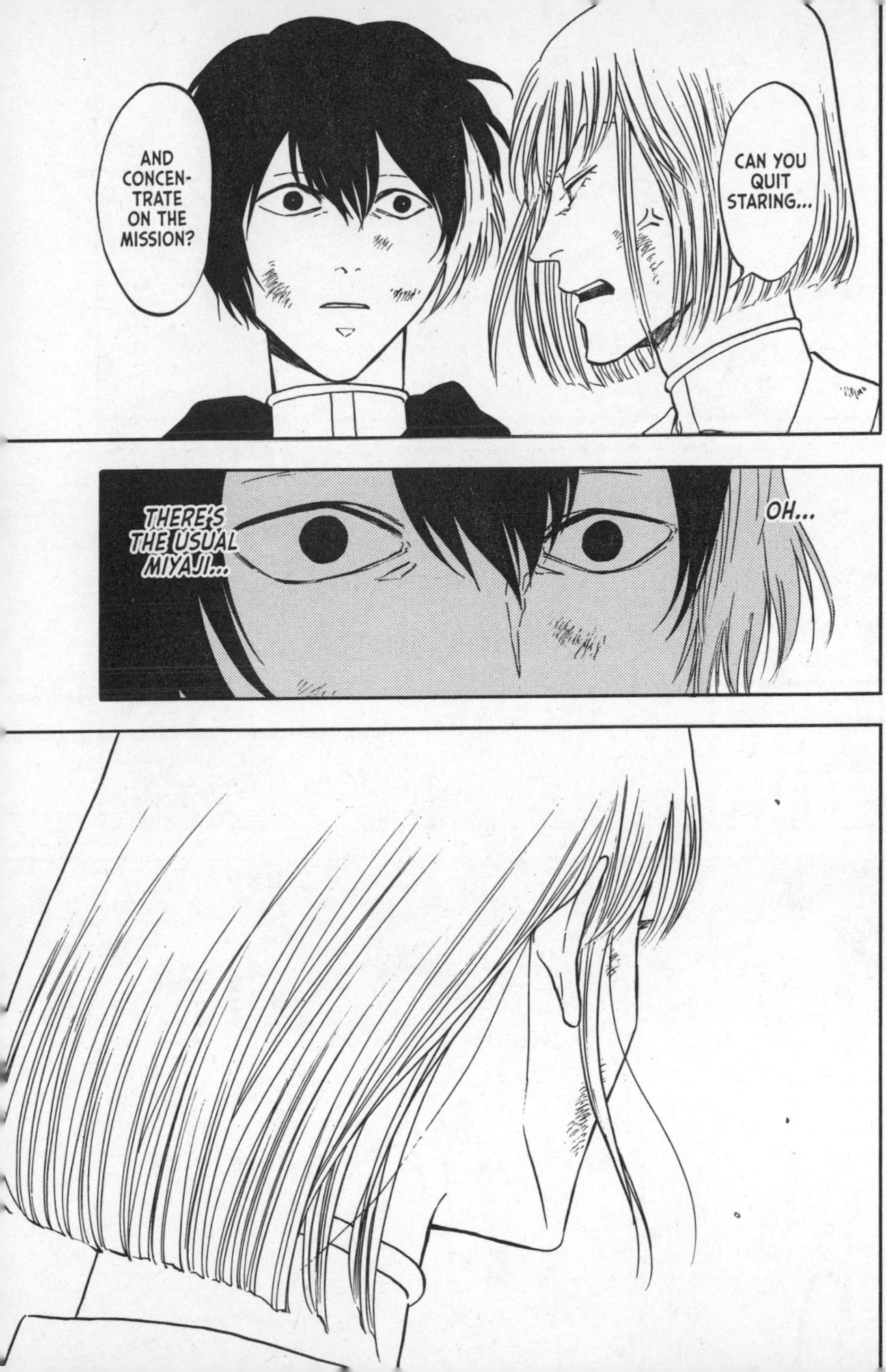
CAN YOU QUIT STARING...
AND CONCEN-TRATE ON THE MISSION?
OH...
THERE'S THE USUAL MIYAJI...

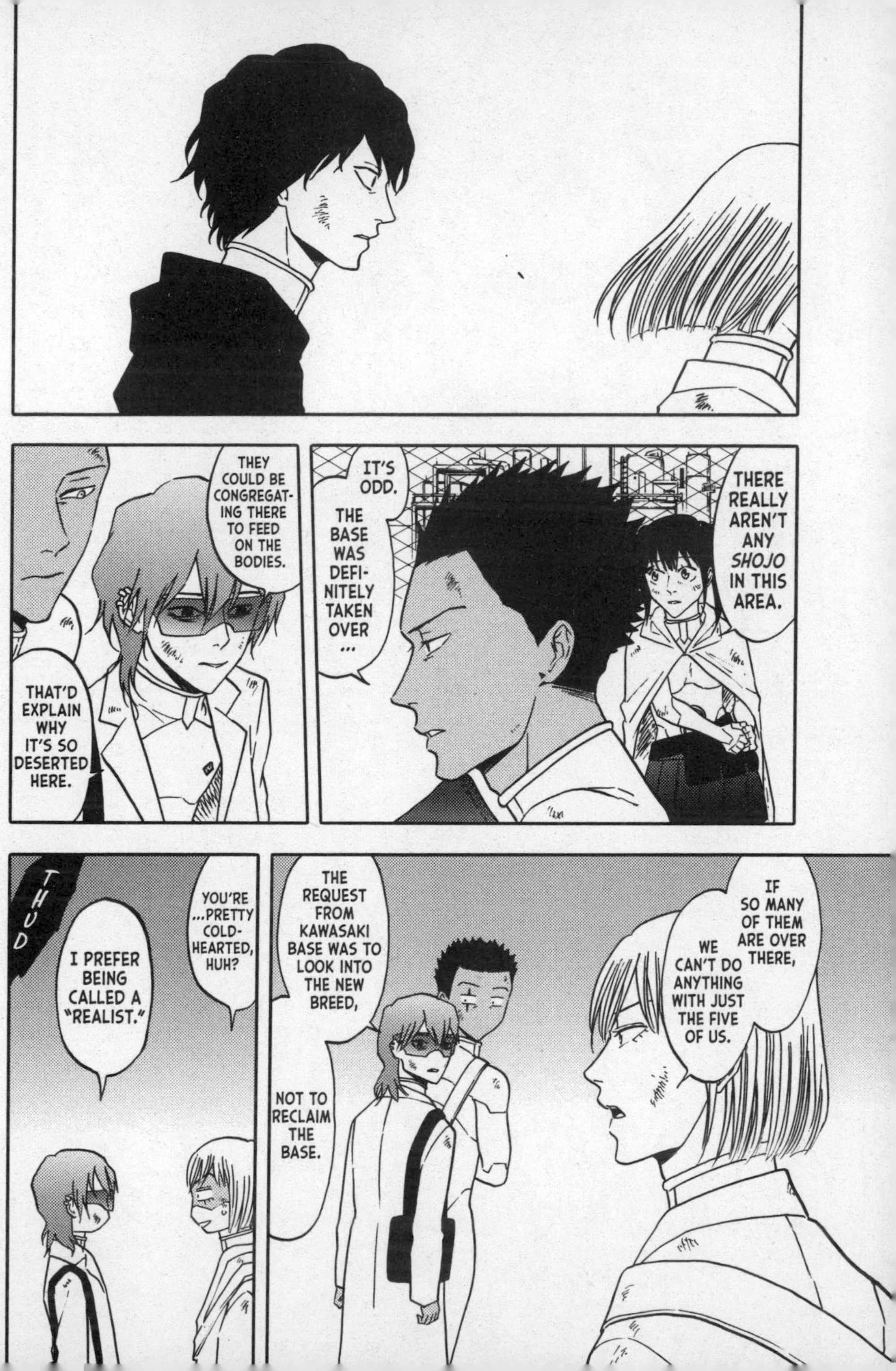
THERE REALLY AREN'T ANY *SHOJO* IN THIS AREA.
IT'S ODD.
THE BASE WAS DEFINITELY TAKEN OVER...
THEY COULD BE CONGREGATING THERE TO FEED ON THE BODIES.
THAT'D EXPLAIN WHY IT'S SO DESERTED HERE.
IF SO MANY OF THEM ARE OVER THERE,
WE CAN'T DO ANYTHING WITH JUST THE FIVE OF US.
THE REQUEST FROM KAWASAKI BASE WAS TO LOOK INTO THE NEW BREED,
NOT TO RECLAIM THE BASE.
YOU'RE ...PRETTY COLD-HEARTED, HUH?
I PREFER BEING CALLED A "REALIST."
THUD

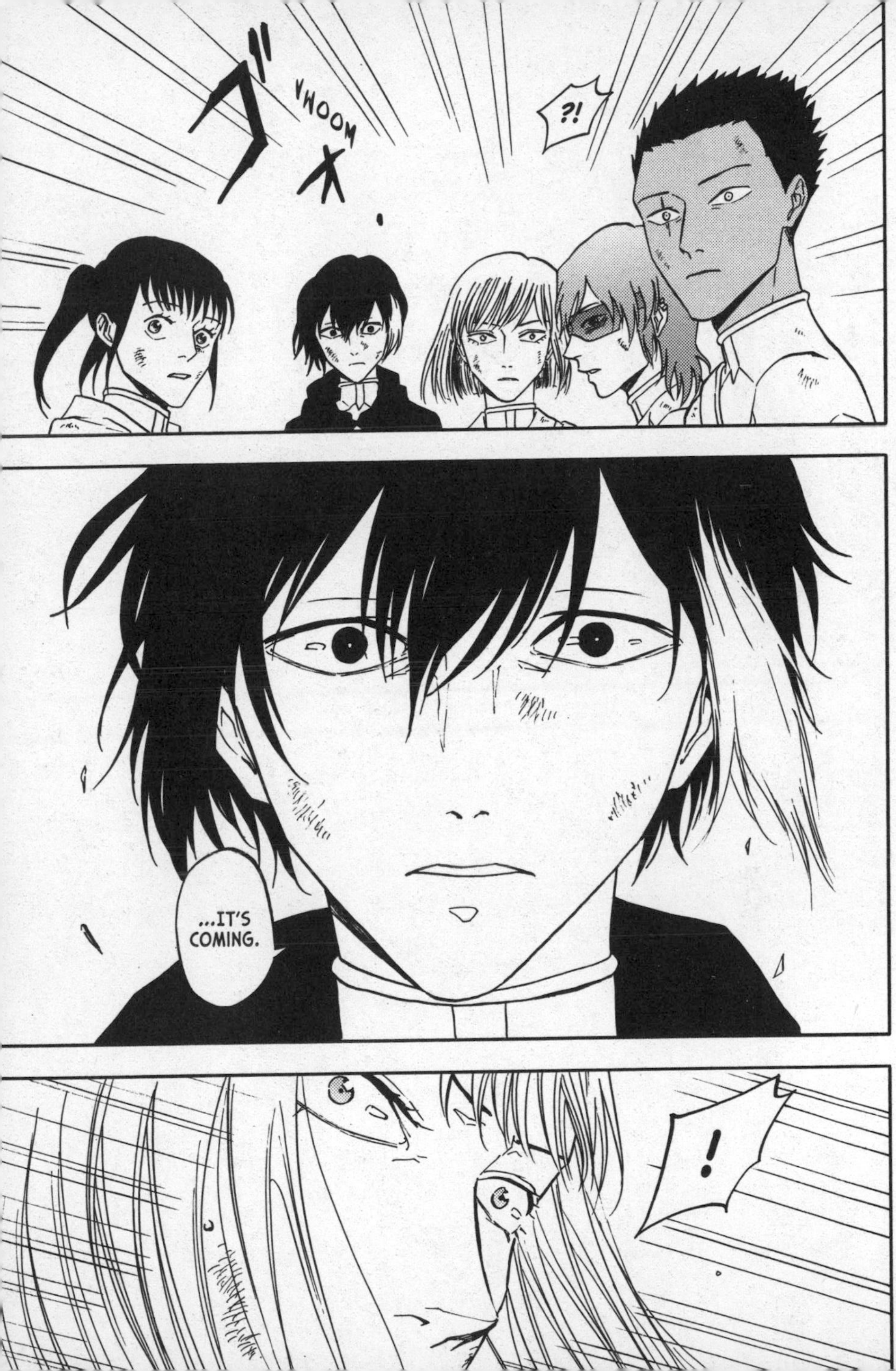
?!
VHOOM
...IT'S COMING.
!

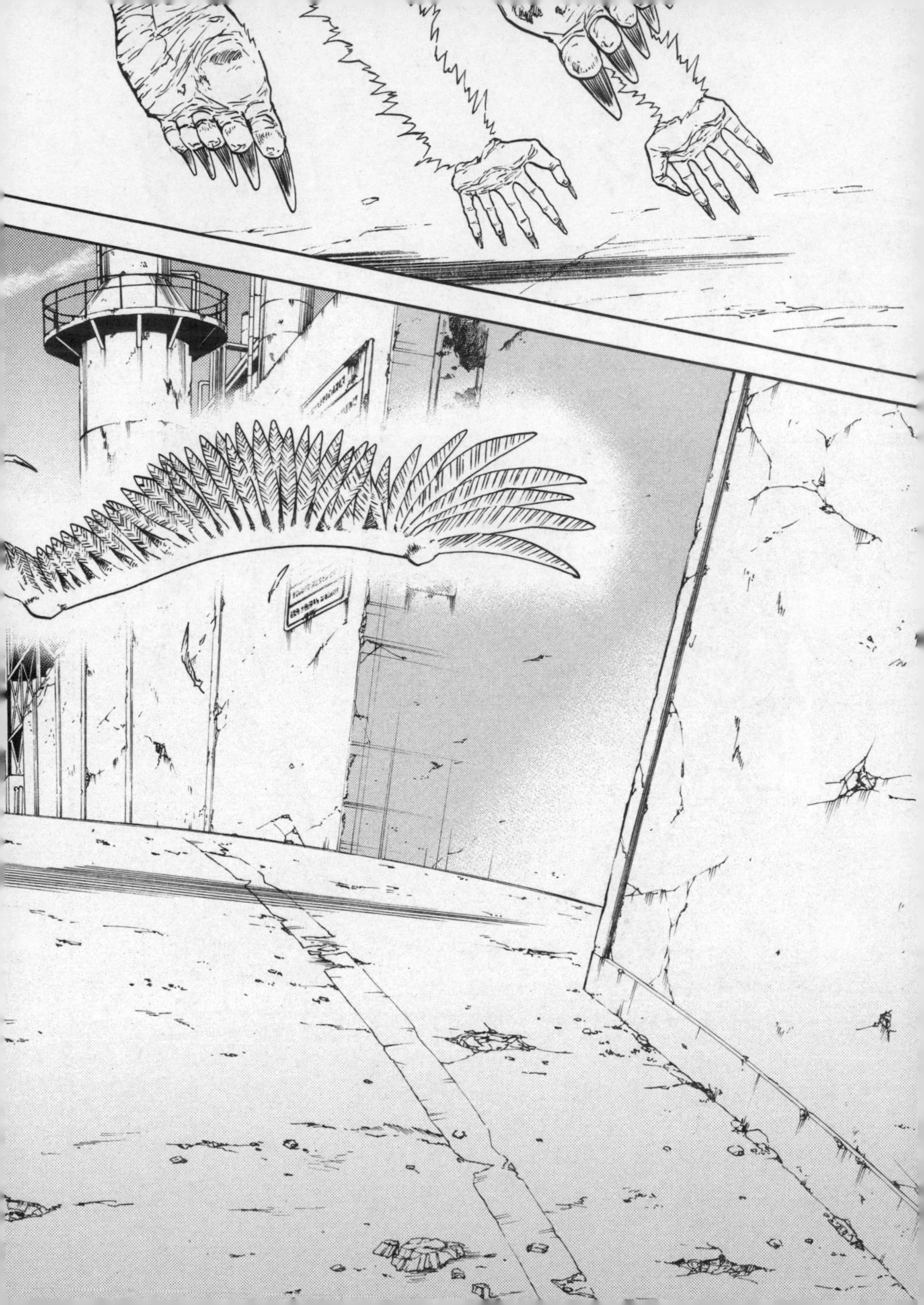

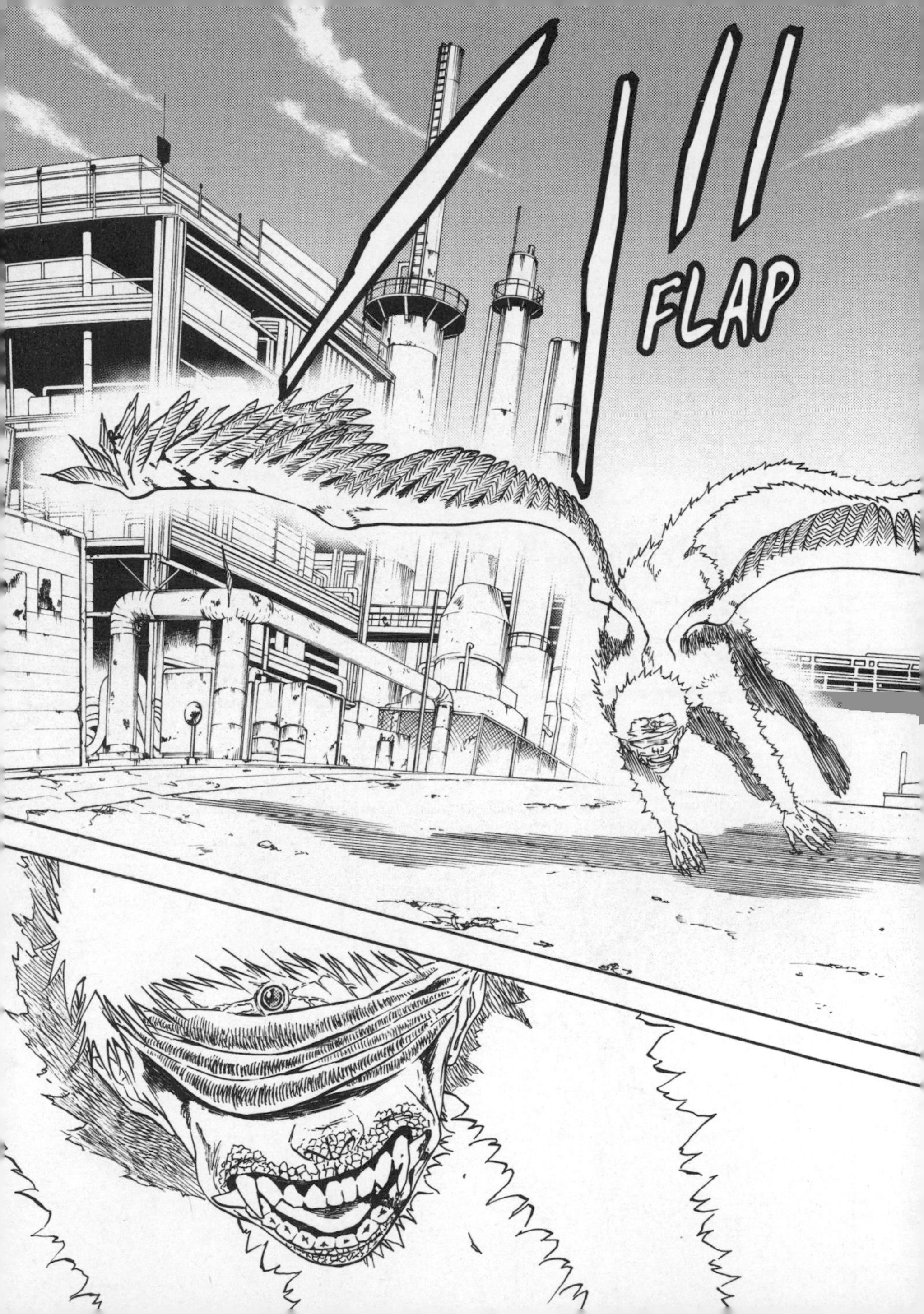
FLAP

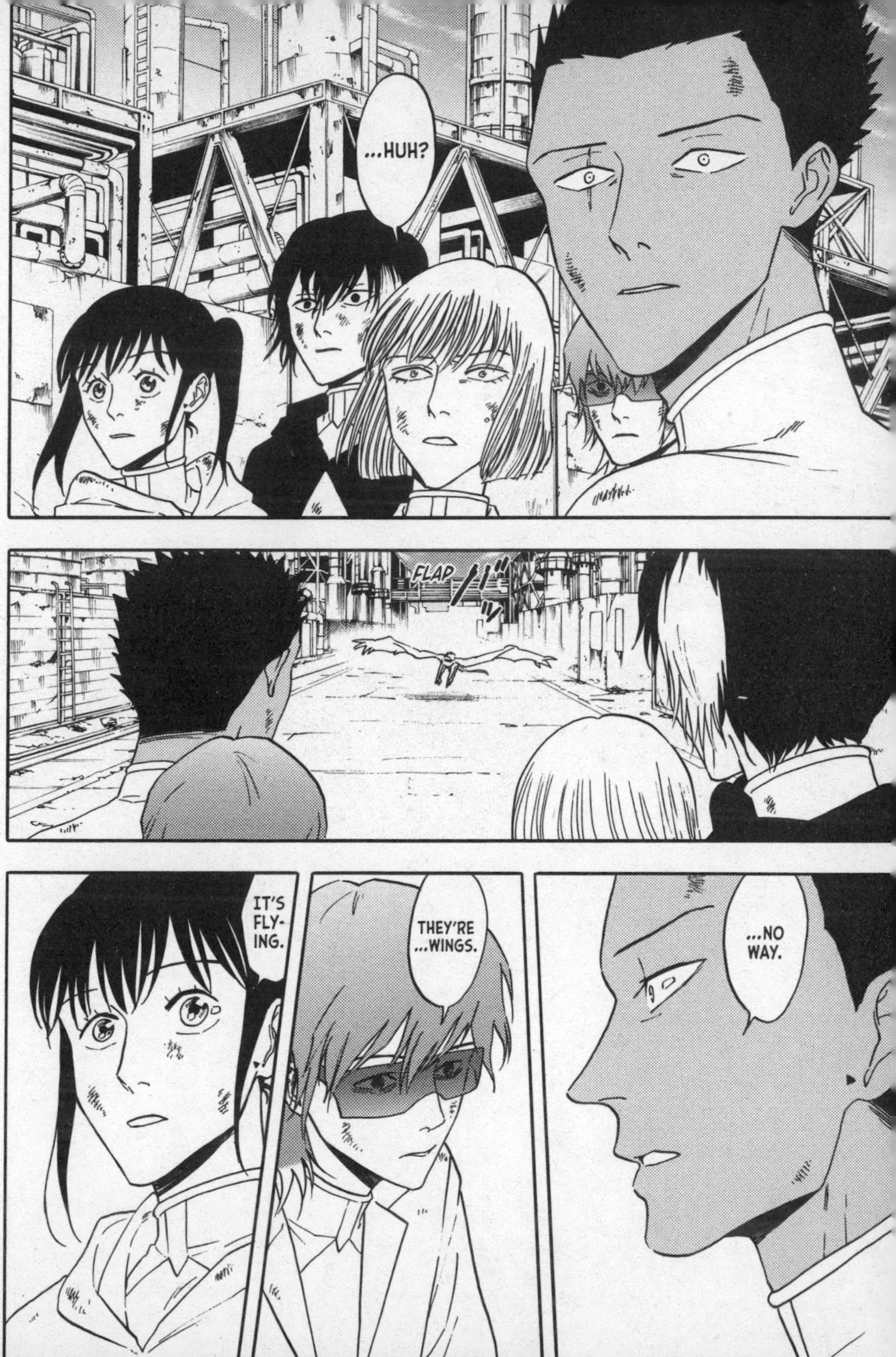
...HUH?
FLAP
...NO WAY.
THEY'RE ...WINGS.
IT'S FLY-ING.

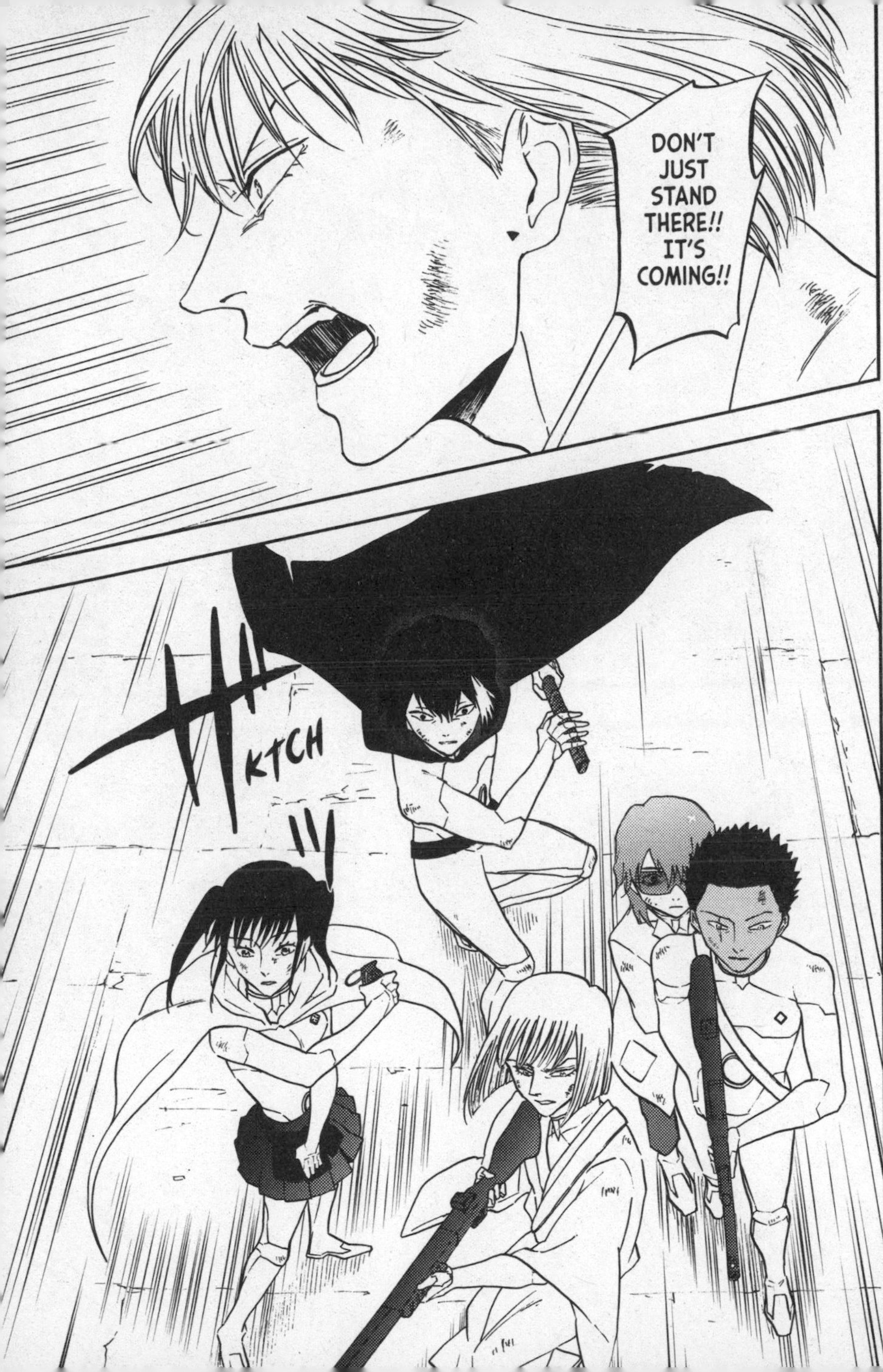
DON'T JUST STAND THERE!! IT'S COMING!!
HKTCH

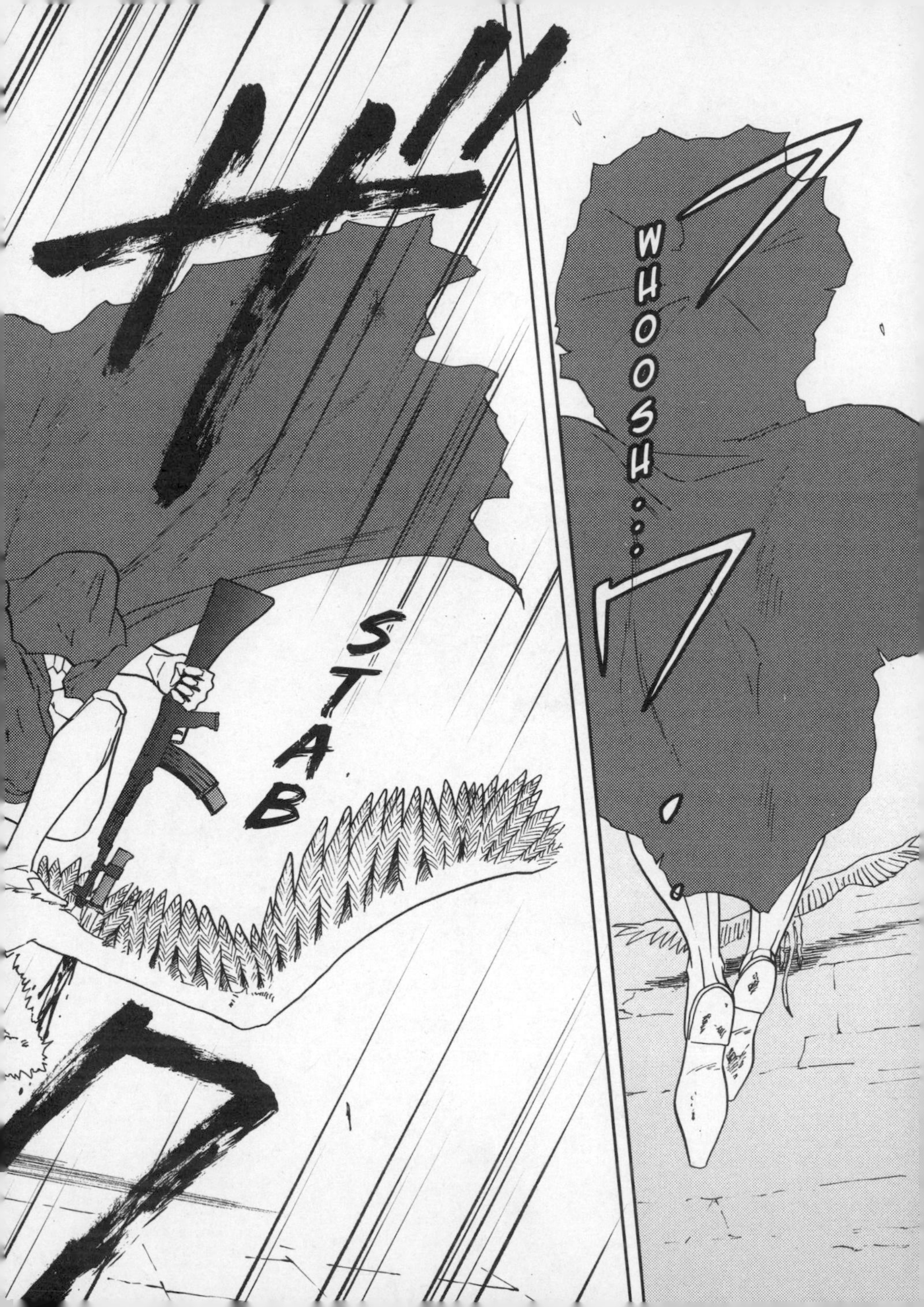
WHOOOSH...
STAB

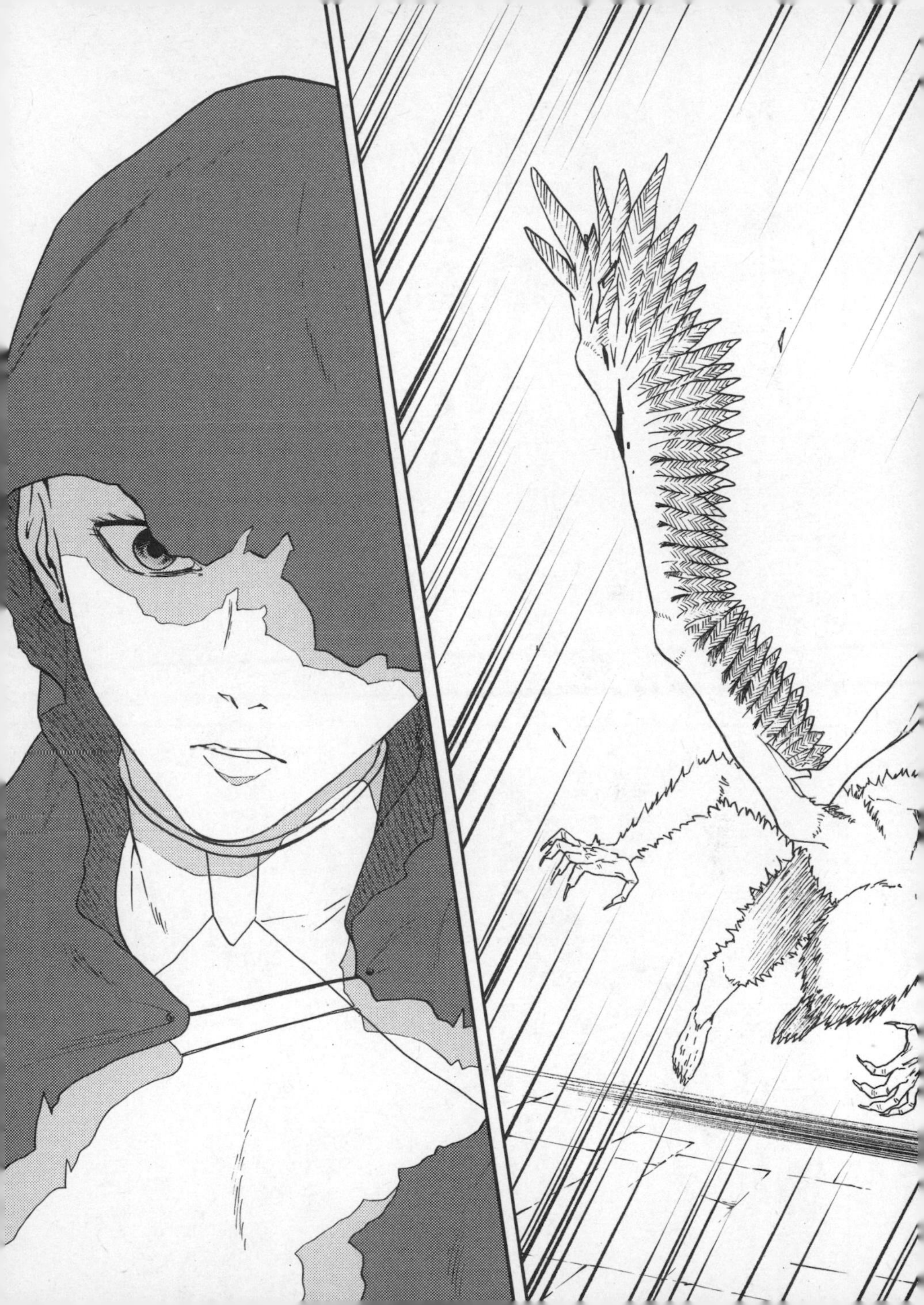

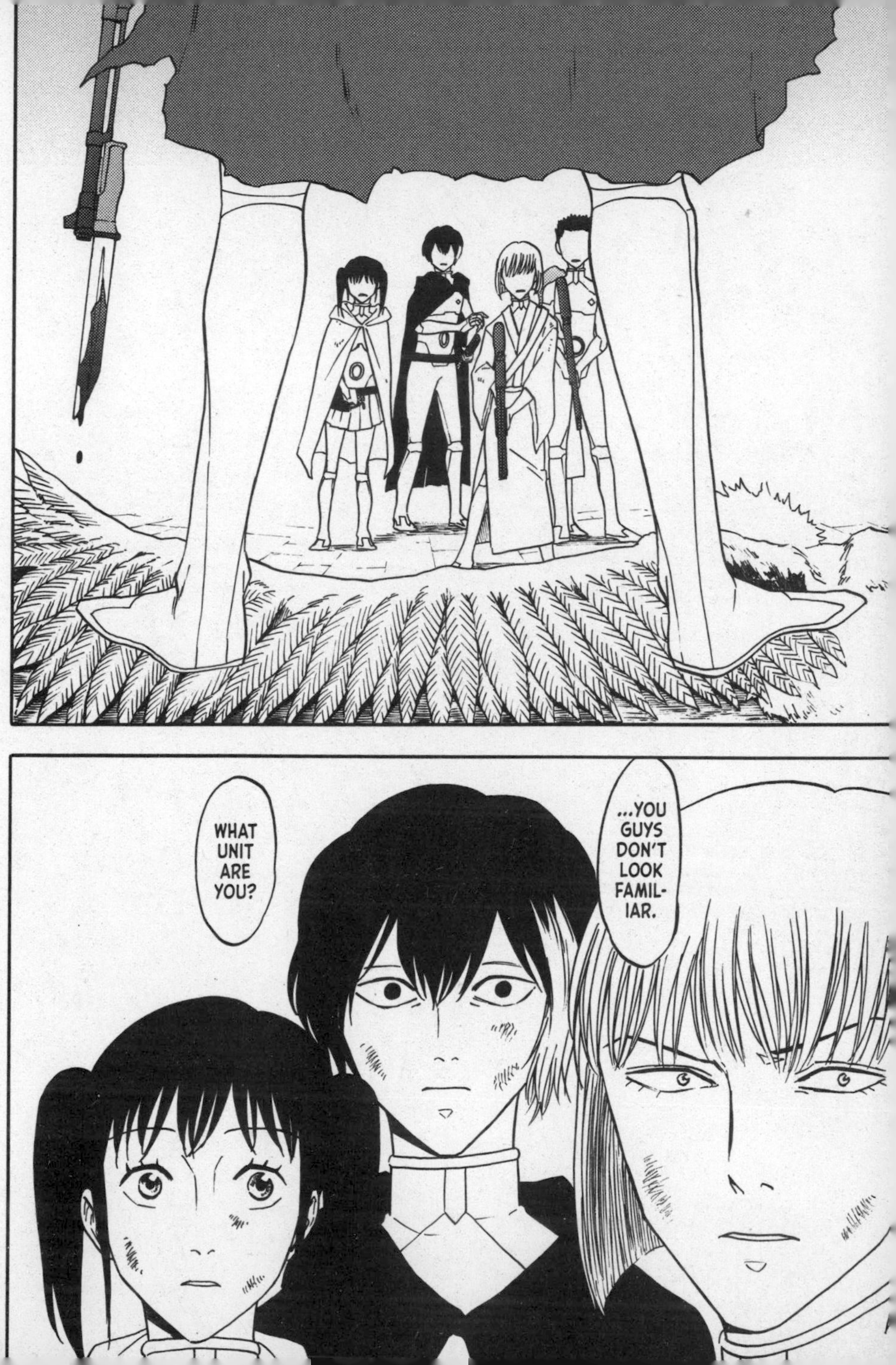
...YOU GUYS DON'T LOOK FAMILIAR.
WHAT UNIT ARE YOU?

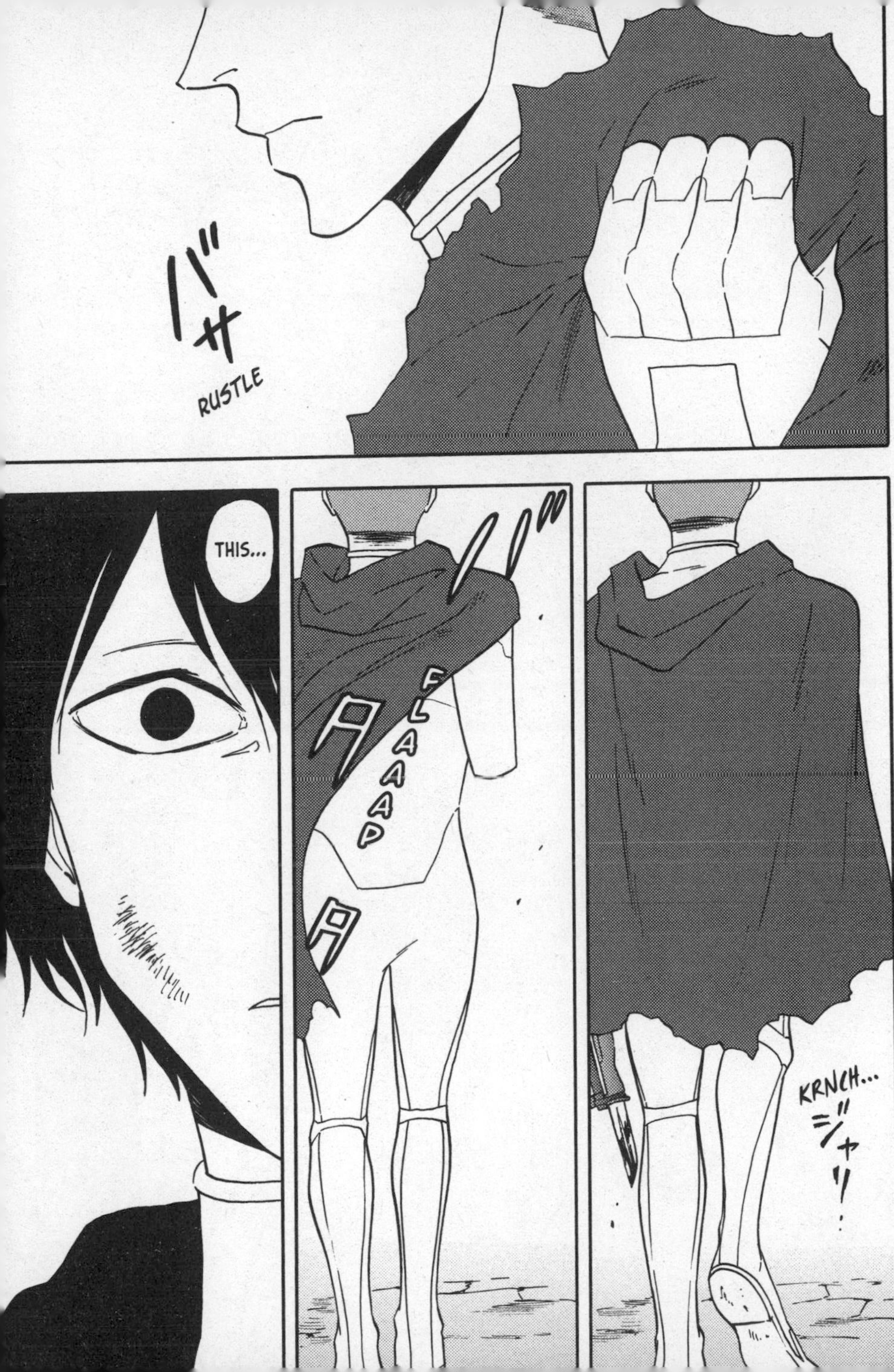
バサ
RUSTLE
KRNCH...
ジャリ!
FLAAAAP
THIS...

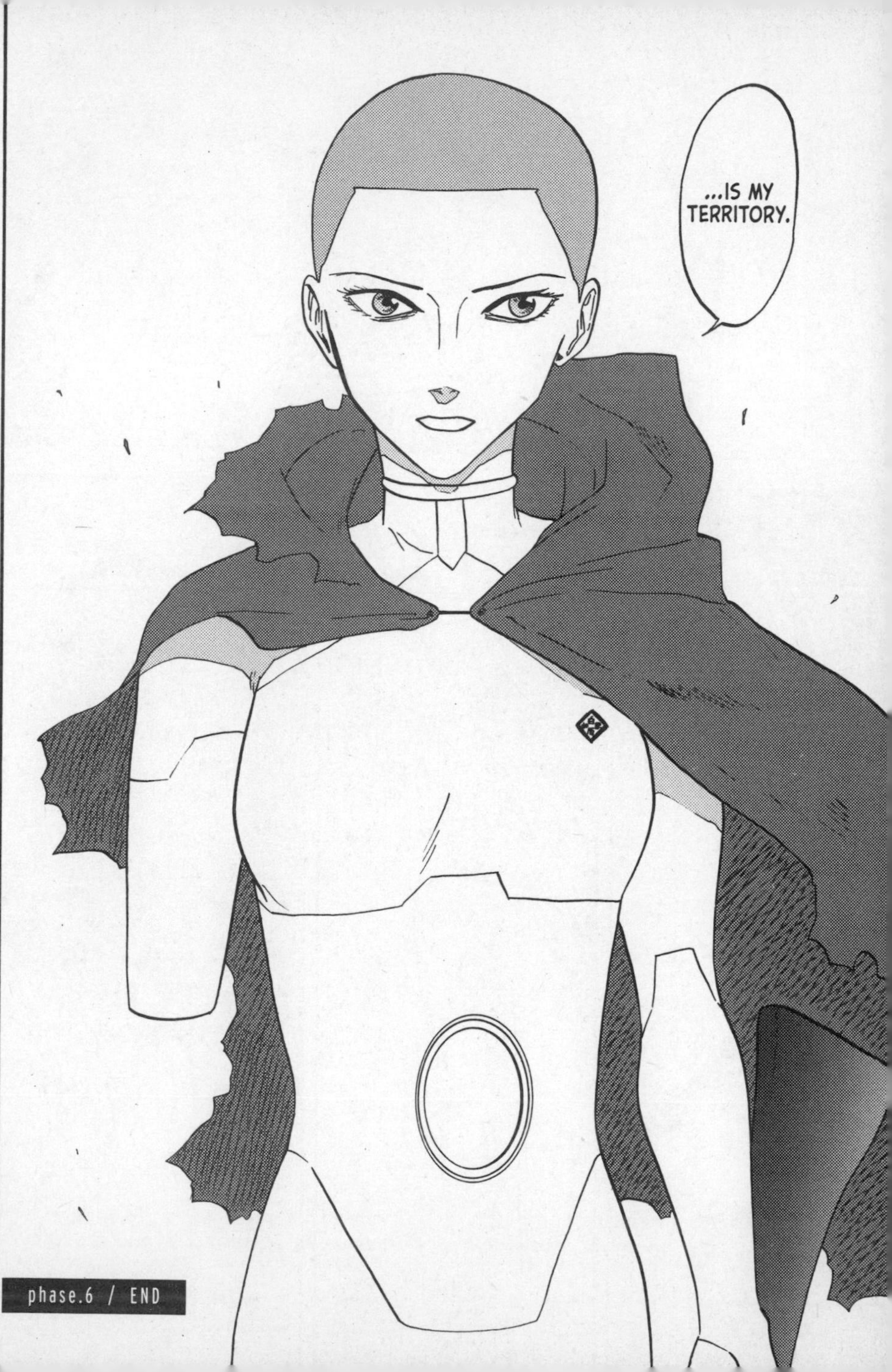
...IS MY TERRITORY.
phase.6 / END

phase.7 Lose It

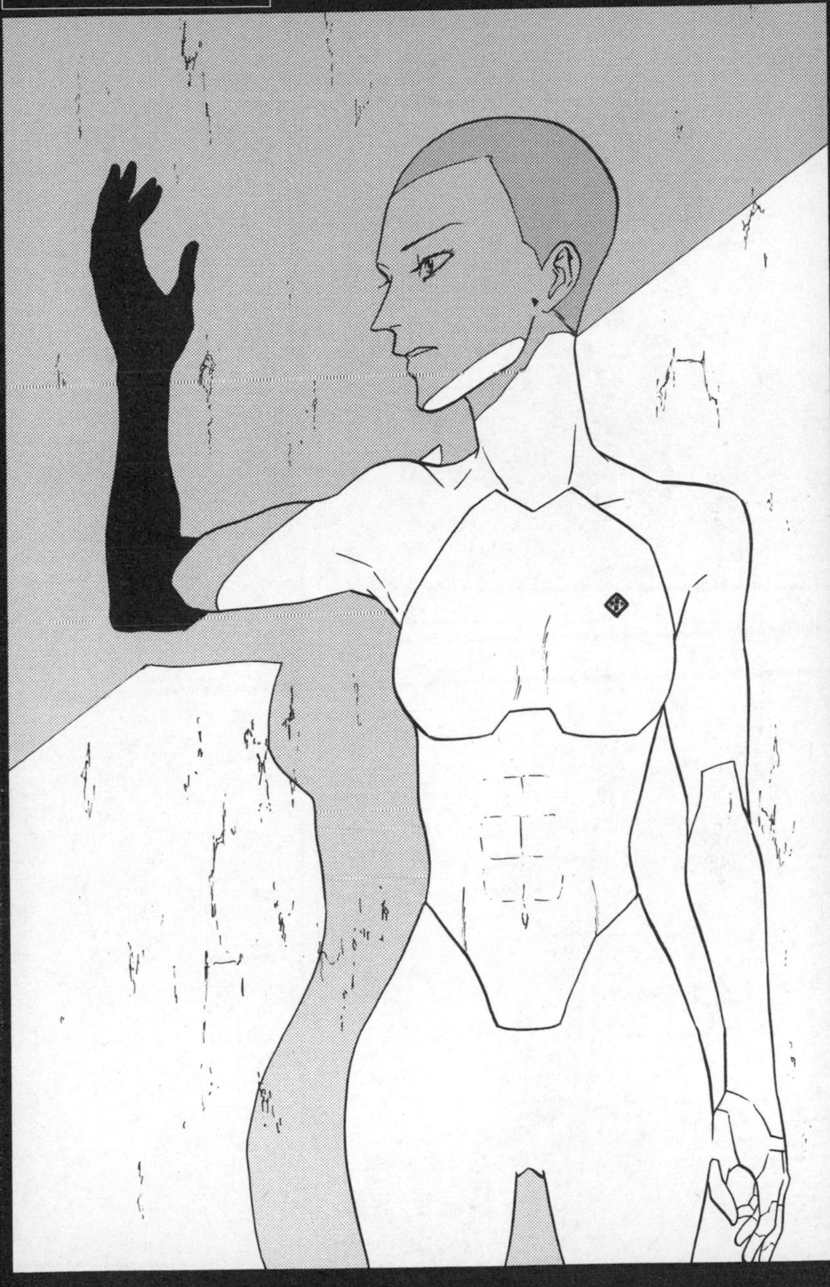

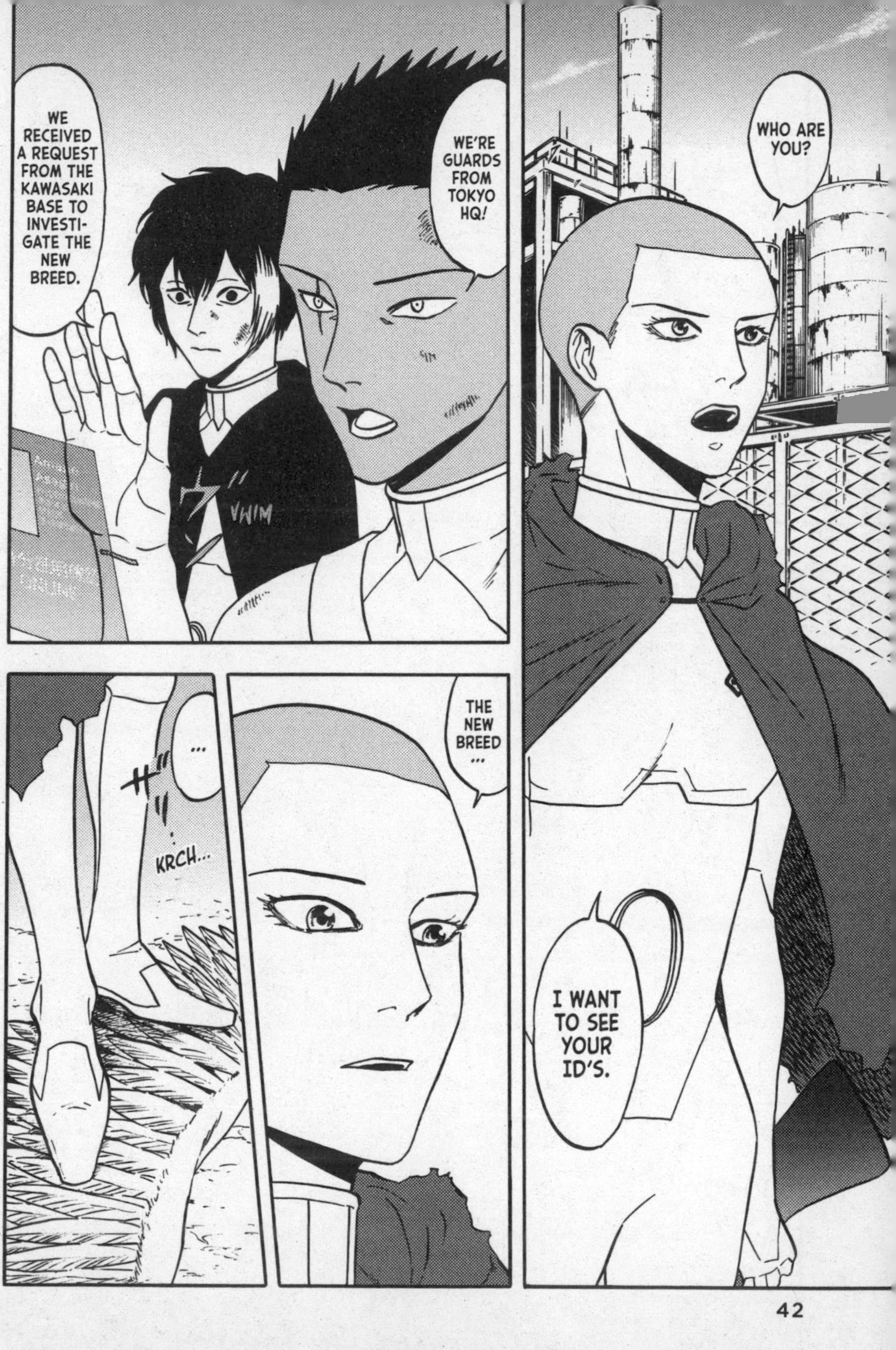
WHO ARE YOU?
I WANT TO SEE YOUR ID'S.
WE'RE GUARDS FROM TOKYO HQ!
WE RECEIVED A REQUEST FROM THE KAWASAKI BASE TO INVESTI-GATE THE NEW BREED.
VWIM
THE NEW BREED...
...
KRCH...

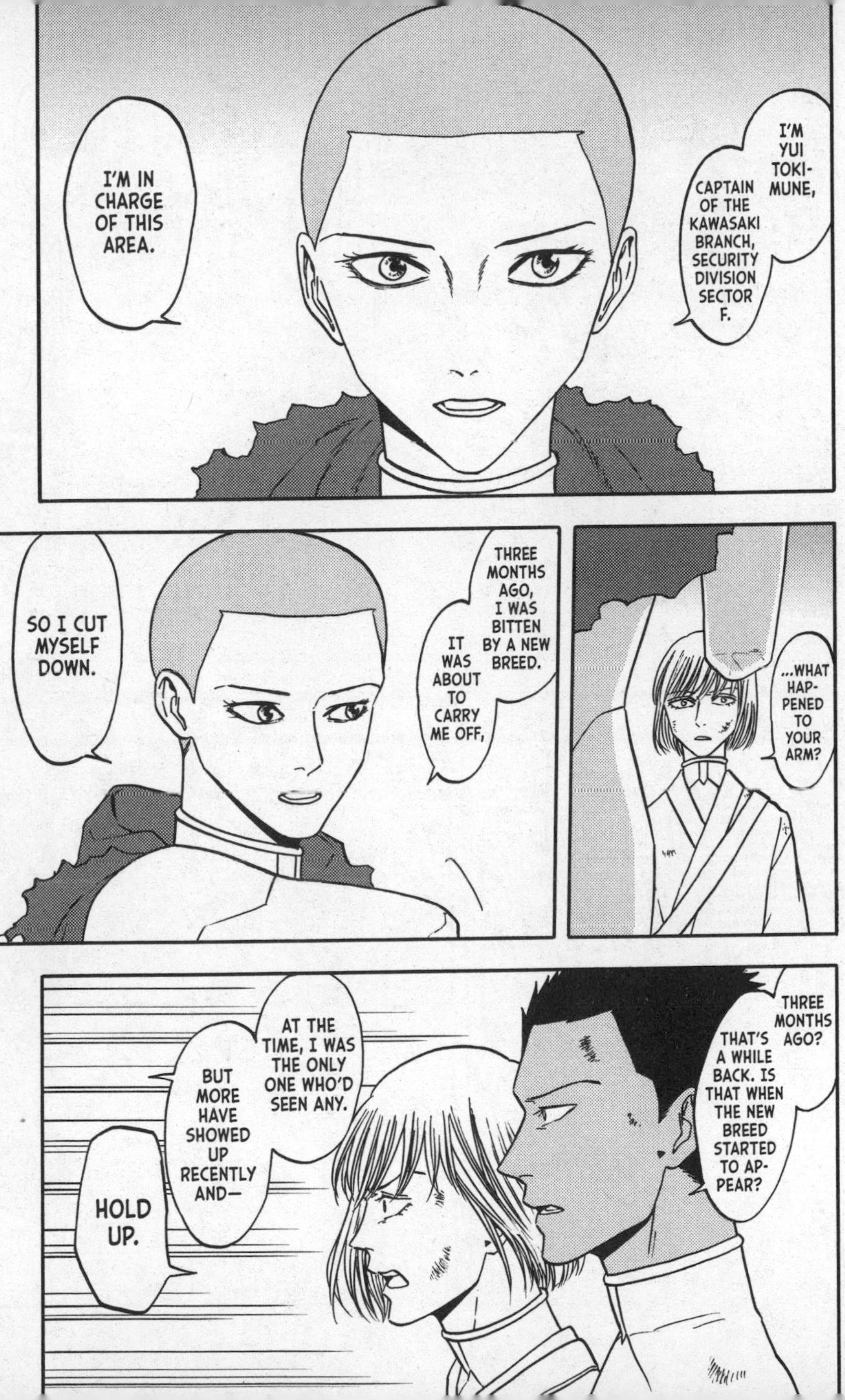
I'M YUI TOKI-MUNE,
CAPTAIN OF THE KAWASAKI BRANCH, SECURITY DIVISION SECTOR F.
I'M IN CHARGE OF THIS AREA.
...WHAT HAP-PENED TO YOUR ARM?
THREE MONTHS AGO, I WAS BITTEN BY A NEW BREED.
IT WAS ABOUT TO CARRY ME OFF,
SO I CUT MYSELF DOWN.
THREE MONTHS AGO?
THAT'S A WHILE BACK. IS THAT WHEN THE NEW BREED STARTED TO AP-PEAR?
AT THE TIME, I WAS THE ONLY ONE WHO'D SEEN ANY.
BUT MORE HAVE SHOWED UP RECENTLY AND—
HOLD UP.

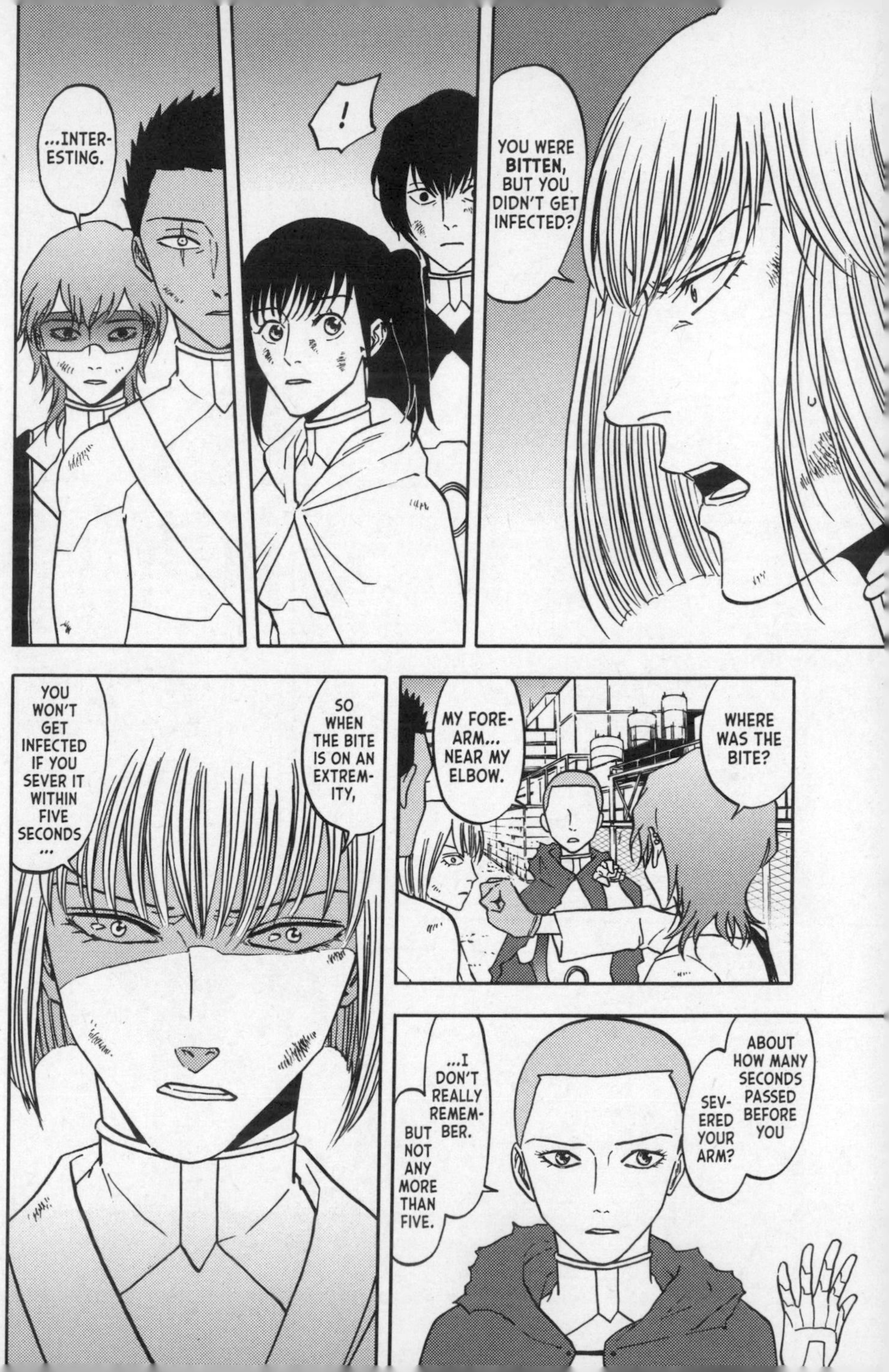
YOU WERE **BITTEN,** BUT YOU DIDN'T GET INFECTED?
!
...INTERESTING.
WHERE WAS THE BITE?
MY FOREARM... NEAR MY ELBOW.
ABOUT HOW MANY SECONDS PASSED BEFORE YOU SEVERED YOUR ARM?
...I DON'T REALLY REMEMBER.
BUT NOT ANY MORE THAN FIVE.
SO WHEN THE BITE IS ON AN EXTREMITY,
YOU WON'T GET INFECTED IF YOU SEVER IT WITHIN FIVE SECONDS...

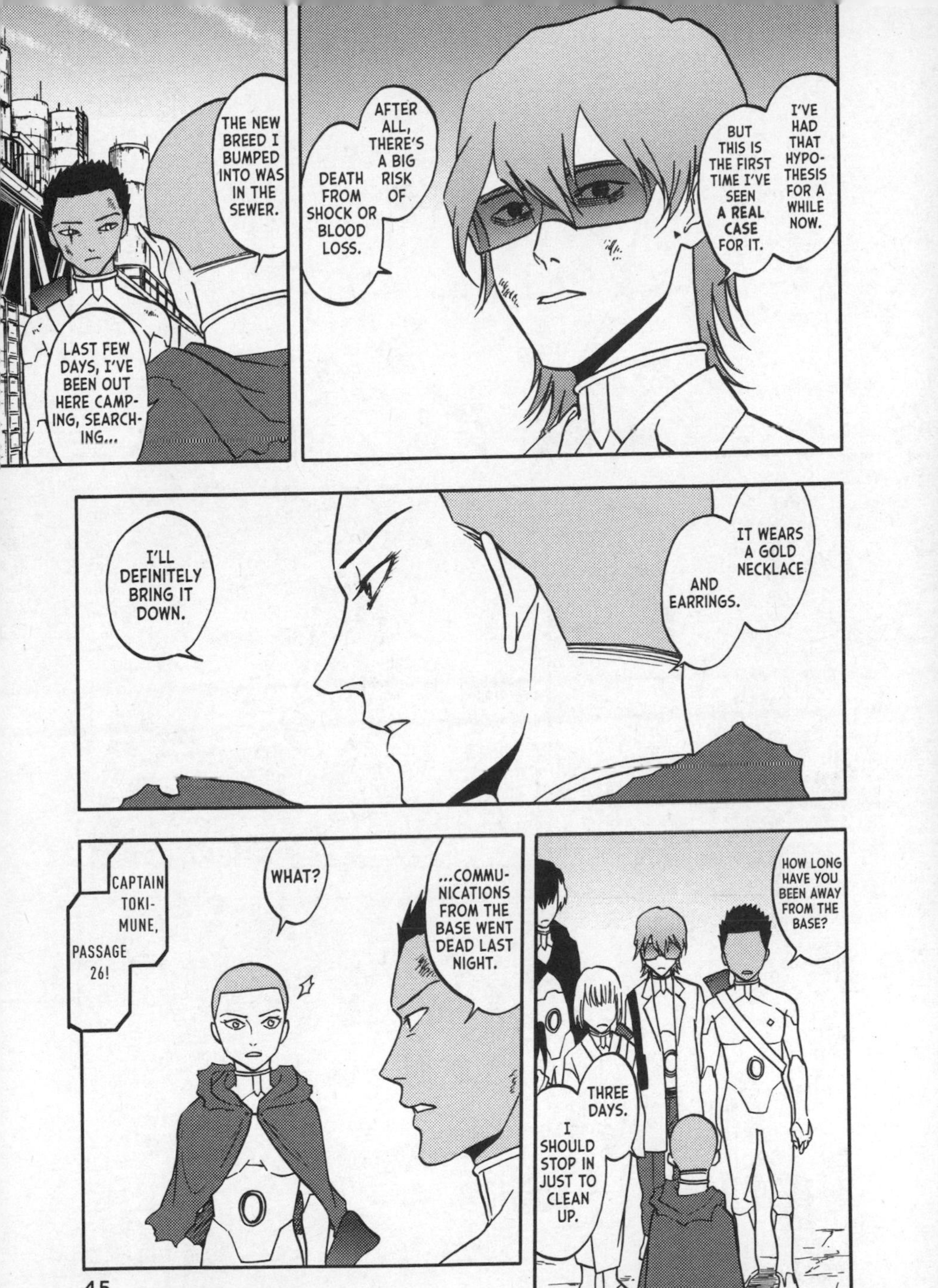
I'VE HAD THAT HYPOTHESIS FOR A WHILE NOW.
BUT THIS IS THE FIRST TIME I'VE SEEN A REAL CASE FOR IT.
AFTER ALL, THERE'S A BIG RISK OF DEATH FROM SHOCK OR BLOOD LOSS.
THE NEW BREED I BUMPED INTO WAS IN THE SEWER.
LAST FEW DAYS, I'VE BEEN OUT HERE CAMPING, SEARCHING...
IT WEARS A GOLD NECKLACE
AND EARRINGS.
I'LL DEFINITELY BRING IT DOWN.
HOW LONG HAVE YOU BEEN AWAY FROM THE BASE?
THREE DAYS.
I SHOULD STOP IN JUST TO CLEAN UP.
...COMMUNICATIONS FROM THE BASE WENT DEAD LAST NIGHT.
WHAT?
CAPTAIN TOKIMUNE,
PASSAGE 26!

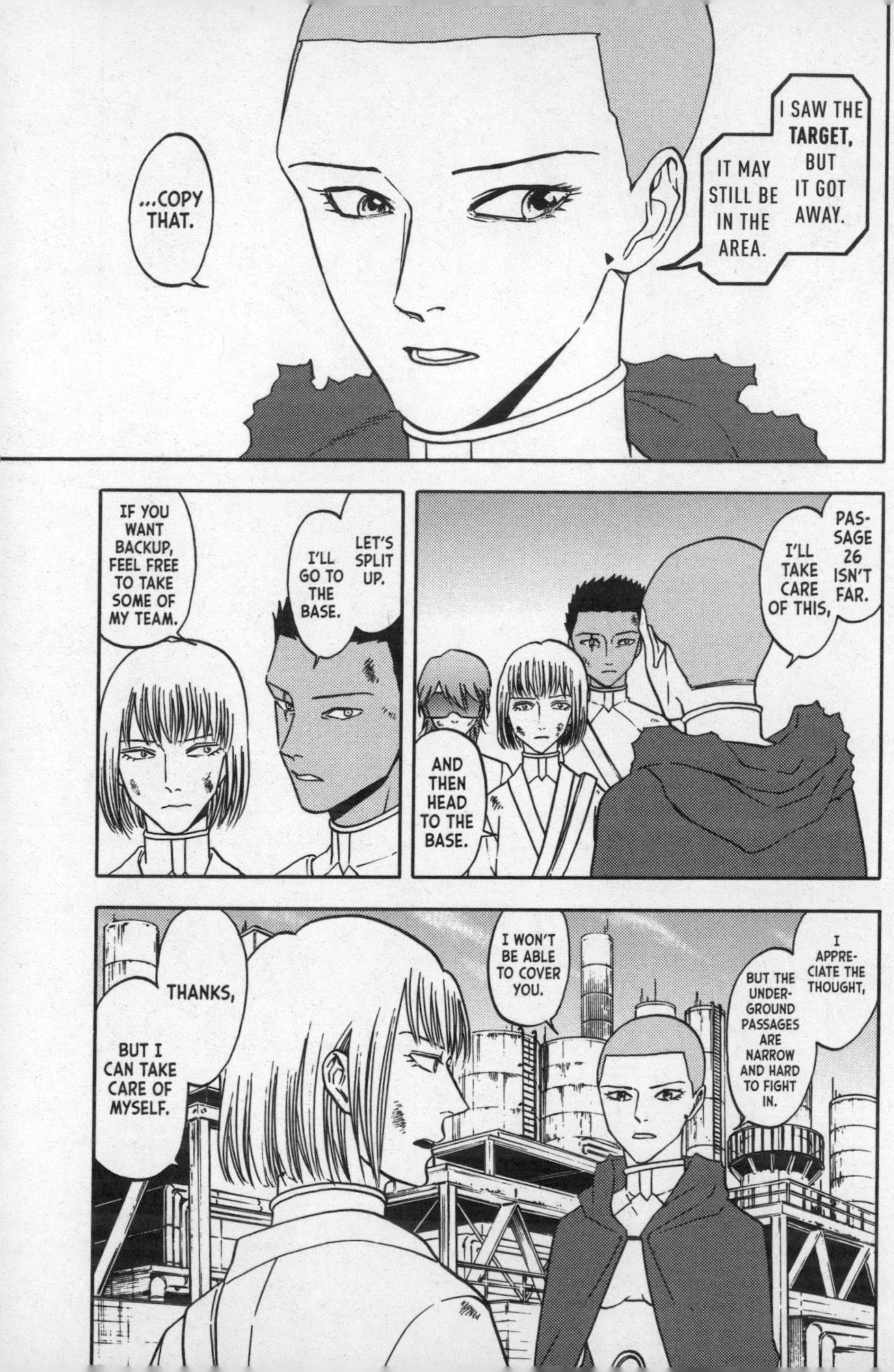
I SAW THE **TARGET,** BUT IT GOT AWAY.
IT MAY STILL BE IN THE AREA.
...COPY THAT.
PASSAGE 26 ISN'T FAR.
I'LL TAKE CARE OF THIS,
AND THEN HEAD TO THE BASE.
LET'S SPLIT UP.
I'LL GO TO THE BASE.
IF YOU WANT BACKUP, FEEL FREE TO TAKE SOME OF MY TEAM.
I APPRECIATE THE THOUGHT,
BUT THE UNDERGROUND PASSAGES ARE NARROW AND HARD TO FIGHT IN.
I WON'T BE ABLE TO COVER YOU.
THANKS,
BUT I CAN TAKE CARE OF MYSELF.

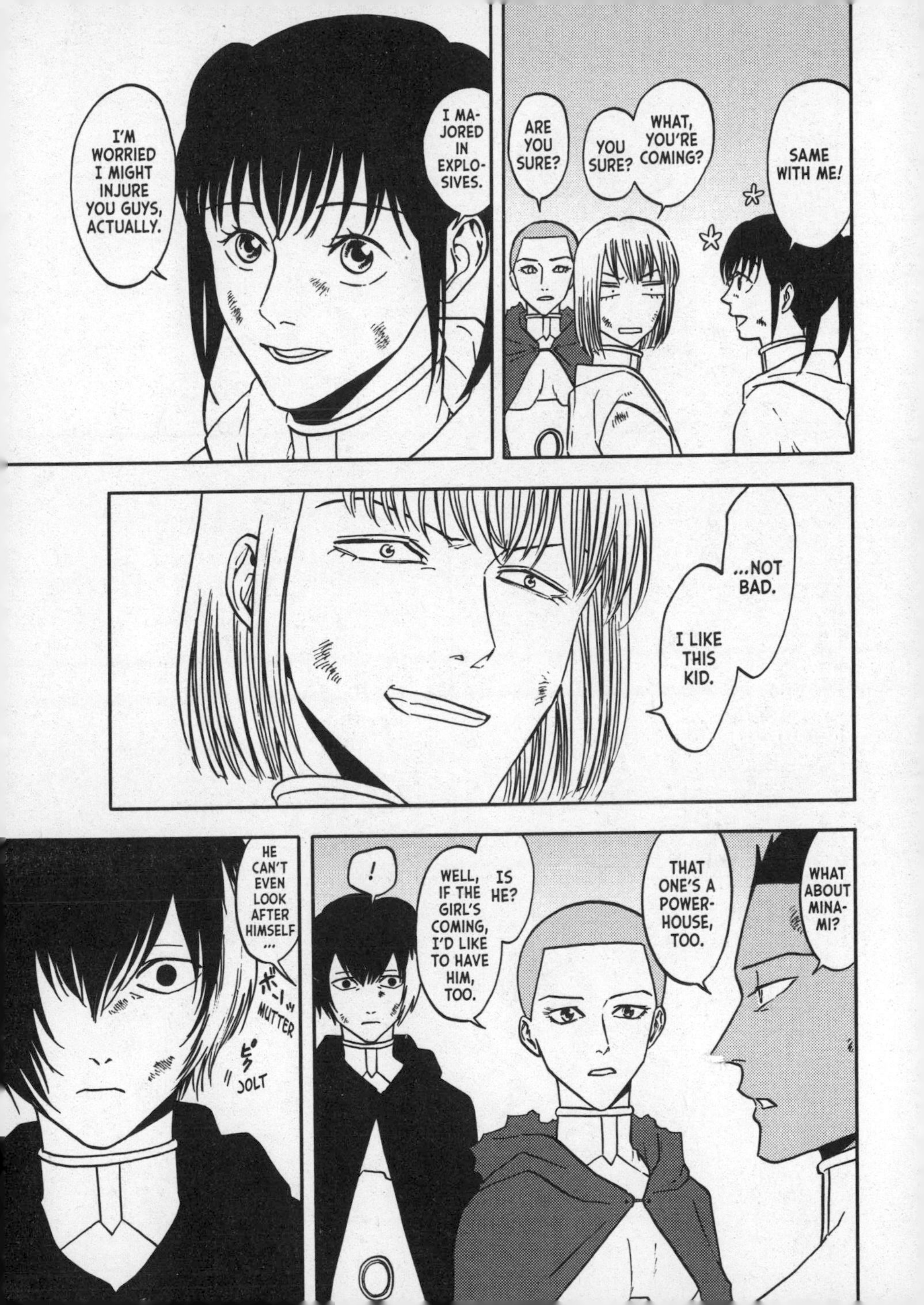
SAME WITH ME!
WHAT, YOU'RE COMING?
YOU SURE?
ARE YOU SURE?
I MAJORED IN EXPLOSIVES.
I'M WORRIED I MIGHT INJURE YOU GUYS, ACTUALLY.
...NOT BAD.
I LIKE THIS KID.
WHAT ABOUT MINAMI?
THAT ONE'S A POWERHOUSE, TOO.
IS HE?
WELL, IF THE GIRL'S COMING, I'D LIKE TO HAVE HIM, TOO.
!
HE CAN'T EVEN LOOK AFTER HIMSELF...
MUTTER
JOLT

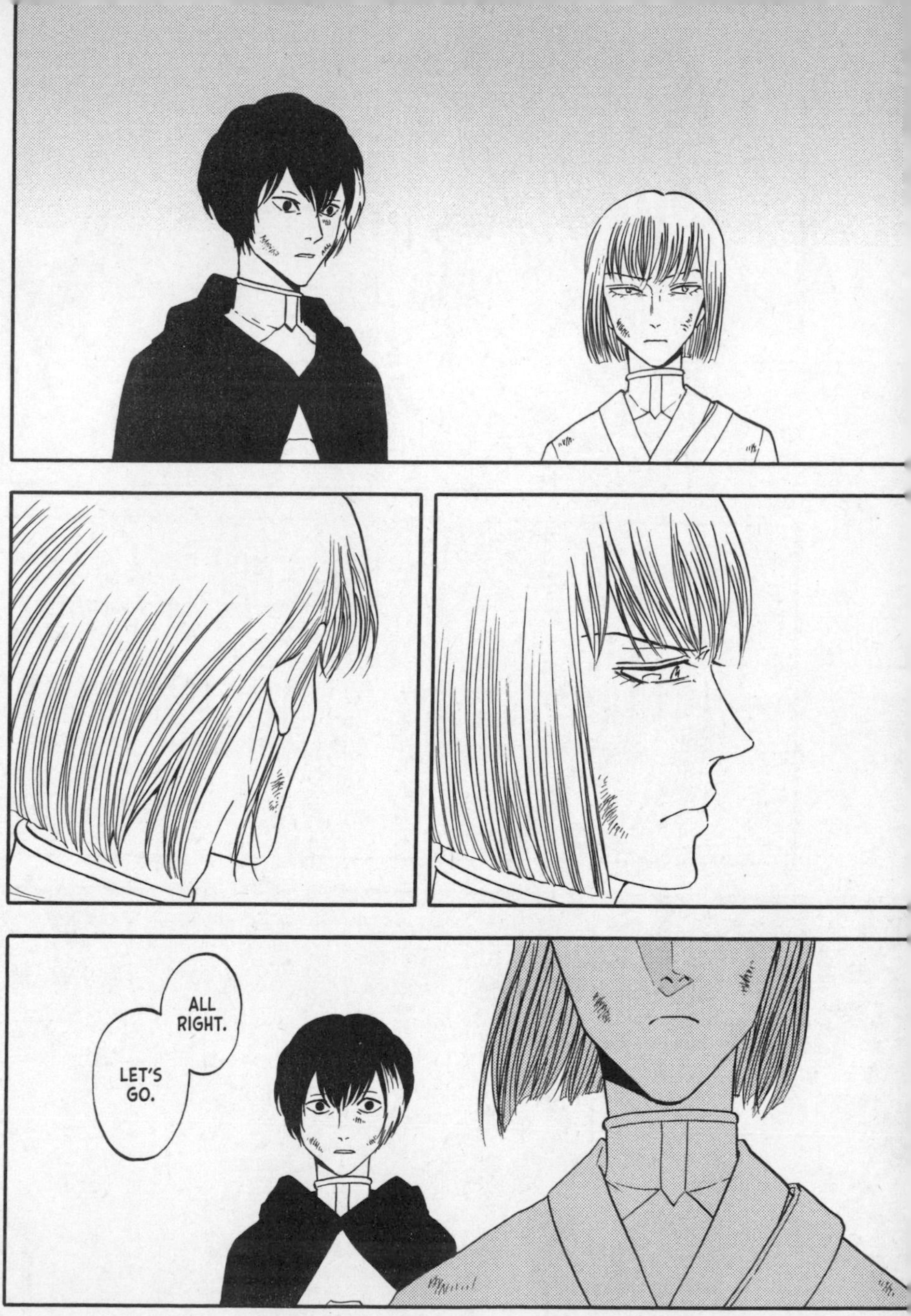
ALL RIGHT.
LET'S GO.

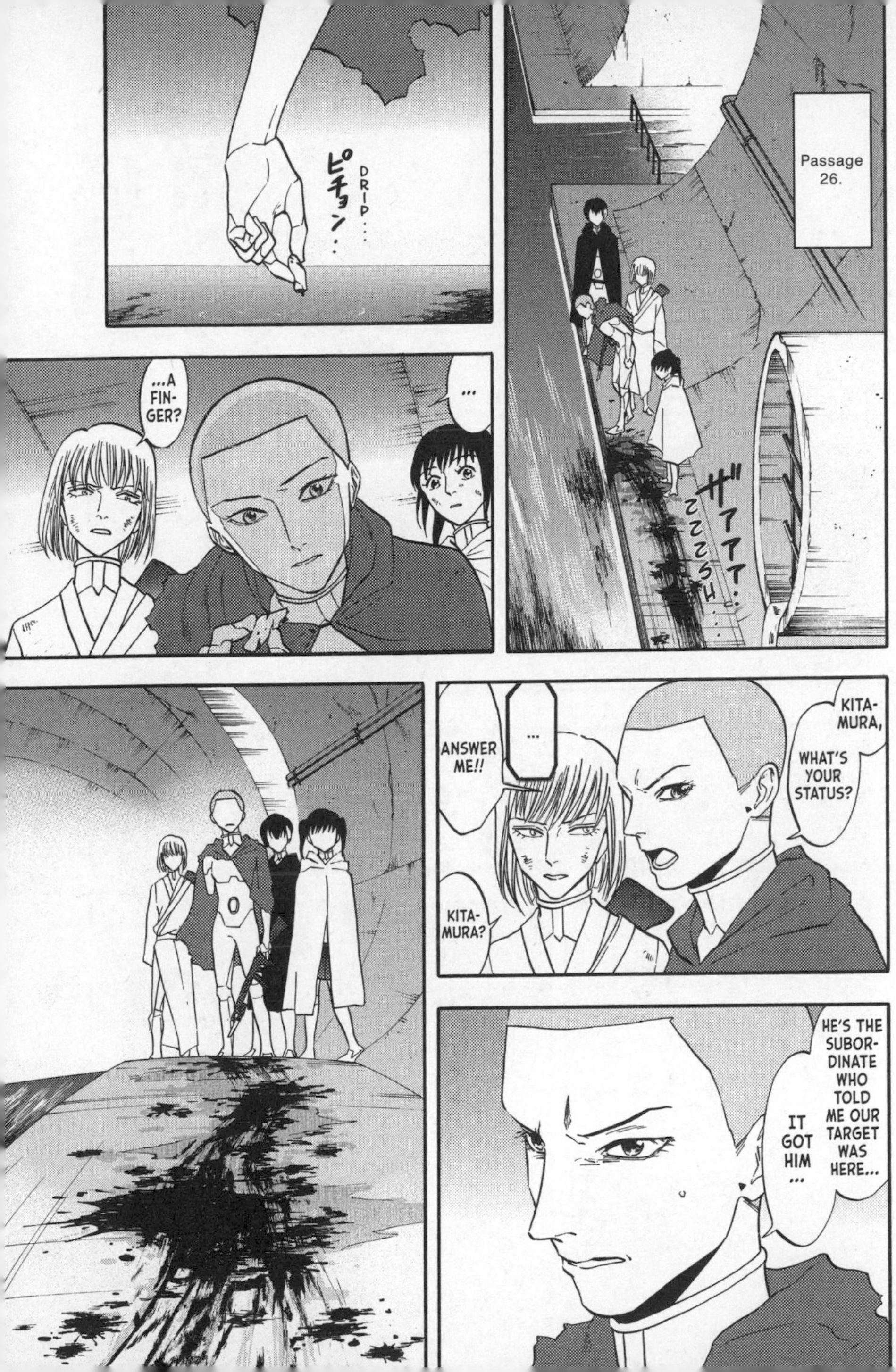
Passage 26.
ザアアア…
ZZZSH
ピチョン…
DRIP…
…
…A FIN-GER?
KITA-MURA, WHAT'S YOUR STATUS?
…
ANSWER ME!!
KITA-MURA?
HE'S THE SUBOR-DINATE WHO TOLD ME OUR TARGET WAS HERE…
IT GOT HIM…

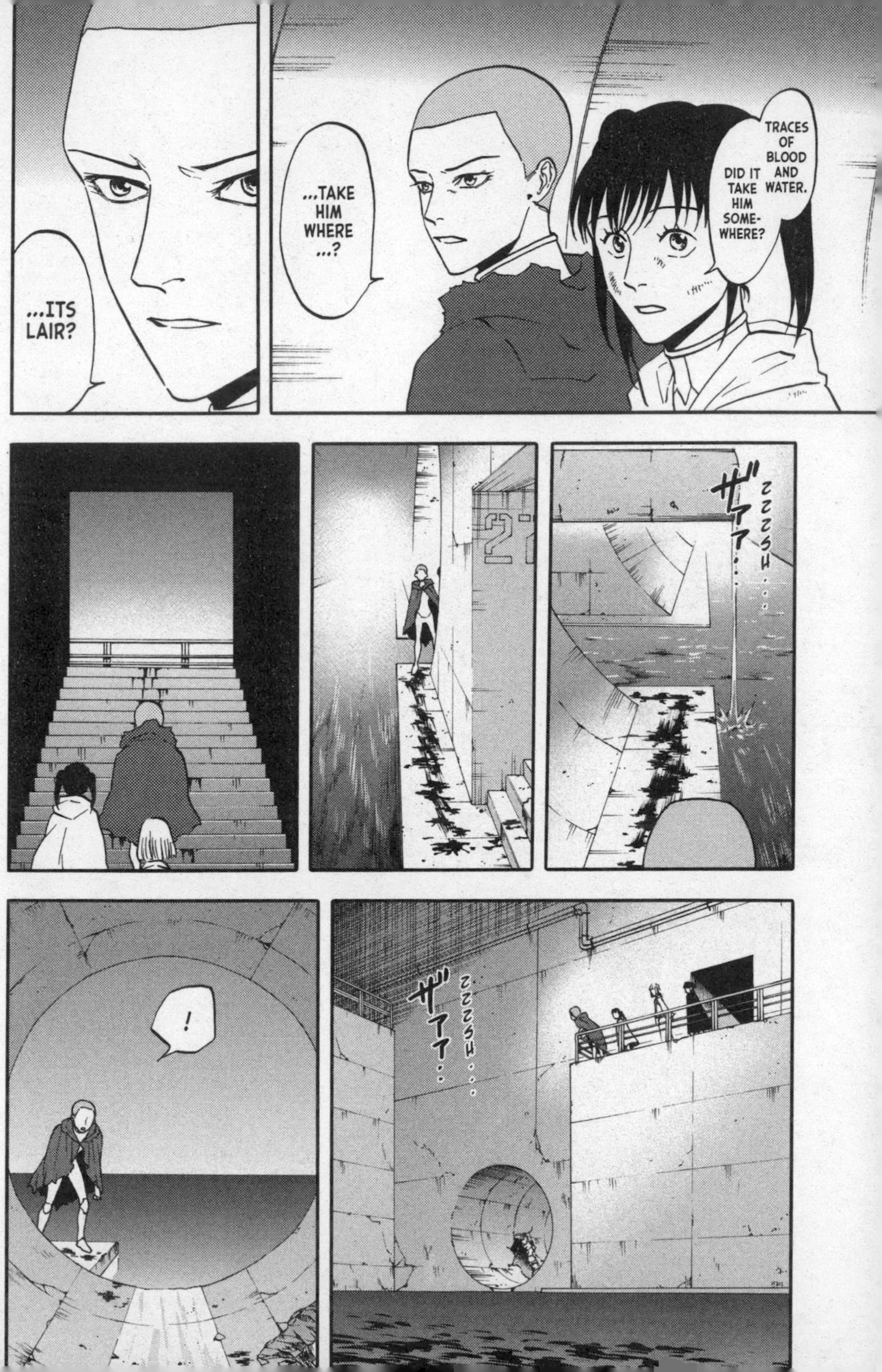
TRACES OF BLOOD AND WATER.
DID IT TAKE HIM SOME-WHERE?
...TAKE HIM WHERE ...?
...ITS LAIR?
ザァア...
ZZZSH...
ザァア...
ZZZSH...
!

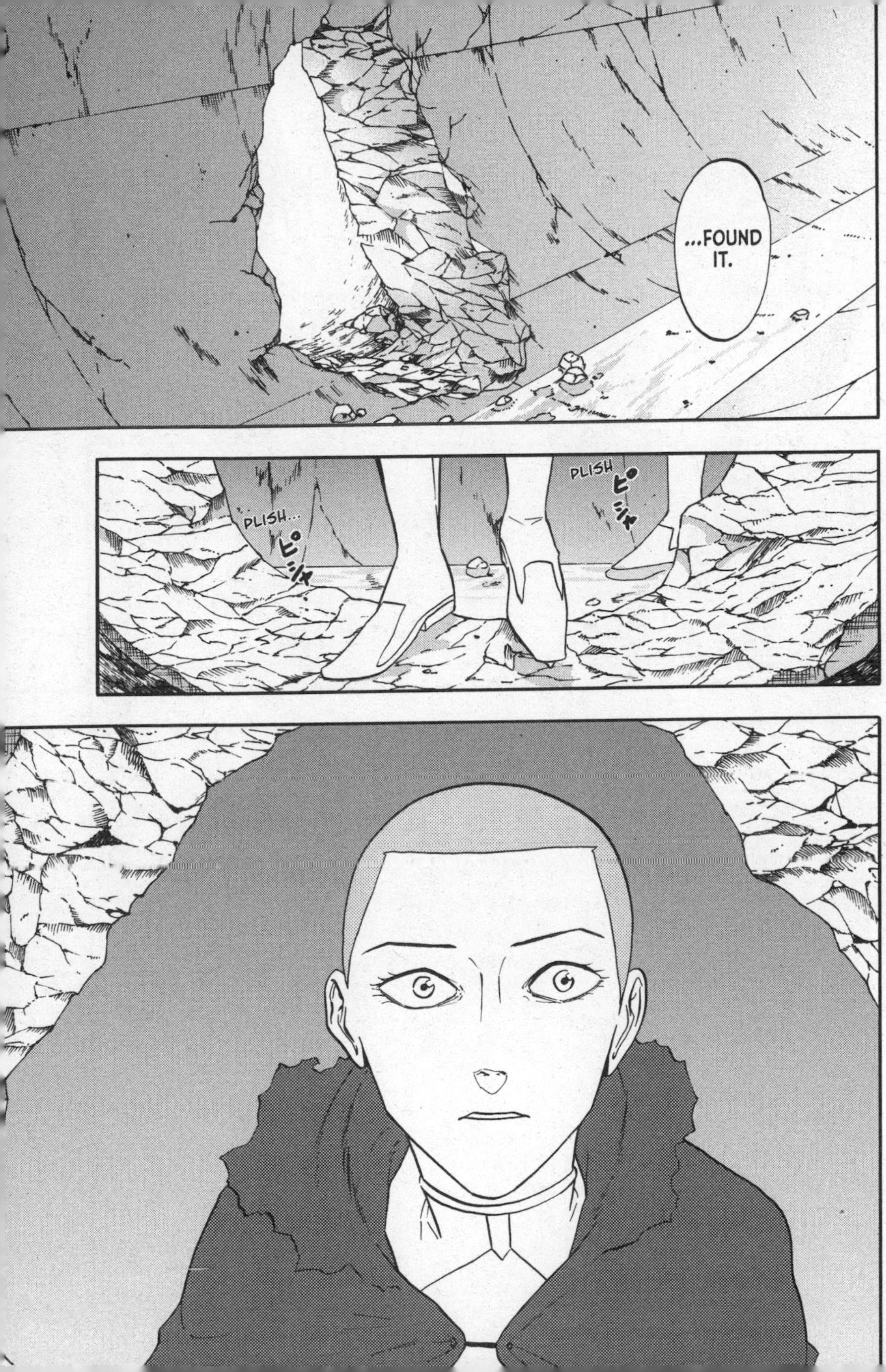
...FOUND IT.
PLISH
ピシャ
PLISH...
ピシャ

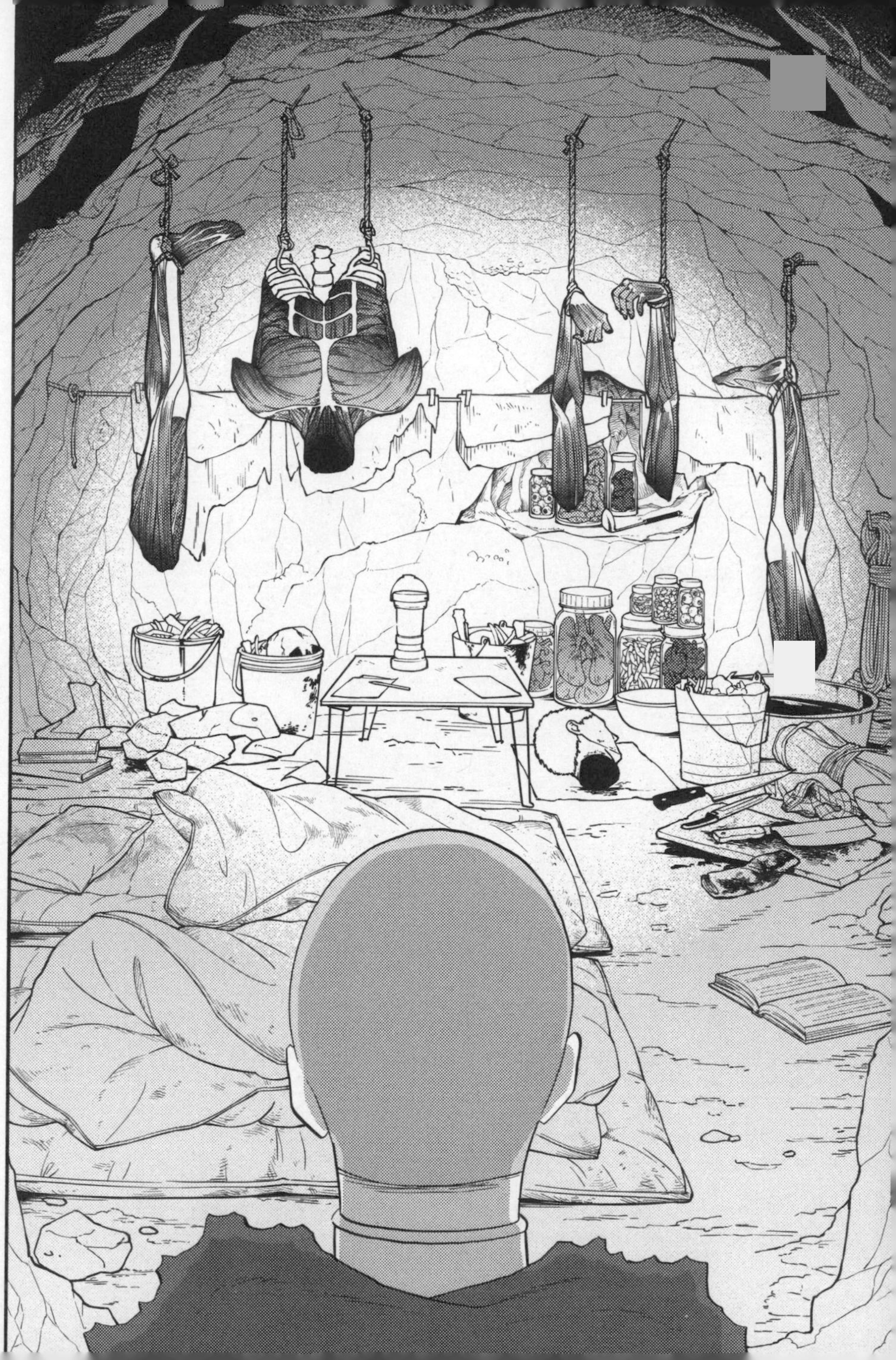

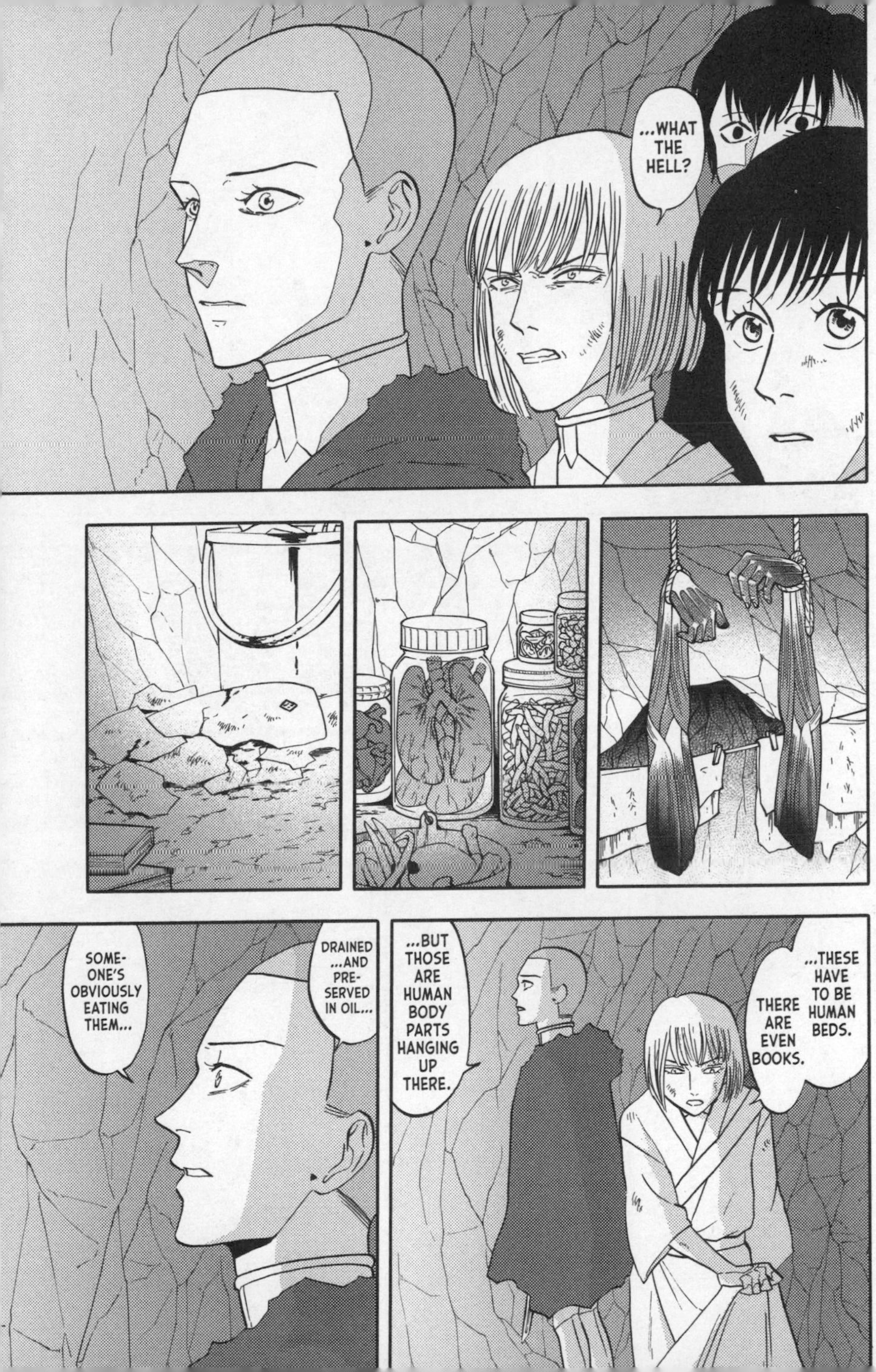
...WHAT THE HELL?
...THESE HAVE TO BE HUMAN BEDS.
THERE ARE EVEN BOOKS.
...BUT THOSE ARE HUMAN BODY PARTS HANGING UP THERE.
DRAINED ...AND PRE-SERVED IN OIL...
SOME-ONE'S OBVIOUSLY EATING THEM...

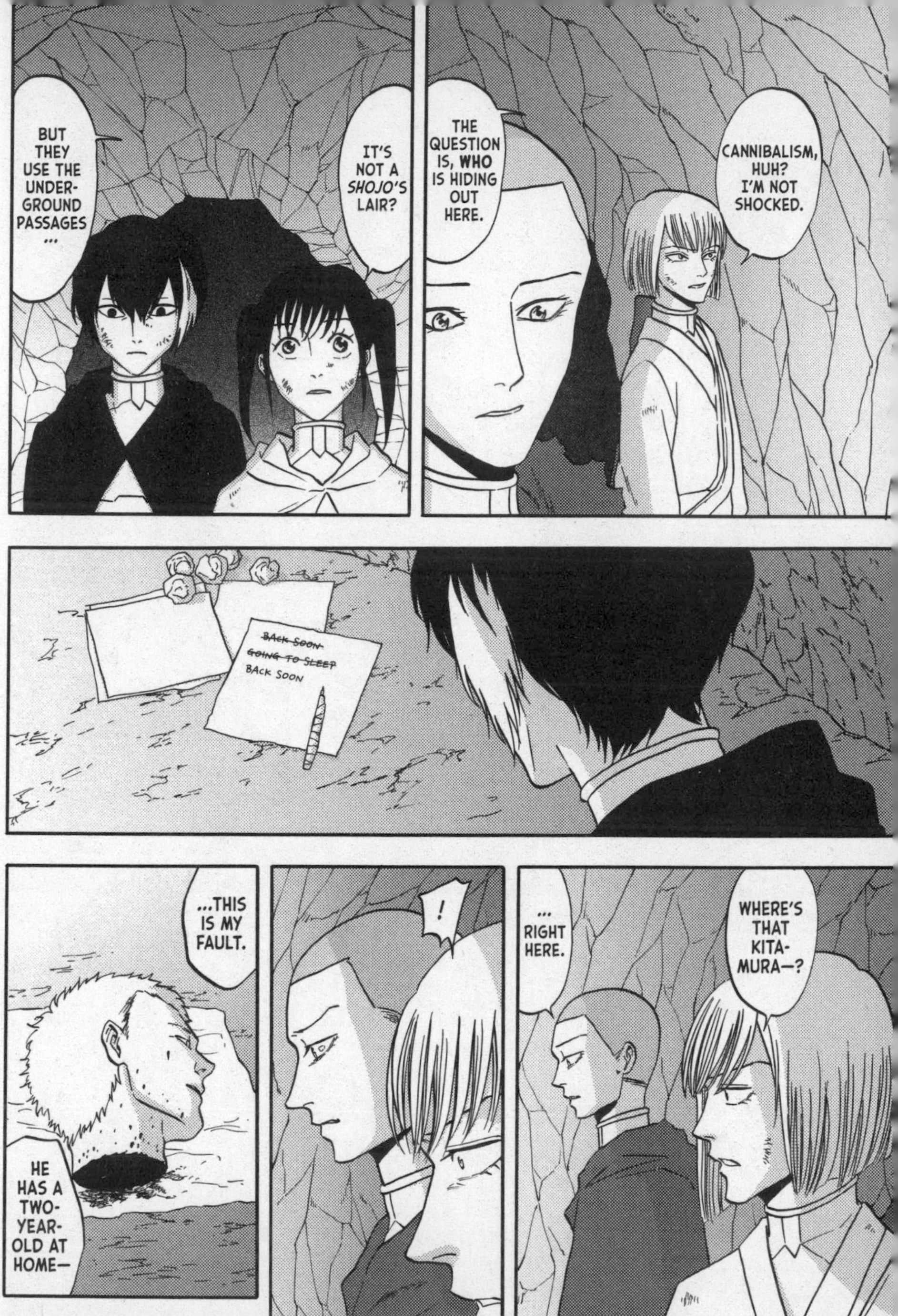
CANNIBALISM, HUH? I'M NOT SHOCKED.
THE QUESTION IS, **WHO** IS HIDING OUT HERE.
IT'S NOT A *SHOJO*'S LAIR?
BUT THEY USE THE UNDER-GROUND PASSAGES...
~~BACK SOON~~
~~GOING TO SLEEP~~
BACK SOON
WHERE'S THAT KITA-MURA—?
... RIGHT HERE.
!
...THIS IS MY FAULT.
HE HAS A TWO-YEAR-OLD AT HOME—

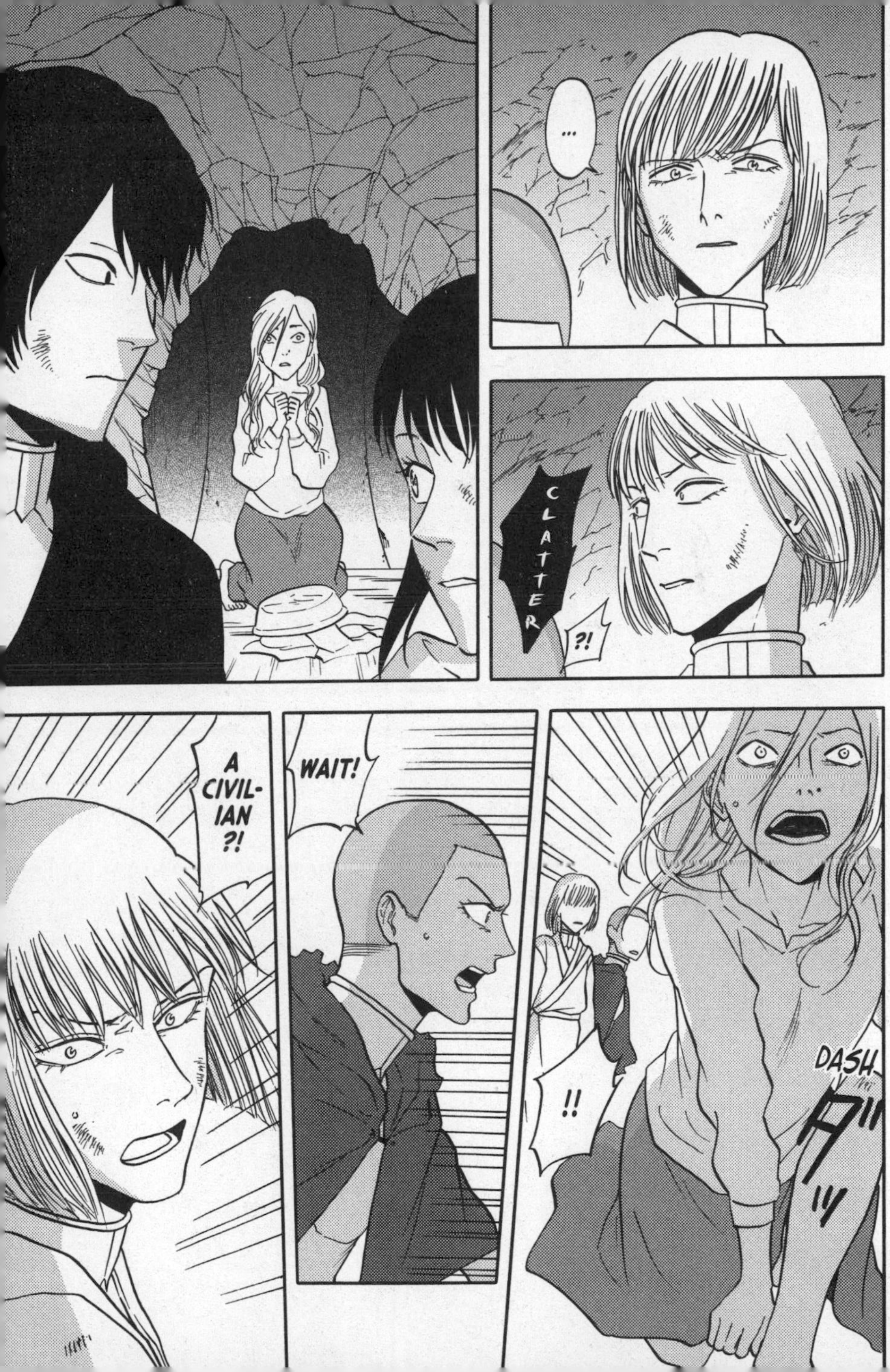
...
CLATTER
?!
DASH
!!
WAIT!
A CIVILIAN?!

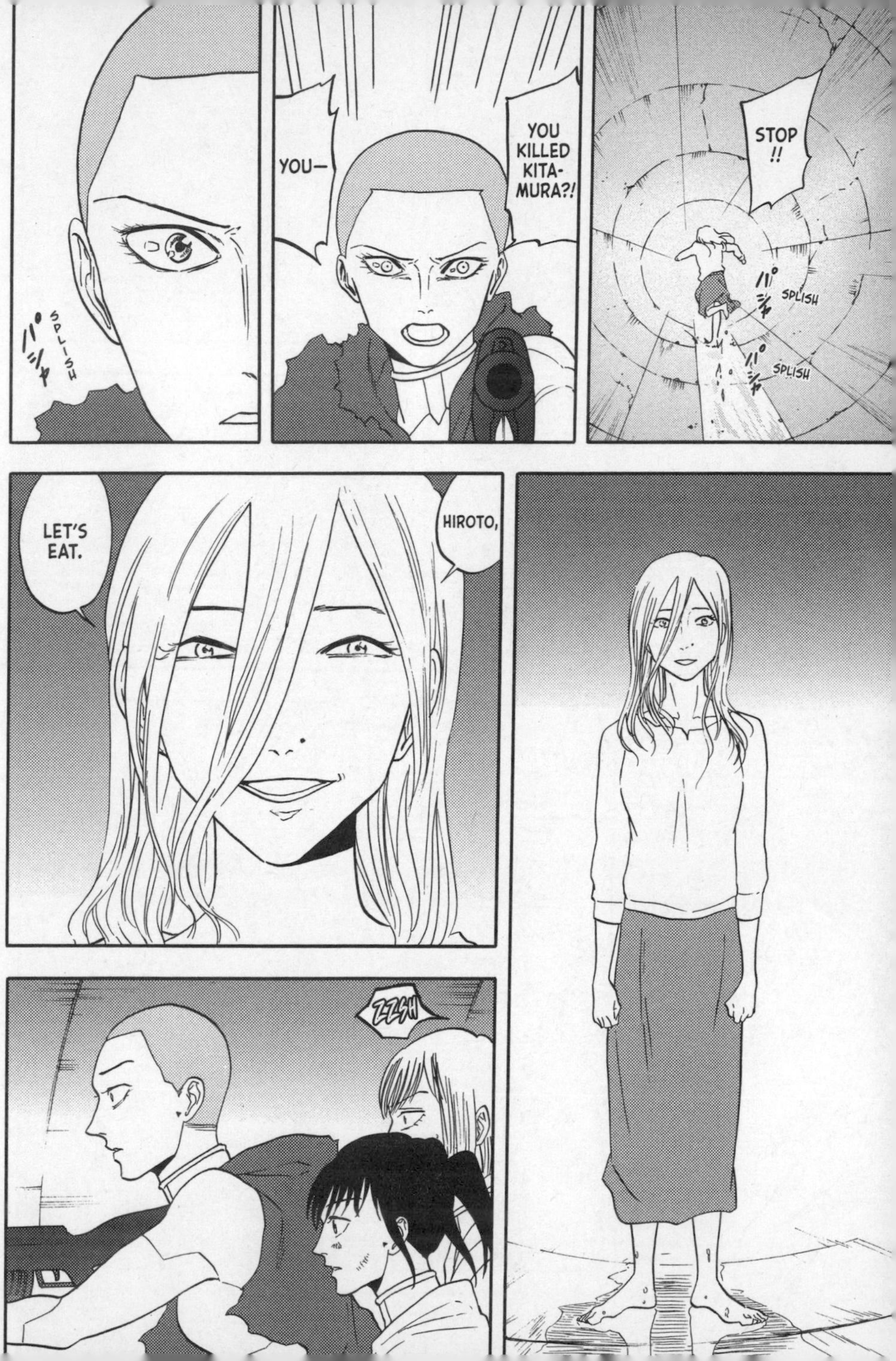
STOP!!
パシャ SPLISH
パシャ SPLISH
YOU KILLED KITA-MURA?!
YOU—
パシャ SPLISH
HIROTO,
LET'S EAT.
ZZSH

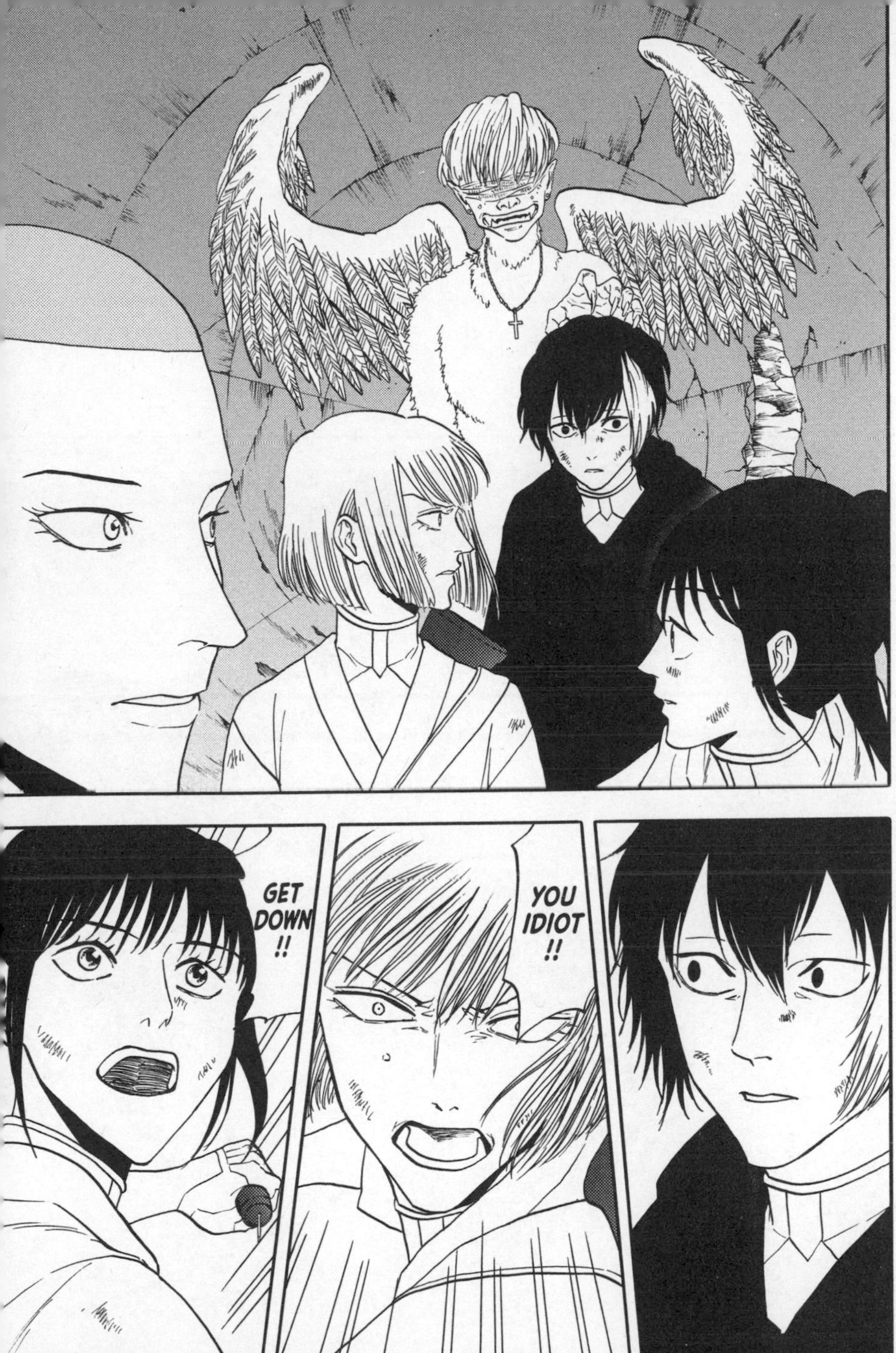
YOU IDIOT !!
GET DOWN !!

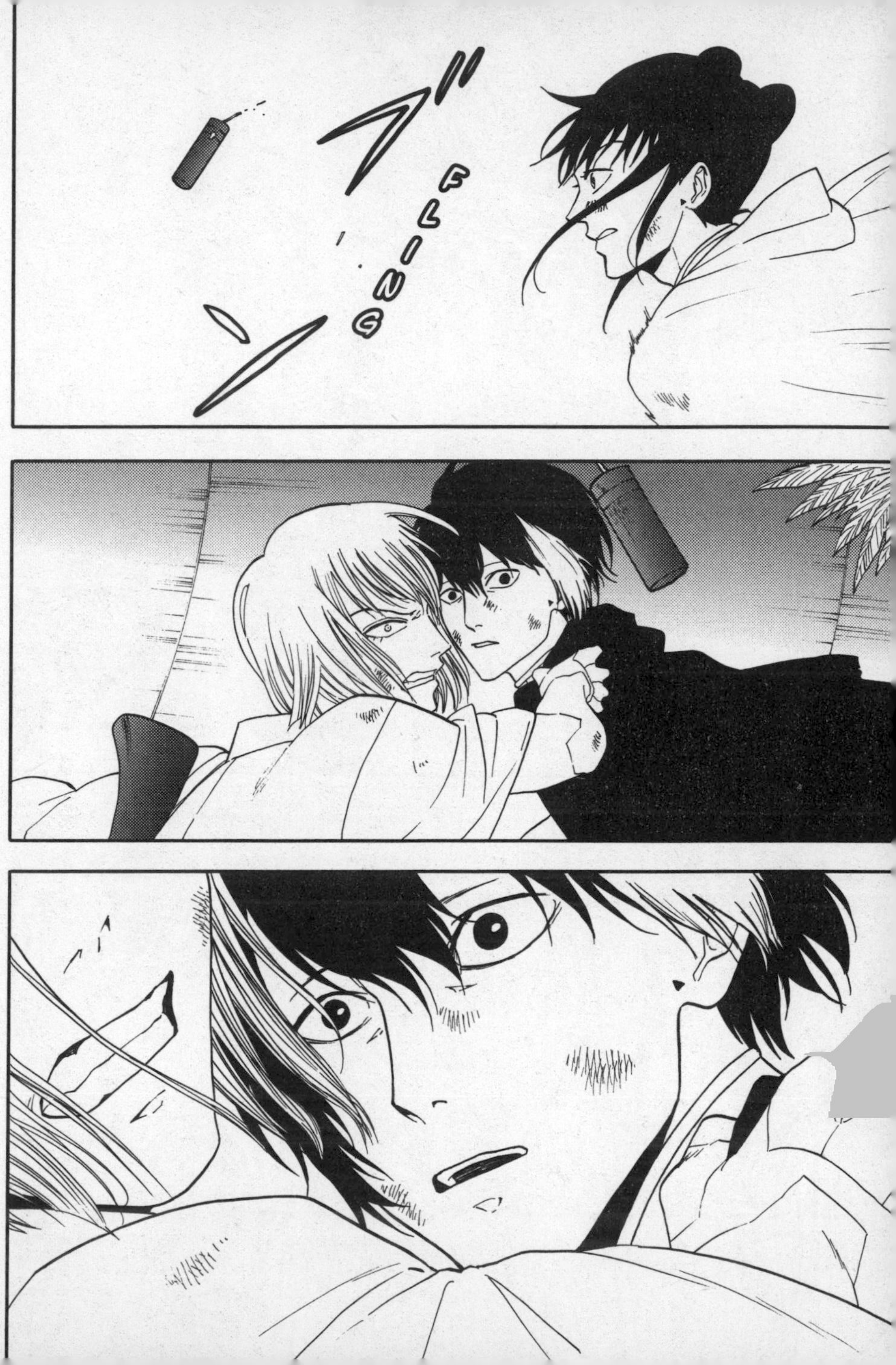
FLING

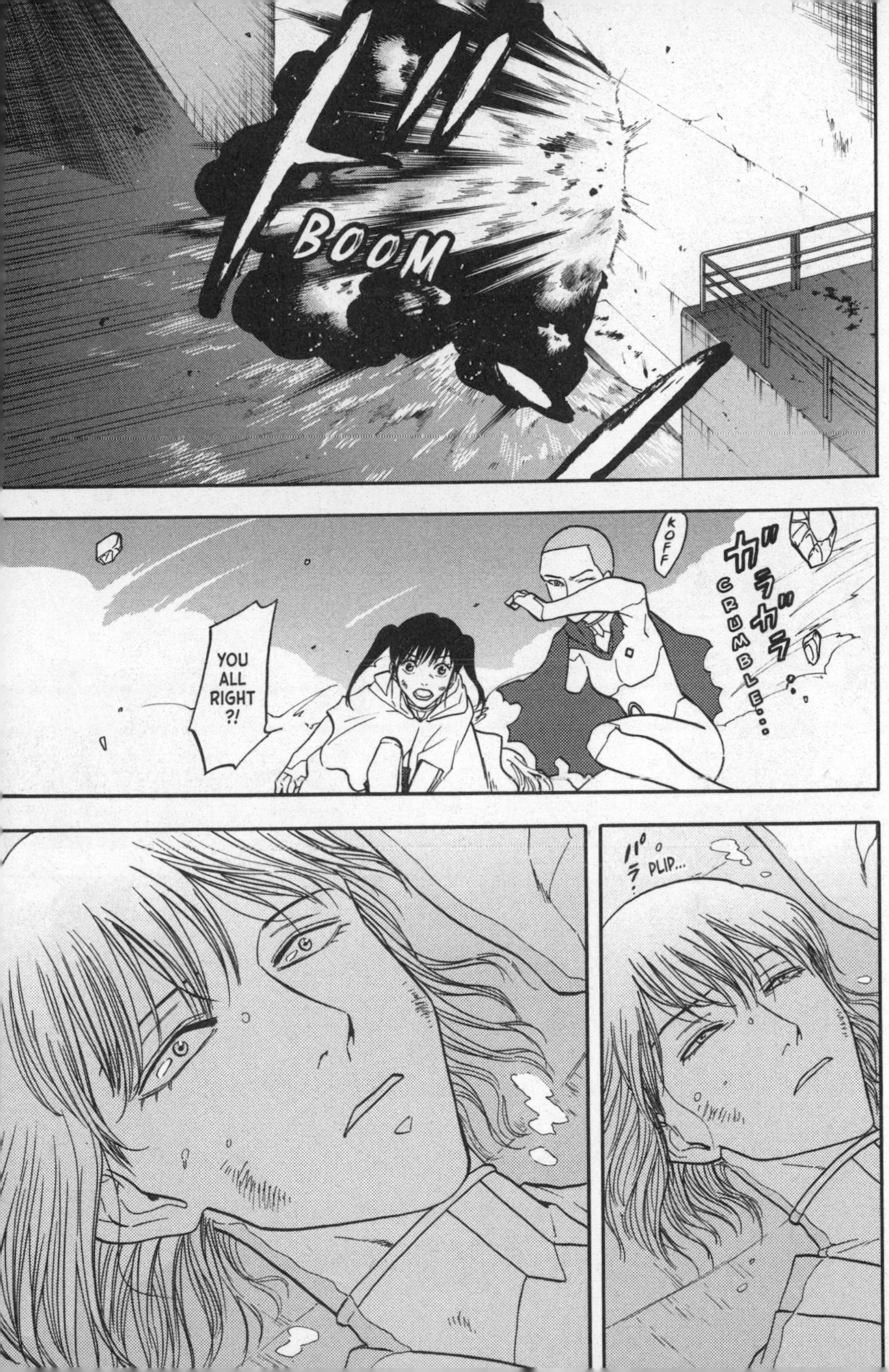

BOOM
KOFF
カラカラ
CRUMBLE...
YOU ALL RIGHT?!
パラ
PLIP...

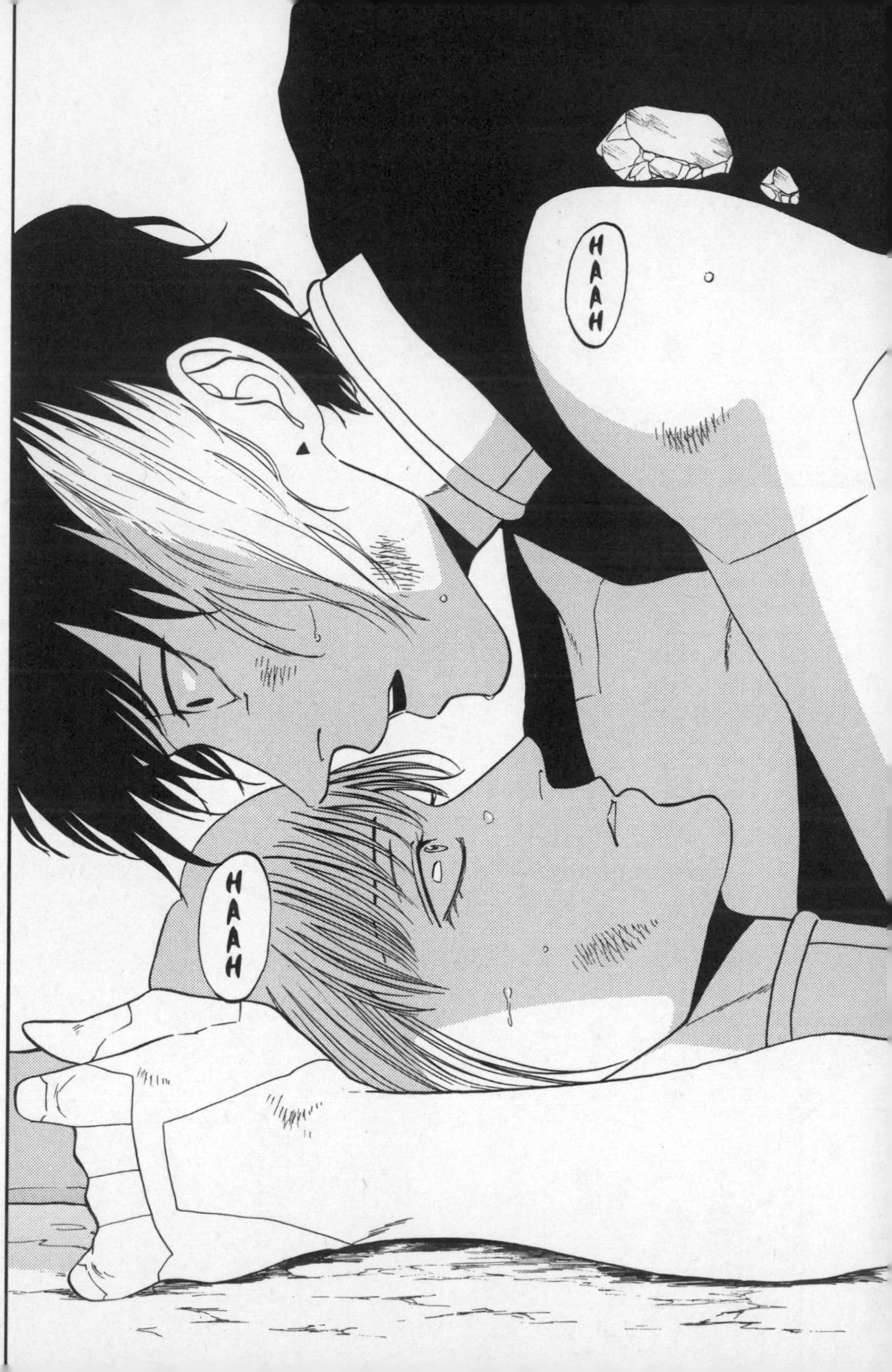
HAAAH
HAAAH

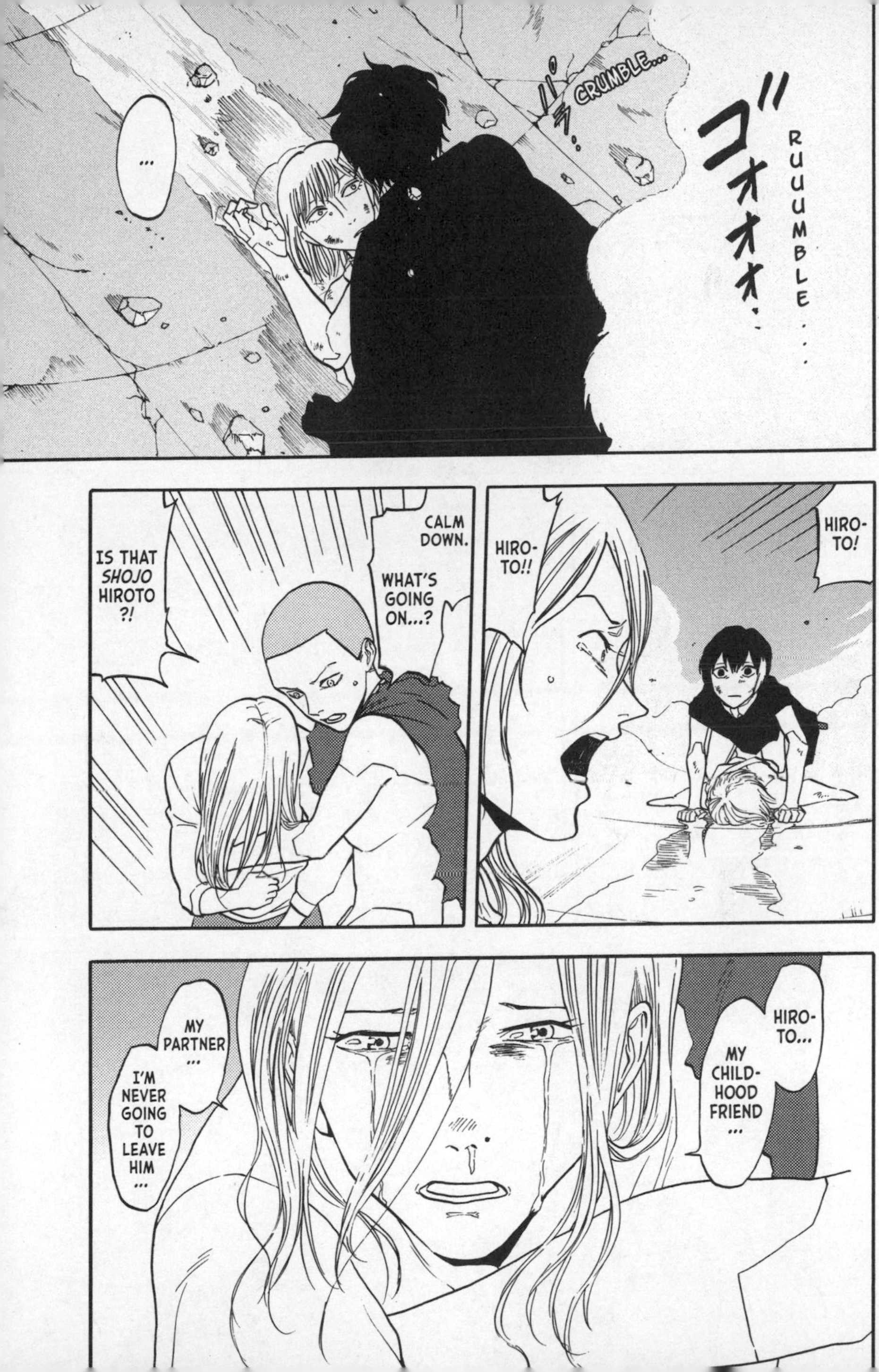

ゴオオオ
RUUUMBLE...
パラ
CRUMBLE...
...
HIRO-TO!
HIRO-TO!!
CALM DOWN.
WHAT'S GOING ON...?
IS THAT *SHOJO* HIROTO?!
HIRO-TO...
MY CHILDHOOD FRIEND...
MY PARTNER...
I'M NEVER GOING TO LEAVE HIM...

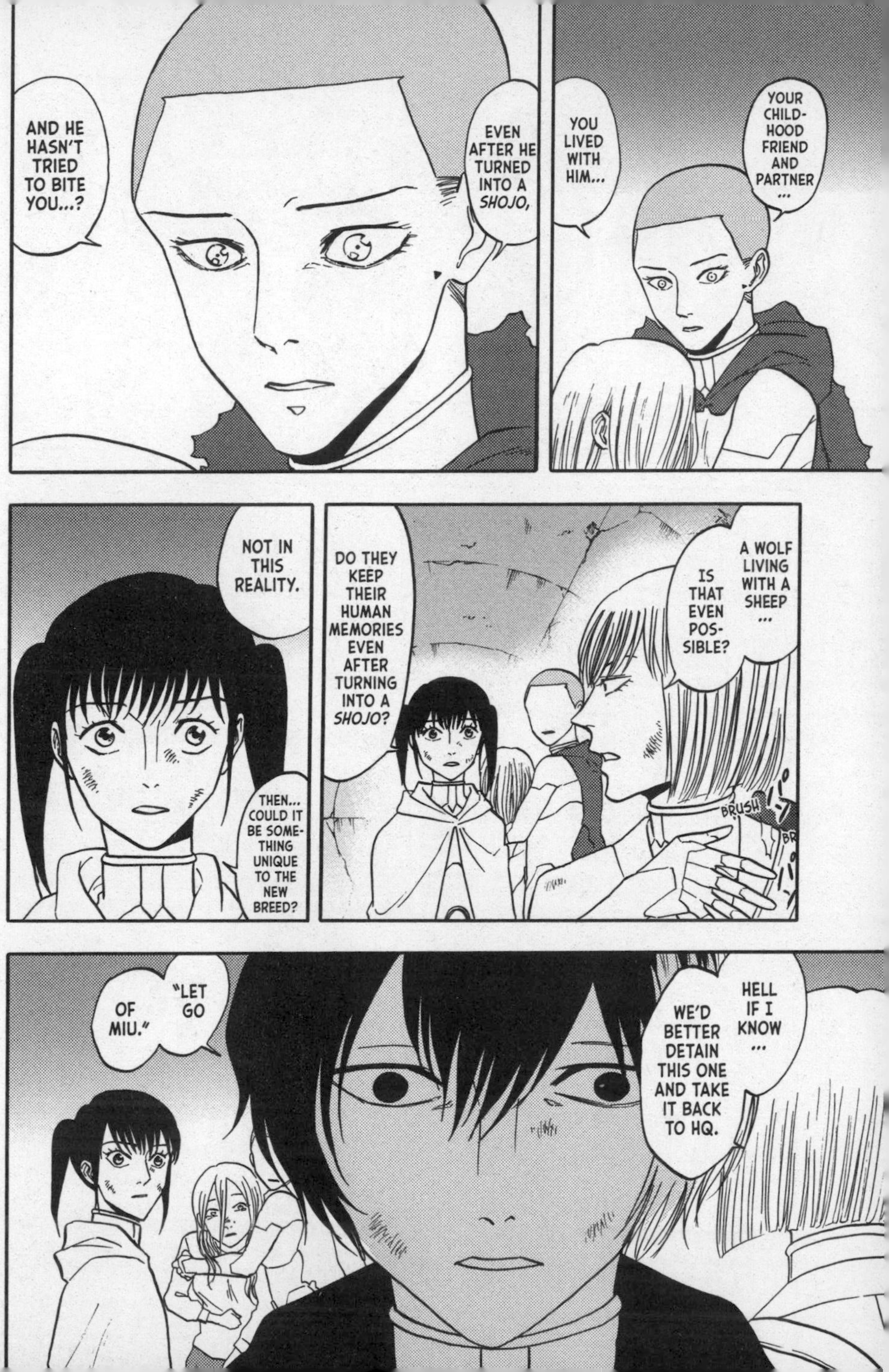
YOUR CHILDHOOD FRIEND AND PARTNER...
YOU LIVED WITH HIM...
EVEN AFTER HE TURNED INTO A *SHOJO*,
AND HE HASN'T TRIED TO BITE YOU...?
A WOLF LIVING WITH A SHEEP...
IS THAT EVEN POSSIBLE?
BRUSH
DO THEY KEEP THEIR HUMAN MEMORIES EVEN AFTER TURNING INTO A *SHOJO*?
NOT IN THIS REALITY.
THEN... COULD IT BE SOMETHING UNIQUE TO THE NEW BREED?
HELL IF I KNOW...
WE'D BETTER DETAIN THIS ONE AND TAKE IT BACK TO HQ.
"LET GO OF MIU."

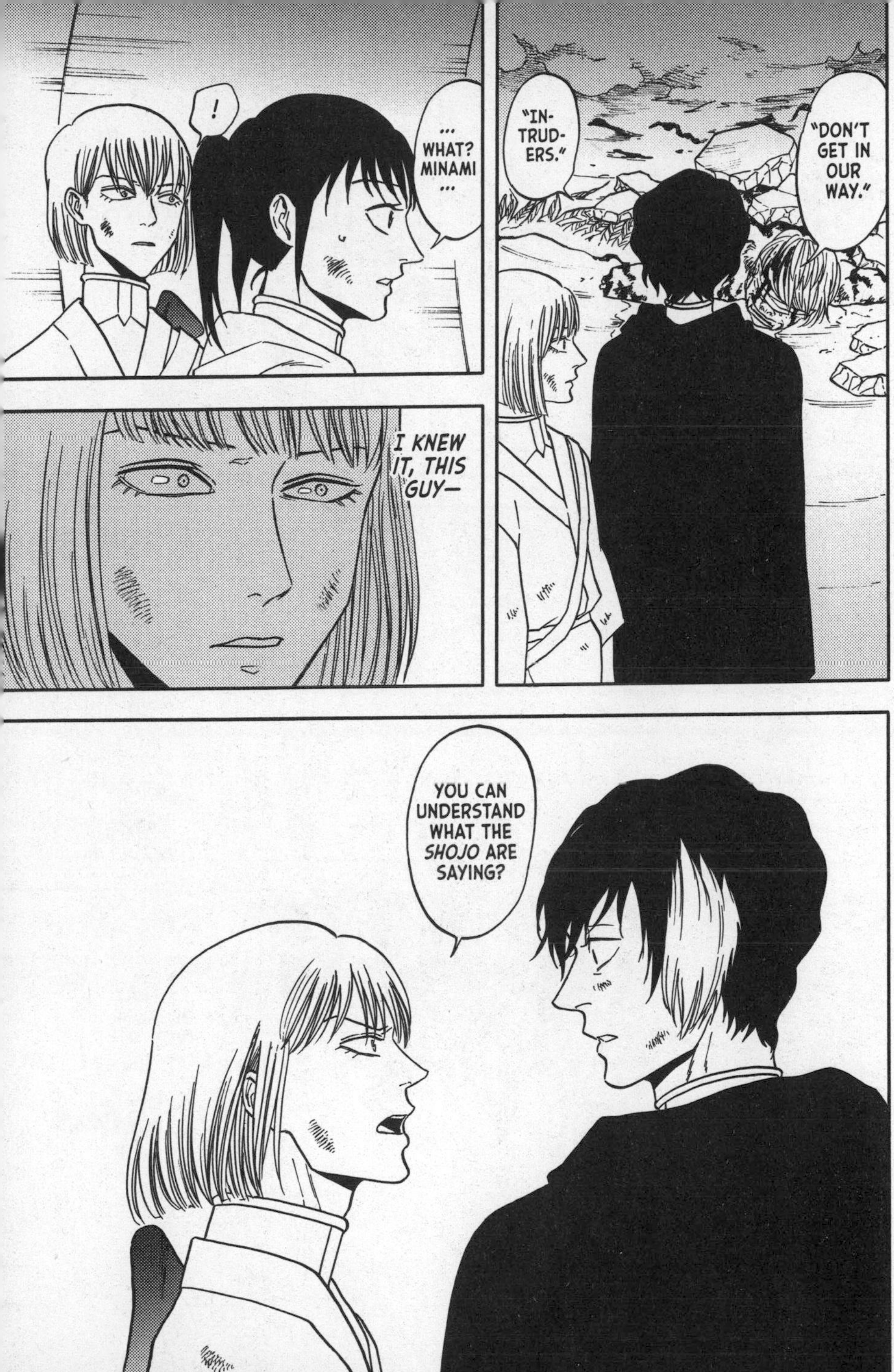
"DON'T GET IN OUR WAY."
"IN-TRUDERS."
... WHAT? MINAMI ...
!
I KNEW IT, THIS GUY—
YOU CAN UNDERSTAND WHAT THE *SHOJO* ARE SAYING?

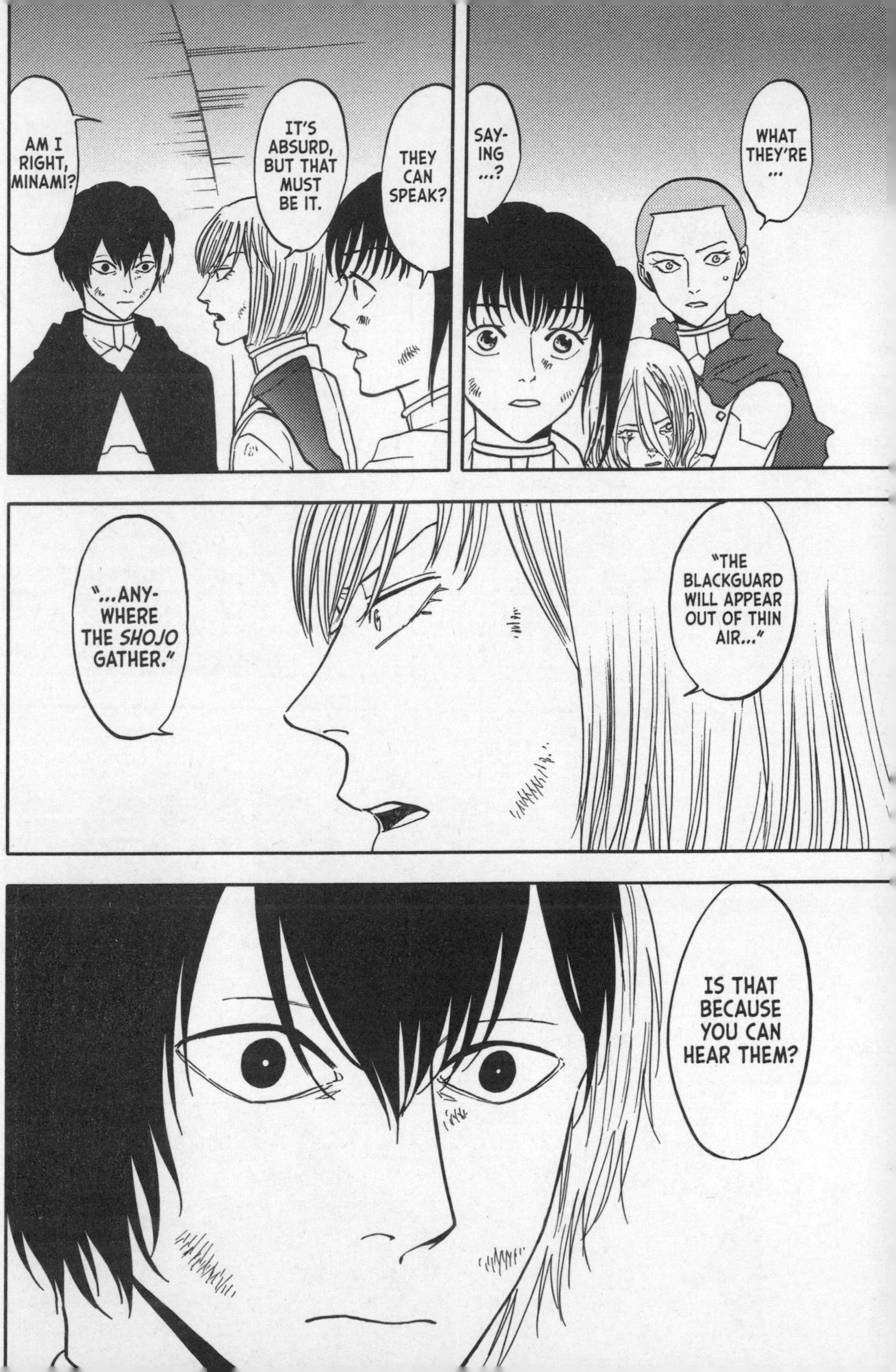
WHAT THEY'RE ...
SAY-ING ...?
THEY CAN SPEAK?
IT'S ABSURD, BUT THAT MUST BE IT.
AM I RIGHT, MINAMI?
"THE BLACKGUARD WILL APPEAR OUT OF THIN AIR..."
"...ANY-WHERE THE *SHOJO* GATHER."
IS THAT BECAUSE YOU CAN HEAR THEM?

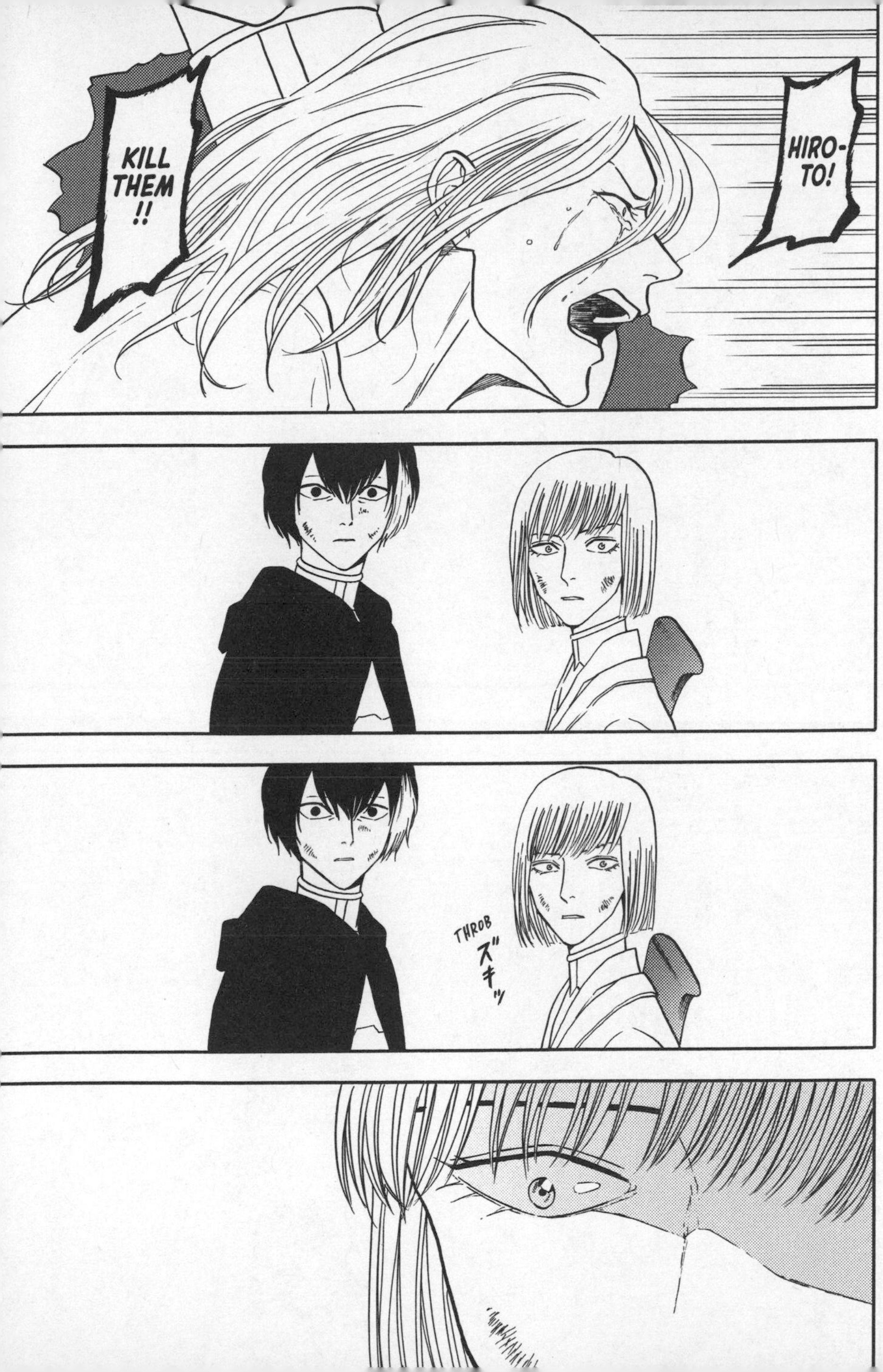
HIRO-TO!
KILL THEM!!
THROB
ズキッ

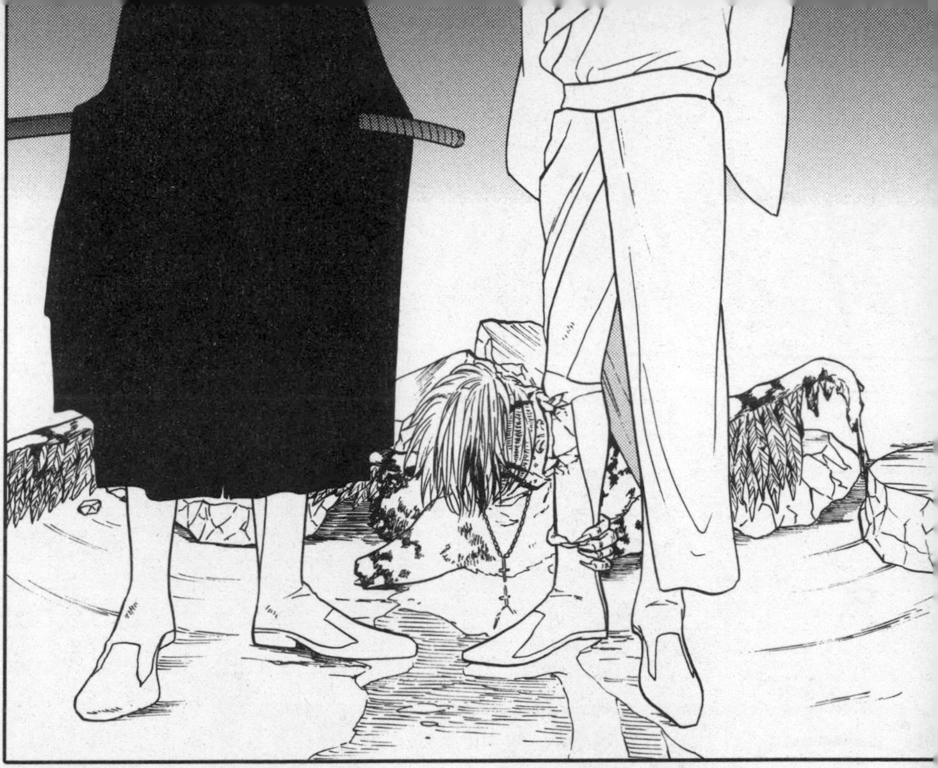
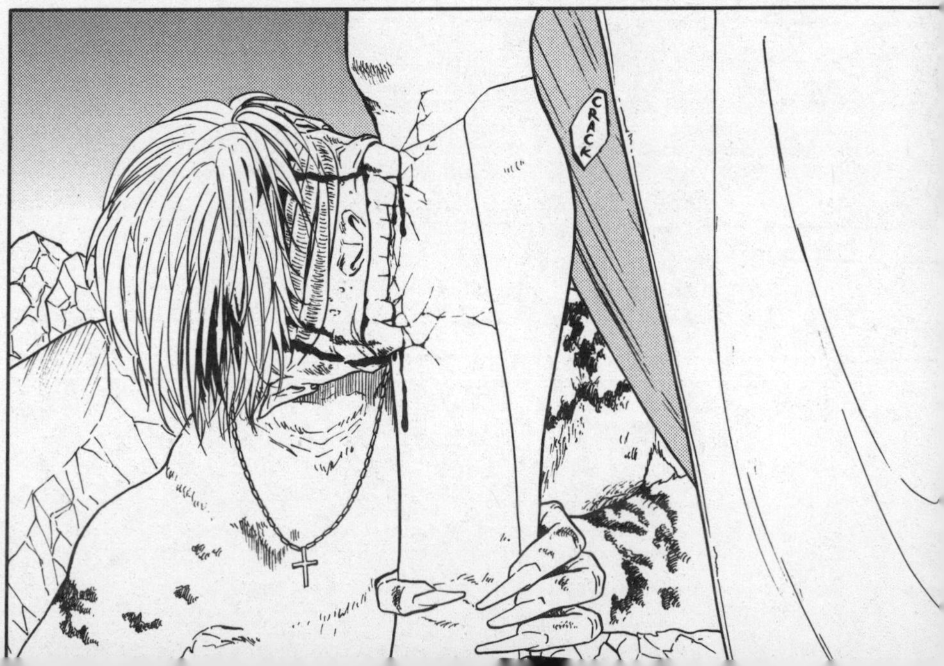
CRACK

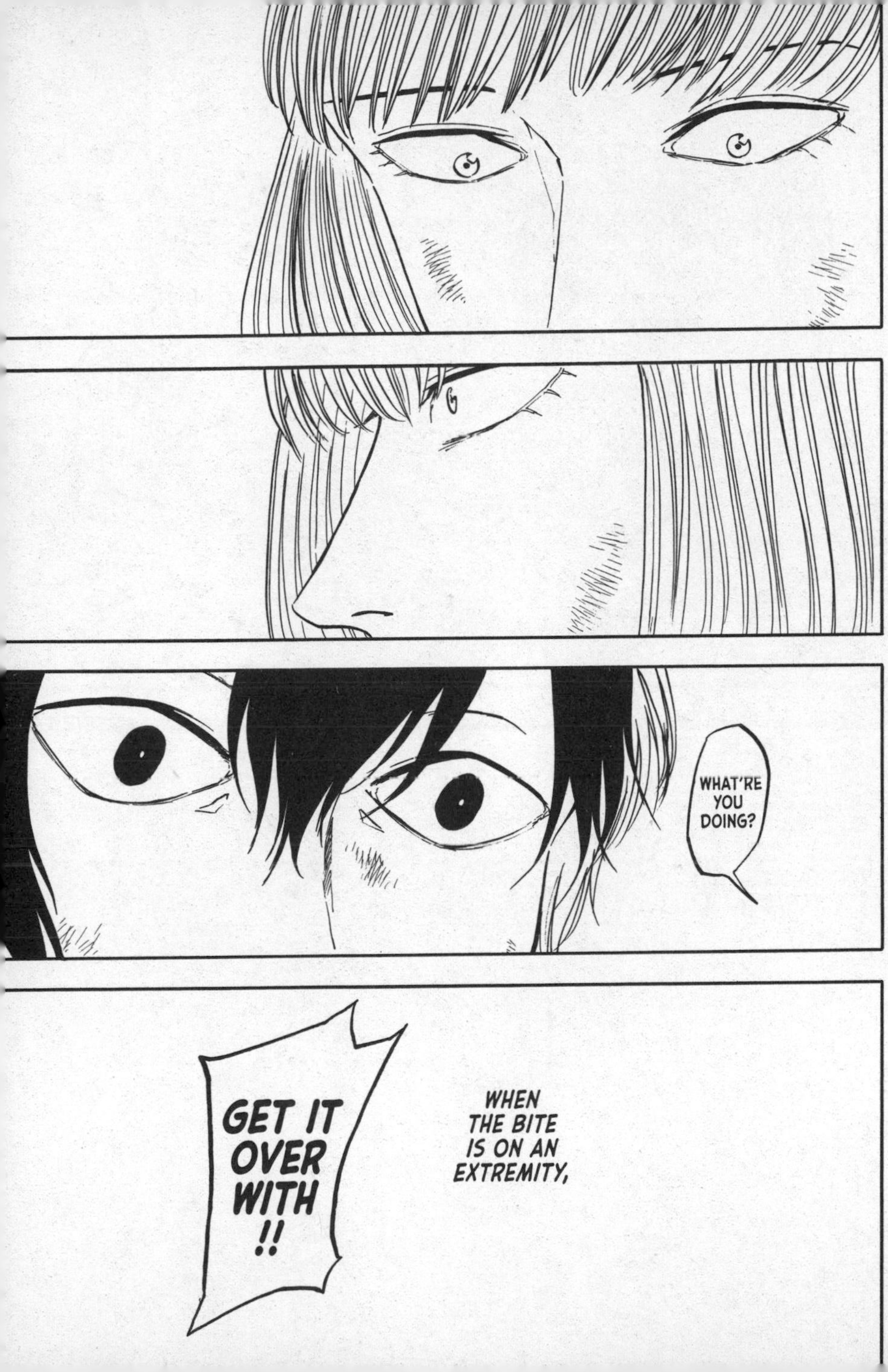
WHAT'RE YOU DOING?
WHEN THE BITE IS ON AN EXTREMITY,
GET IT OVER WITH!!

YOU WON'T GET
INFECTED IF
YOU SEVER
IT WITHIN FIVE
SECONDS.

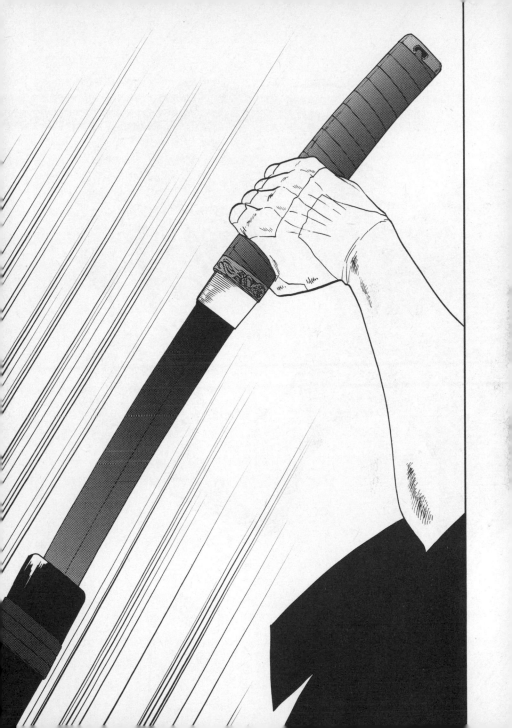

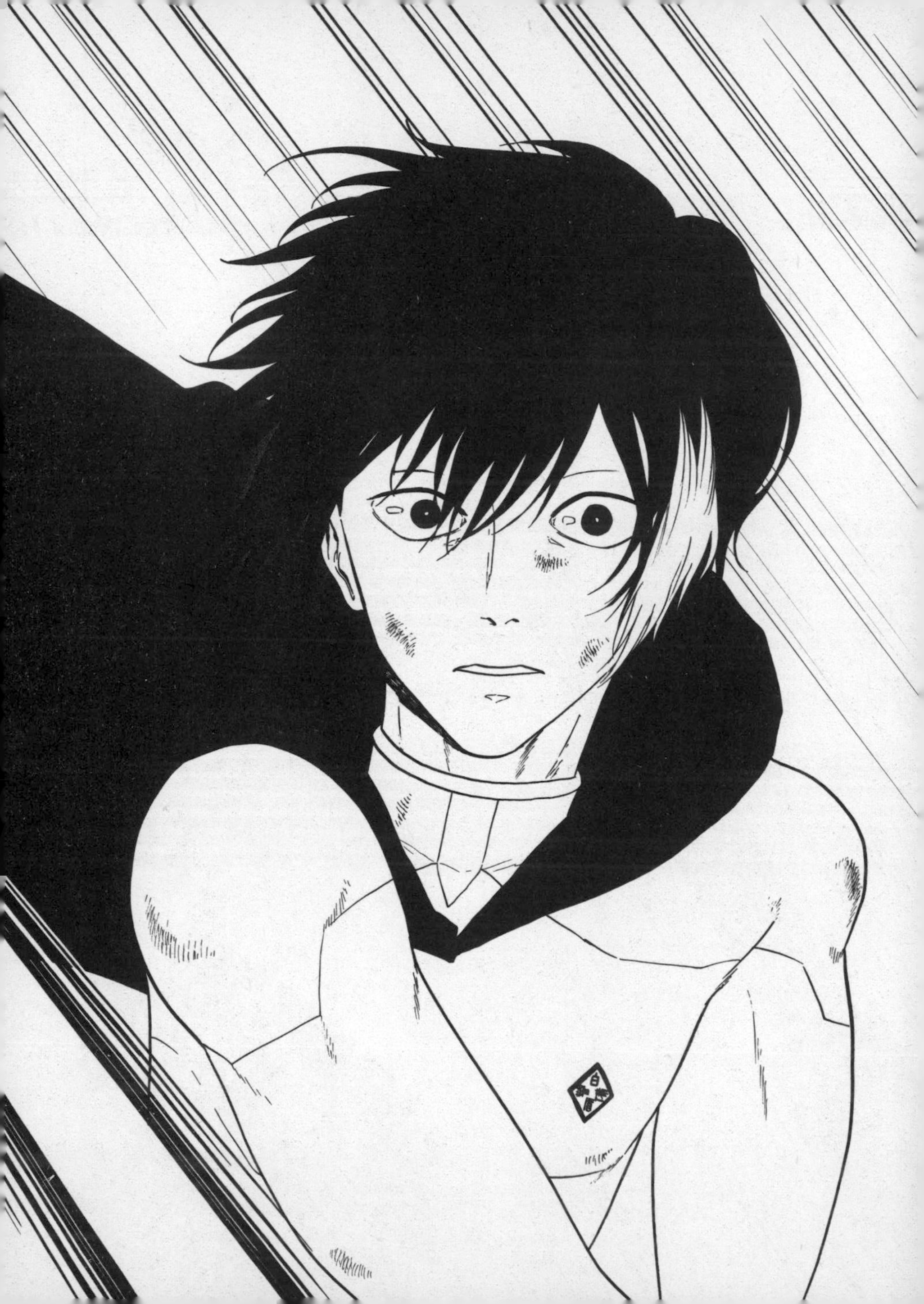

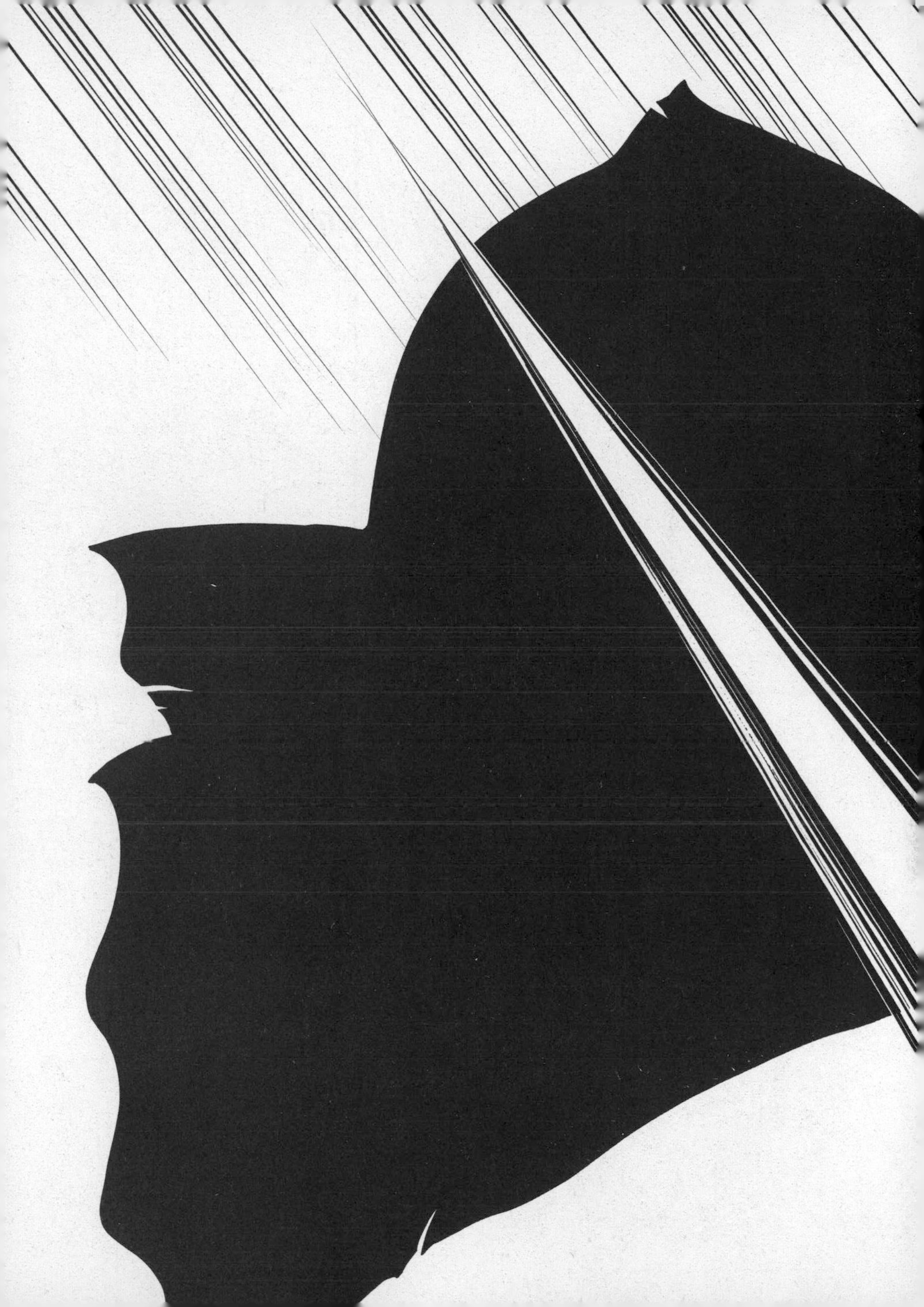

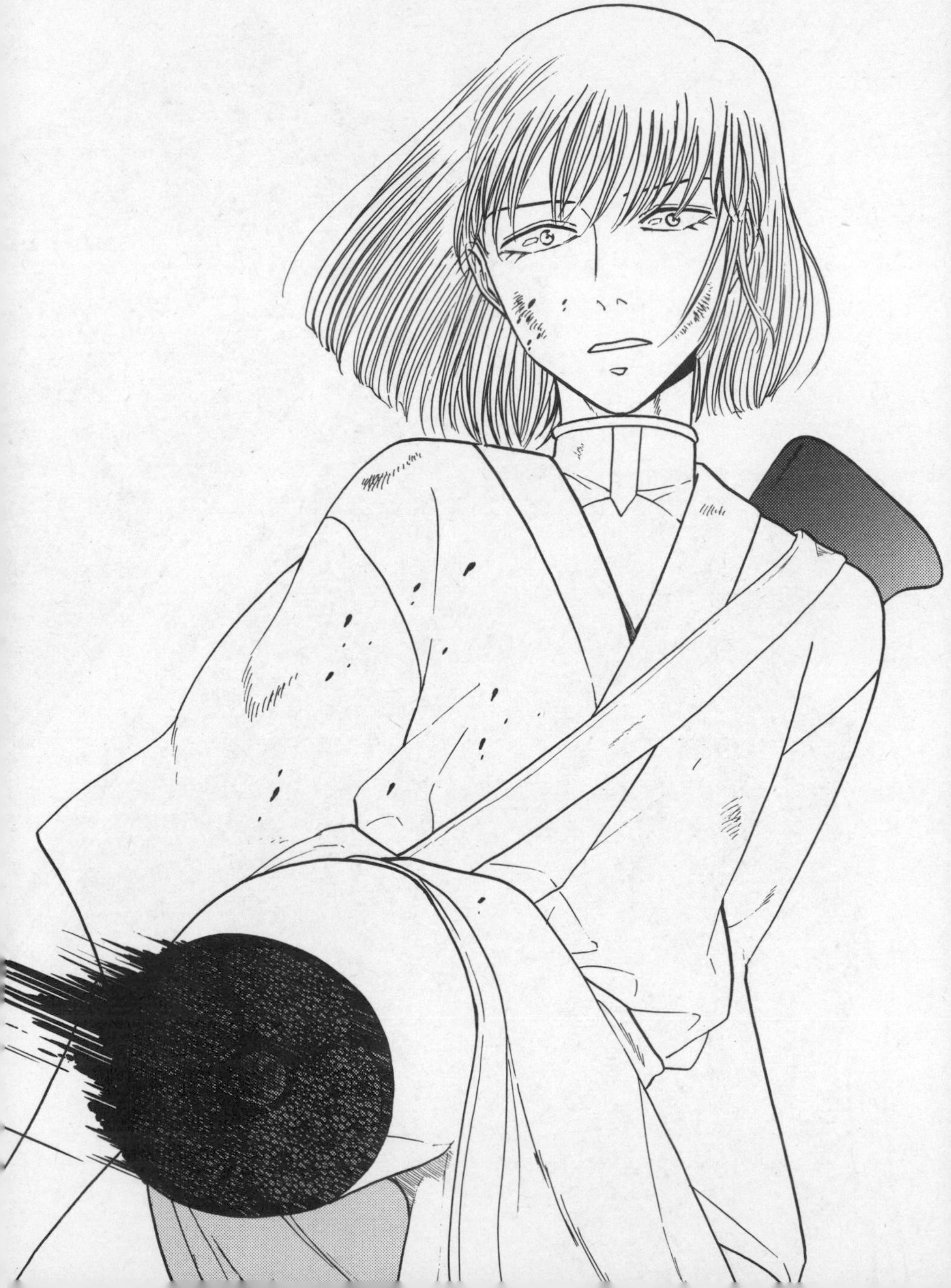

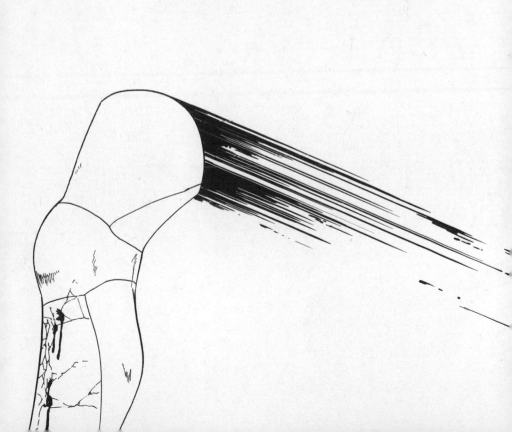

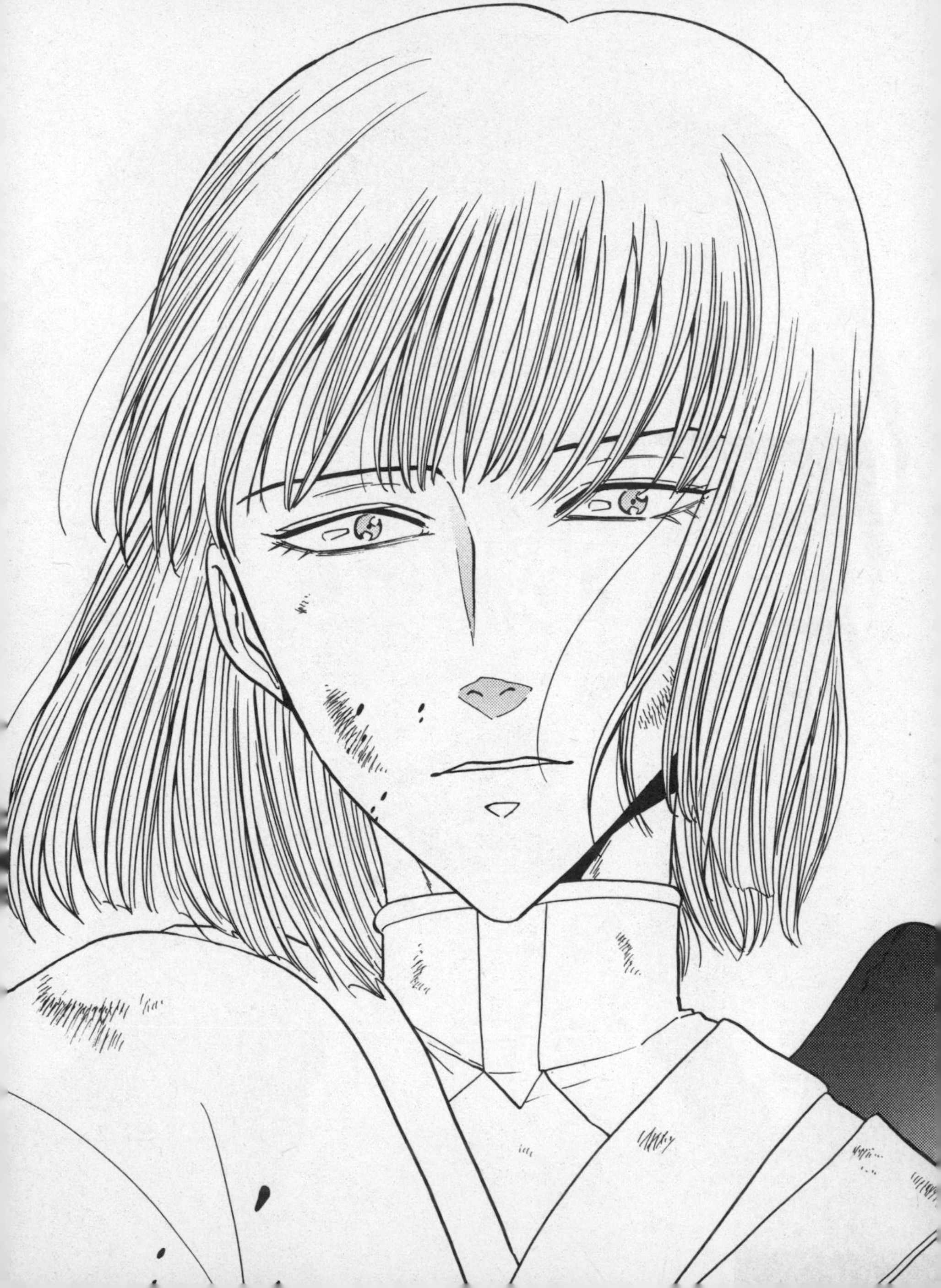

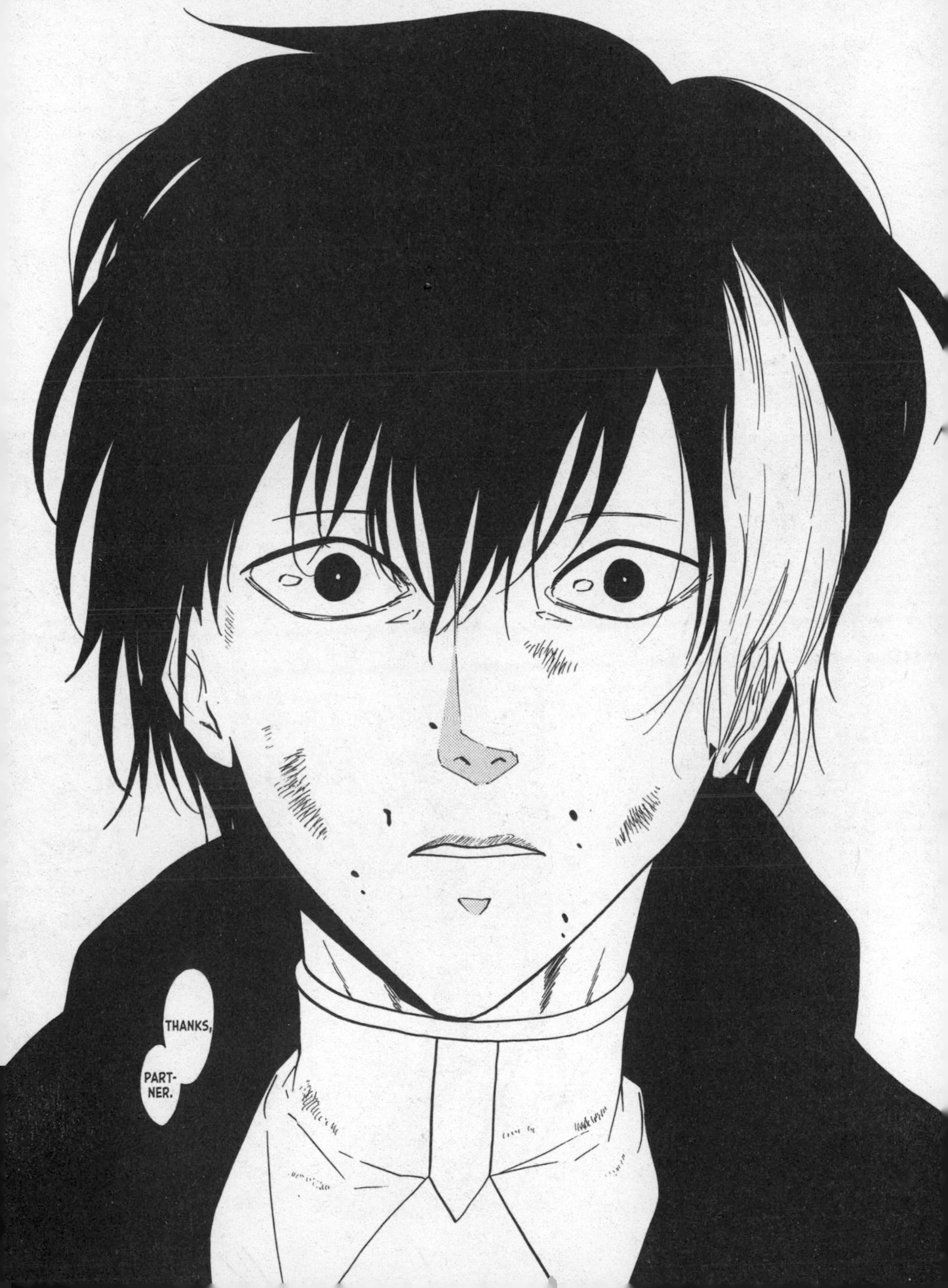
THANKS, PARTNER.

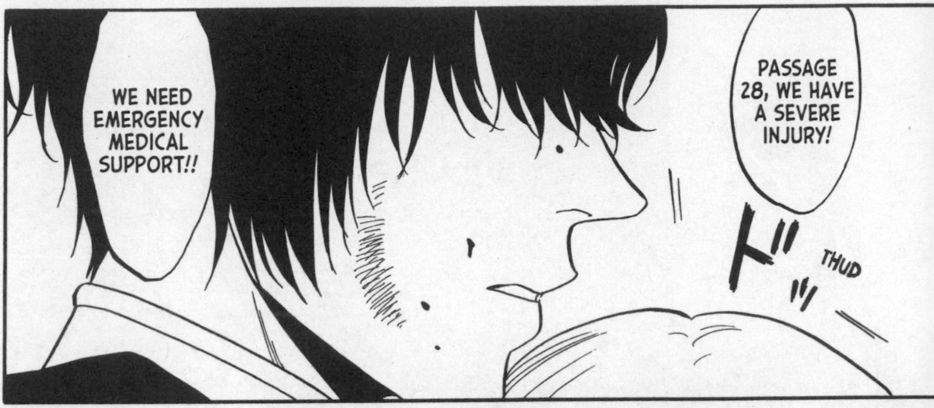
PASSAGE 28, WE HAVE A SEVERE INJURY!
ドッ
THUD
WE NEED EMERGENCY MEDICAL SUPPORT!!

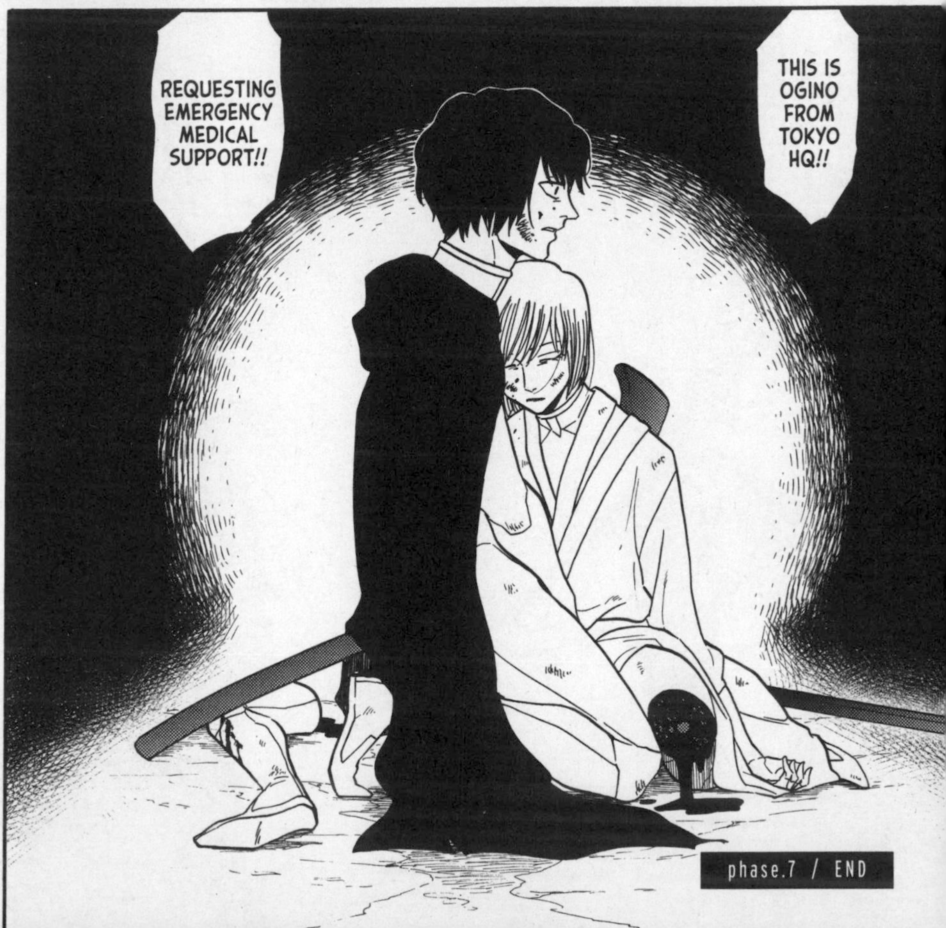
THIS IS OGINO FROM TOKYO HQ!!
REQUESTING EMERGENCY MEDICAL SUPPORT!!
phase.7 / END

phase.8 Stopped

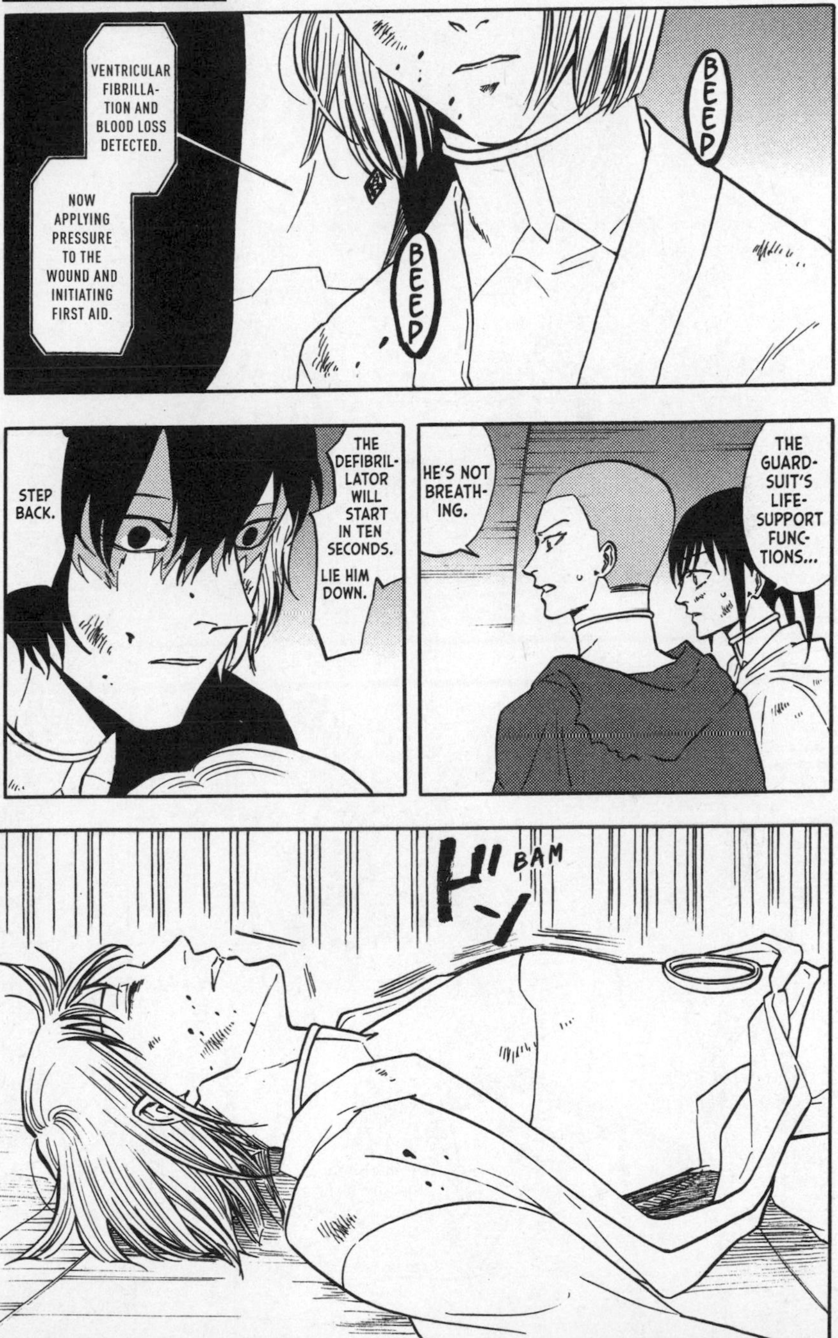
BEEP
BEEP
VENTRICULAR FIBRILLATION AND BLOOD LOSS DETECTED.
NOW APPLYING PRESSURE TO THE WOUND AND INITIATING FIRST AID.
THE GUARD-SUIT'S LIFE-SUPPORT FUNCTIONS...
HE'S NOT BREATHING.
THE DEFIBRILLATOR WILL START IN TEN SECONDS.
LIE HIM DOWN.
STEP BACK.
BAM

phase.8 Stopped

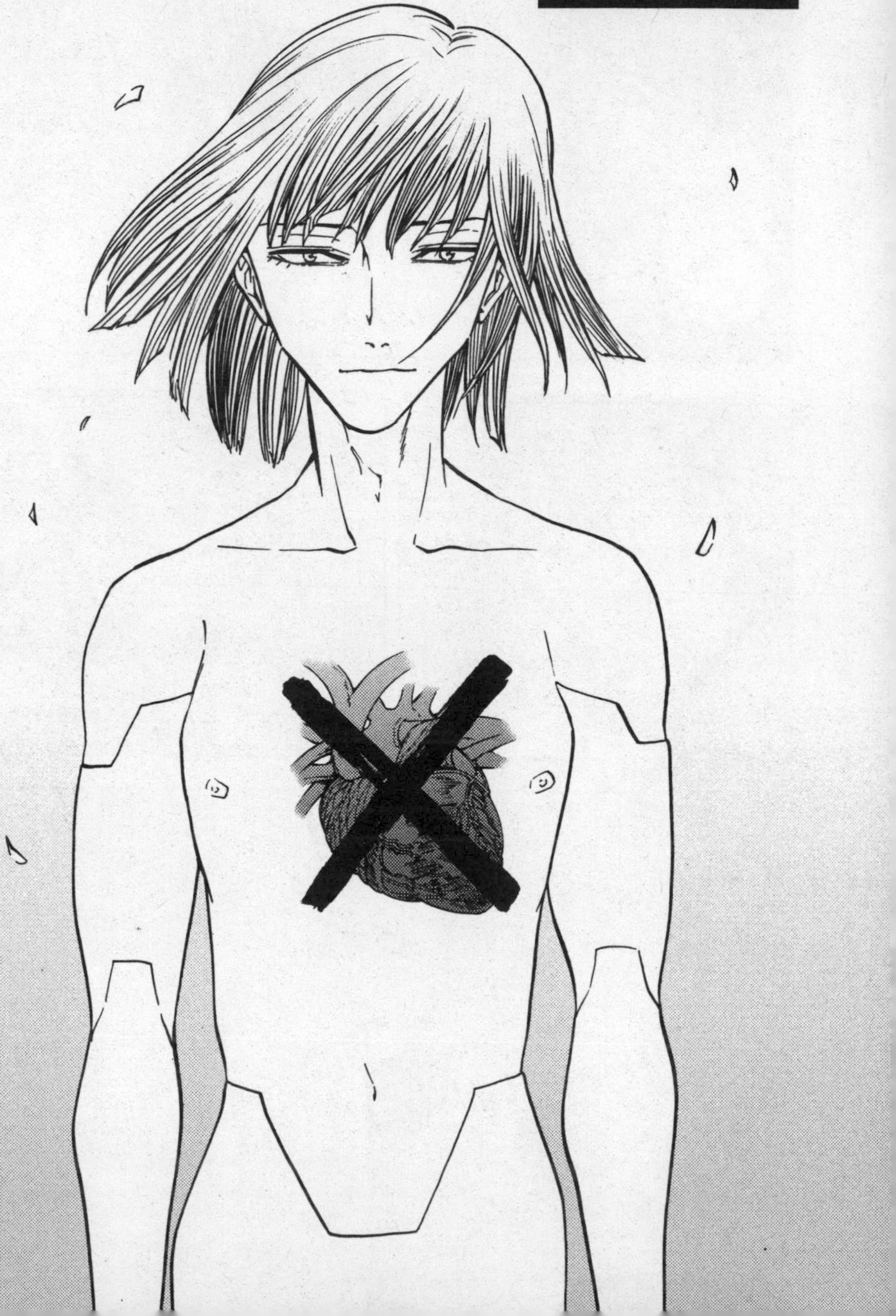

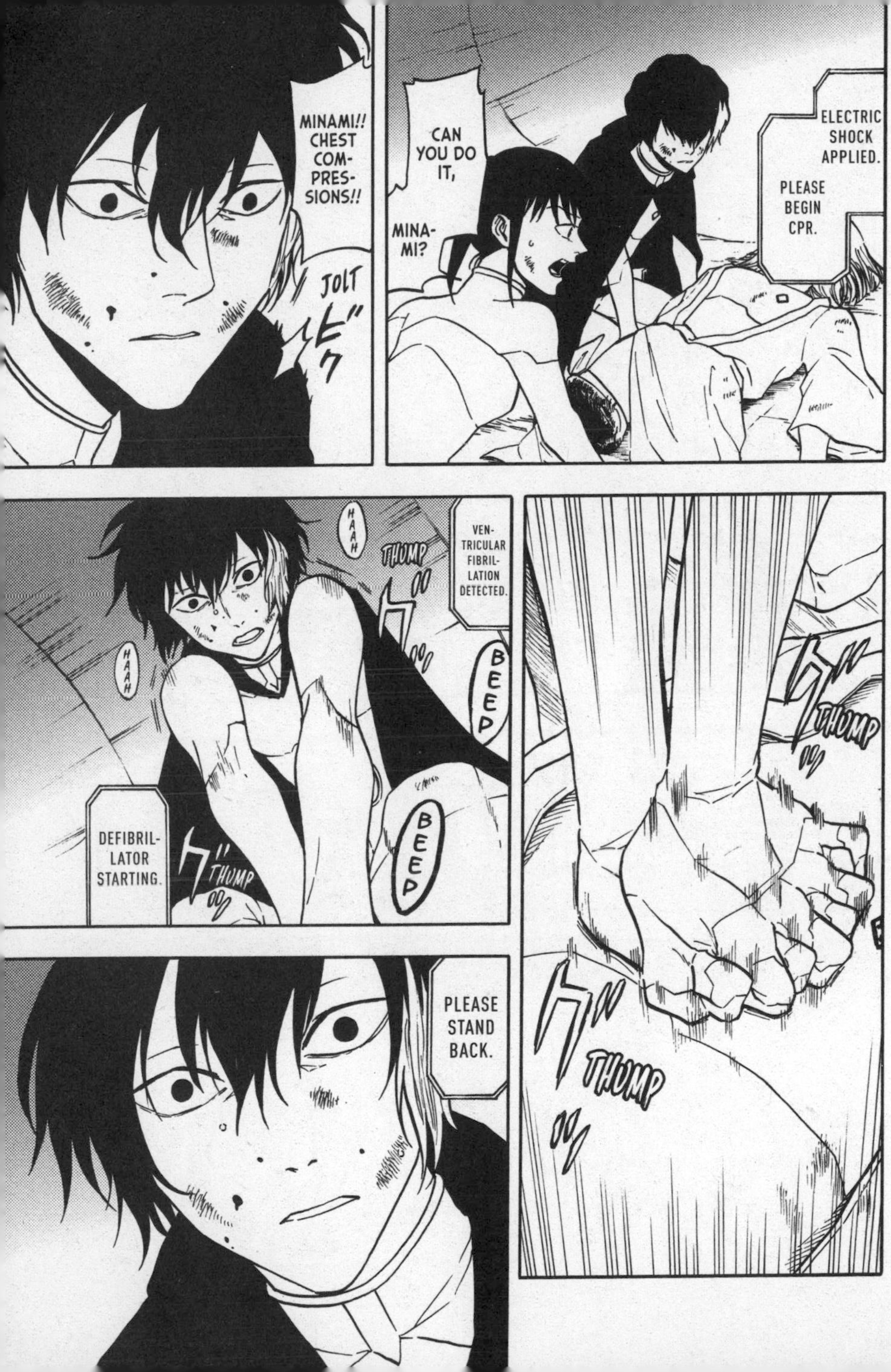
ELECTRIC SHOCK APPLIED.
PLEASE BEGIN CPR.
CAN YOU DO IT,
MINAMI?
MINAMI!! CHEST COMPRESSIONS!!
JOLT
THUMP
THUMP
VENTRICULAR FIBRILLATION DETECTED.
HAAH
THUMP
BEEP
HAAH
BEEP
DEFIBRILLATOR STARTING.
THUMP
PLEASE STAND BACK.

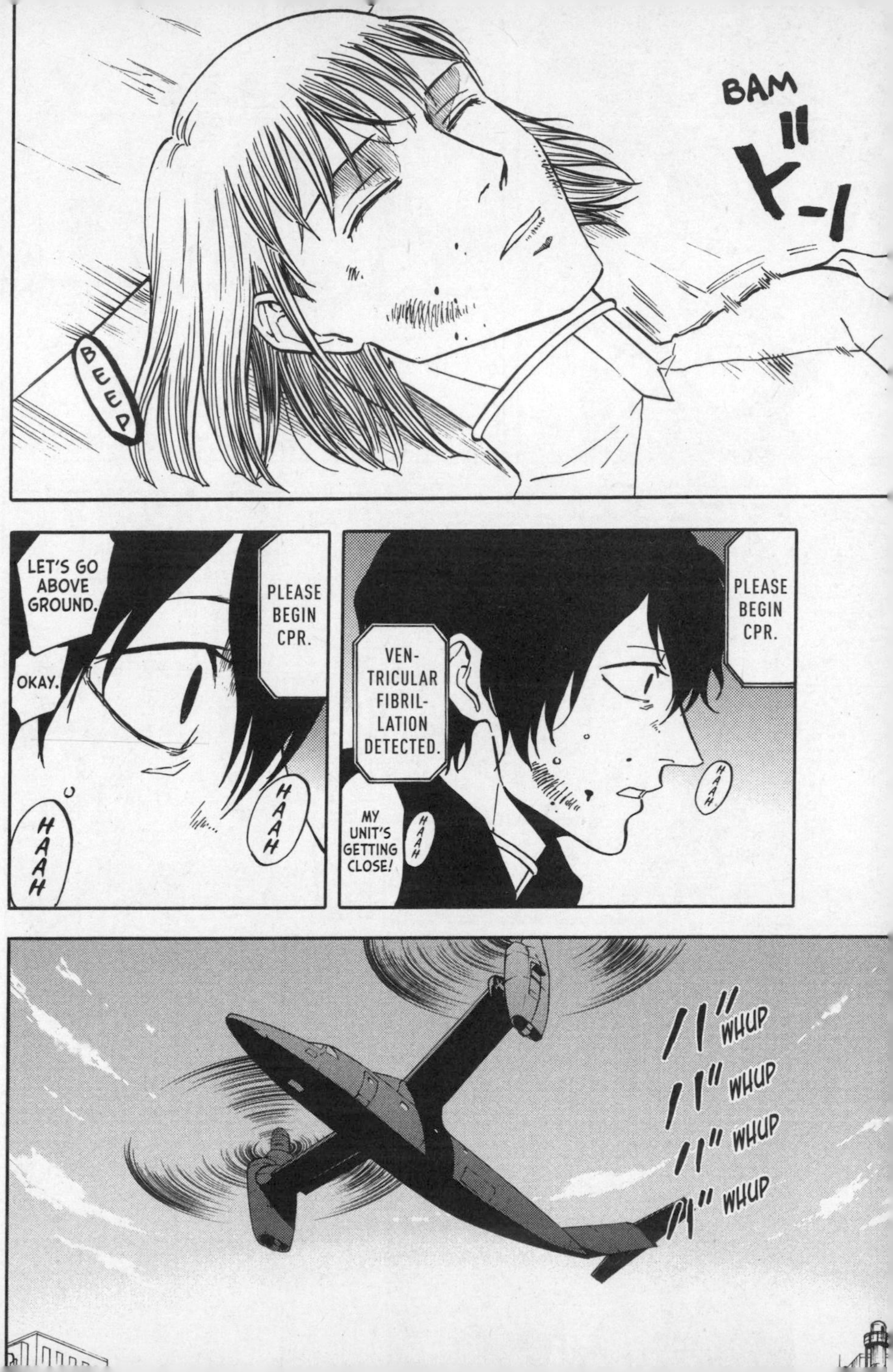
BAM
BEEP
PLEASE BEGIN CPR.
VEN-TRICULAR FIBRIL-LATION DETECTED.
HAAH
MY UNIT'S GETTING CLOSE!
HAAH
PLEASE BEGIN CPR.
LET'S GO ABOVE GROUND.
OKAY.
HAAH
HAAH
WHUP
WHUP
WHUP
WHUP

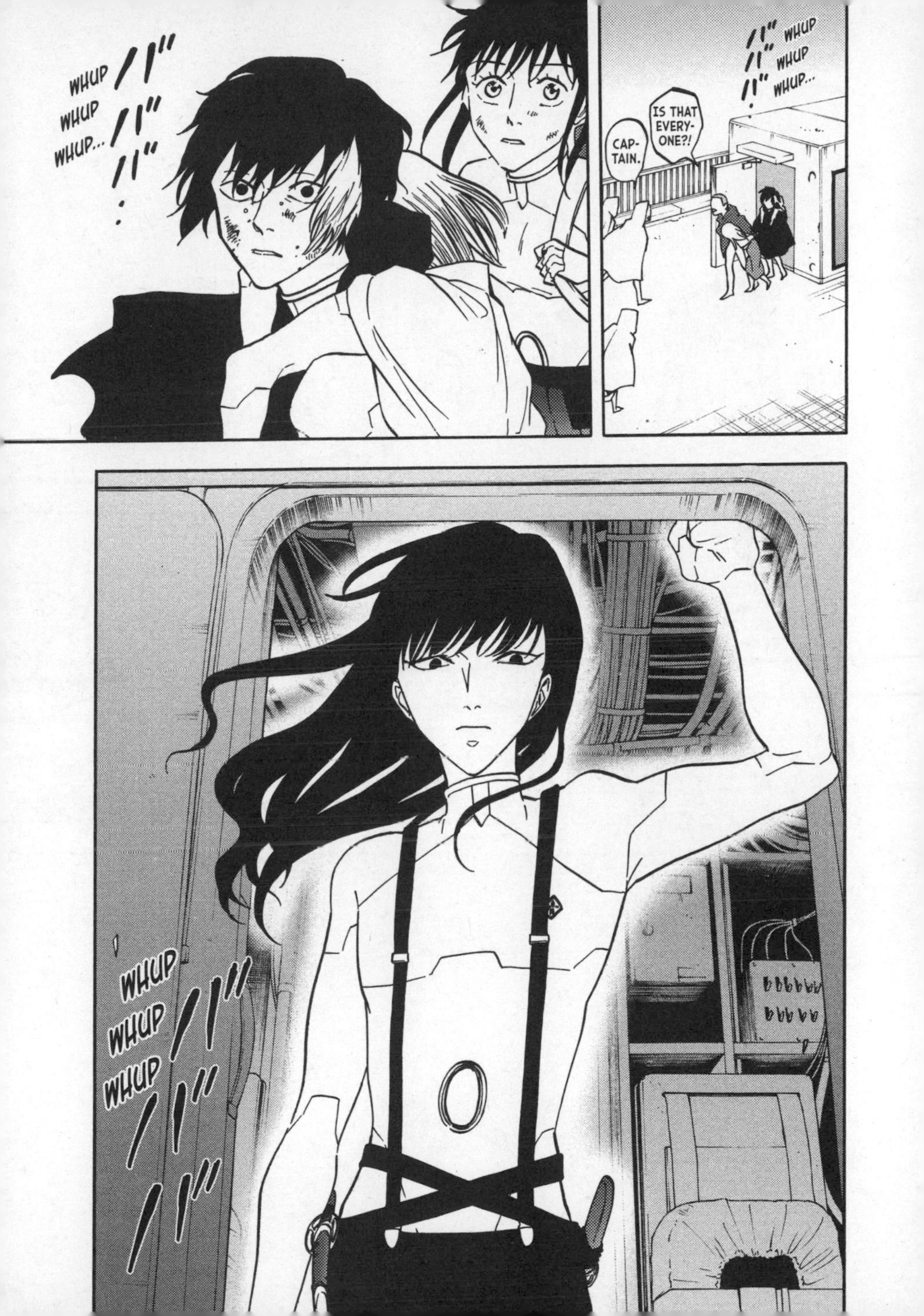
WHUP WHUP WHUP...
IS THAT EVERY-ONE?!
CAP-TAIN.
WHUP WHUP WHUP...
WHUP WHUP WHUP

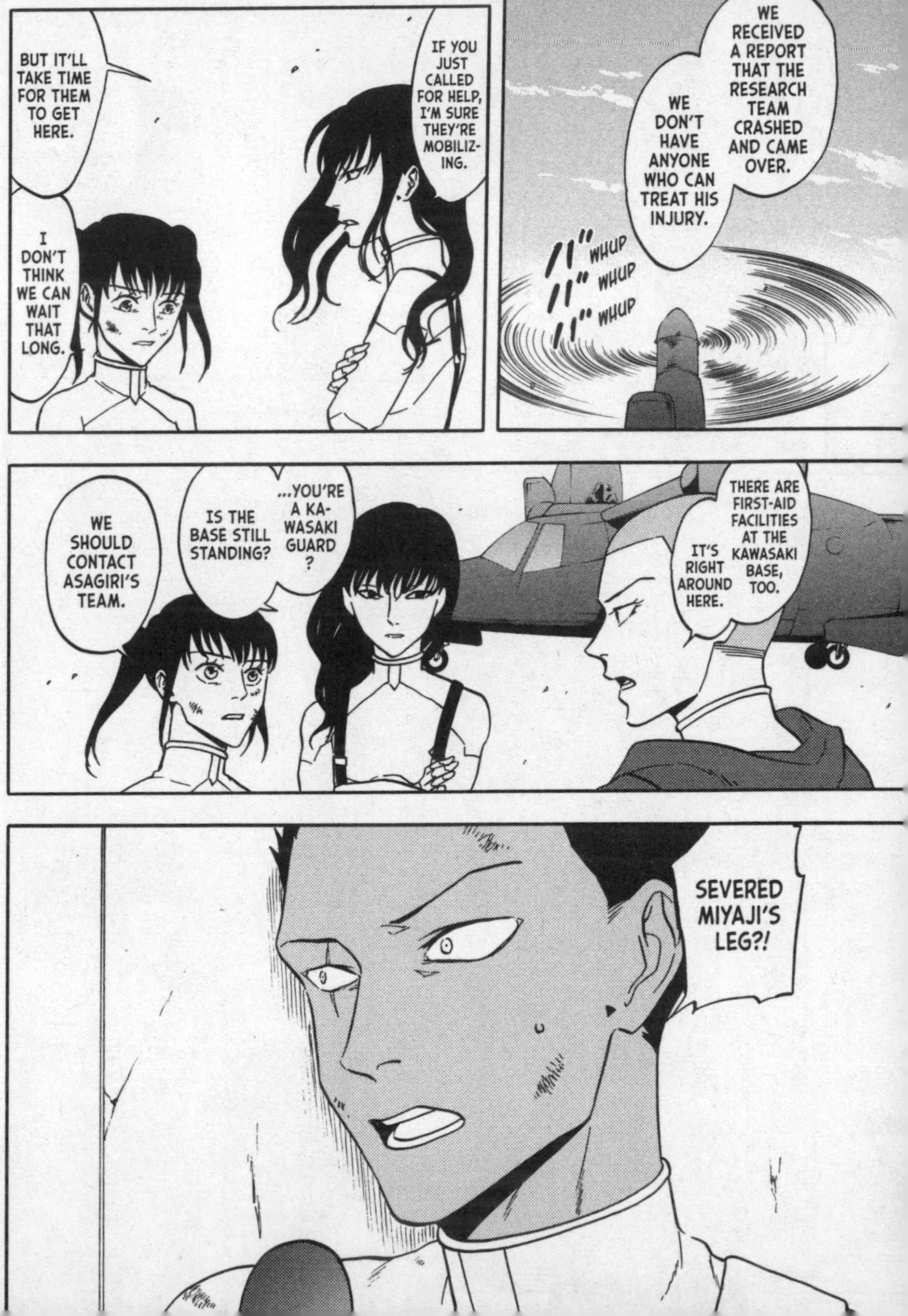
WE RECEIVED A REPORT THAT THE RESEARCH TEAM CRASHED AND CAME OVER.
WE DON'T HAVE ANYONE WHO CAN TREAT HIS INJURY.
WHUP
WHUP
WHUP
IF YOU JUST CALLED FOR HELP, I'M SURE THEY'RE MOBILIZING.
BUT IT'LL TAKE TIME FOR THEM TO GET HERE.
I DON'T THINK WE CAN WAIT THAT LONG.
THERE ARE FIRST-AID FACILITIES AT THE KAWASAKI BASE, TOO.
IT'S RIGHT AROUND HERE.
...YOU'RE A KAWASAKI GUARD?
IS THE BASE STILL STANDING?
WE SHOULD CONTACT ASAGIRI'S TEAM.
SEVERED MIYAJI'S LEG?!

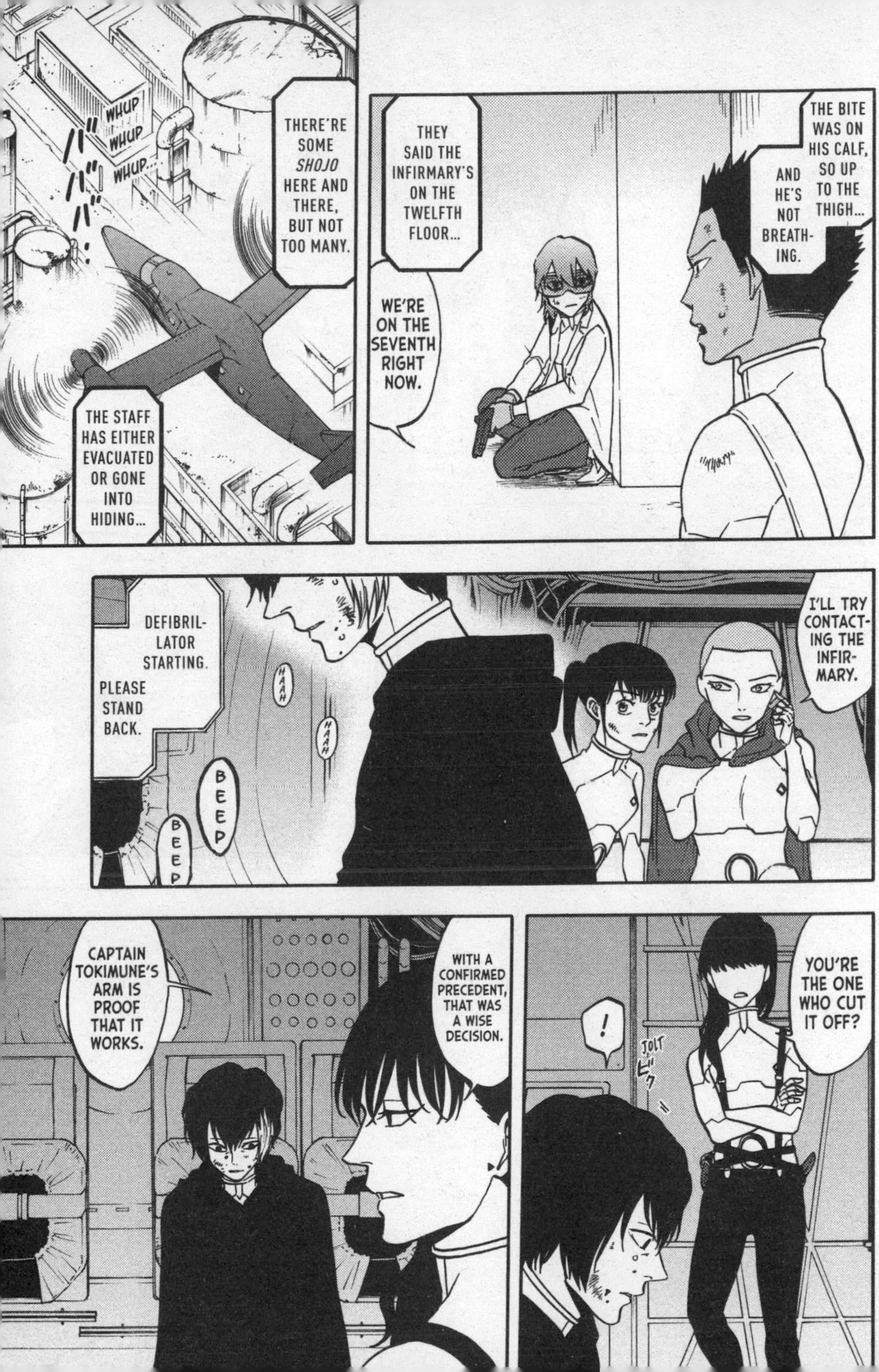
THE BITE WAS ON HIS CALF, SO UP TO THE THIGH...
AND HE'S NOT BREATHING.
THEY SAID THE INFIRMARY'S ON THE TWELFTH FLOOR...
WE'RE ON THE SEVENTH RIGHT NOW.
THERE'RE SOME *SHOJO* HERE AND THERE, BUT NOT TOO MANY.
WHUP WHUP WHUP...
THE STAFF HAS EITHER EVACUATED OR GONE INTO HIDING...
I'LL TRY CONTACTING THE INFIRMARY.
DEFIBRILLATOR STARTING.
PLEASE STAND BACK.
HAAH
HAAH
BEEP
BEEP
YOU'RE THE ONE WHO CUT IT OFF?
JOLT
!
WITH A CONFIRMED PRECEDENT, THAT WAS A WISE DECISION.
CAPTAIN TOKIMUNE'S ARM IS PROOF THAT IT WORKS.

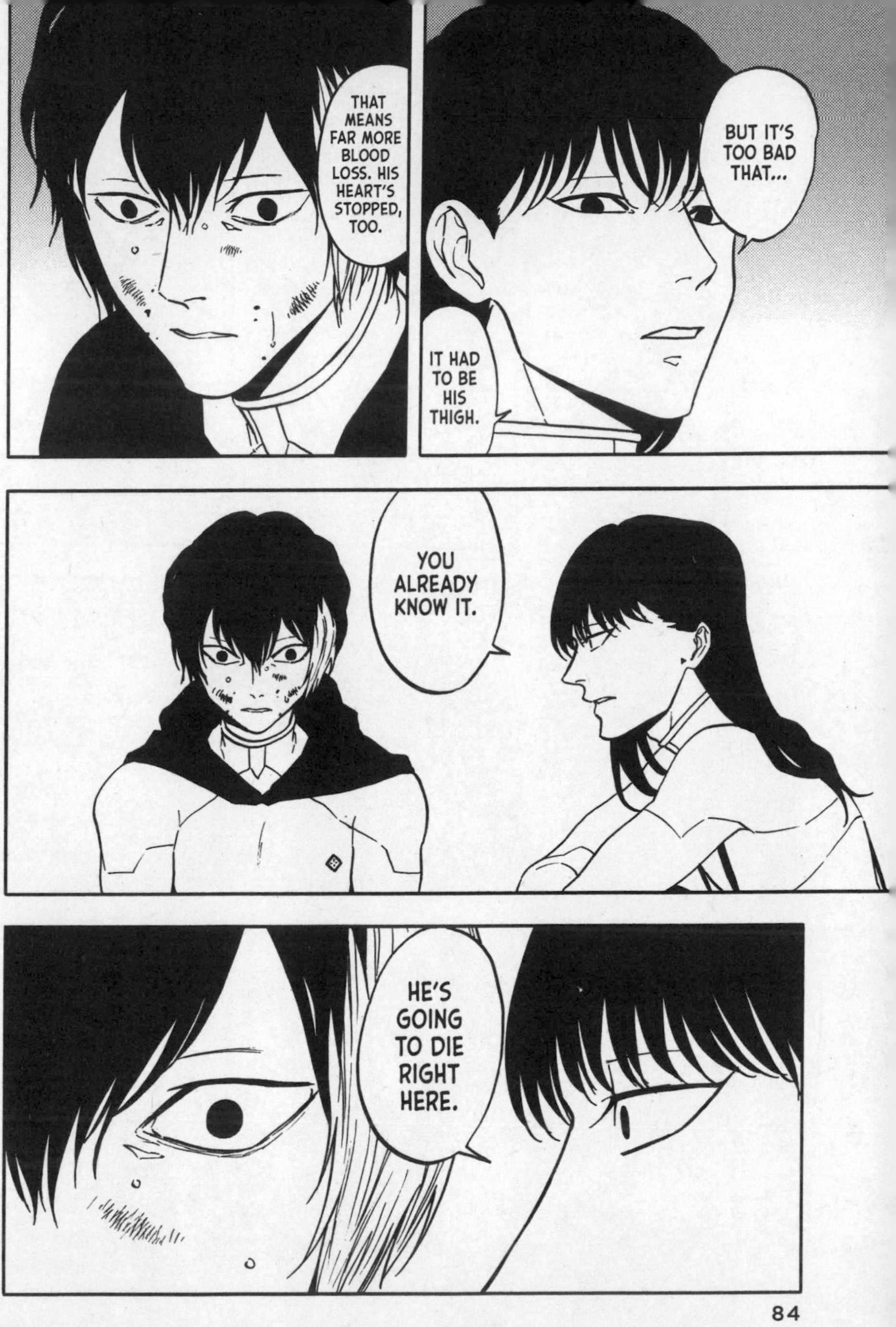
BUT IT'S TOO BAD THAT...
IT HAD TO BE HIS THIGH.
THAT MEANS FAR MORE BLOOD LOSS. HIS HEART'S STOPPED, TOO.
YOU ALREADY KNOW IT.
HE'S GOING TO DIE RIGHT HERE.

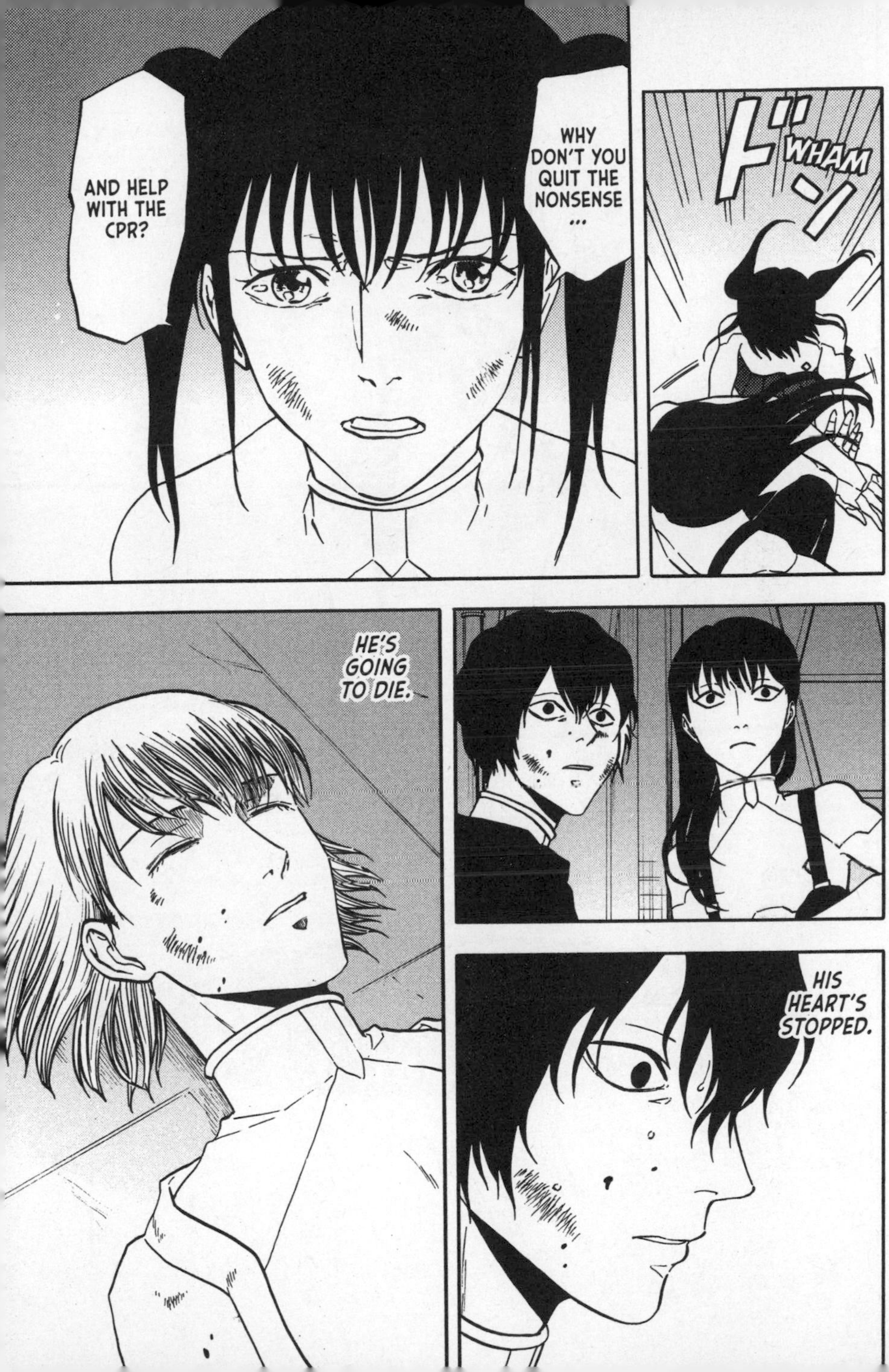
WHAM
WHY DON'T YOU QUIT THE NONSENSE ...
AND HELP WITH THE CPR?
HIS HEART'S STOPPED.
HE'S GOING TO DIE.

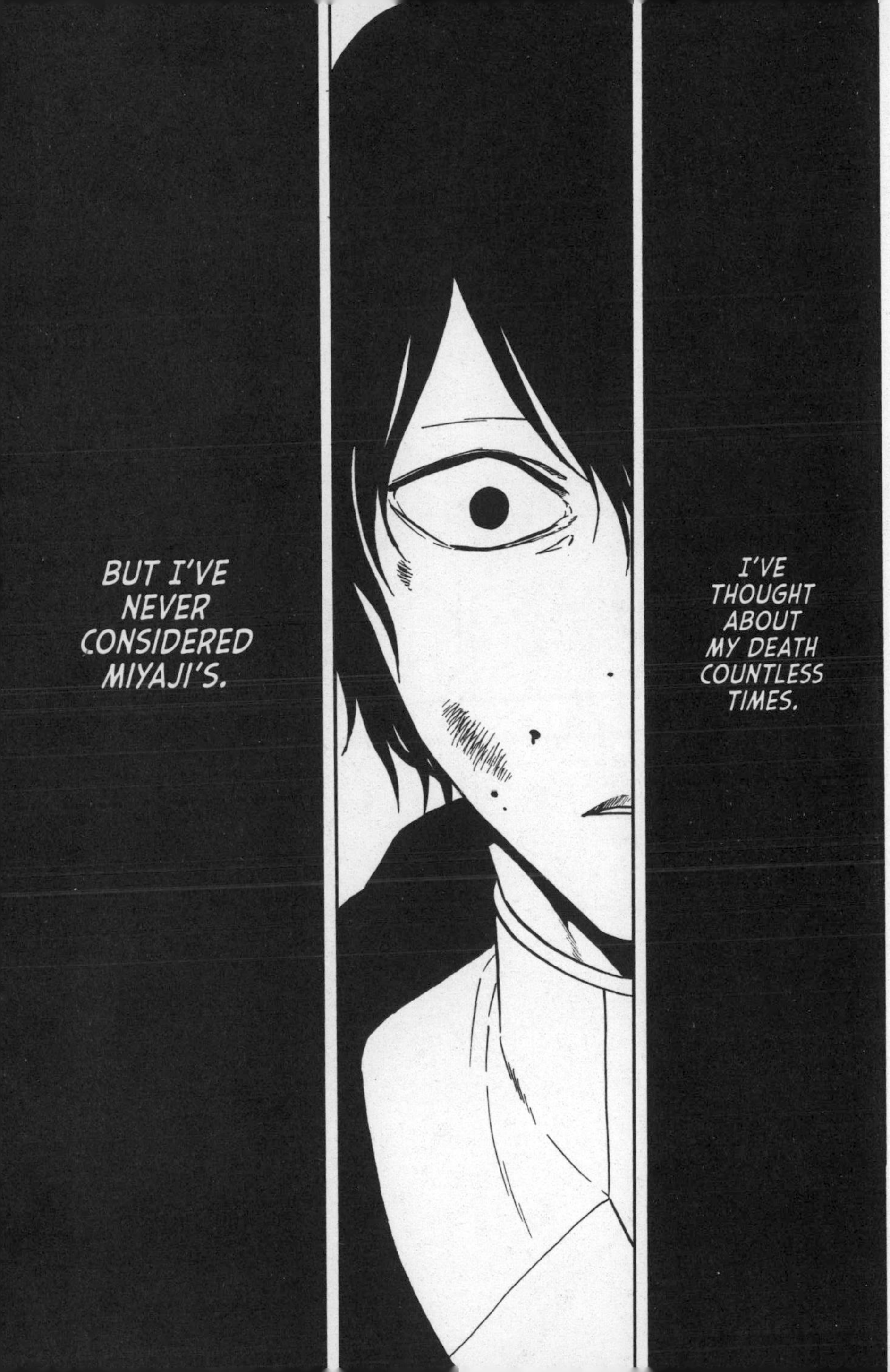
I'VE THOUGHT ABOUT MY DEATH COUNTLESS TIMES.
BUT I'VE NEVER CONSIDERED MIYAJI'S.

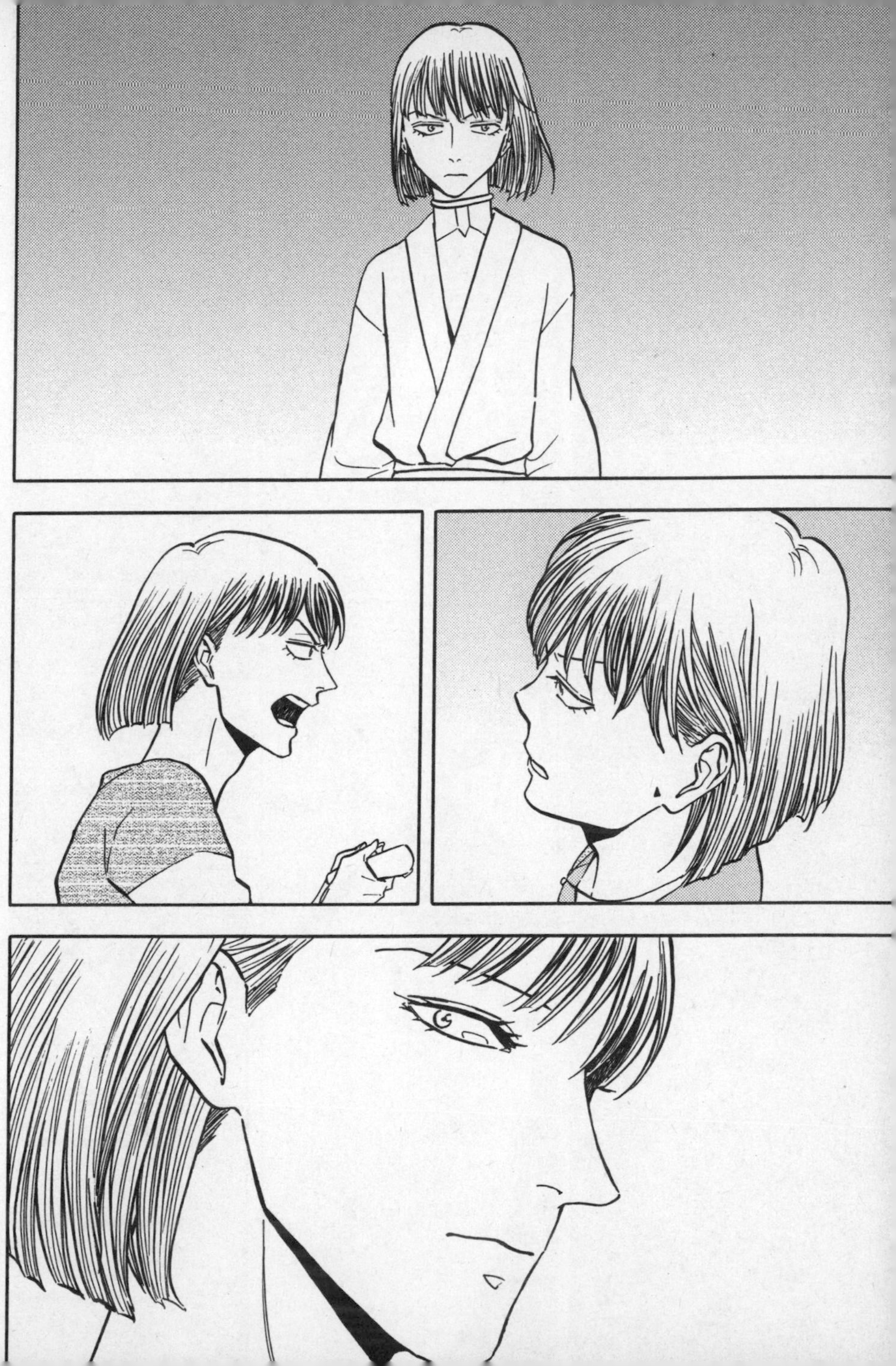

CHRIS
MIYAJI
IS GOING
TO DIE.

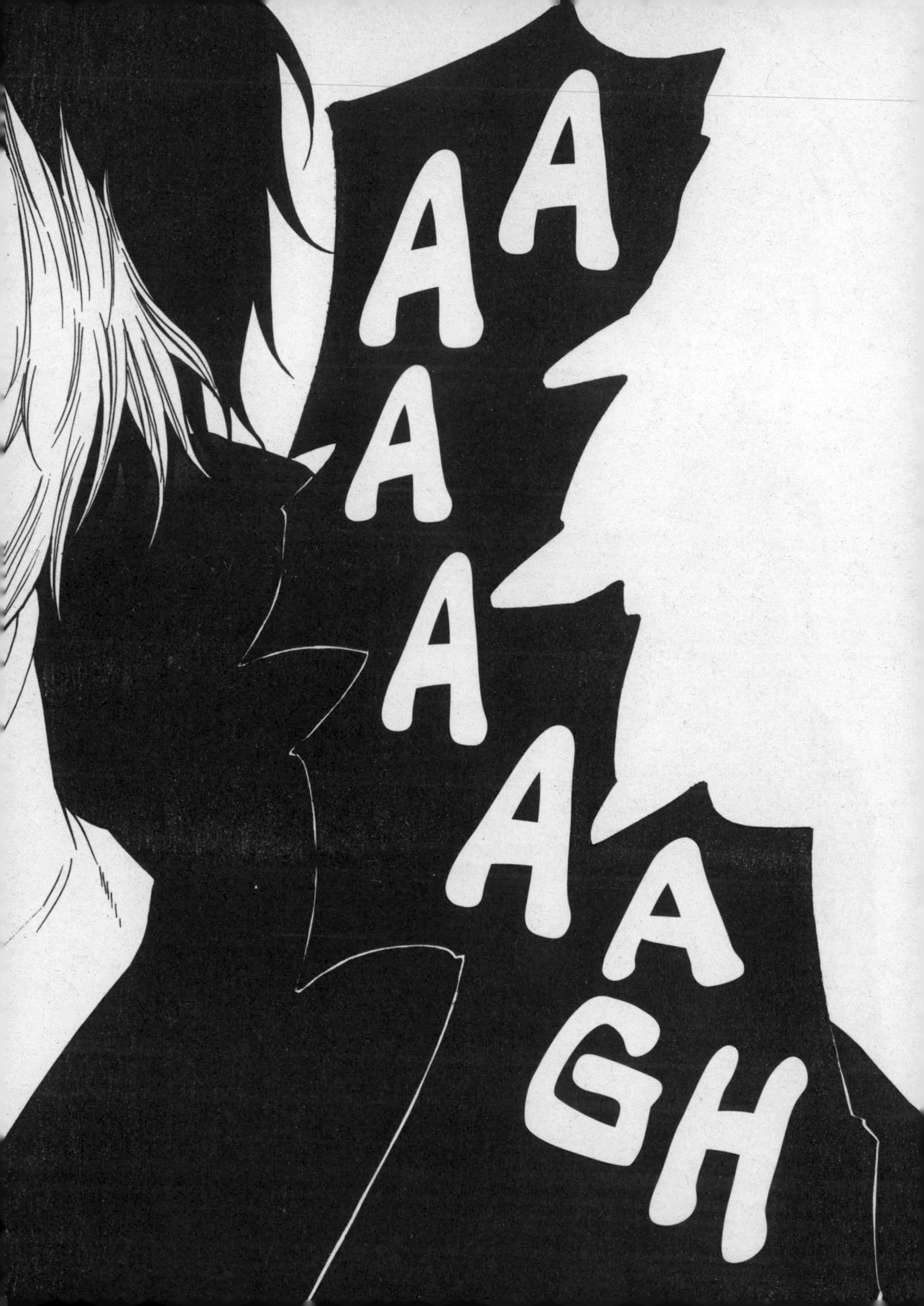
AAAAAAAAGH

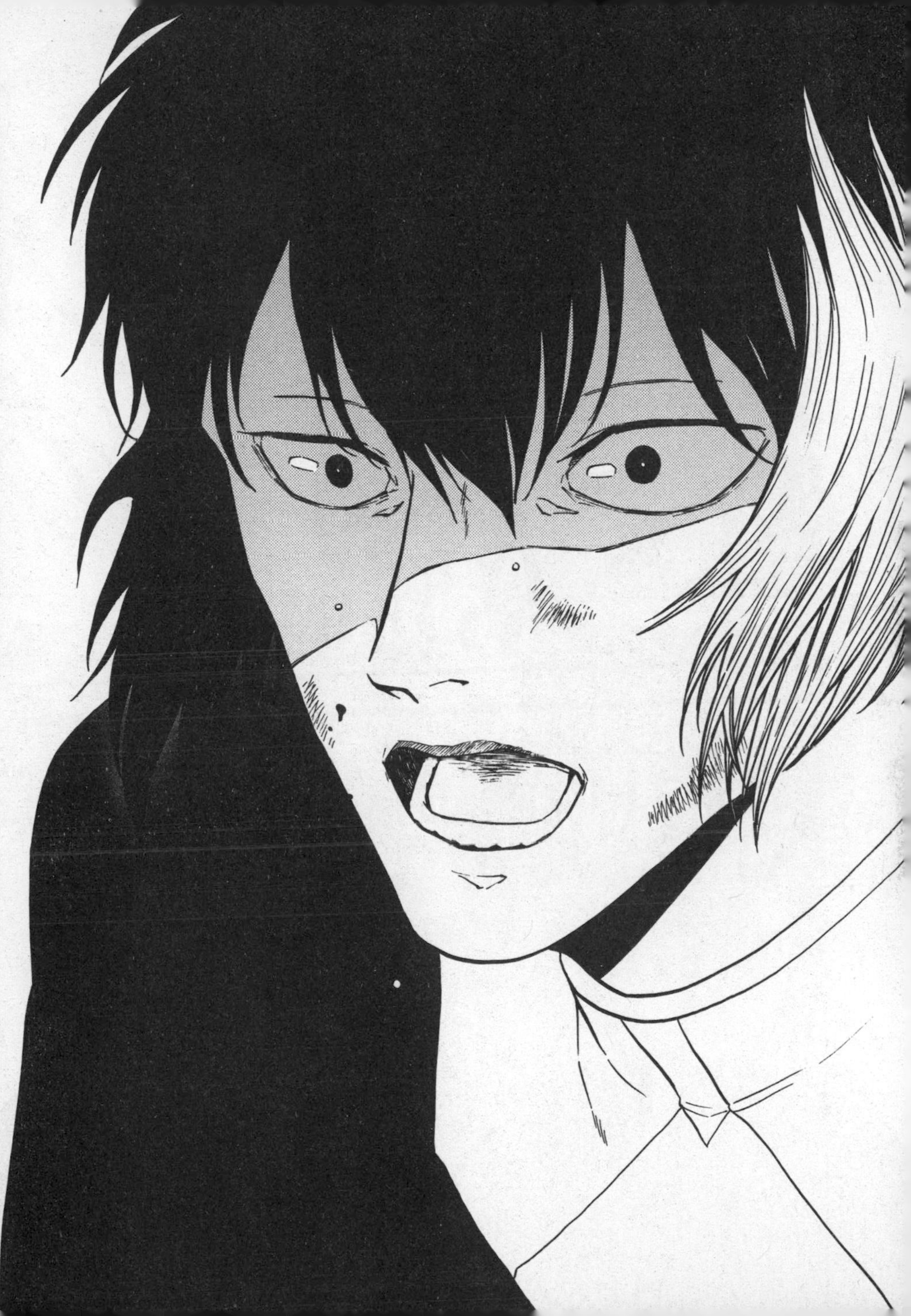

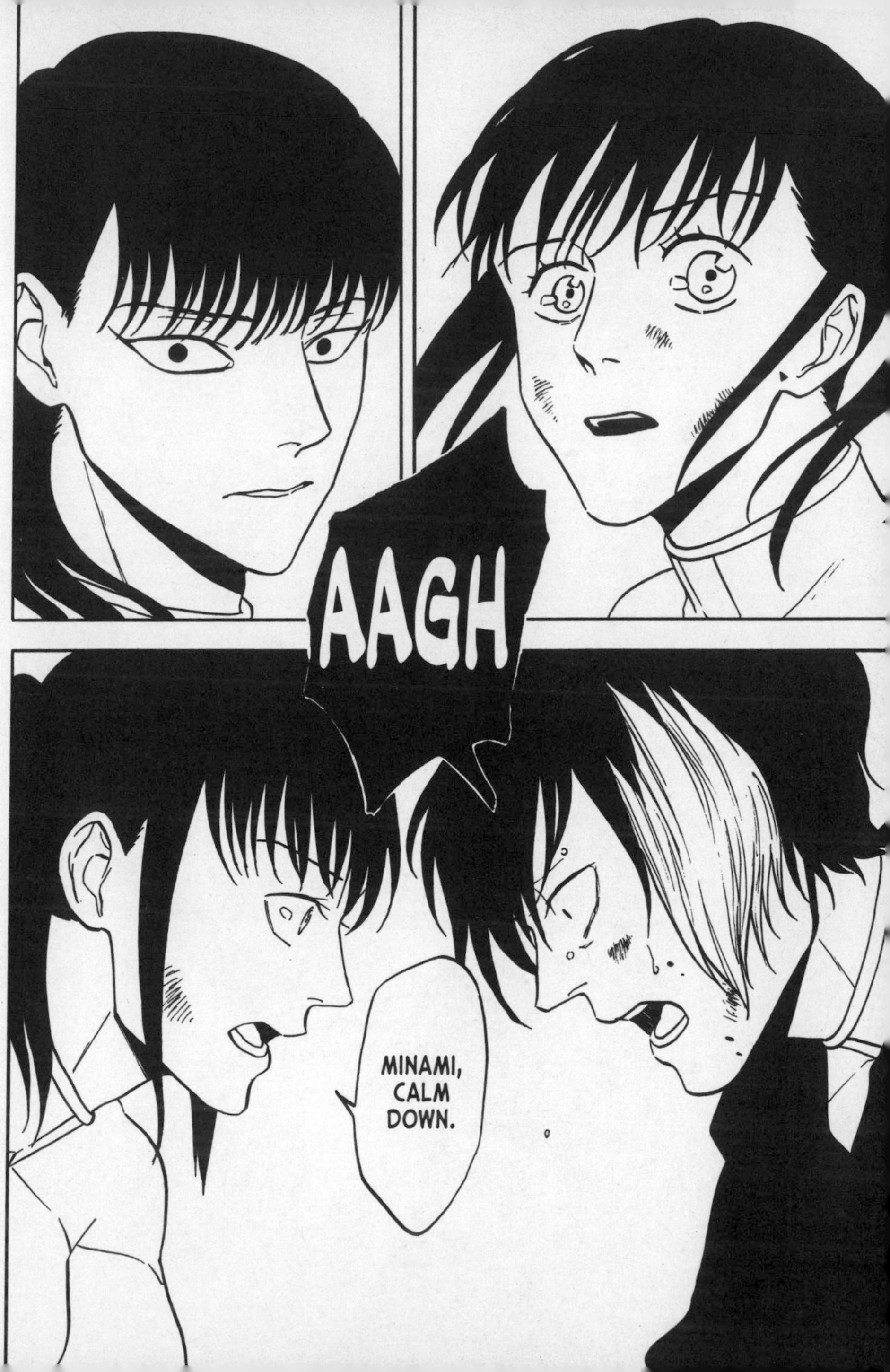
AAGH
MINAMI, CALM DOWN.

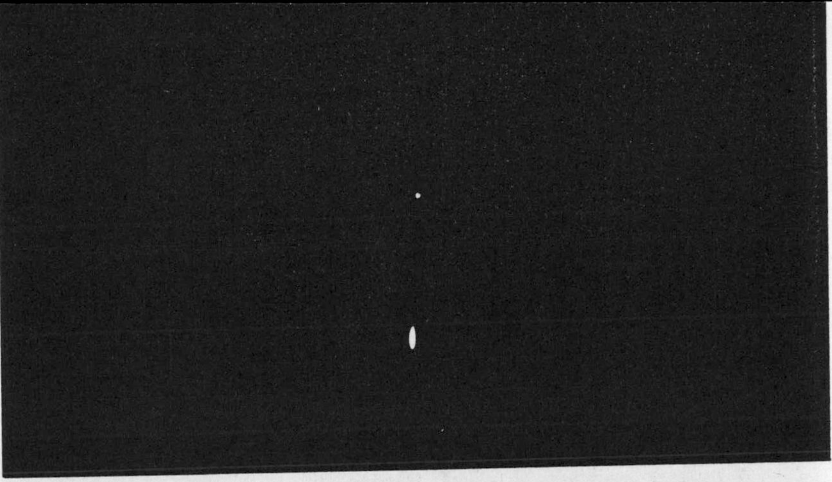
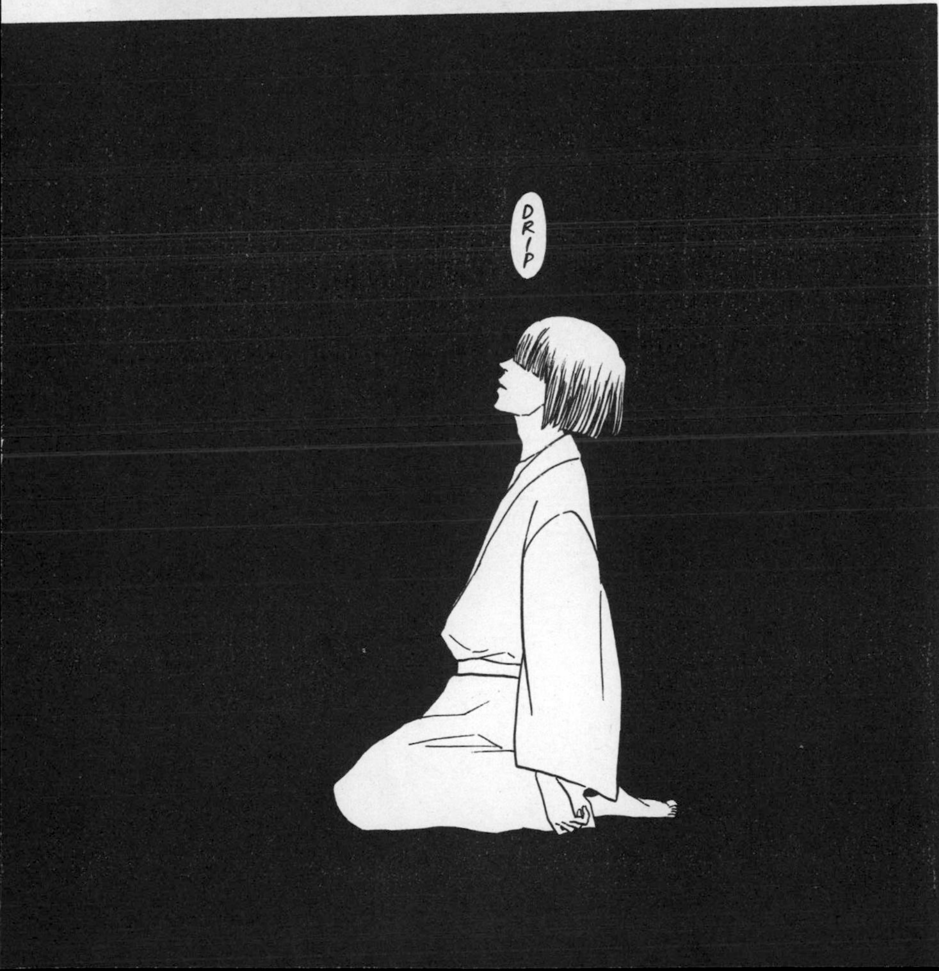
DRIP

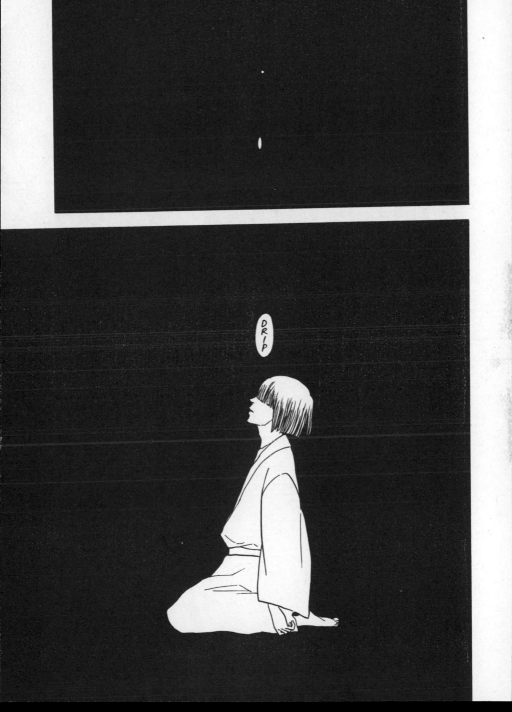

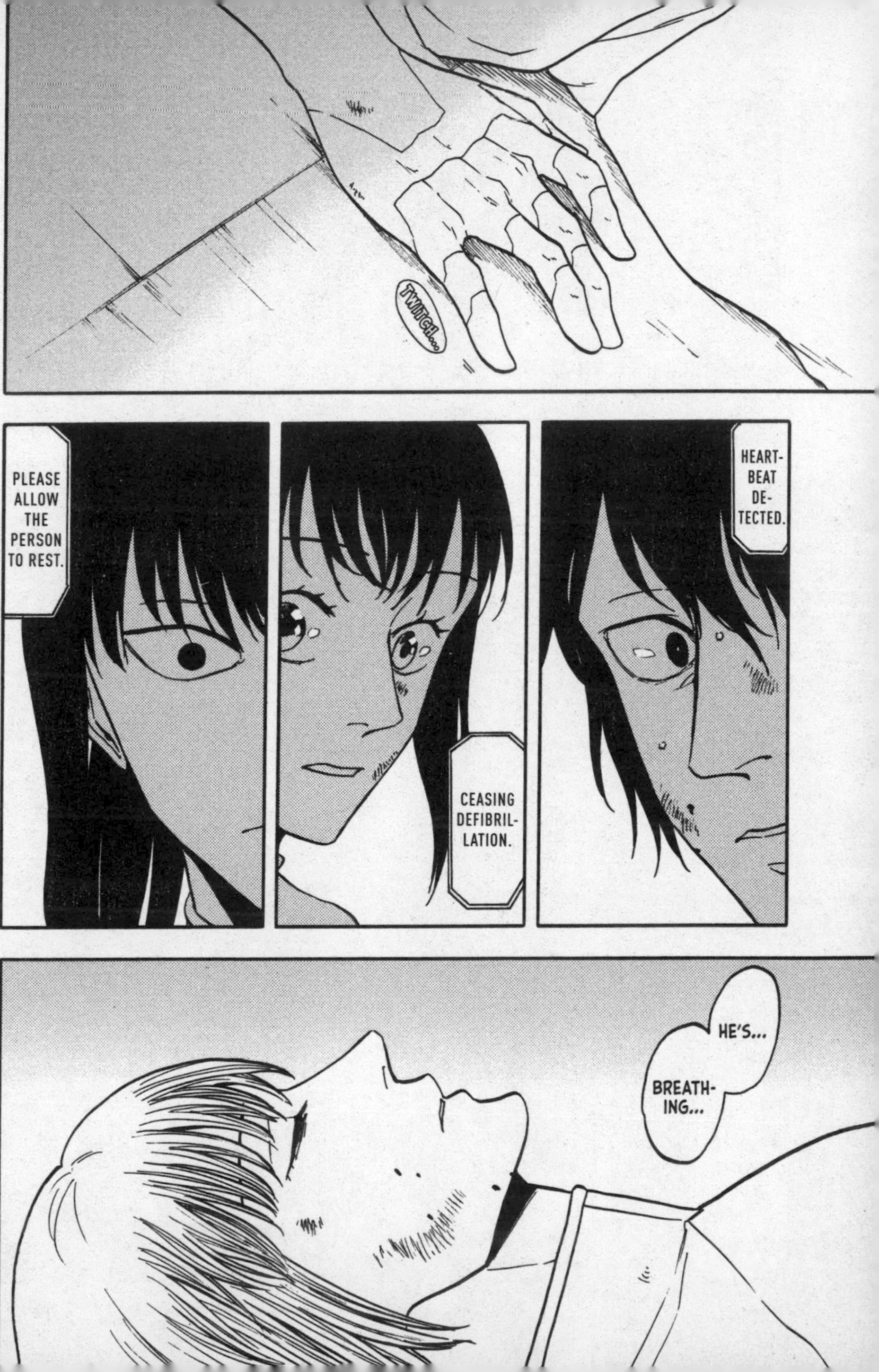
TWITCH...
HEART-BEAT DE-TECTED.
CEASING DEFIBRIL-LATION.
PLEASE ALLOW THE PERSON TO REST.
HE'S...
BREATH-ING...

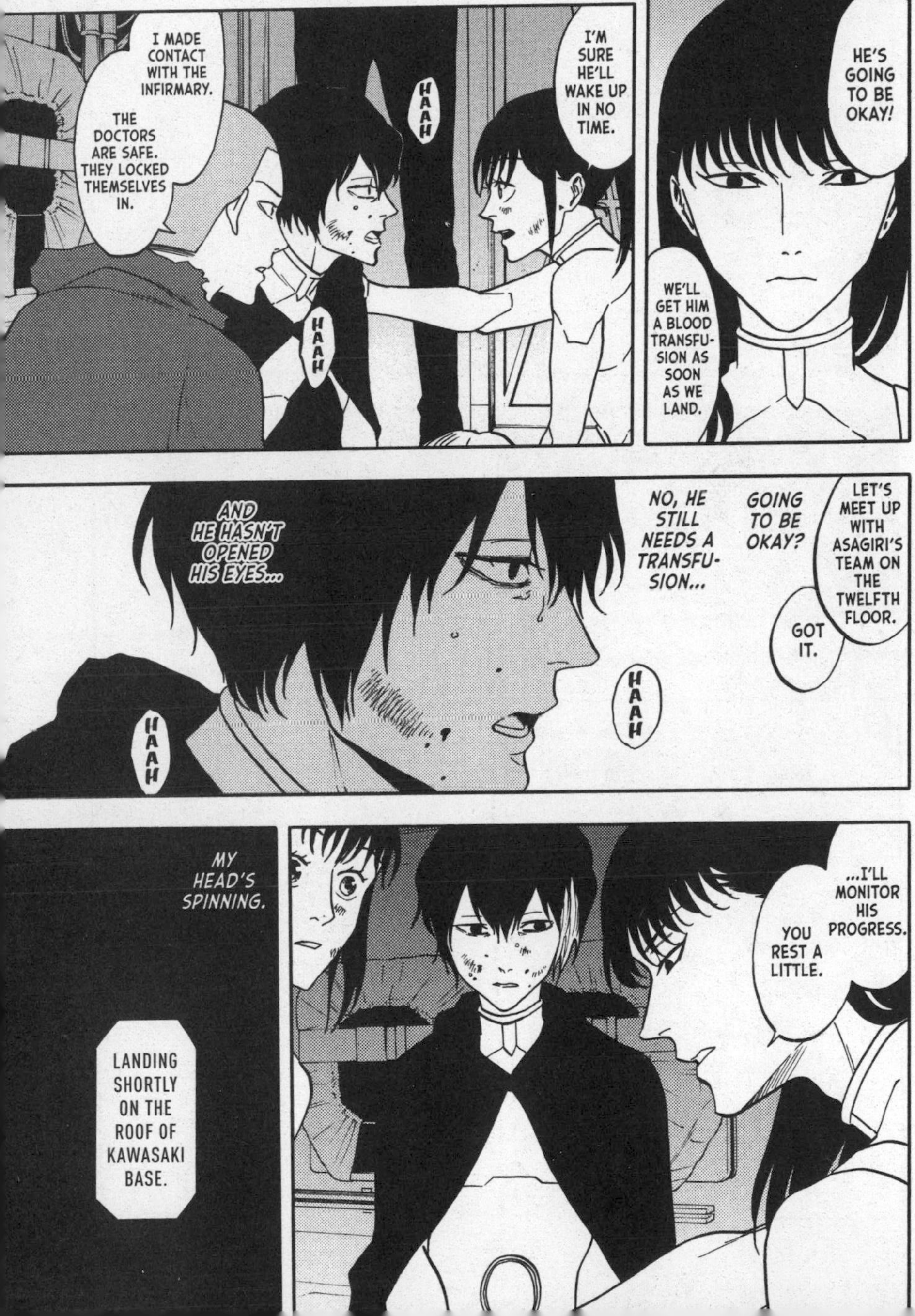
HE'S GOING TO BE OKAY!
WE'LL GET HIM A BLOOD TRANSFUSION AS SOON AS WE LAND.
I'M SURE HE'LL WAKE UP IN NO TIME.
HAAH
I MADE CONTACT WITH THE INFIRMARY.
THE DOCTORS ARE SAFE. THEY LOCKED THEMSELVES IN.
HAAH
LET'S MEET UP WITH ASAGIRI'S TEAM ON THE TWELFTH FLOOR.
GOT IT.
GOING TO BE OKAY?
NO, HE STILL NEEDS A TRANSFUSION...
HAAH
AND HE HASN'T OPENED HIS EYES...
HAAH
...I'LL MONITOR HIS PROGRESS.
YOU REST A LITTLE.
MY HEAD'S SPINNING.
LANDING SHORTLY ON THE ROOF OF KAWASAKI BASE.

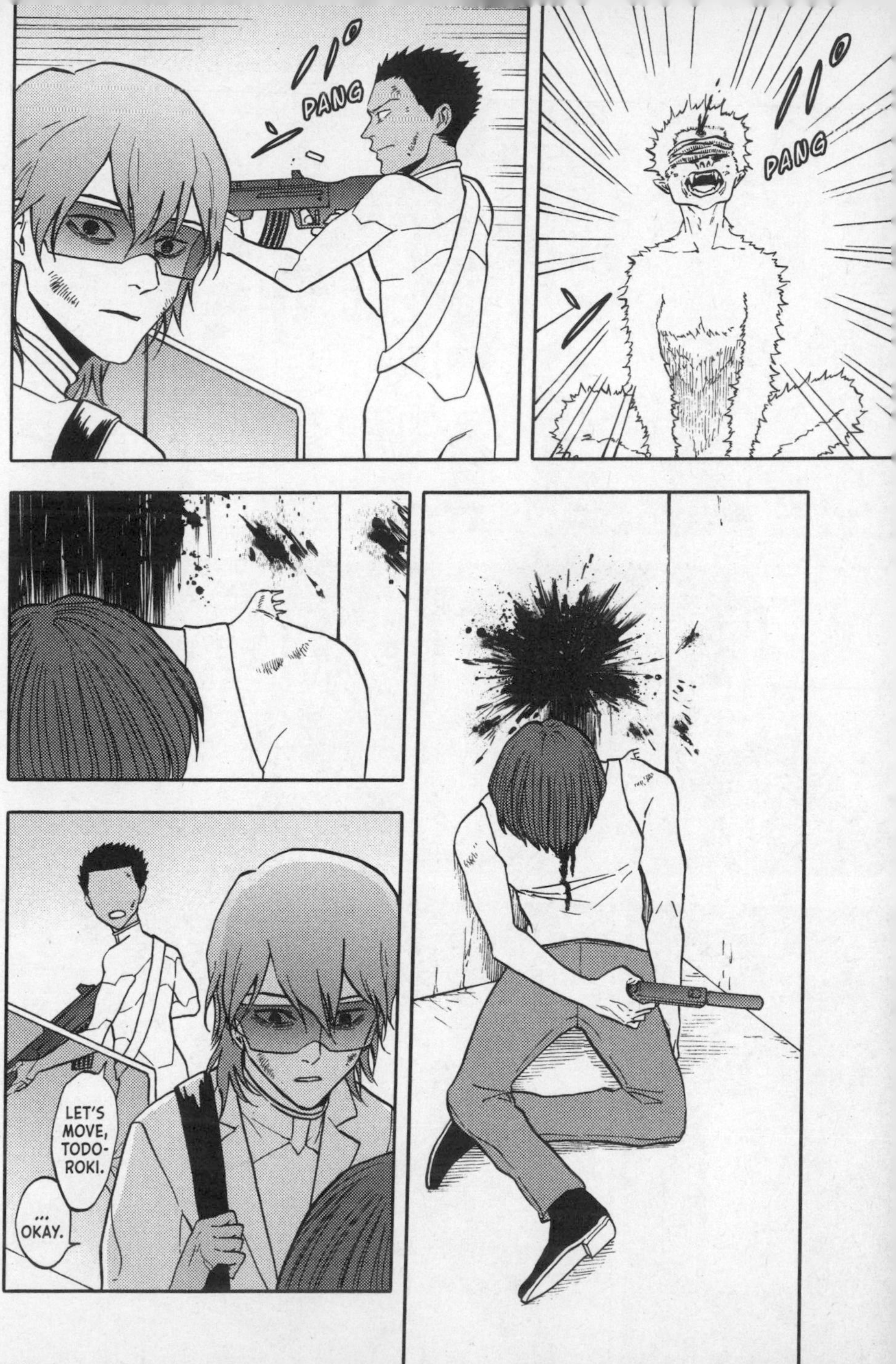
PANG
PANG
LET'S MOVE, TODO-ROKI.
...OKAY.

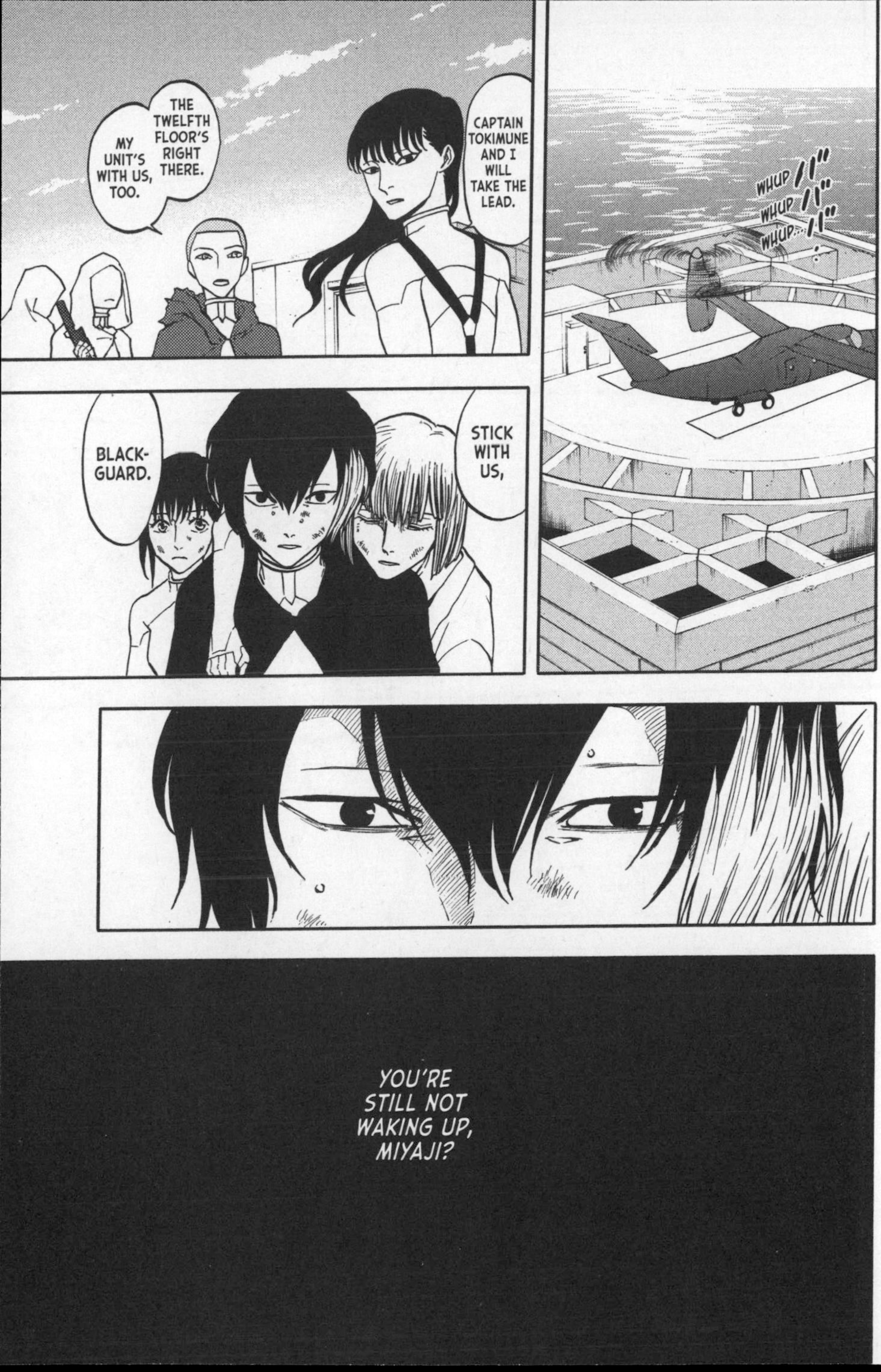
WHUP
WHUP
WHUP...
CAPTAIN TOKIMUNE AND I WILL TAKE THE LEAD.
THE TWELFTH FLOOR'S RIGHT THERE.
MY UNIT'S WITH US, TOO.
STICK WITH US,
BLACK-GUARD.
YOU'RE STILL NOT WAKING UP, MIYAJI?

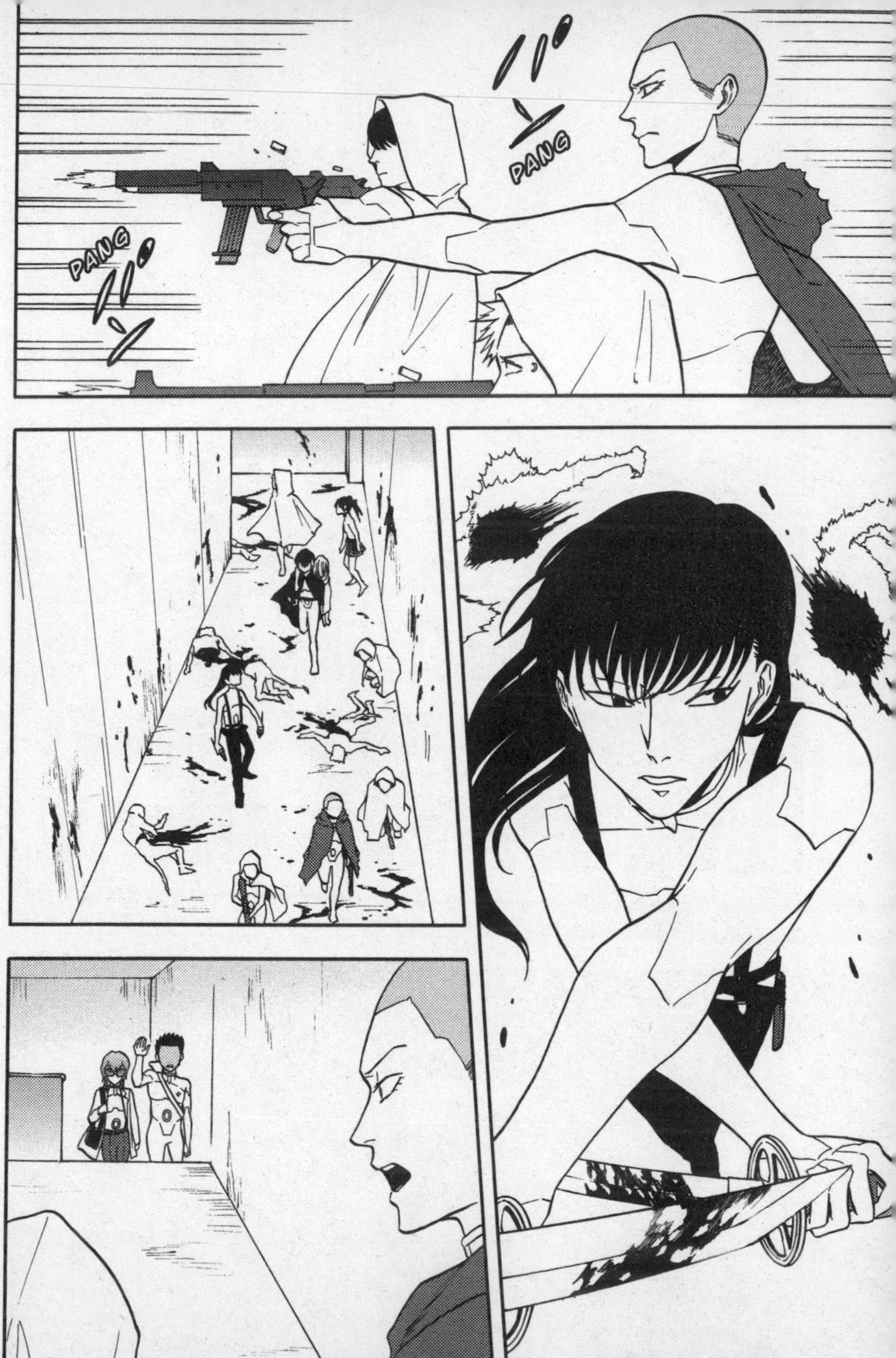
PANG
PANG

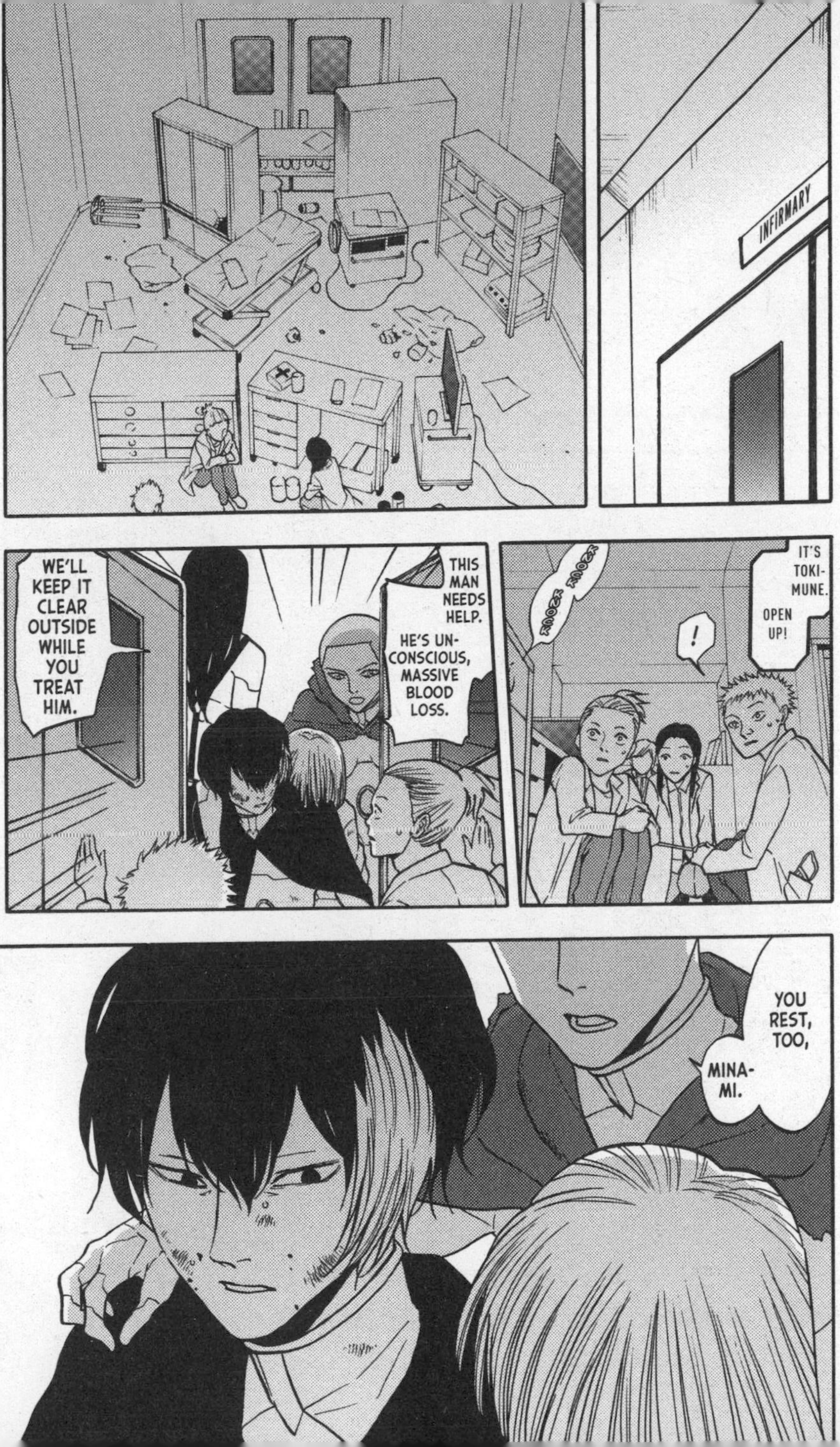
INFIRMARY
IT'S TOKI-MUNE.
OPEN UP!
KNOCK KNOCK
!
THIS MAN NEEDS HELP.
HE'S UN-CONSCIOUS, MASSIVE BLOOD LOSS.
WE'LL KEEP IT CLEAR OUTSIDE WHILE YOU TREAT HIM.
YOU REST, TOO,
MINA-MI.

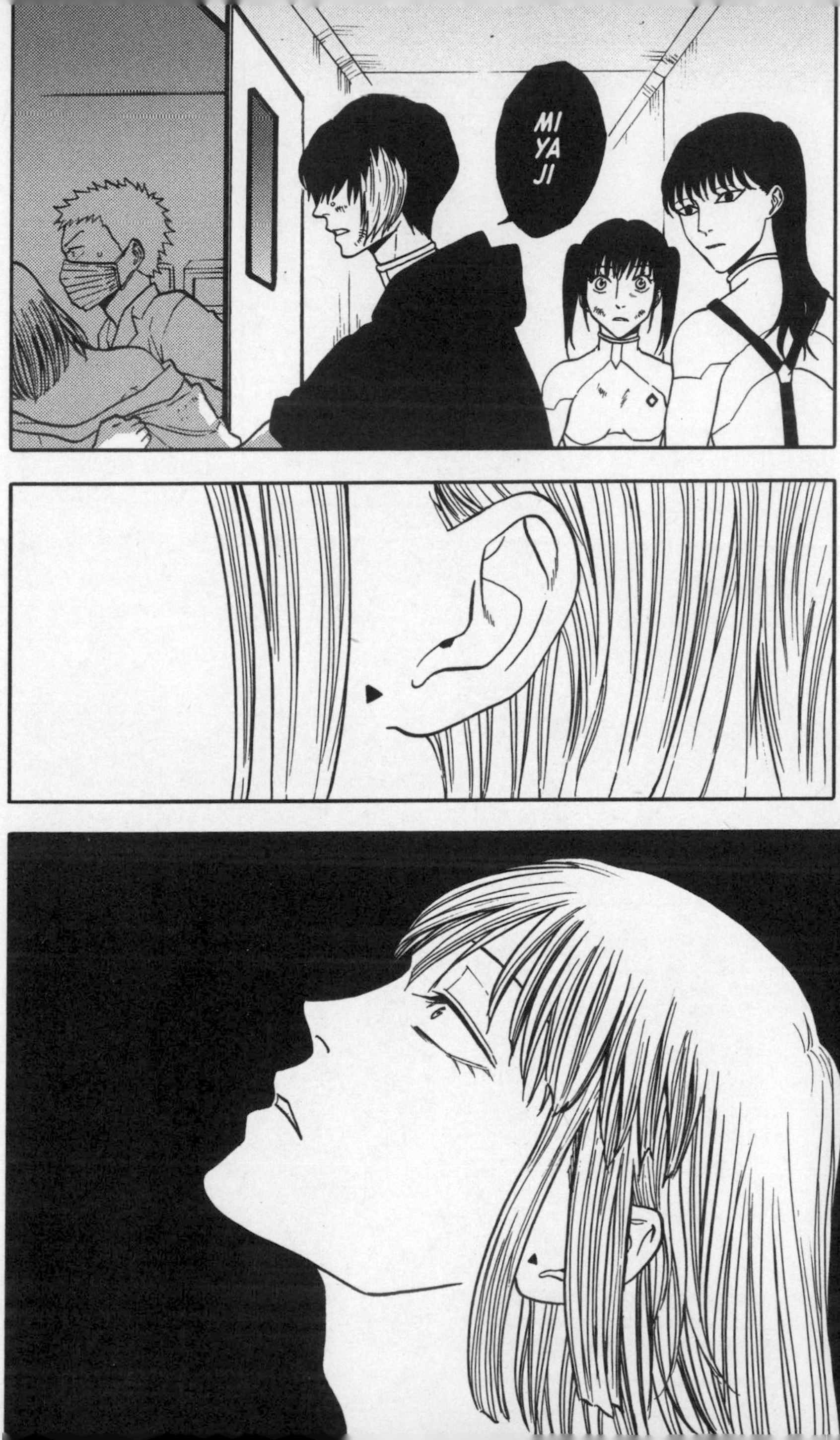
MI YA JI

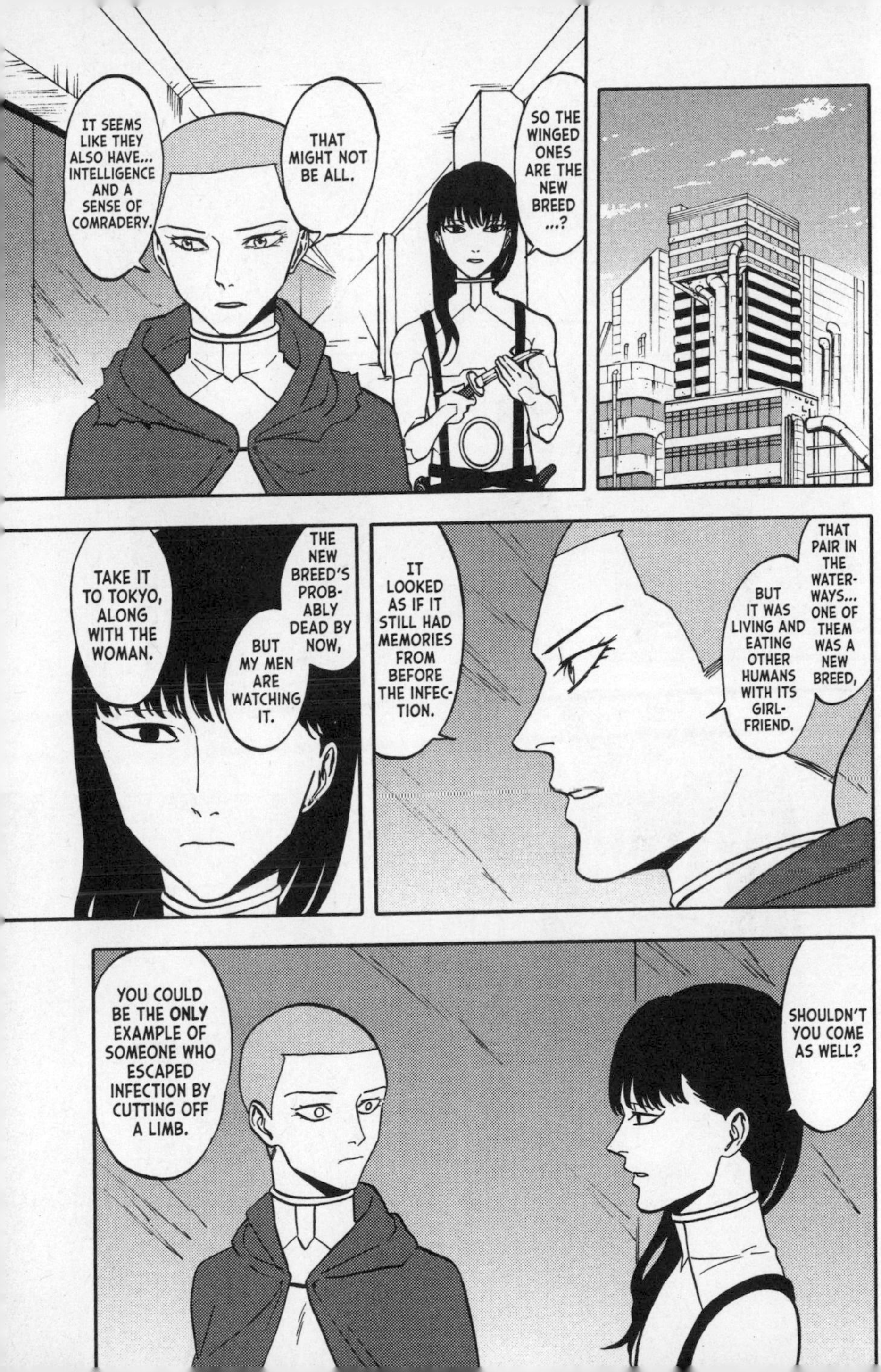
SO THE WINGED ONES ARE THE NEW BREED ...?
THAT MIGHT NOT BE ALL.
IT SEEMS LIKE THEY ALSO HAVE... INTELLIGENCE AND A SENSE OF COMRADERY.
THAT PAIR IN THE WATERWAYS... ONE OF THEM WAS A NEW BREED,
BUT IT WAS LIVING AND EATING OTHER HUMANS WITH ITS GIRLFRIEND.
IT LOOKED AS IF IT STILL HAD MEMORIES FROM BEFORE THE INFECTION.
THE NEW BREED'S PROBABLY DEAD BY NOW,
BUT MY MEN ARE WATCHING IT.
TAKE IT TO TOKYO, ALONG WITH THE WOMAN.
SHOULDN'T YOU COME AS WELL?
YOU COULD BE THE **ONLY** EXAMPLE OF SOMEONE WHO ESCAPED INFECTION BY CUTTING OFF A LIMB.

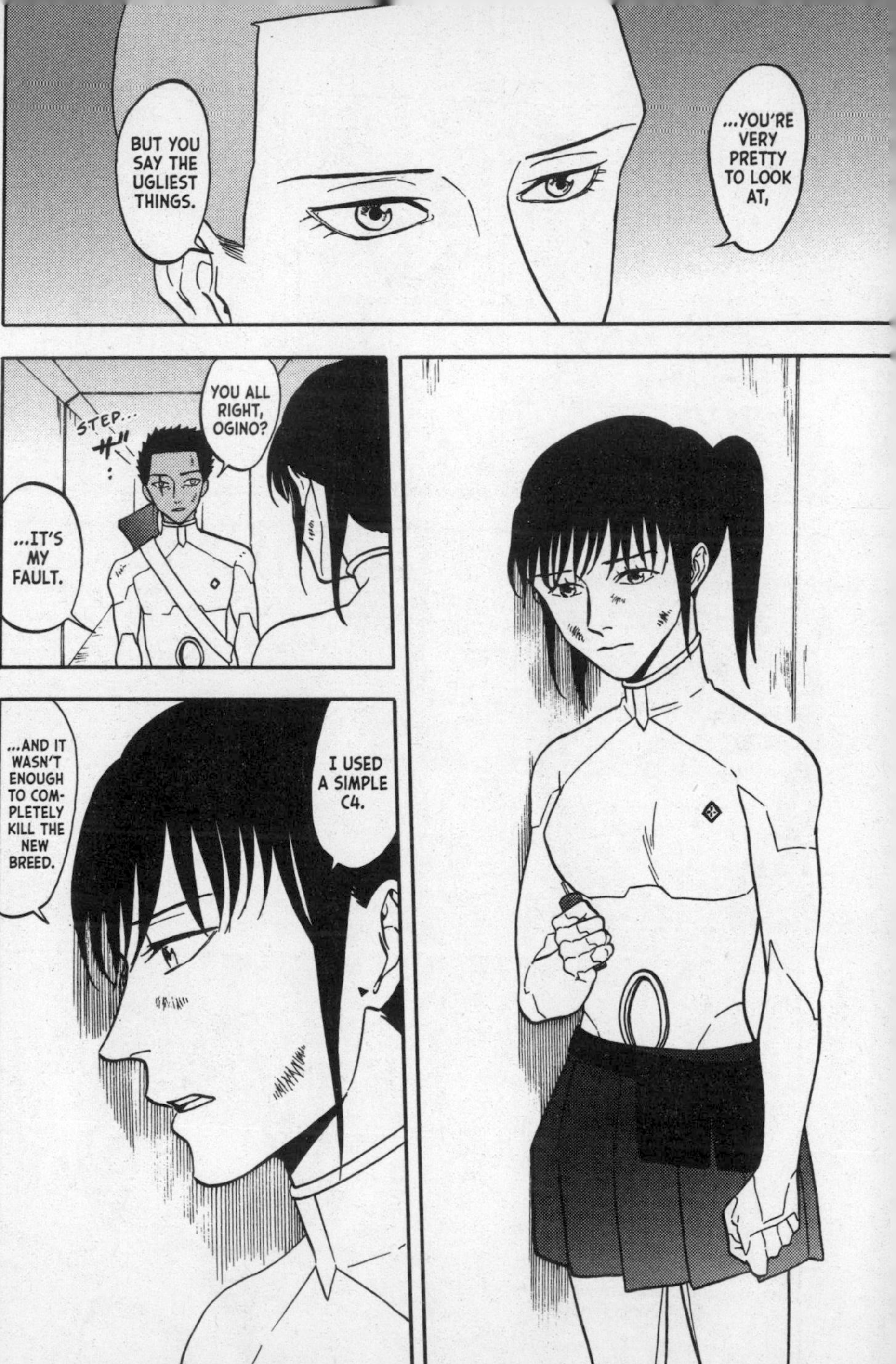
...YOU'RE VERY PRETTY TO LOOK AT,
BUT YOU SAY THE UGLIEST THINGS.
YOU ALL RIGHT, OGINO?
STEP...
...IT'S MY FAULT.
I USED A SIMPLE C4.
...AND IT WASN'T ENOUGH TO COM-PLETELY KILL THE NEW BREED.

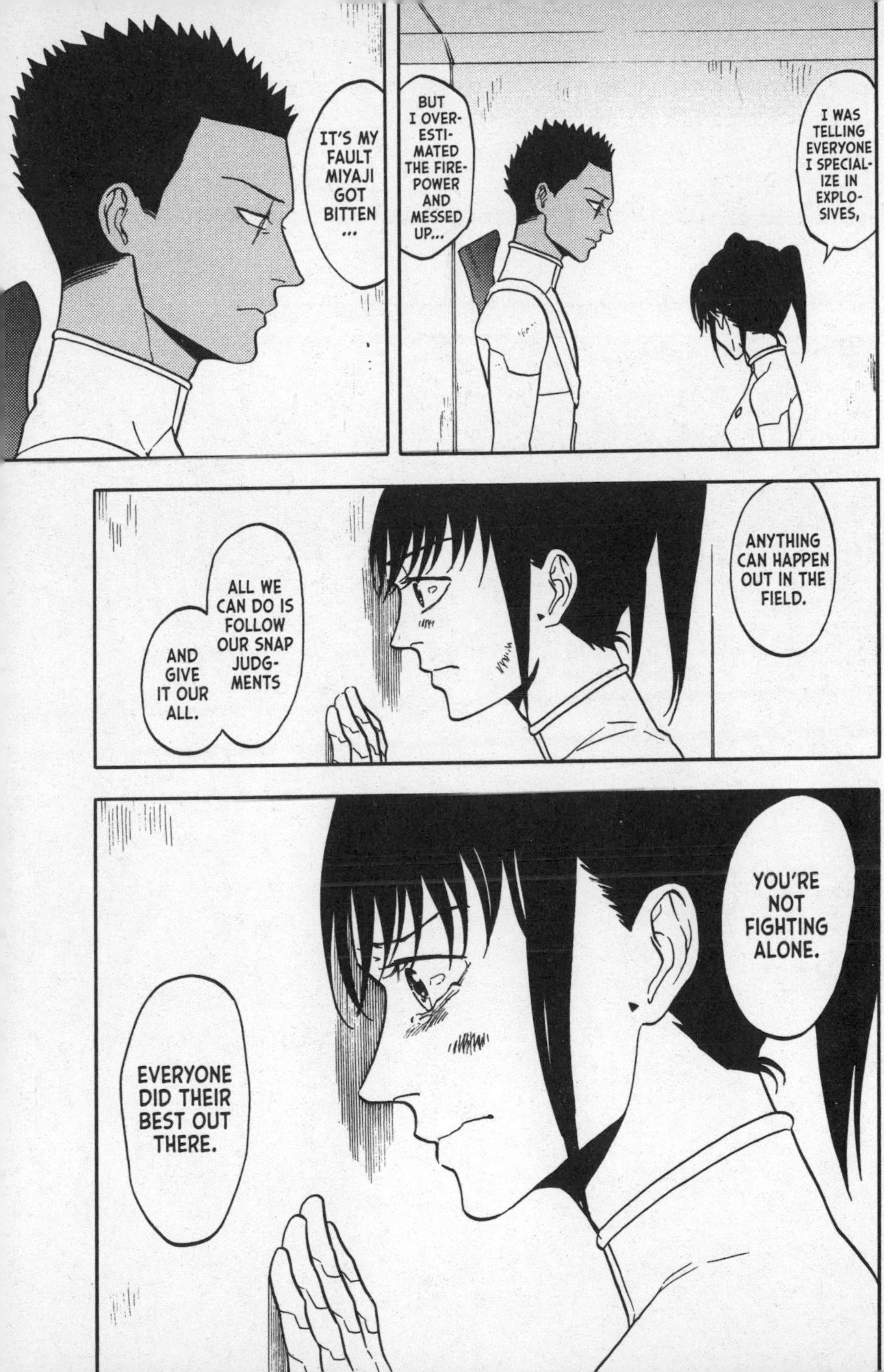
I WAS TELLING EVERYONE I SPECIALIZE IN EXPLOSIVES,
BUT I OVERESTIMATED THE FIREPOWER AND MESSED UP...
IT'S MY FAULT MIYAJI GOT BITTEN...
ANYTHING CAN HAPPEN OUT IN THE FIELD.
ALL WE CAN DO IS FOLLOW OUR SNAP JUDGMENTS
AND GIVE IT OUR ALL.
YOU'RE NOT FIGHTING ALONE.
EVERYONE DID THEIR BEST OUT THERE.

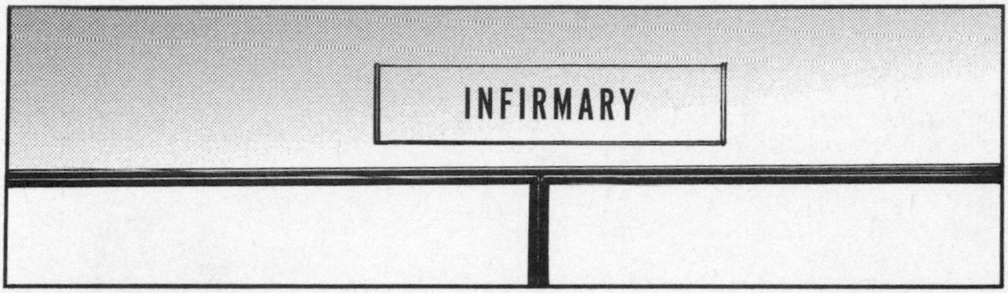
INFIRMARY
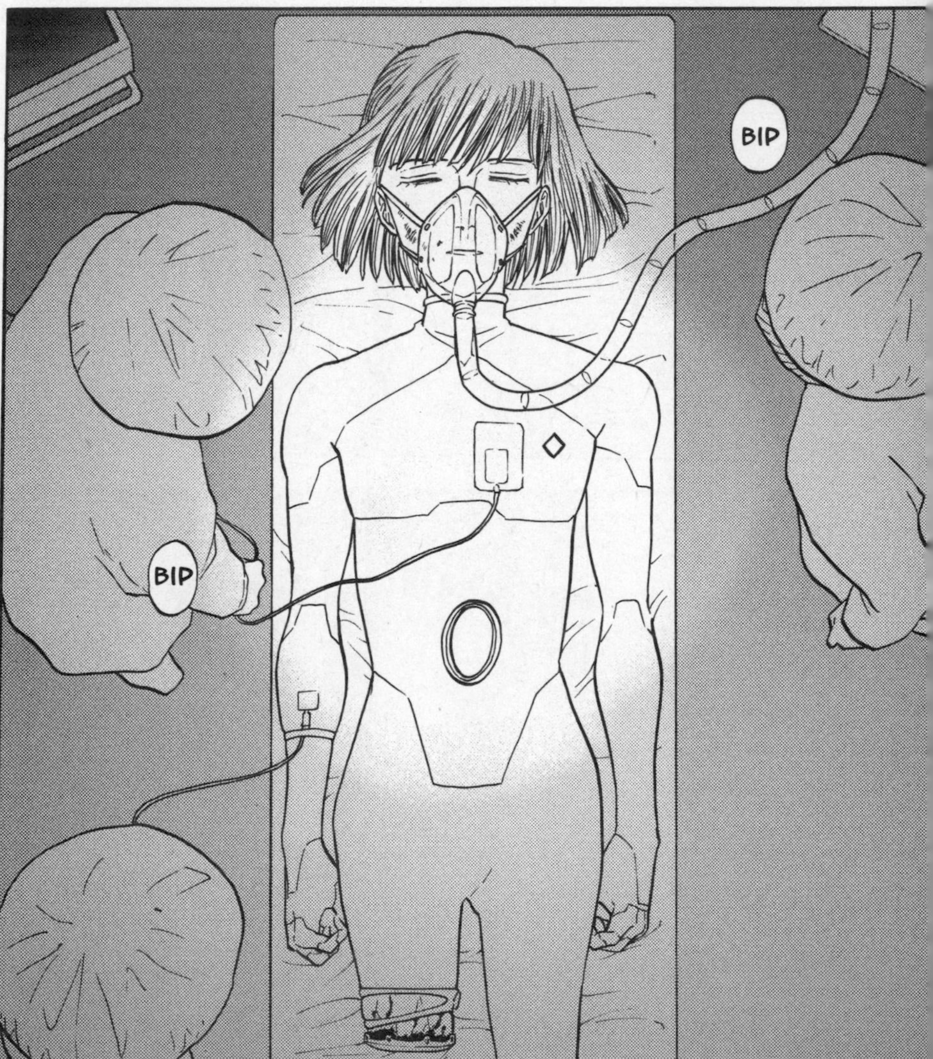
BIP
BIP

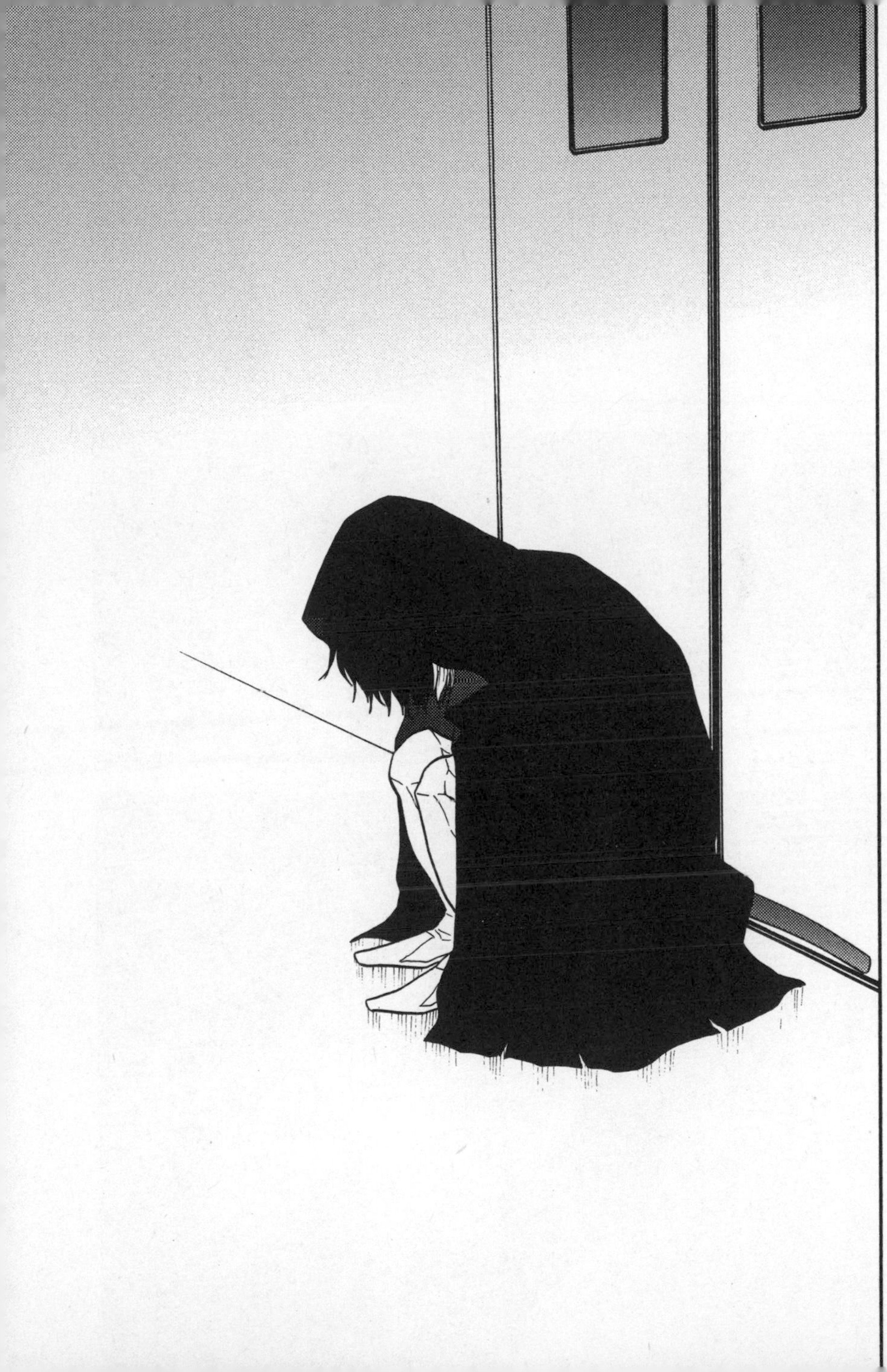

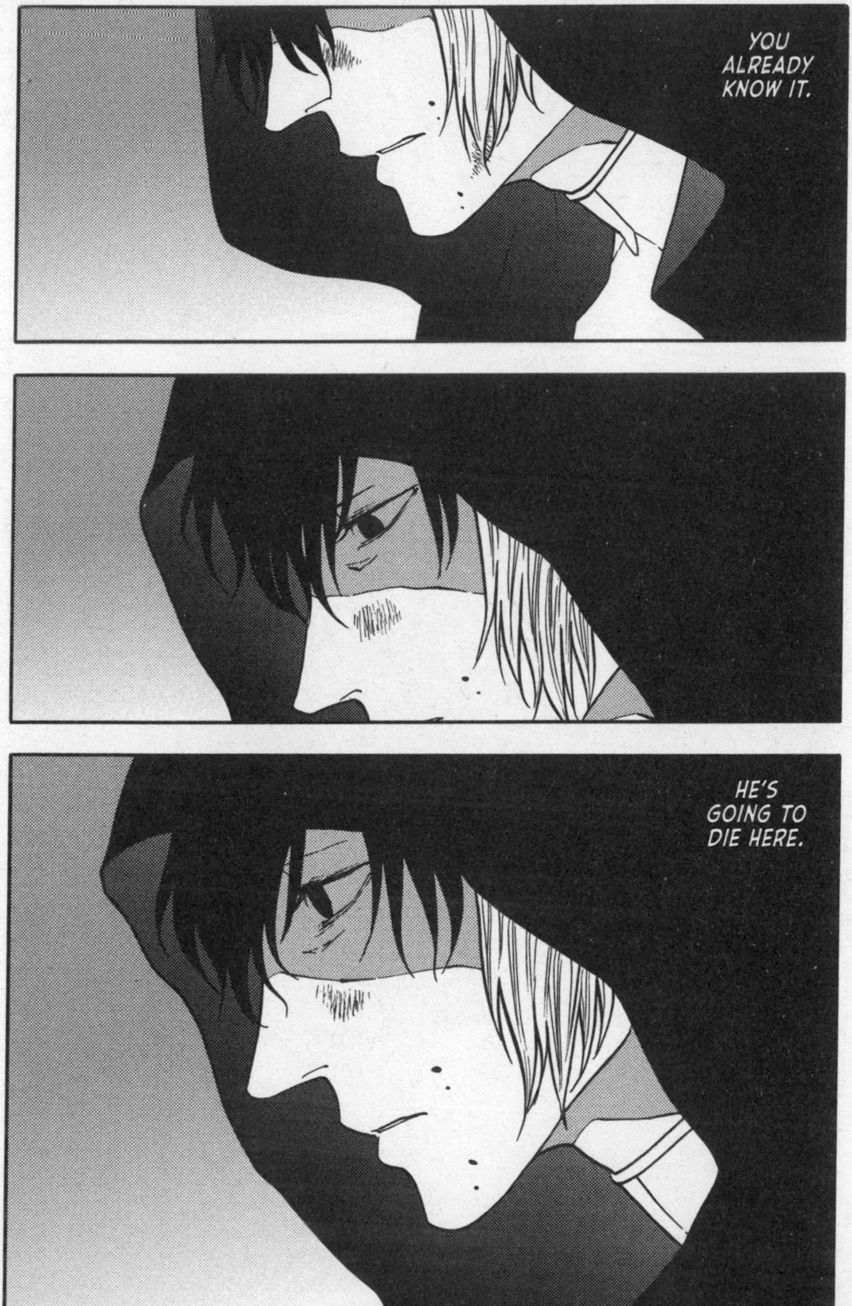
YOU ALREADY KNOW IT.
HE'S GOING TO DIE HERE.

RATTLE

WE FINISHED TREATING HIM.

BAM

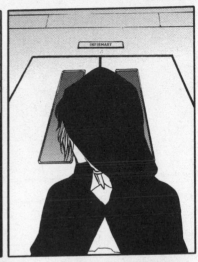

INFIRMARY

HE'S NO LONGER IN CRITICAL CONDITION.

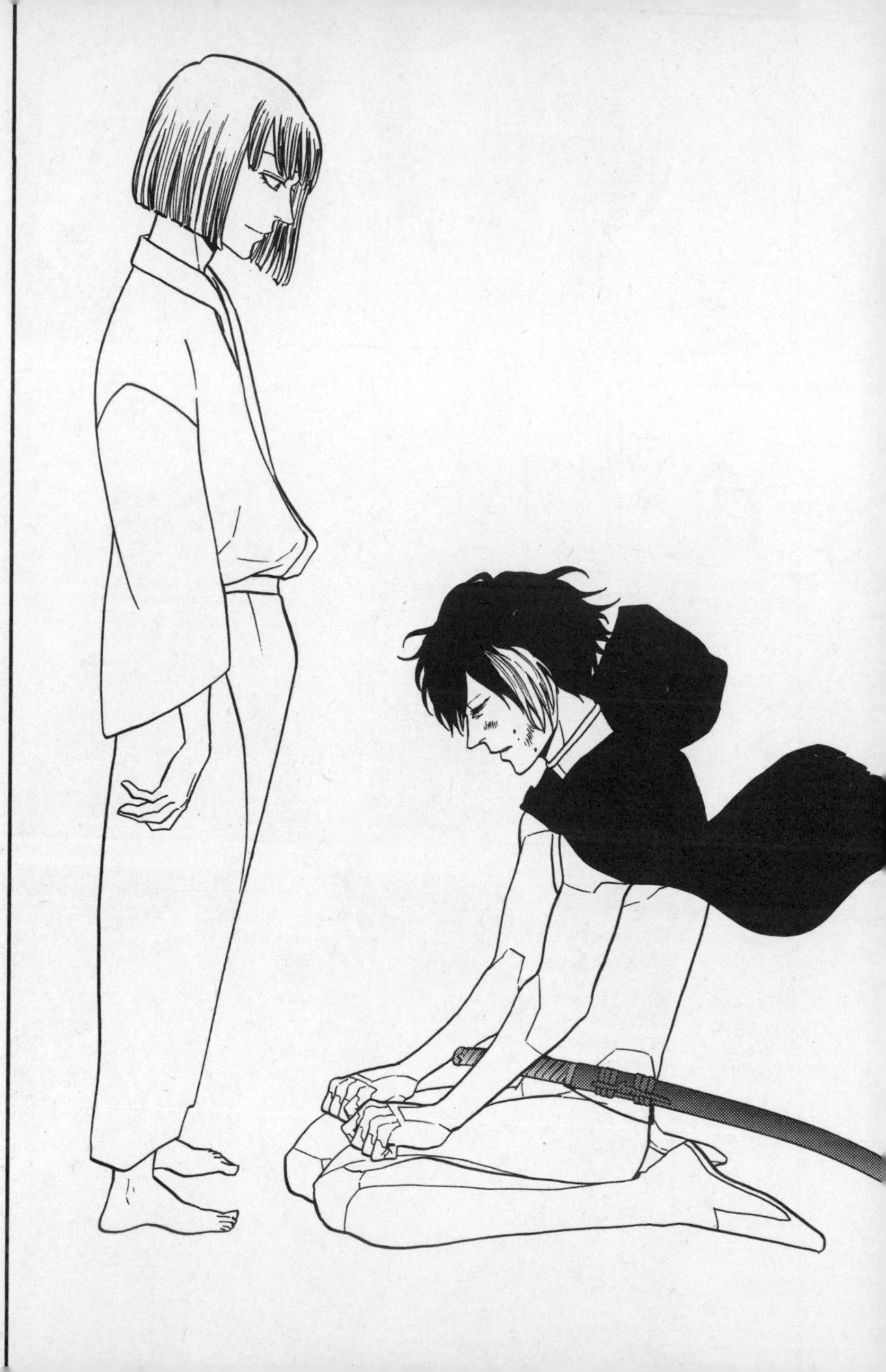

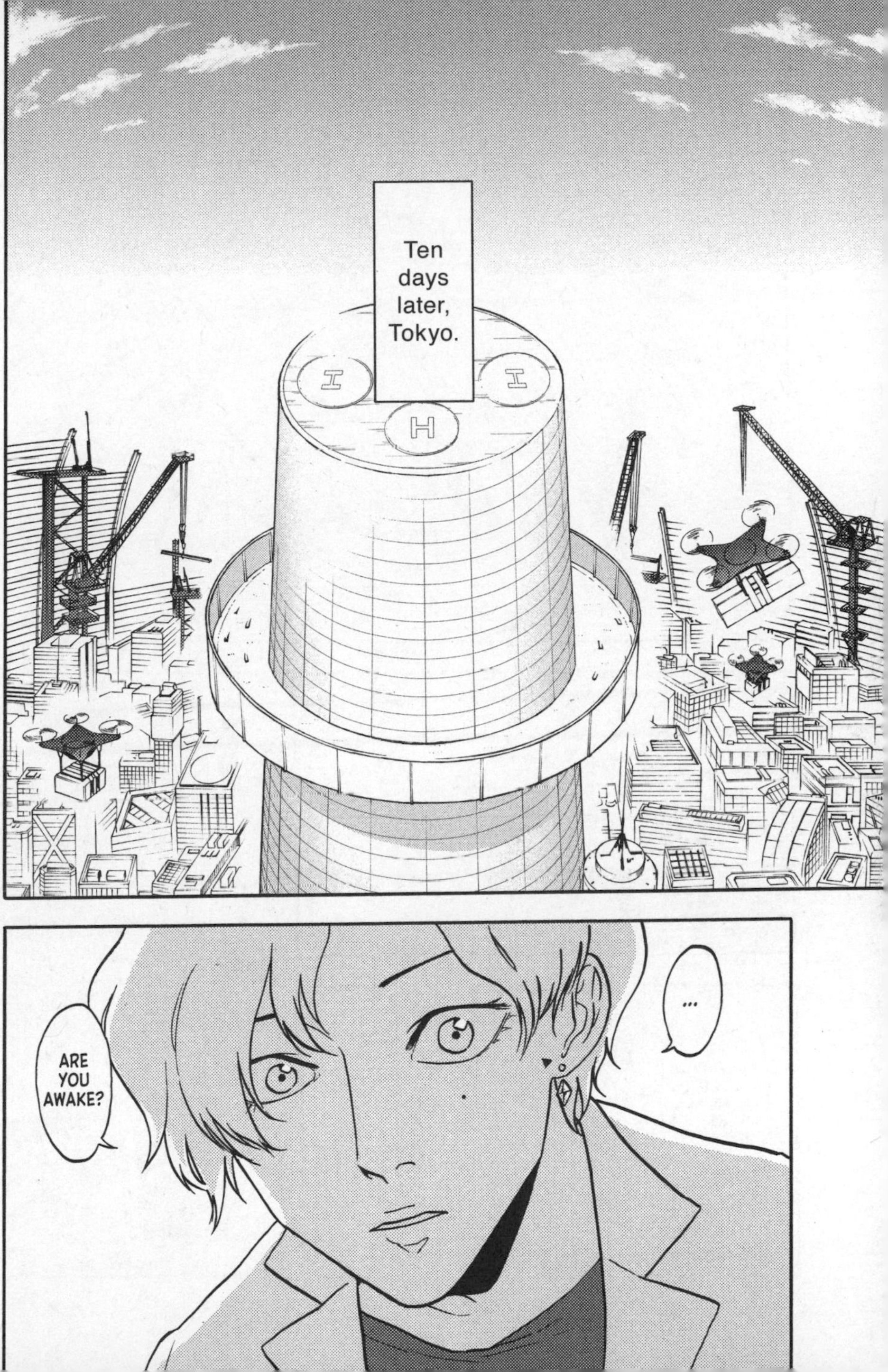
Ten days later, Tokyo.
...
ARE YOU AWAKE?

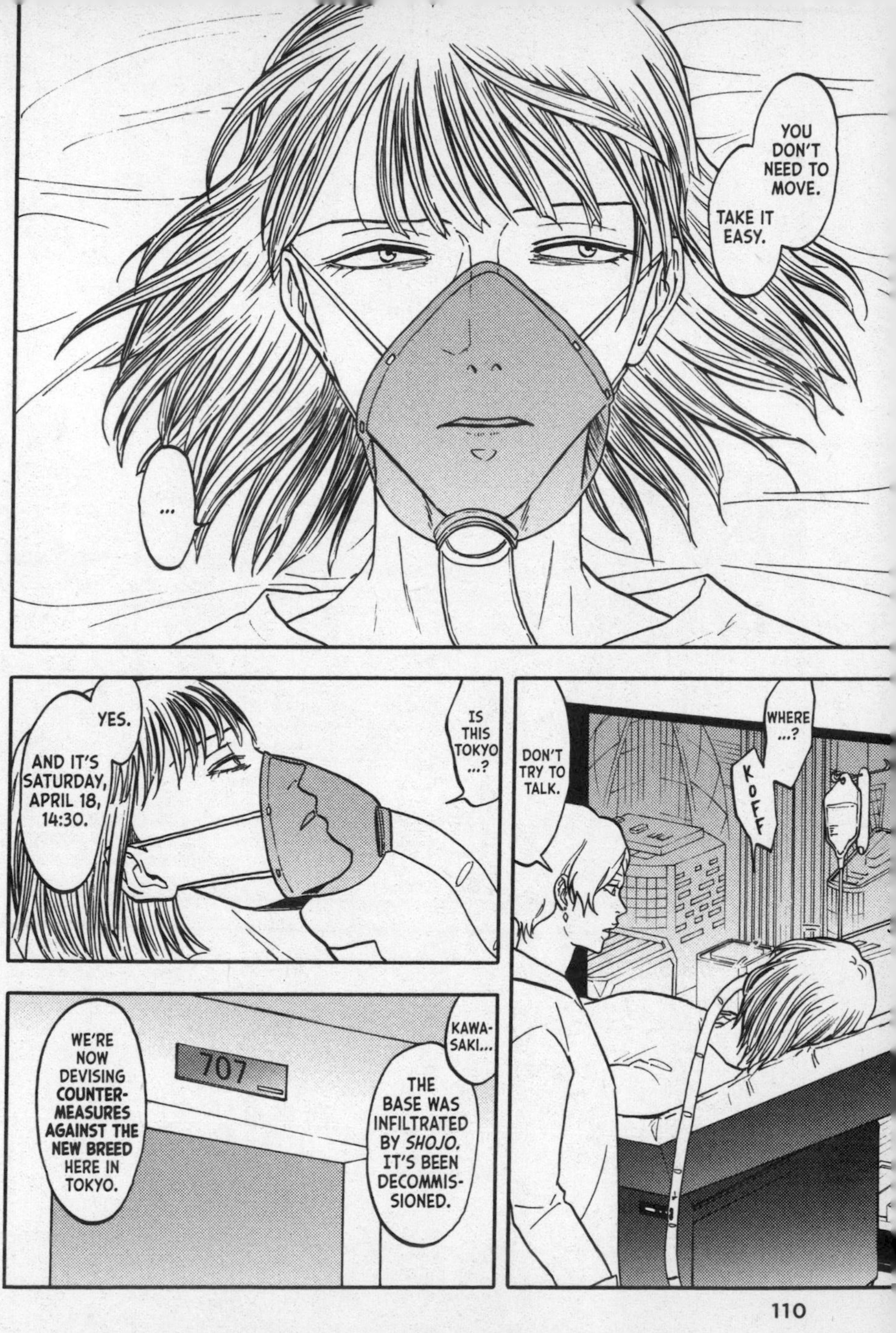
YOU DON'T NEED TO MOVE.
TAKE IT EASY.
...
WHERE ...?
KOFF
DON'T TRY TO TALK.
IS THIS TOKYO ...?
YES.
AND IT'S SATURDAY, APRIL 18, 14:30.
KAWASAKI...
THE BASE WAS INFILTRATED BY *SHOJO.* IT'S BEEN DECOMMISSIONED.
707
WE'RE NOW DEVISING **COUNTERMEASURES AGAINST THE NEW BREED** HERE IN TOKYO.

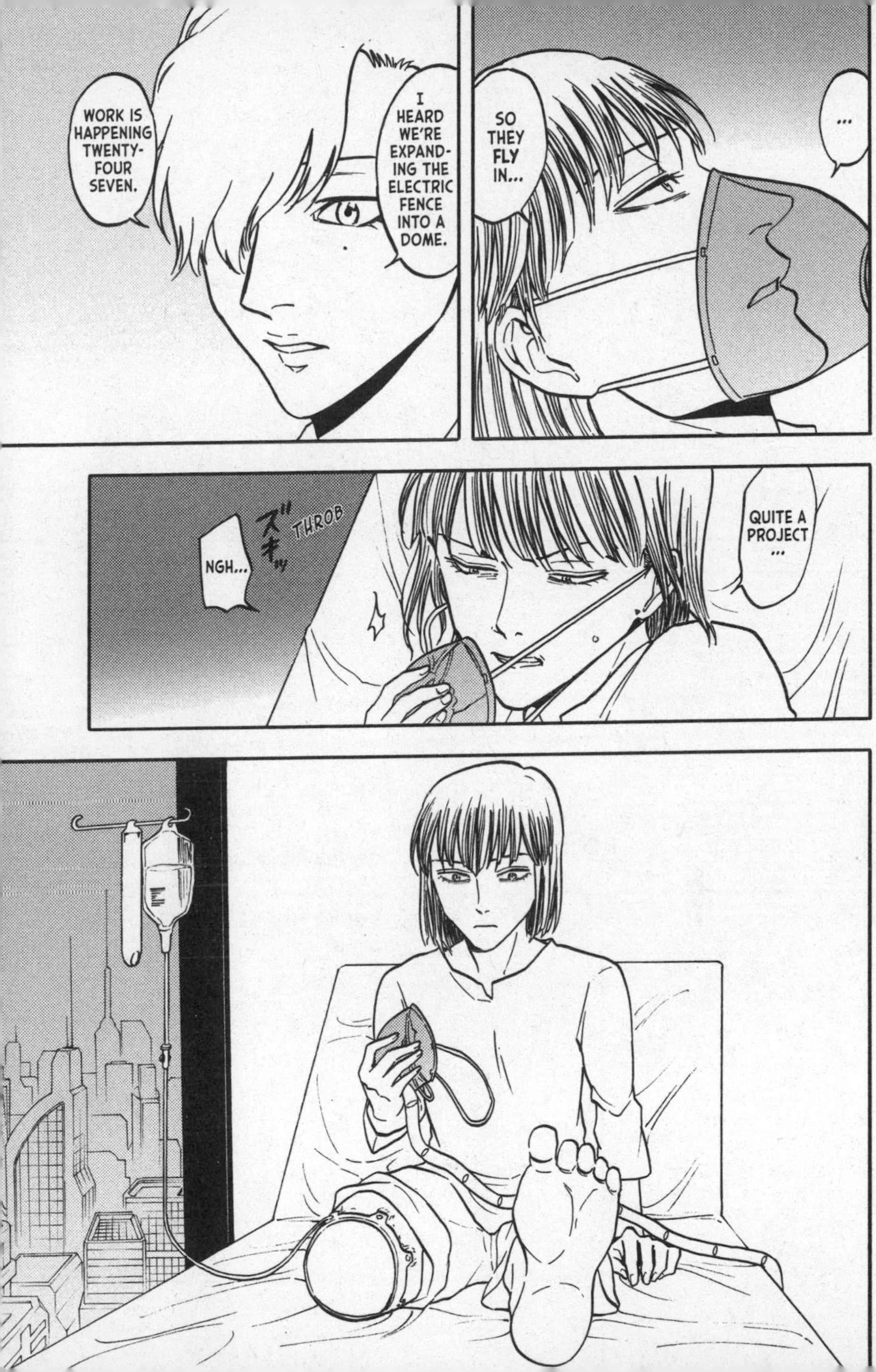
...
SO THEY FLY IN...
I HEARD WE'RE EXPANDING THE ELECTRIC FENCE INTO A DOME.
WORK IS HAPPENING TWENTY-FOUR SEVEN.
QUITE A PROJECT...
ズキッ THROB
NGH...

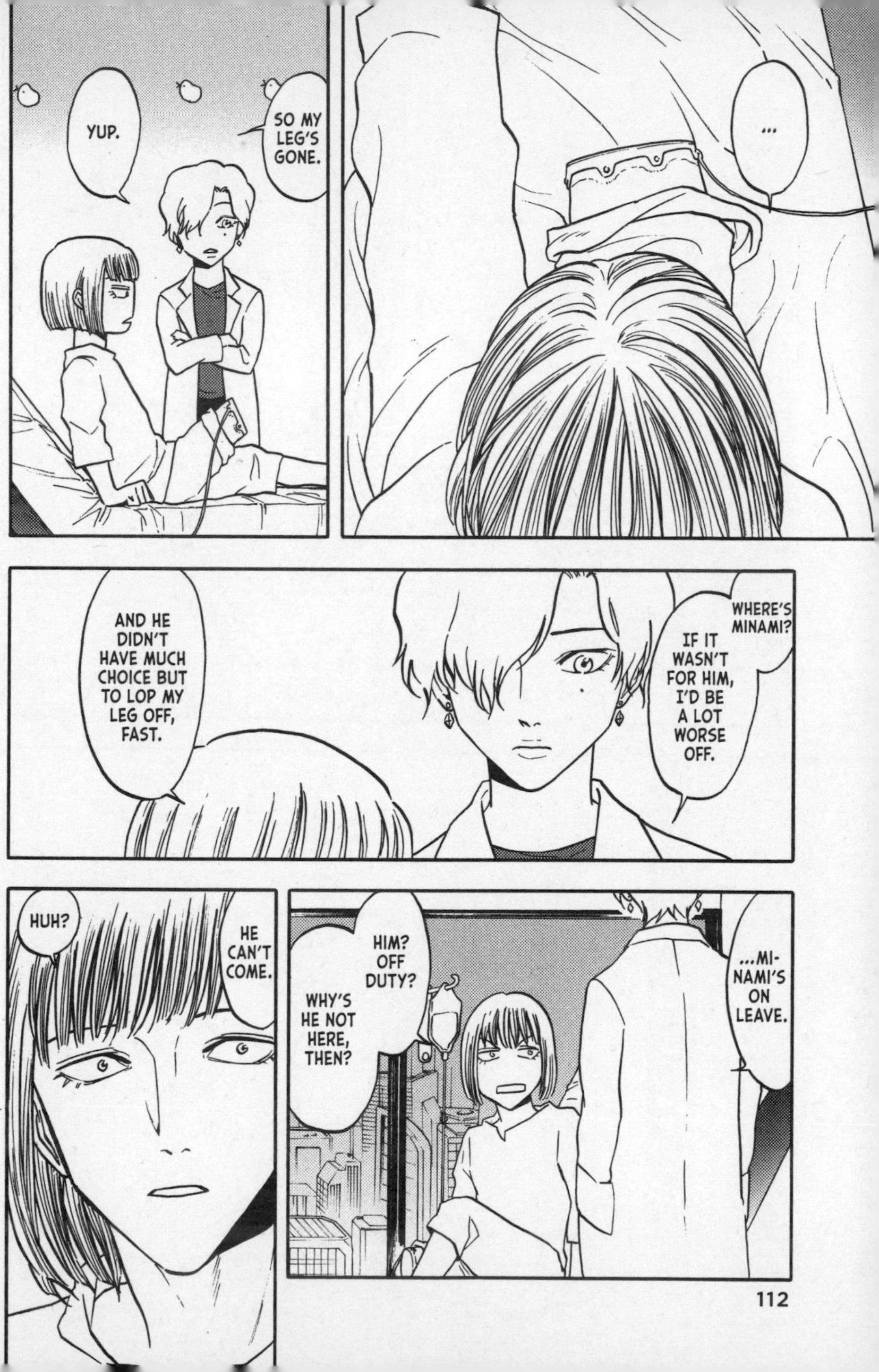
...
SO MY LEG'S GONE.
YUP.
WHERE'S MINAMI?
IF IT WASN'T FOR HIM, I'D BE A LOT WORSE OFF.
AND HE DIDN'T HAVE MUCH CHOICE BUT TO LOP MY LEG OFF, FAST.
...MI-NAMI'S ON LEAVE.
HIM? OFF DUTY?
WHY'S HE NOT HERE, THEN?
HE CAN'T COME.
HUH?

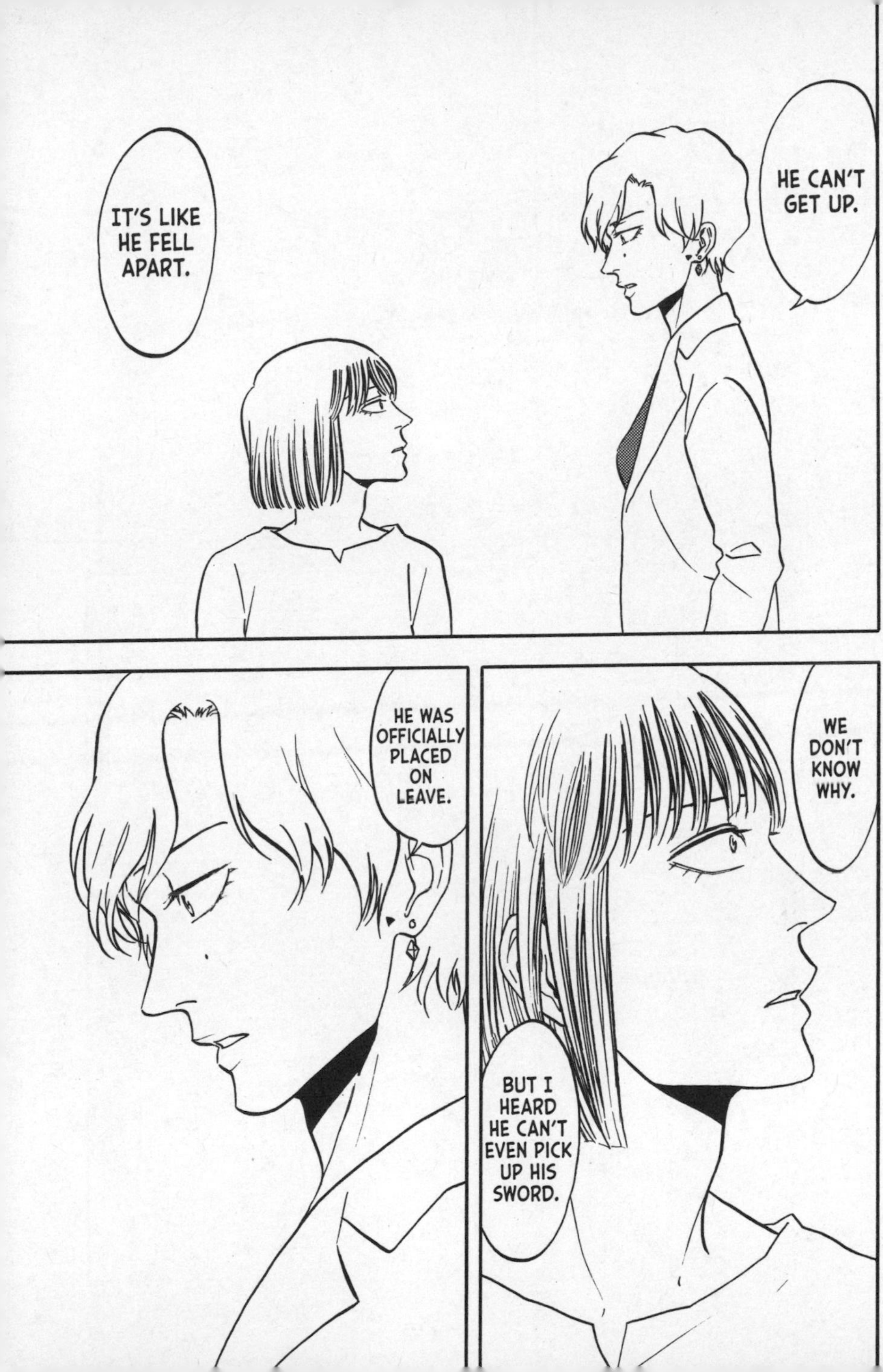
HE CAN'T GET UP.
IT'S LIKE HE FELL APART.
WE DON'T KNOW WHY.
BUT I HEARD HE CAN'T EVEN PICK UP HIS SWORD.
HE WAS OFFICIALLY PLACED ON LEAVE.

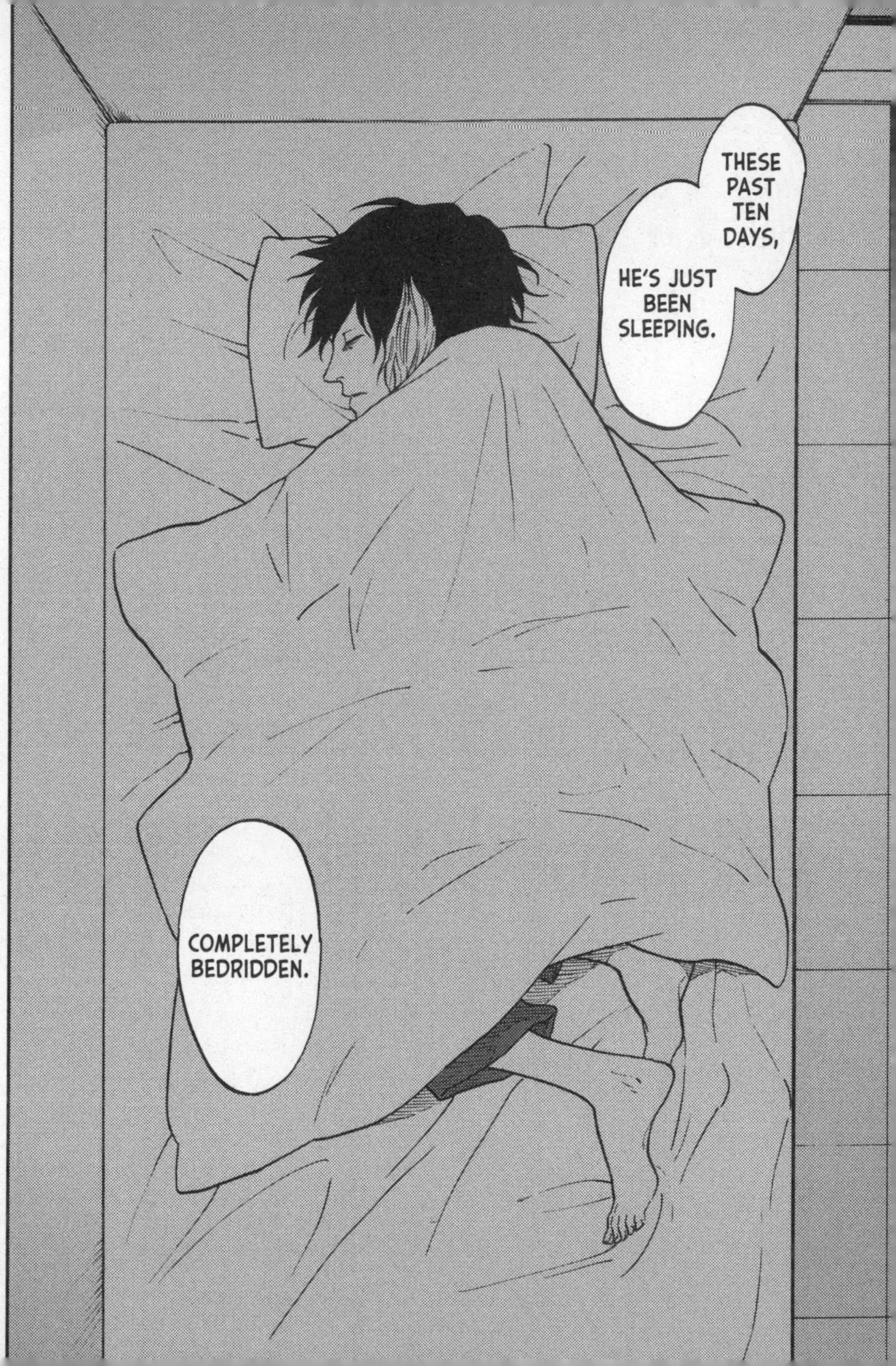
THESE PAST TEN DAYS,
HE'S JUST BEEN SLEEPING.
COMPLETELY BEDRIDDEN.

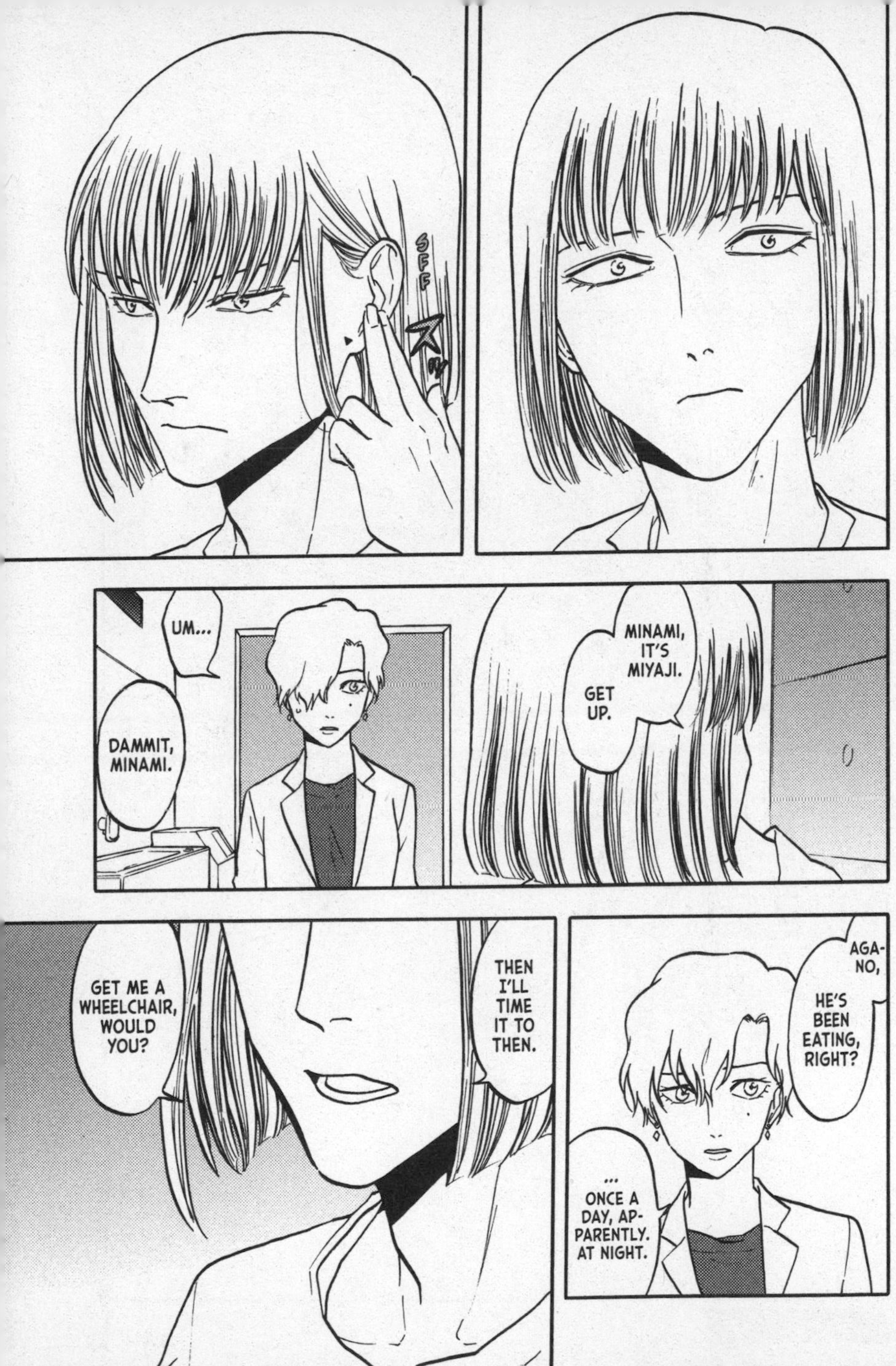
SFF
スッ
MINAMI, IT'S MIYAJI.
GET UP.
UM...
DAMMIT, MINAMI.
AGA-NO,
HE'S BEEN EATING, RIGHT?
... ONCE A DAY, AP-PARENTLY. AT NIGHT.
THEN I'LL TIME IT TO THEN.
GET ME A WHEELCHAIR, WOULD YOU?

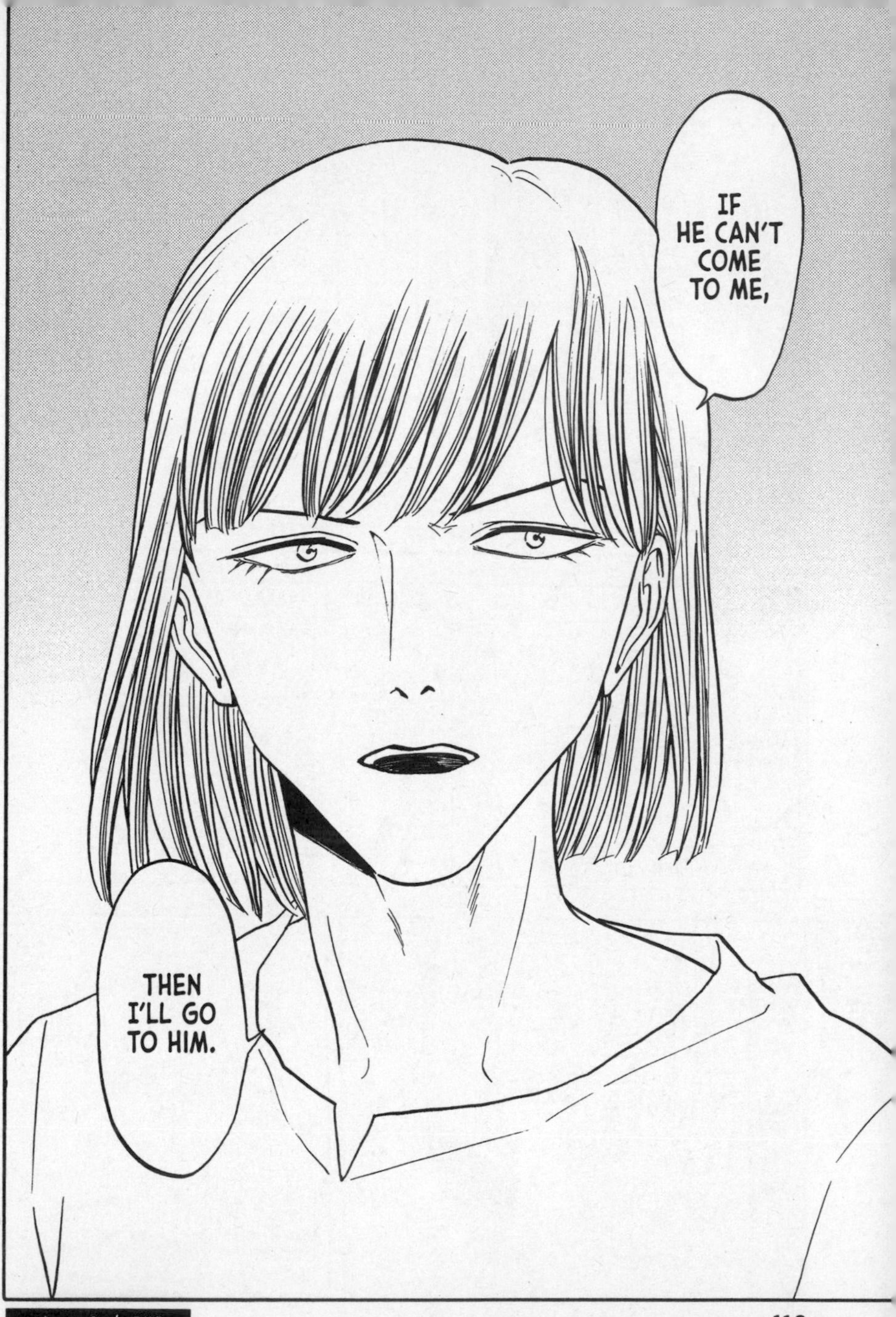
IF HE CAN'T COME TO ME,
THEN I'LL GO TO HIM.

phase.9 Voice of the Wild

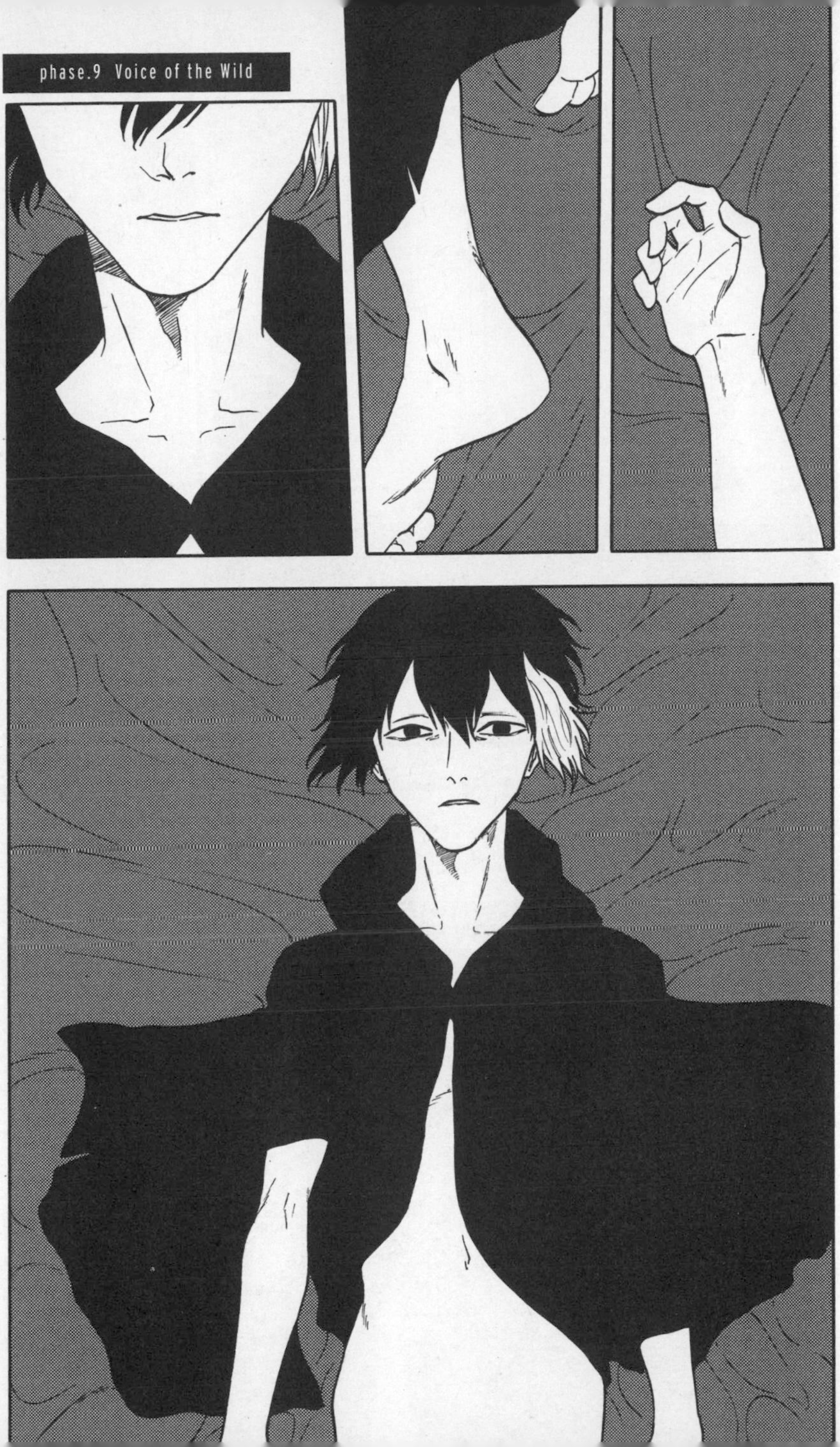

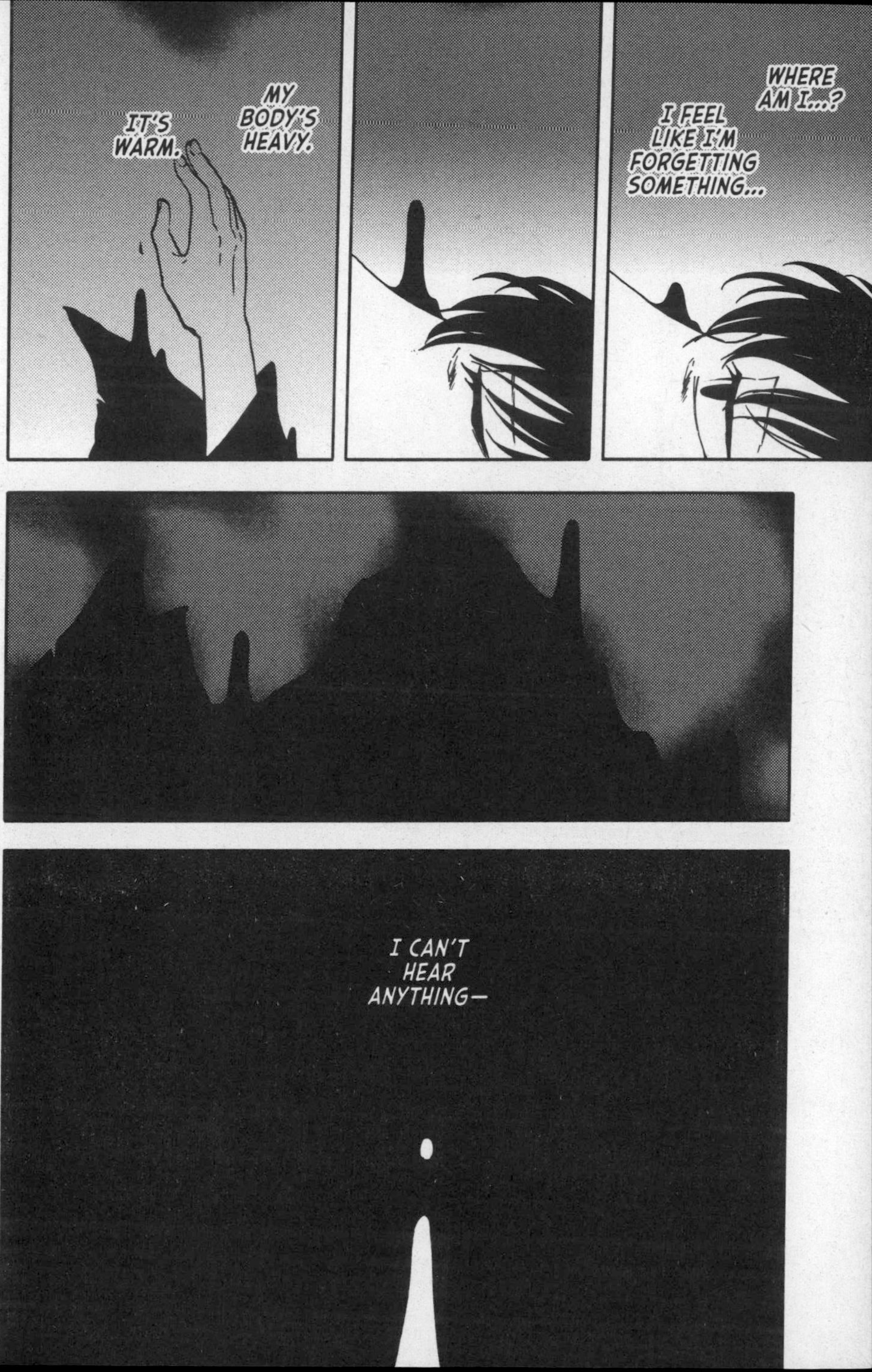
WHERE AM I...?
I FEEL LIKE I'M FORGETTING SOMETHING...
MY BODY'S HEAVY.
IT'S WARM.
I CAN'T HEAR ANYTHING—

phase.9 Voice of the Wild

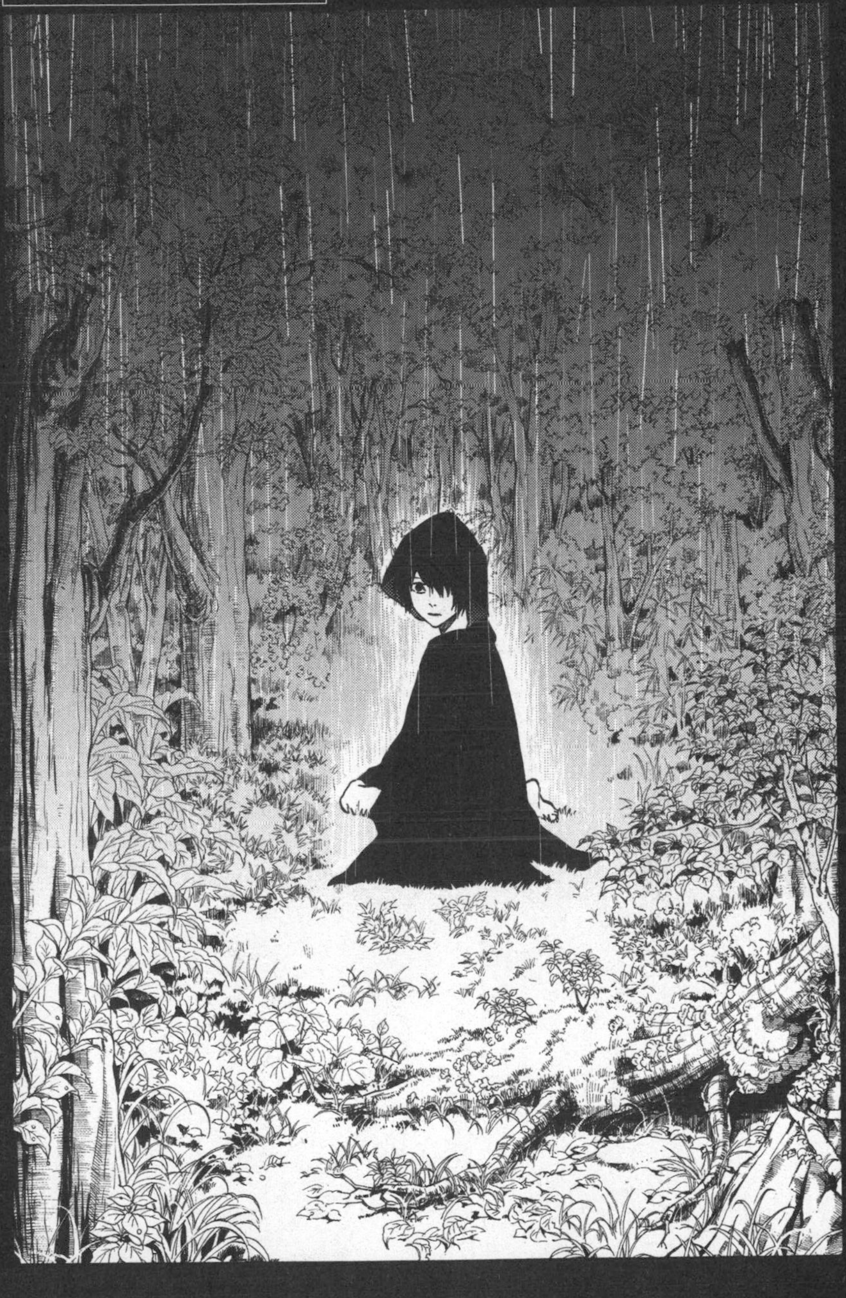

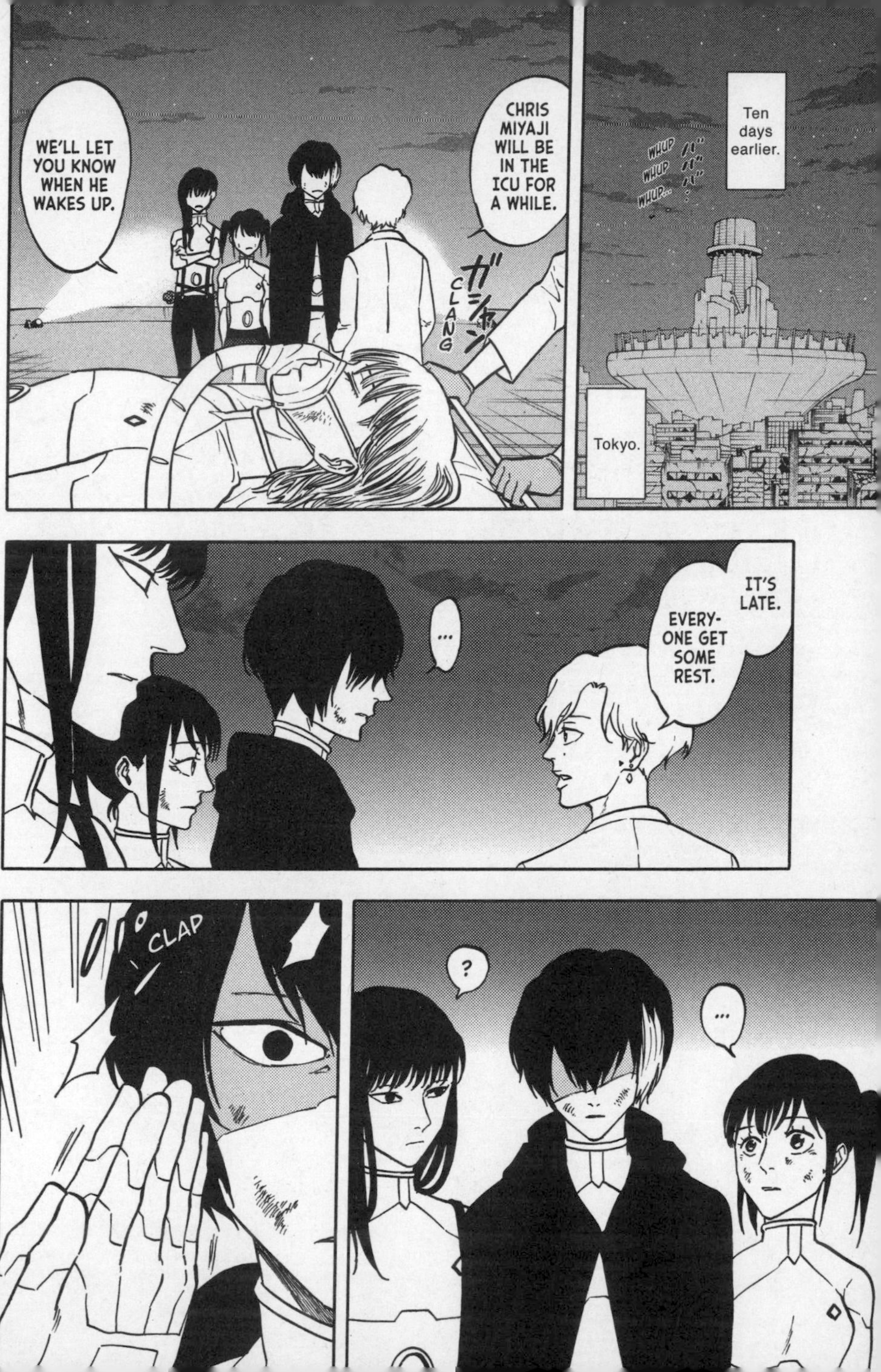
Ten days earlier.
WHUP WHUP WHUP...
Tokyo.
CHRIS MIYAJI WILL BE IN THE ICU FOR A WHILE.
ガシャン
CLANG
WE'LL LET YOU KNOW WHEN HE WAKES UP.
IT'S LATE. EVERYONE GET SOME REST.
...
...
?
CLAP

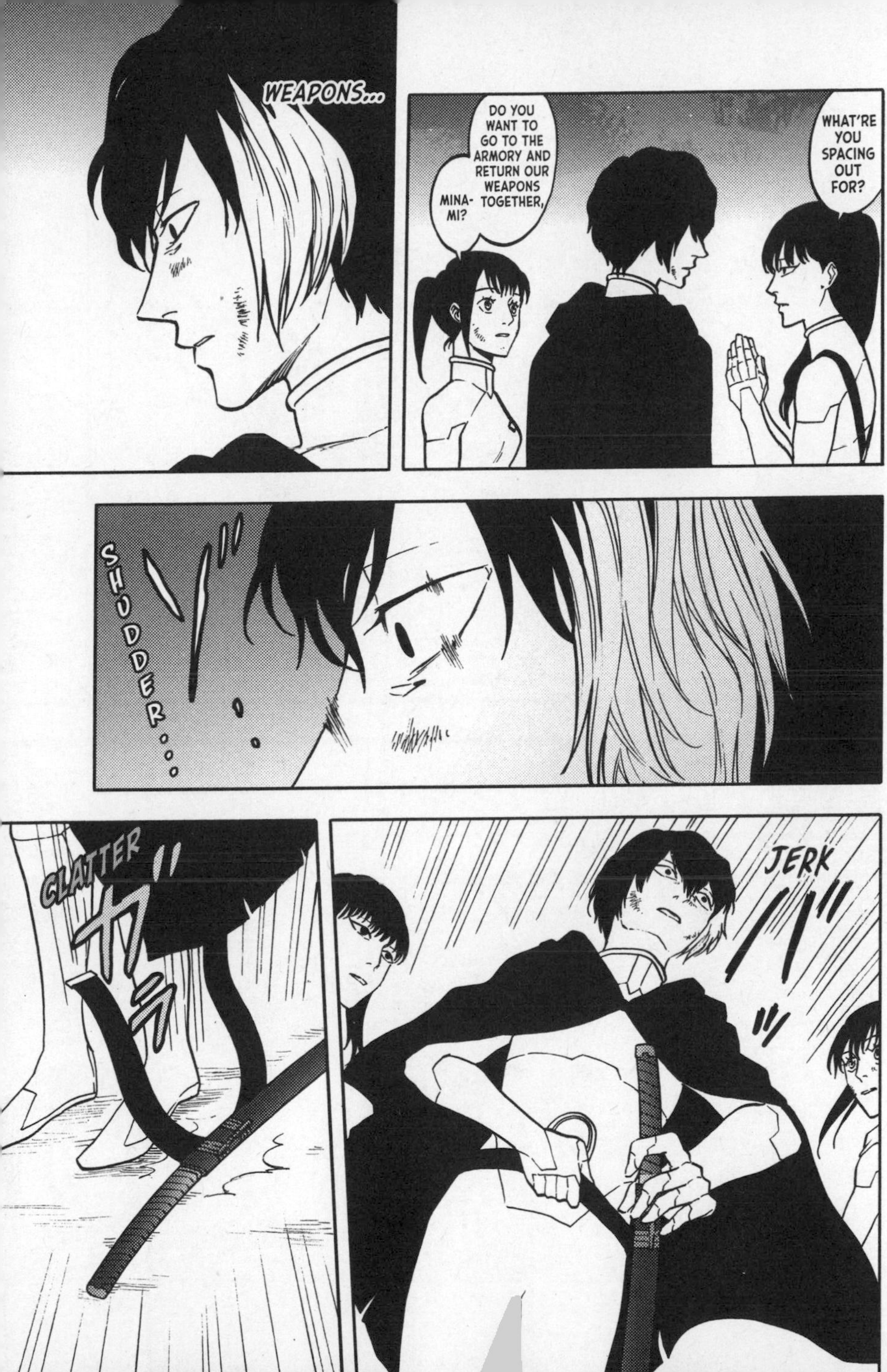
WHAT'RE YOU SPACING OUT FOR?
DO YOU WANT TO GO TO THE ARMORY AND RETURN OUR WEAPONS TOGETHER, MINA-MI?
WEAPONS...
SHUDDER...
JERK
CLATTER

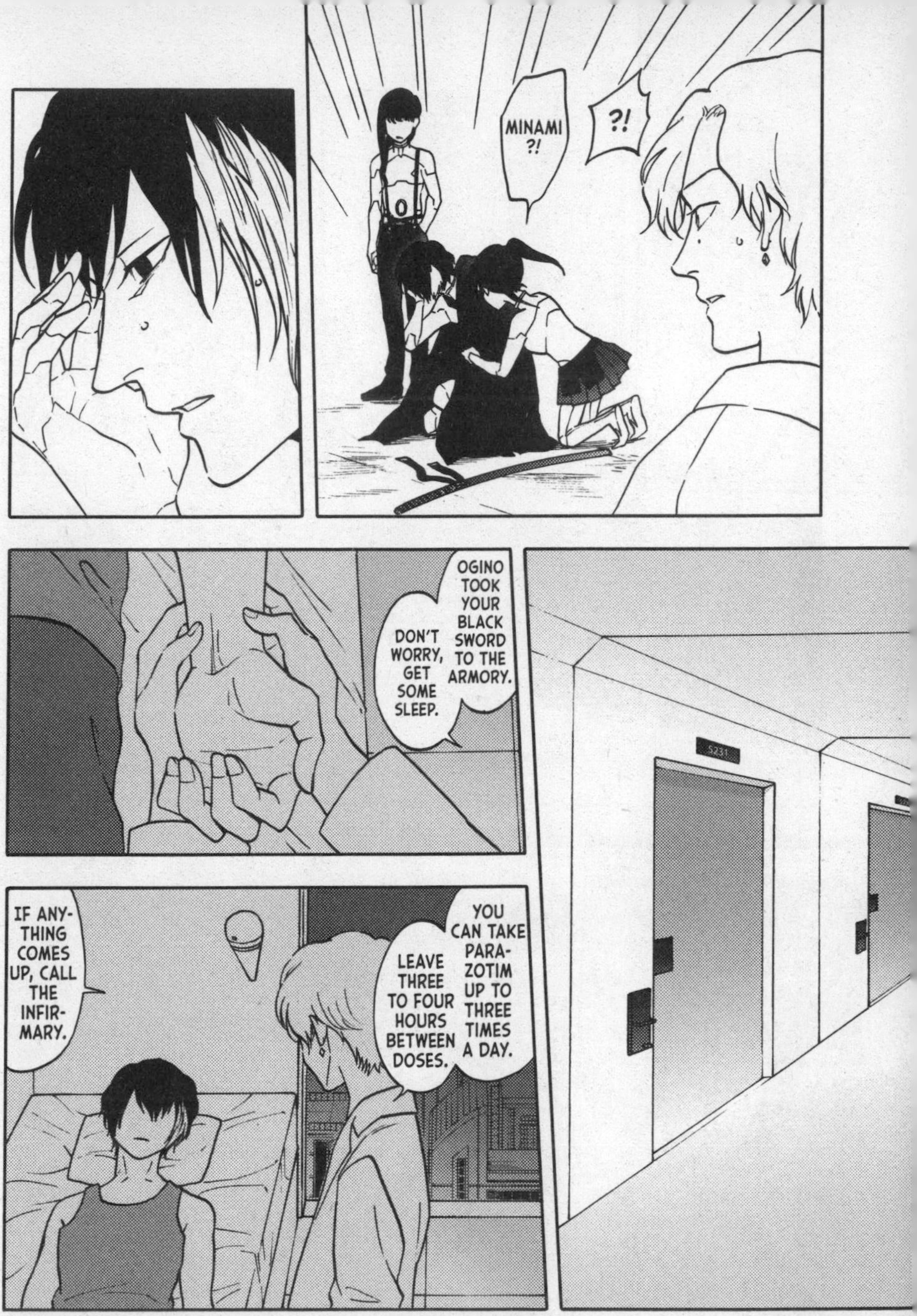
?!
MINAMI ?!
OGINO TOOK YOUR BLACK SWORD TO THE ARMORY.
DON'T WORRY, GET SOME SLEEP.
YOU CAN TAKE PARAZOTIM UP TO THREE TIMES A DAY.
LEAVE THREE TO FOUR HOURS BETWEEN DOSES.
IF ANYTHING COMES UP, CALL THE INFIRMARY.

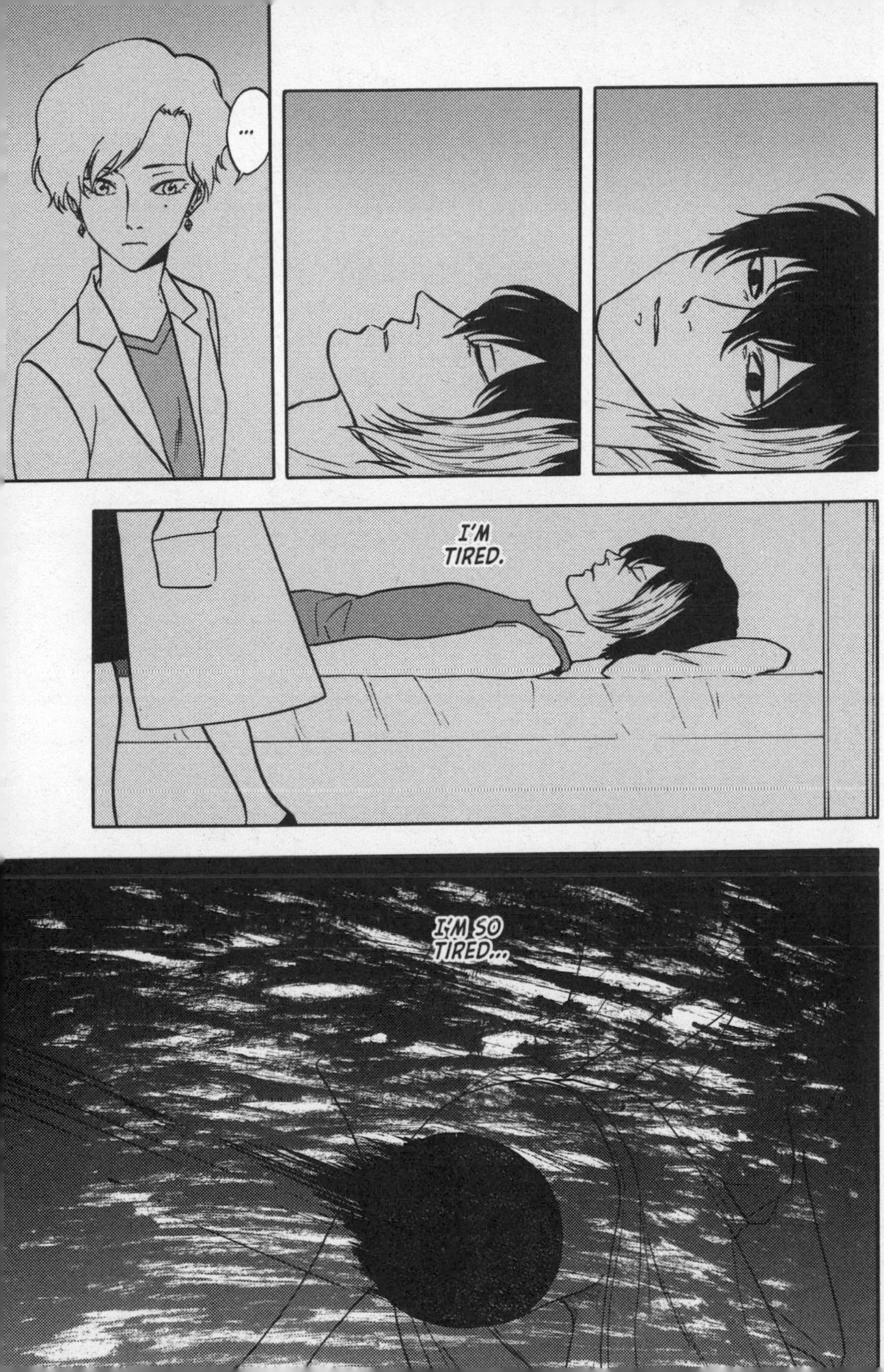
...
I'M TIRED.
I'M SO TIRED...

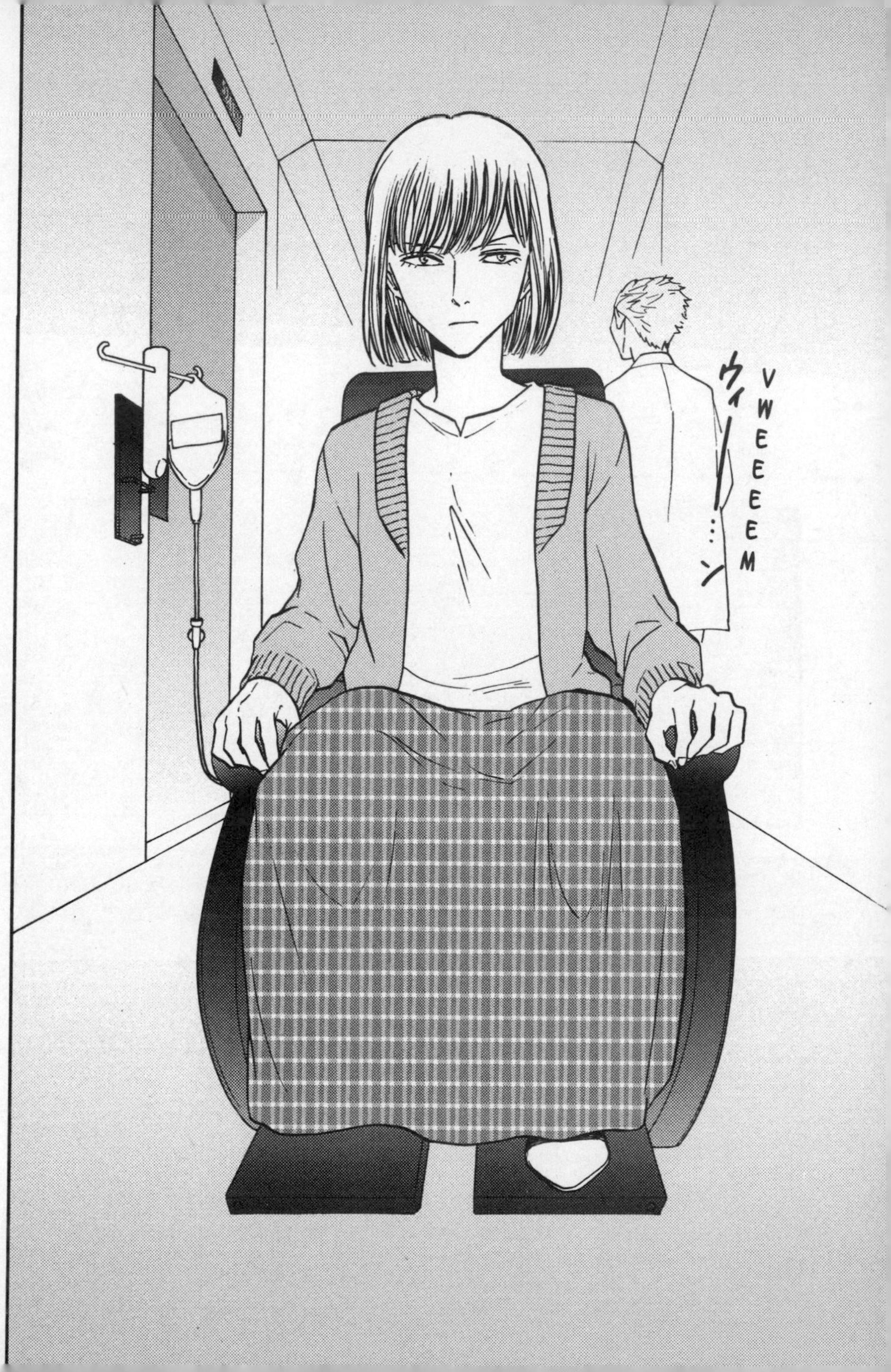
ウィ ー ー…ン
VWEEEEM

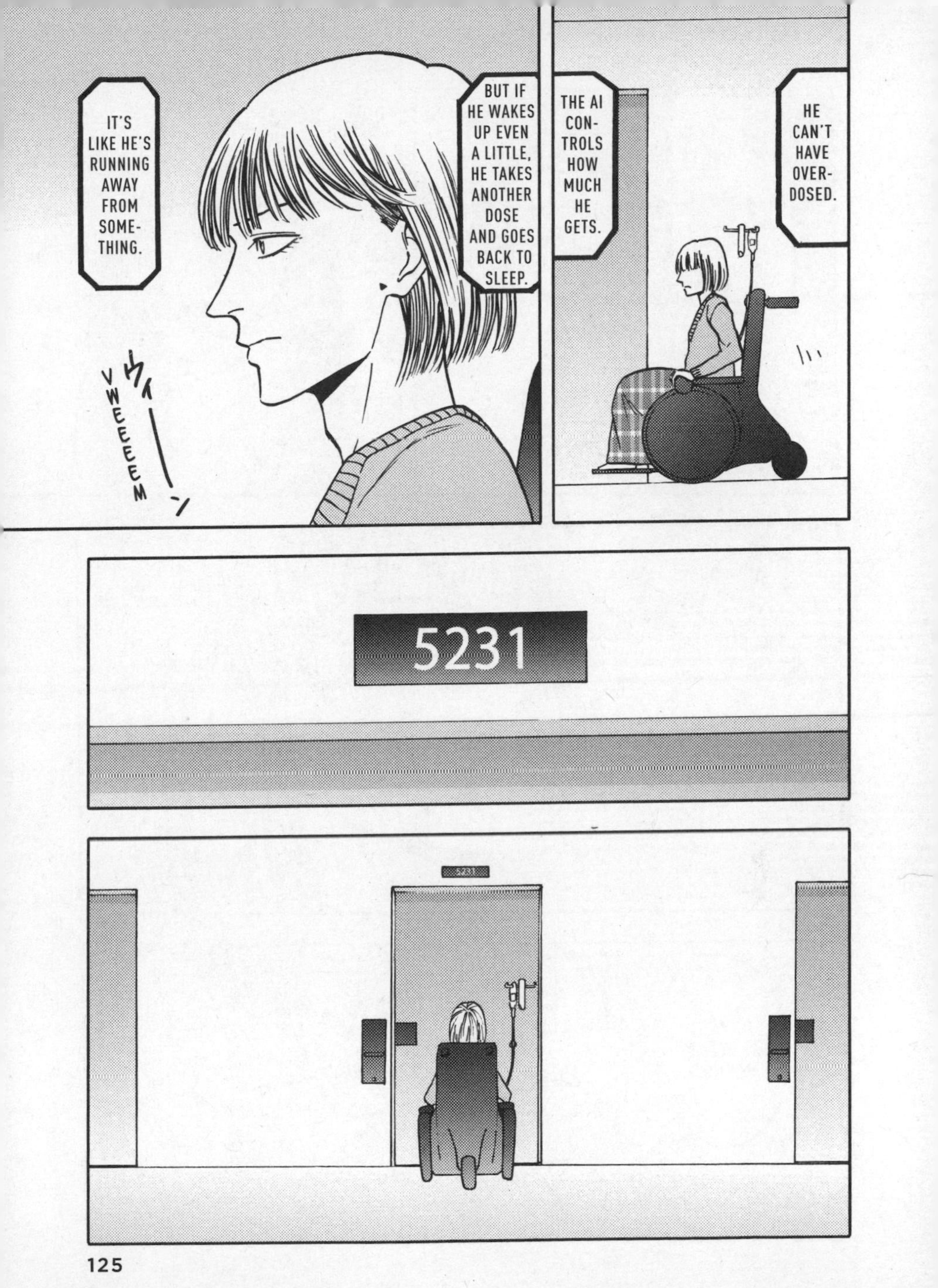
HE CAN'T HAVE OVER-DOSED.
THE AI CON-TROLS HOW MUCH HE GETS.
BUT IF HE WAKES UP EVEN A LITTLE, HE TAKES ANOTHER DOSE AND GOES BACK TO SLEEP.
IT'S LIKE HE'S RUNNING AWAY FROM SOME-THING.
ウィーン
VWEEEEM
5231

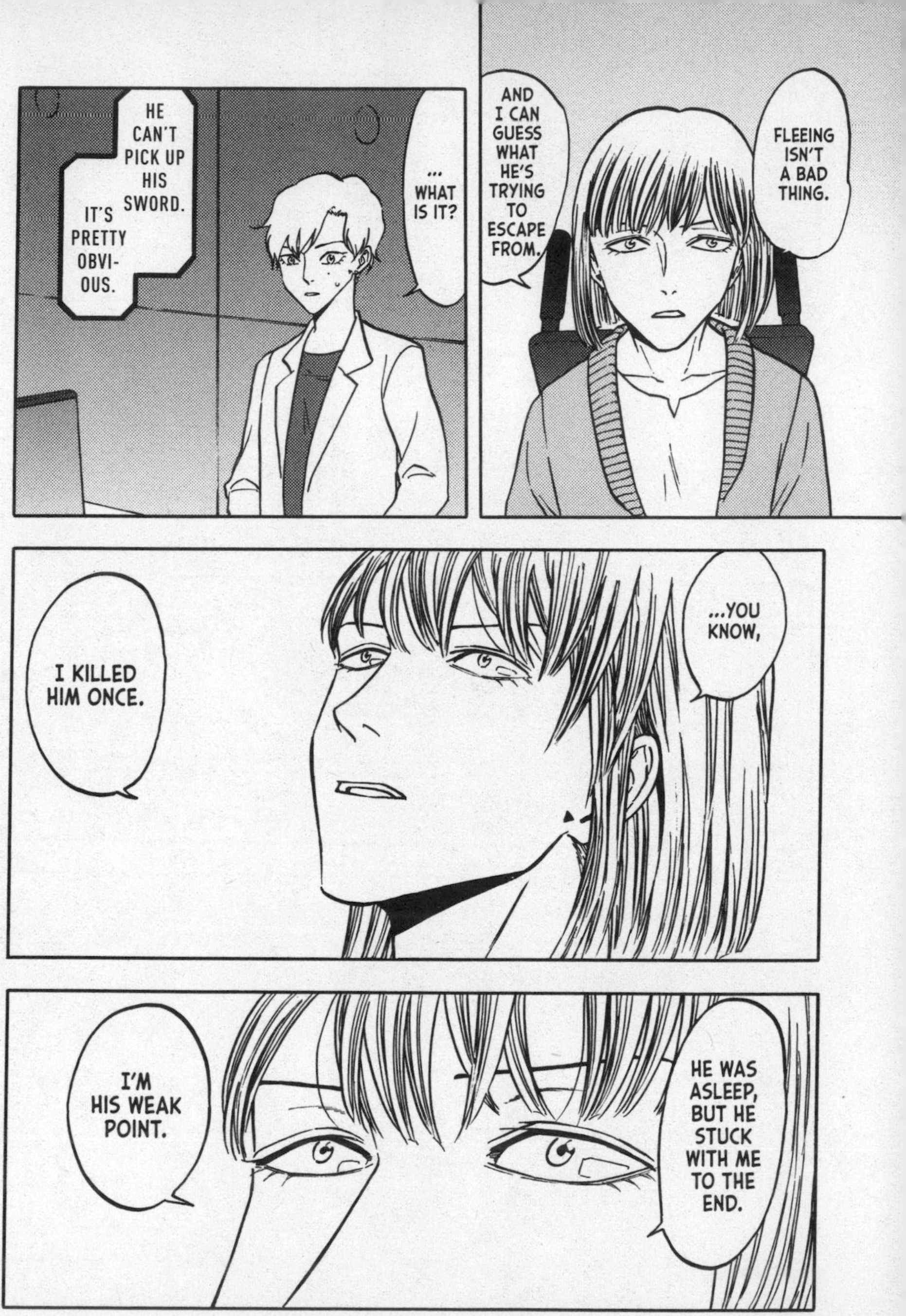
FLEEING ISN'T A BAD THING.
AND I CAN GUESS WHAT HE'S TRYING TO ESCAPE FROM.
... WHAT IS IT?
HE CAN'T PICK UP HIS SWORD.
IT'S PRETTY OBVI-OUS.
...YOU KNOW,
I KILLED HIM ONCE.
HE WAS ASLEEP, BUT HE STUCK WITH ME TO THE END.
I'M HIS WEAK POINT.

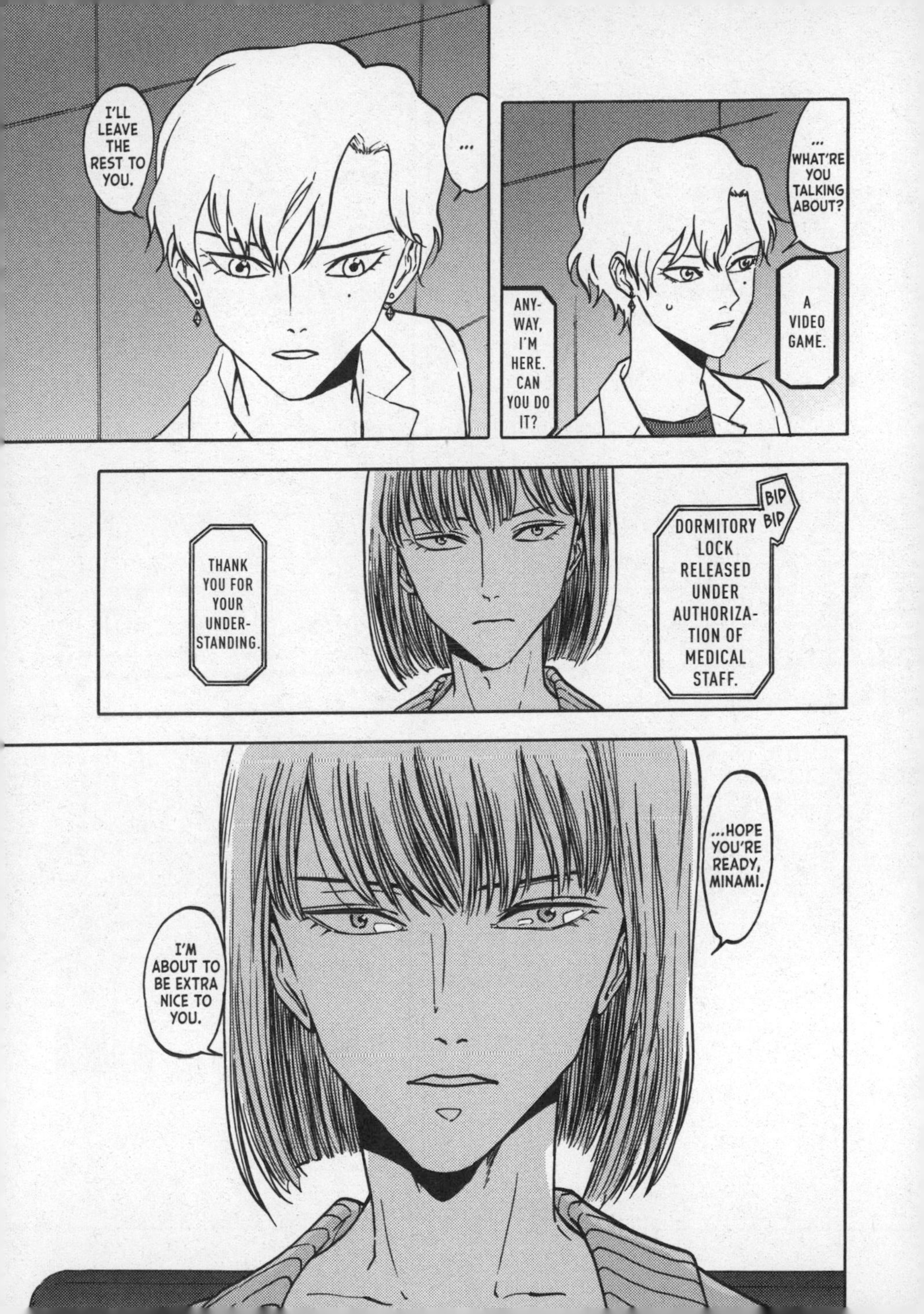
...WHAT'RE YOU TALKING ABOUT?
A VIDEO GAME.
ANYWAY, I'M HERE. CAN YOU DO IT?
...
I'LL LEAVE THE REST TO YOU.
BIP BIP
DORMITORY LOCK RELEASED UNDER AUTHORIZATION OF MEDICAL STAFF.
THANK YOU FOR YOUR UNDERSTANDING.
...HOPE YOU'RE READY, MINAMI.
I'M ABOUT TO BE EXTRA NICE TO YOU.

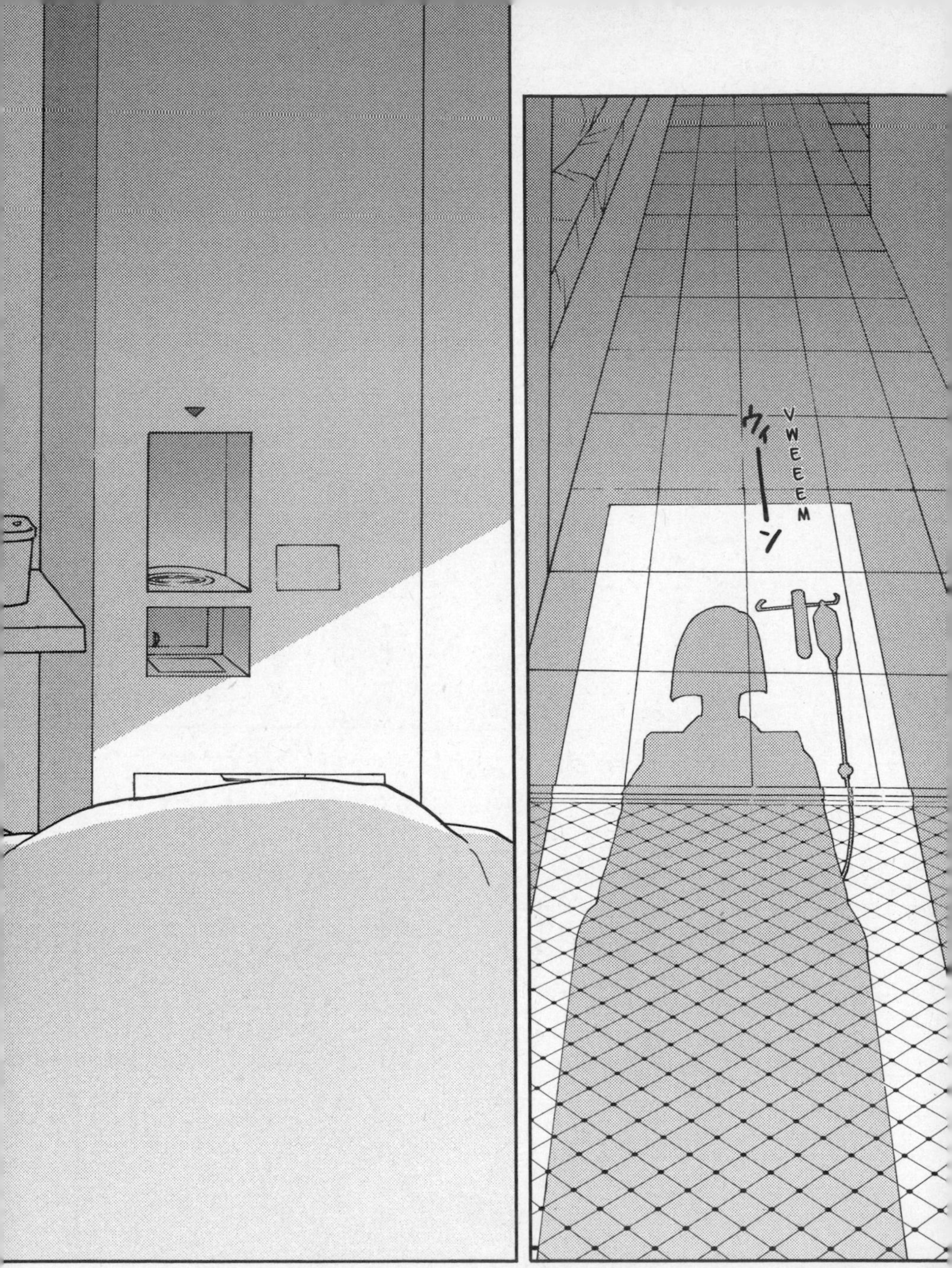
ウィーン
VWEEEM

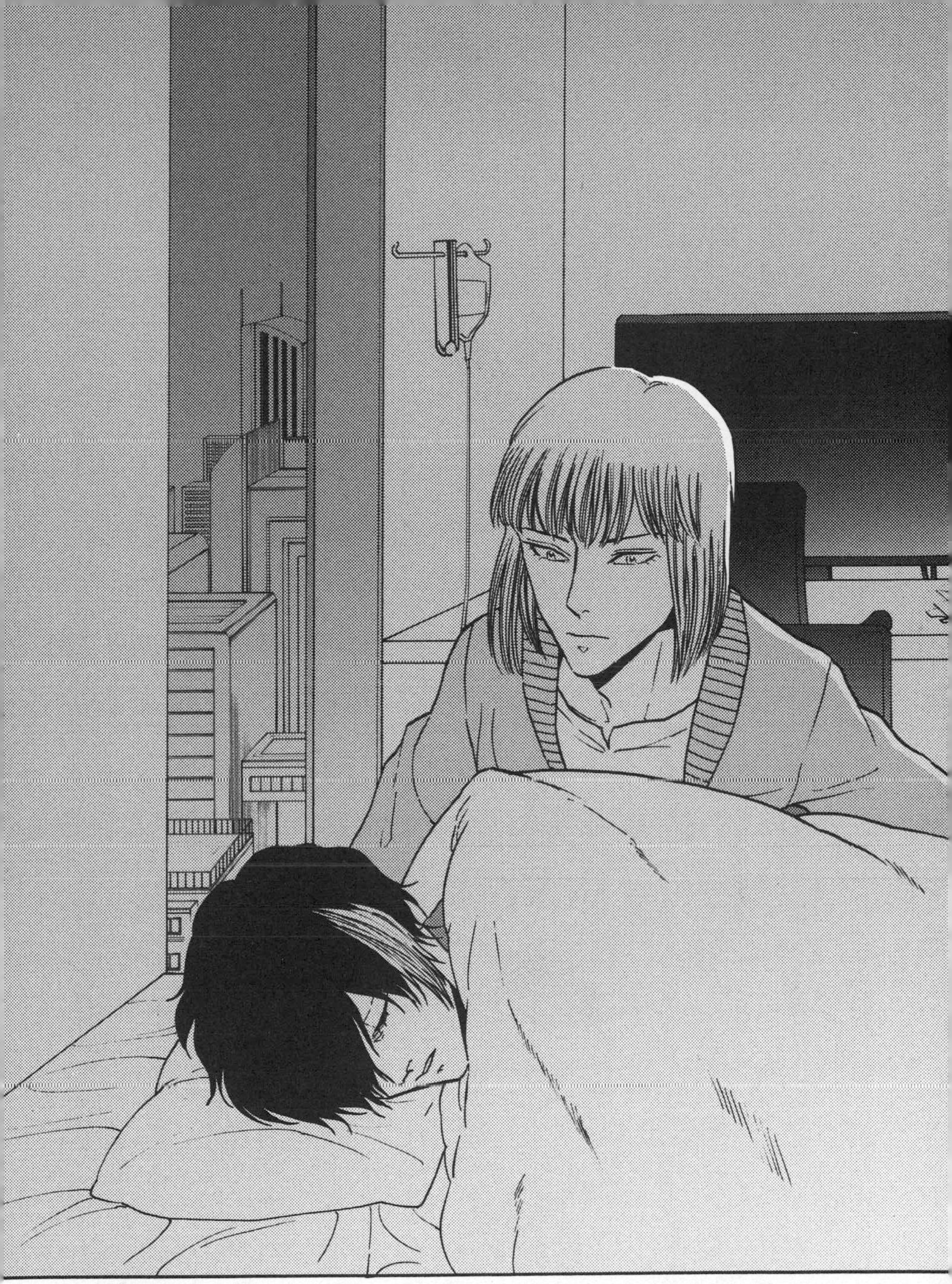

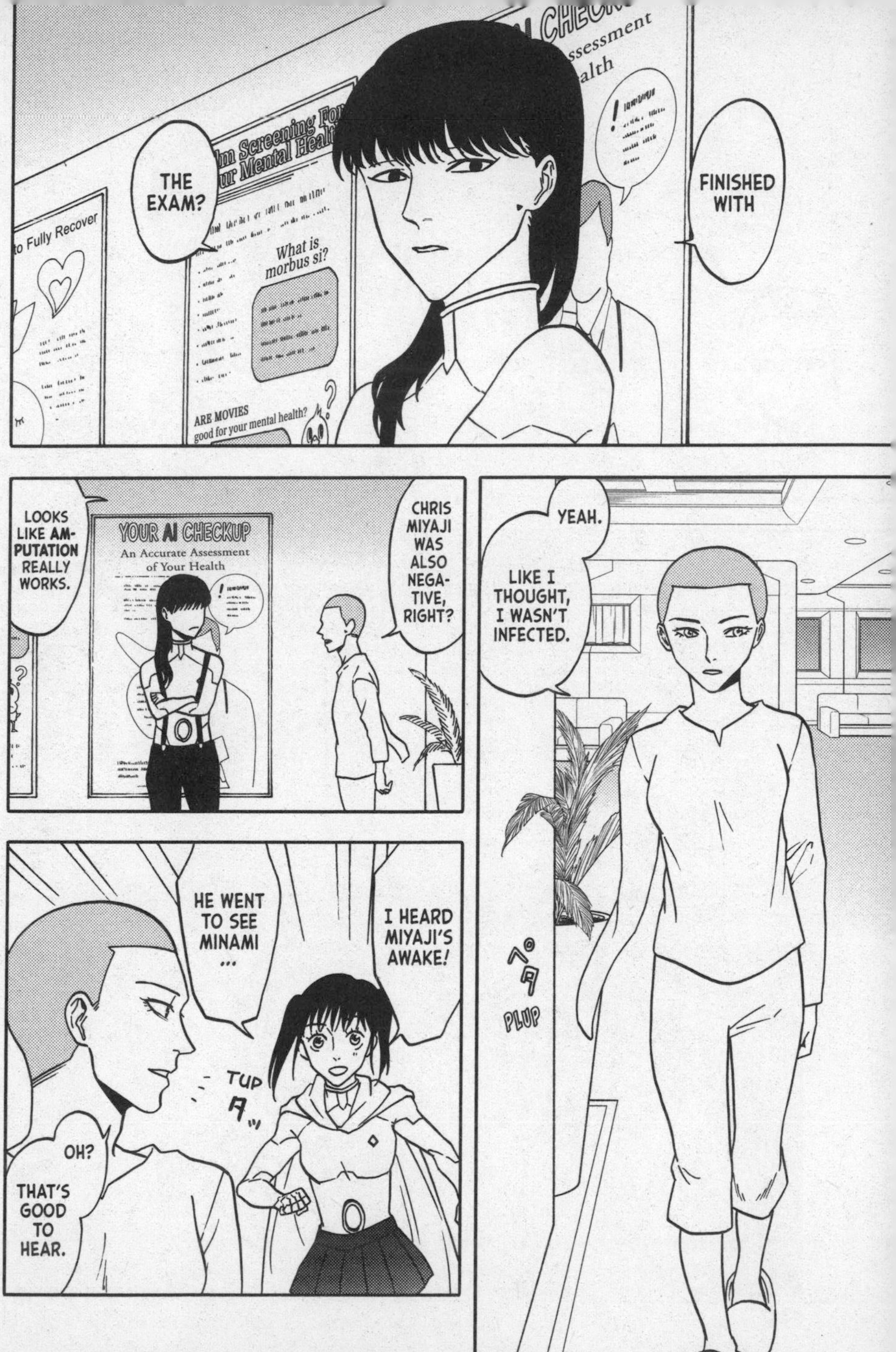
FINISHED WITH
THE EXAM?
Film Screening For Your Mental Health
What is morbus si?
ARE MOVIES good for your mental health?
to Fully Recover
YEAH.
LIKE I THOUGHT, I WASN'T INFECTED.
ペタ
PLUP
CHRIS MIYAJI WAS ALSO NEGATIVE, RIGHT?
LOOKS LIKE AMPUTATION REALLY WORKS.
YOUR AI CHECKUP
An Accurate Assessment of Your Health
I HEARD MIYAJI'S AWAKE!
HE WENT TO SEE MINAMI...
TUP
タッ
OH?
THAT'S GOOD TO HEAR.

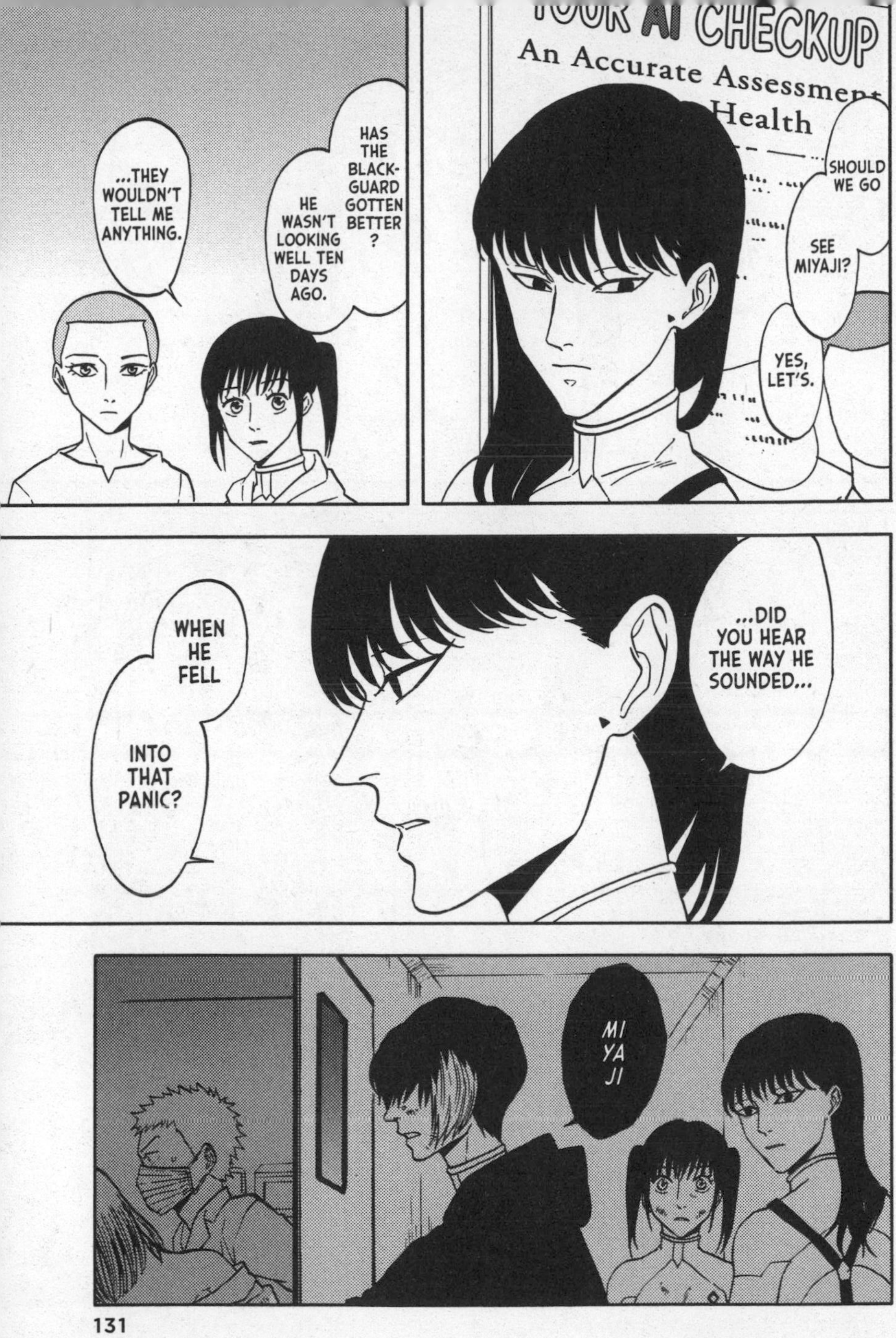
AI CHECKUP
An Accurate Assessment
Health
SHOULD WE GO SEE MIYAJI?
YES, LET'S.
HAS THE BLACKGUARD GOTTEN BETTER?
HE WASN'T LOOKING WELL TEN DAYS AGO.
...THEY WOULDN'T TELL ME ANYTHING.
...DID YOU HEAR THE WAY HE SOUNDED...
WHEN HE FELL INTO THAT PANIC?
MIYAJI

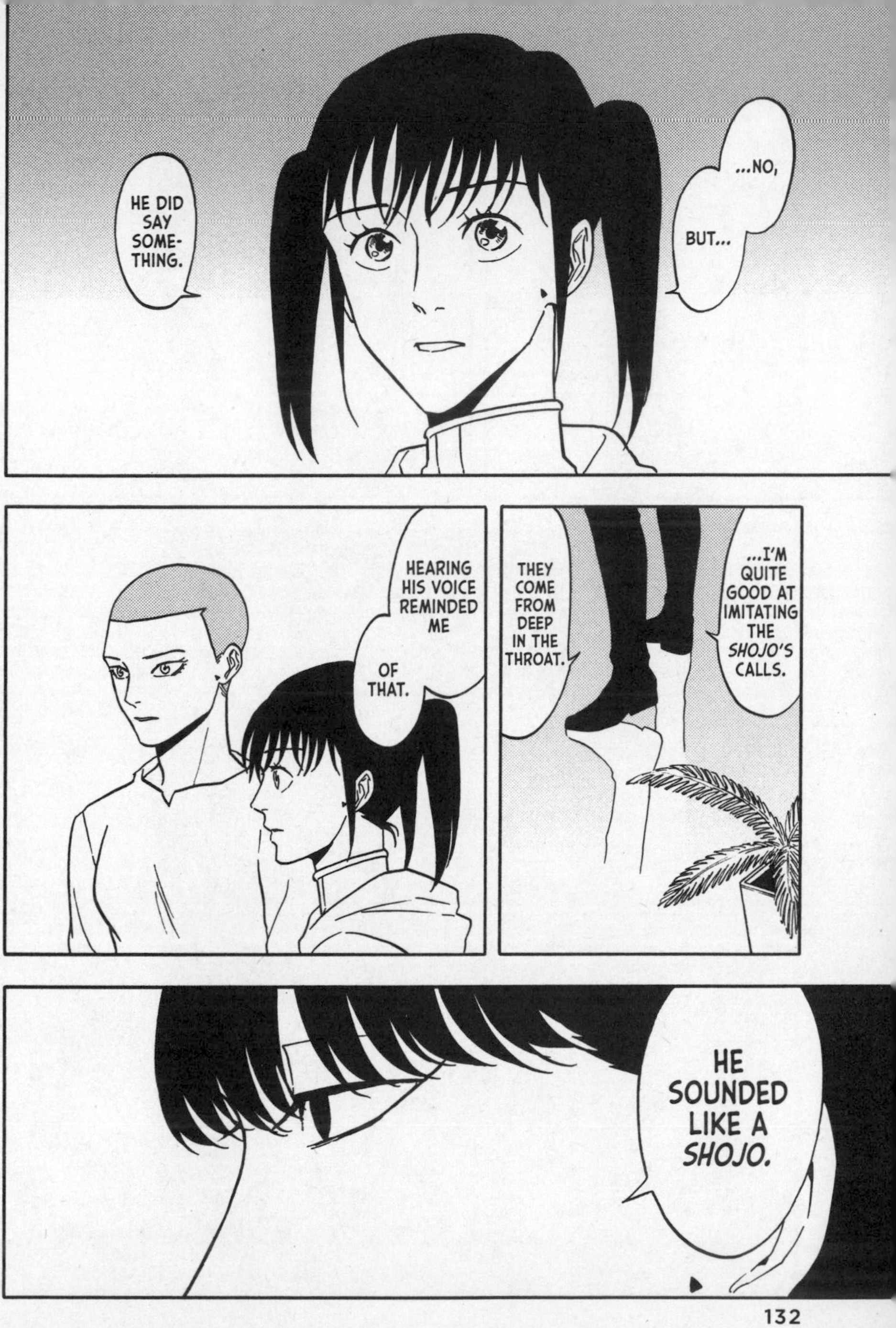
...NO, BUT...
HE DID SAY SOME-THING.
...I'M QUITE GOOD AT IMITATING THE *SHOJO*'S CALLS.
THEY COME FROM DEEP IN THE THROAT.
HEARING HIS VOICE REMINDED ME OF THAT.
HE SOUNDED LIKE A *SHOJO.*

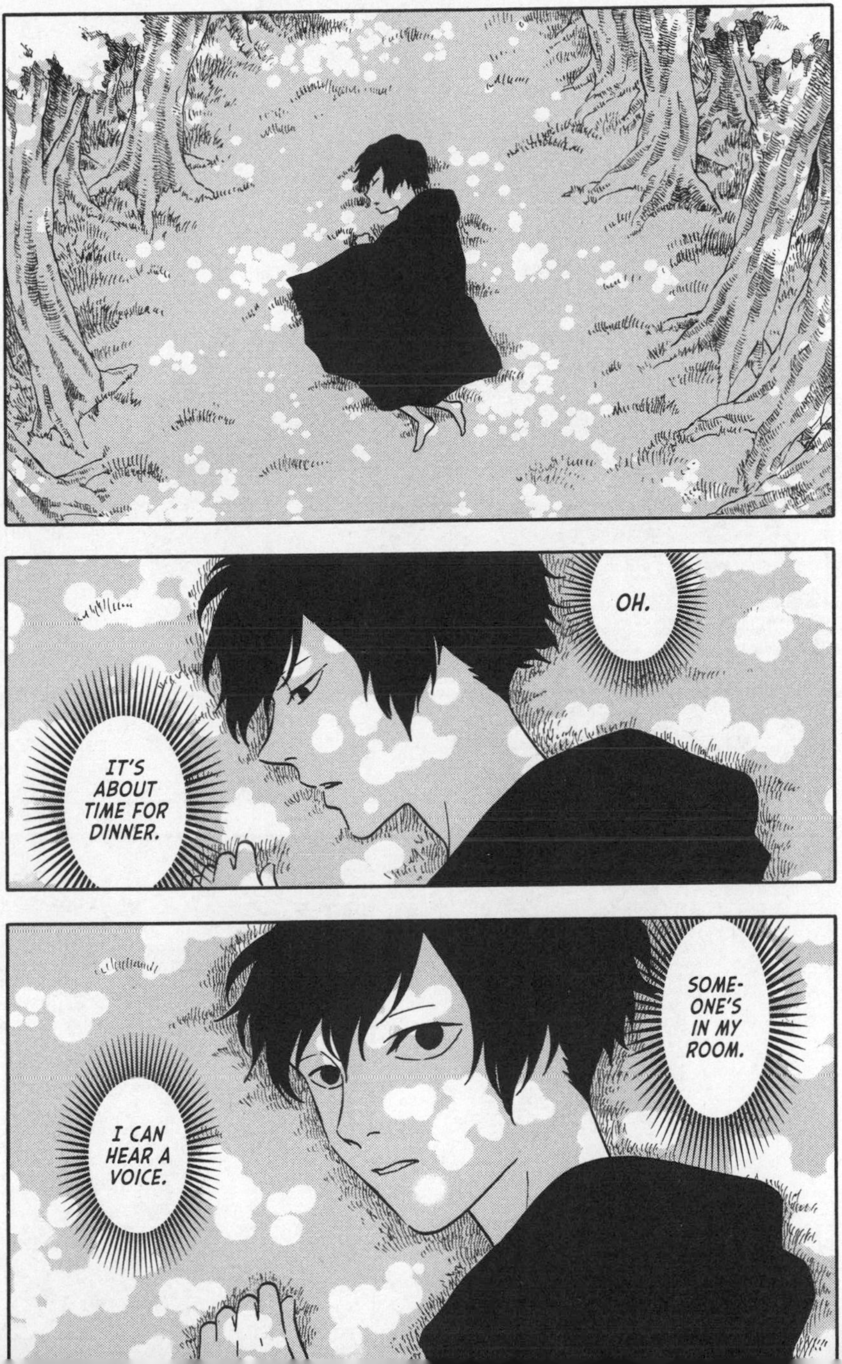
OH.
IT'S ABOUT TIME FOR DINNER.
SOME-ONE'S IN MY ROOM.
I CAN HEAR A VOICE.

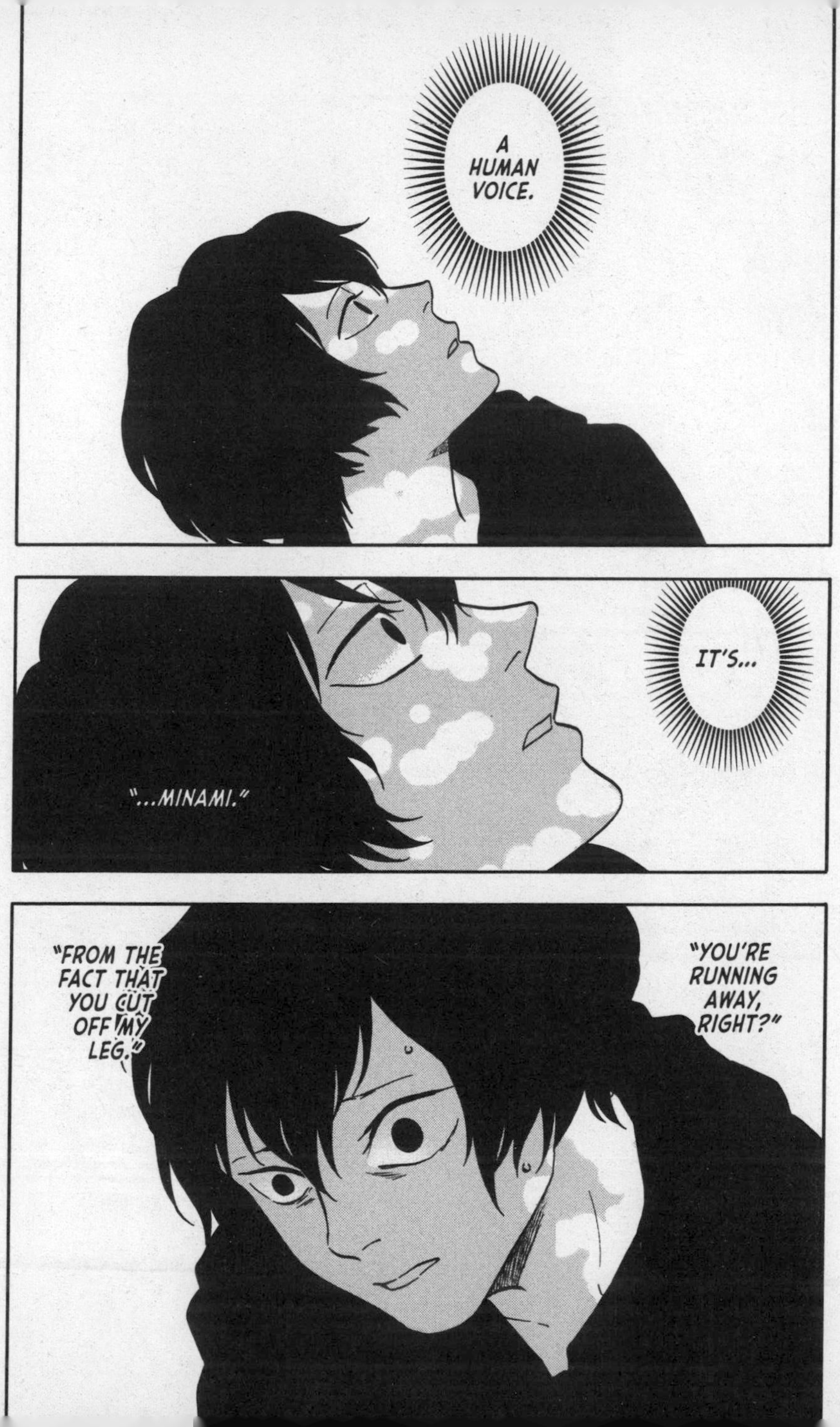
A HUMAN VOICE.
IT'S...
"...MINAMI."
"YOU'RE RUNNING AWAY, RIGHT?"
"FROM THE FACT THAT YOU CUT OFF MY LEG."

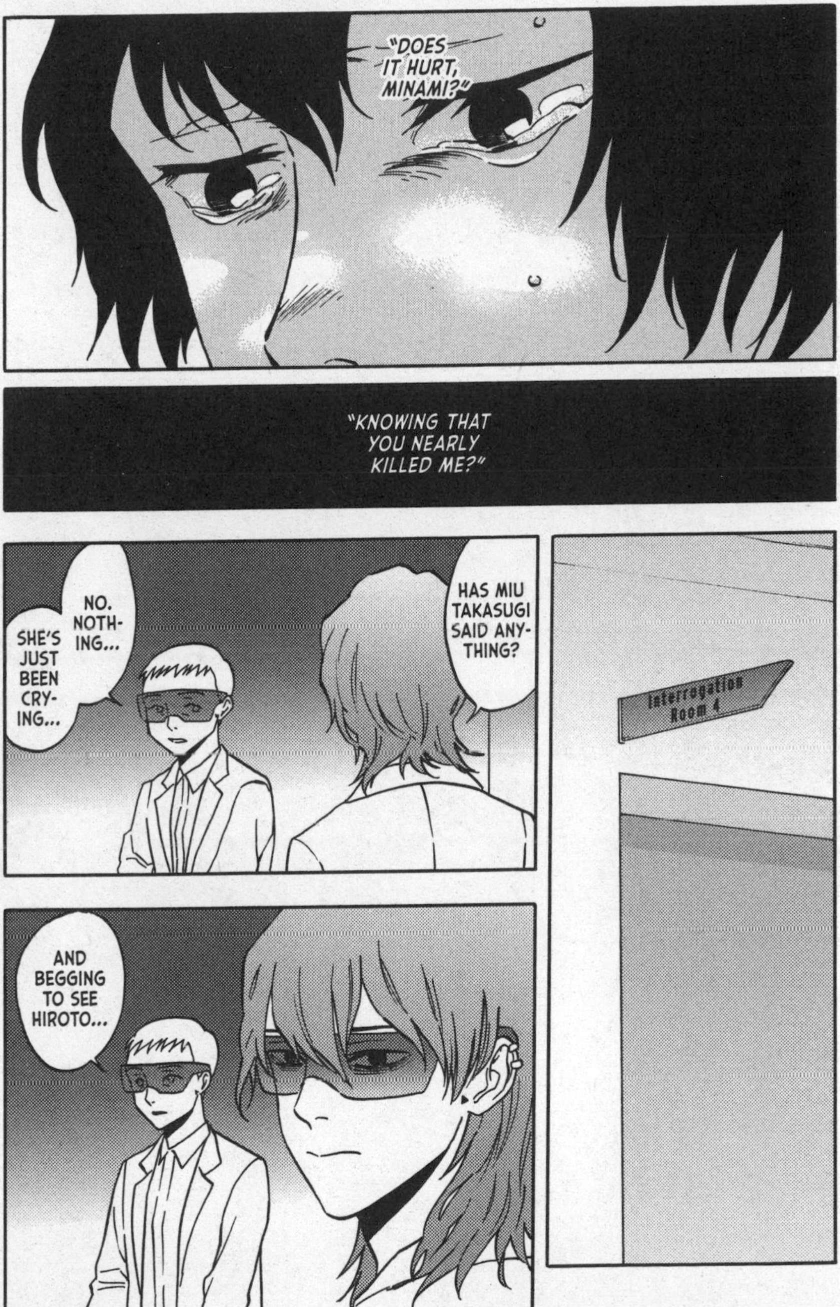
"DOES IT HURT, MINAMI?"
"KNOWING THAT YOU NEARLY KILLED ME?"
Interrogation Room 4
HAS MIU TAKASUGI SAID ANYTHING?
NO. NOTHING...
SHE'S JUST BEEN CRYING...
AND BEGGING TO SEE HIROTO...

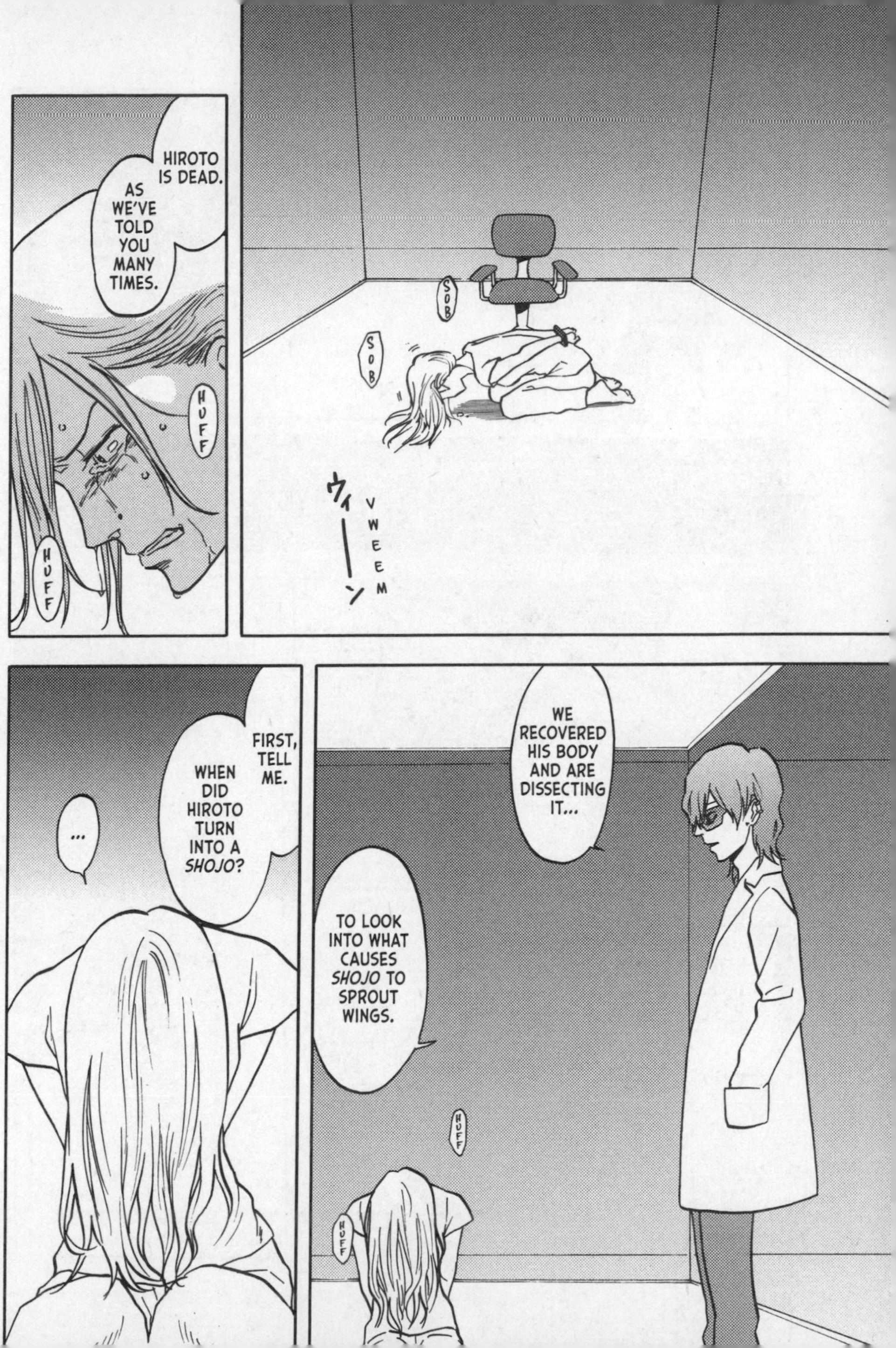
SOB
SOB
ウィーーン
VWEEM
HIROTO IS DEAD.
AS WE'VE TOLD YOU MANY TIMES.
HUFF
HUFF
WE RECOVERED HIS BODY AND ARE DISSECTING IT...
TO LOOK INTO WHAT CAUSES *SHOJO* TO SPROUT WINGS.
HUFF
HUFF
FIRST, TELL ME.
WHEN DID HIROTO TURN INTO A *SHOJO*?
...

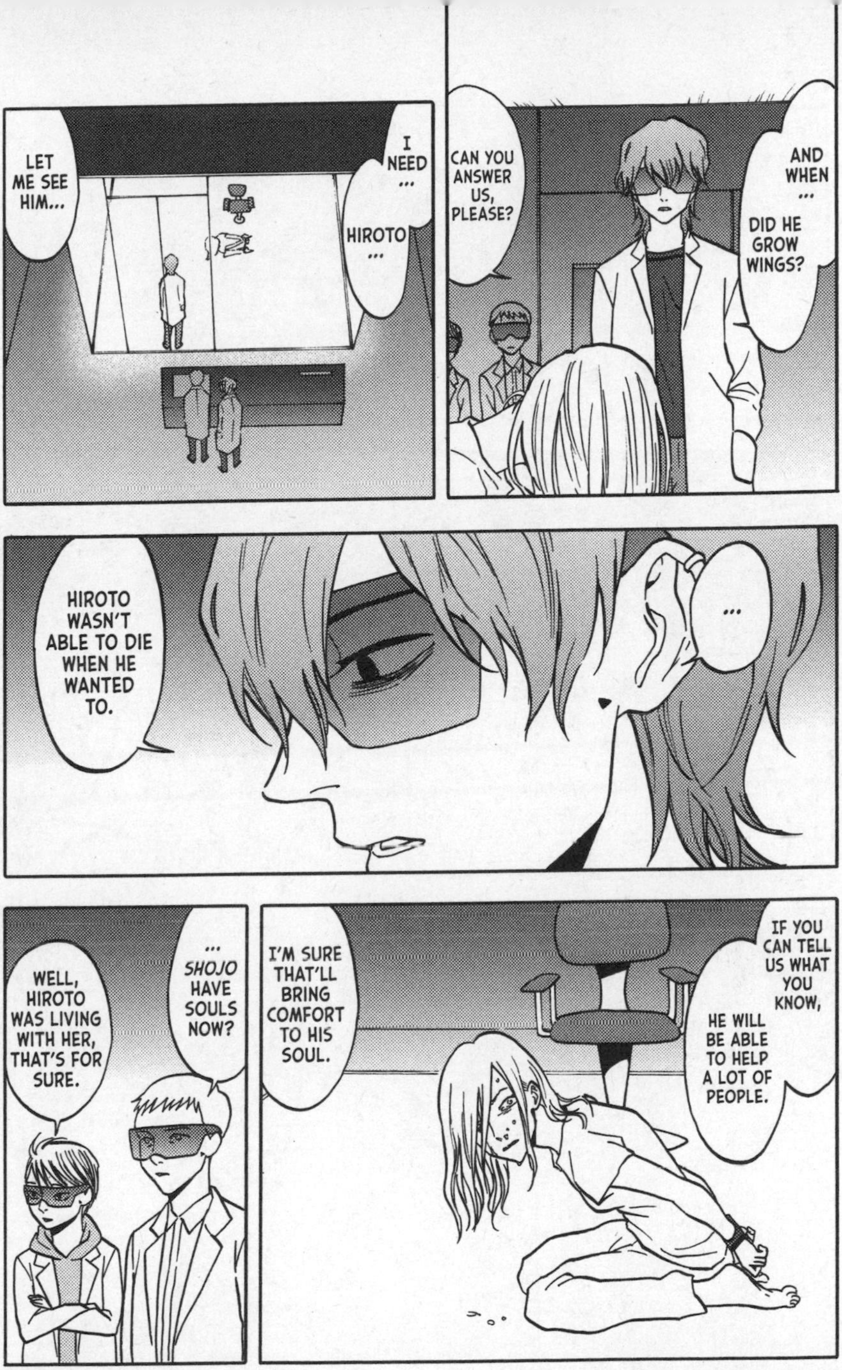
AND WHEN ... DID HE GROW WINGS?
CAN YOU ANSWER US, PLEASE?
I NEED ... HIROTO ...
LET ME SEE HIM...
...
HIROTO WASN'T ABLE TO DIE WHEN HE WANTED TO.
IF YOU CAN TELL US WHAT YOU KNOW, HE WILL BE ABLE TO HELP A LOT OF PEOPLE.
I'M SURE THAT'LL BRING COMFORT TO HIS SOUL.
... *SHOJO* HAVE SOULS NOW?
WELL, HIROTO WAS LIVING WITH HER, THAT'S FOR SURE.

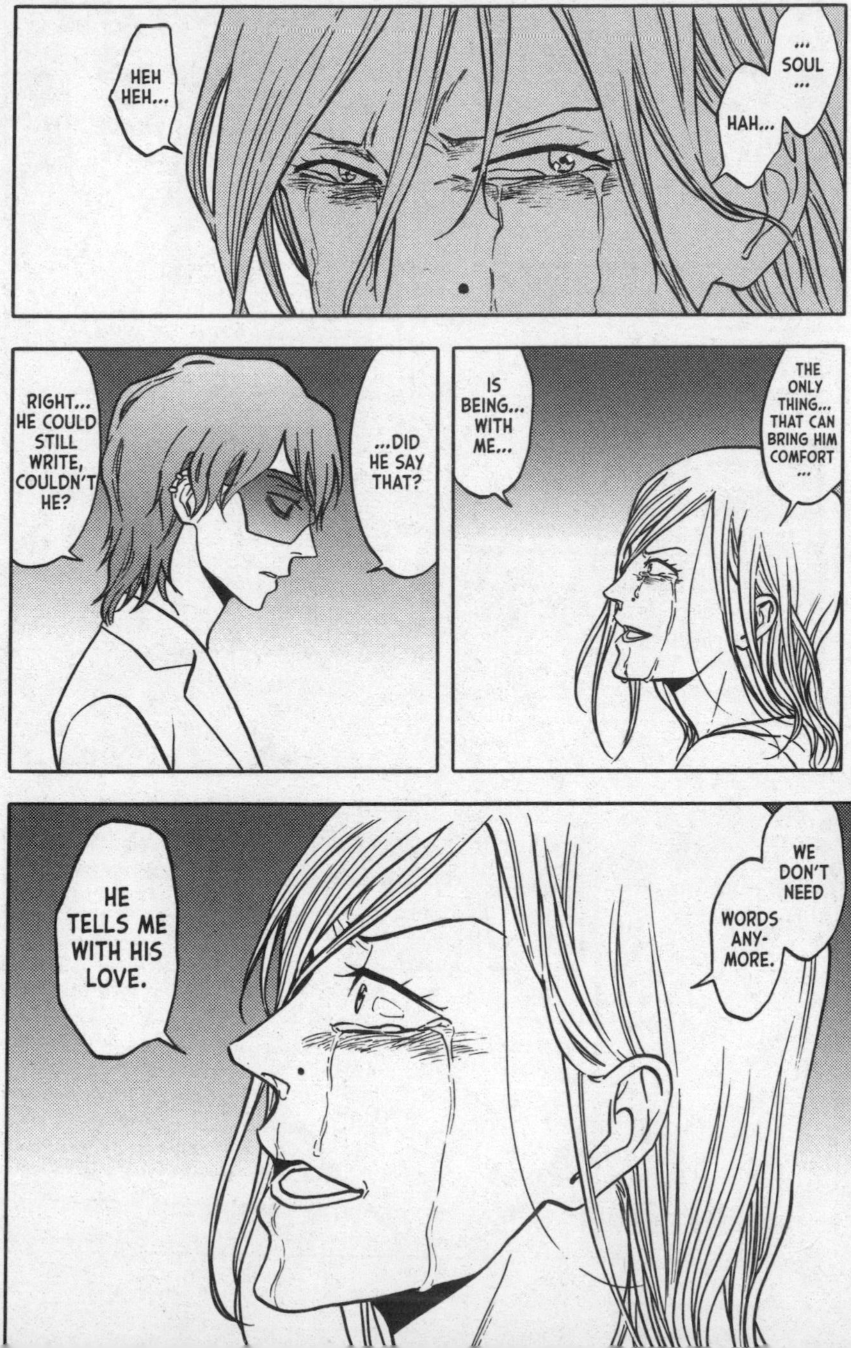
... SOUL ... HAH...
HEH HEH...
THE ONLY THING... THAT CAN BRING HIM COMFORT ...
IS BEING... WITH ME...
...DID HE SAY THAT?
RIGHT... HE COULD STILL WRITE, COULDN'T HE?
WE DON'T NEED WORDS ANY-MORE.
HE TELLS ME WITH HIS LOVE.

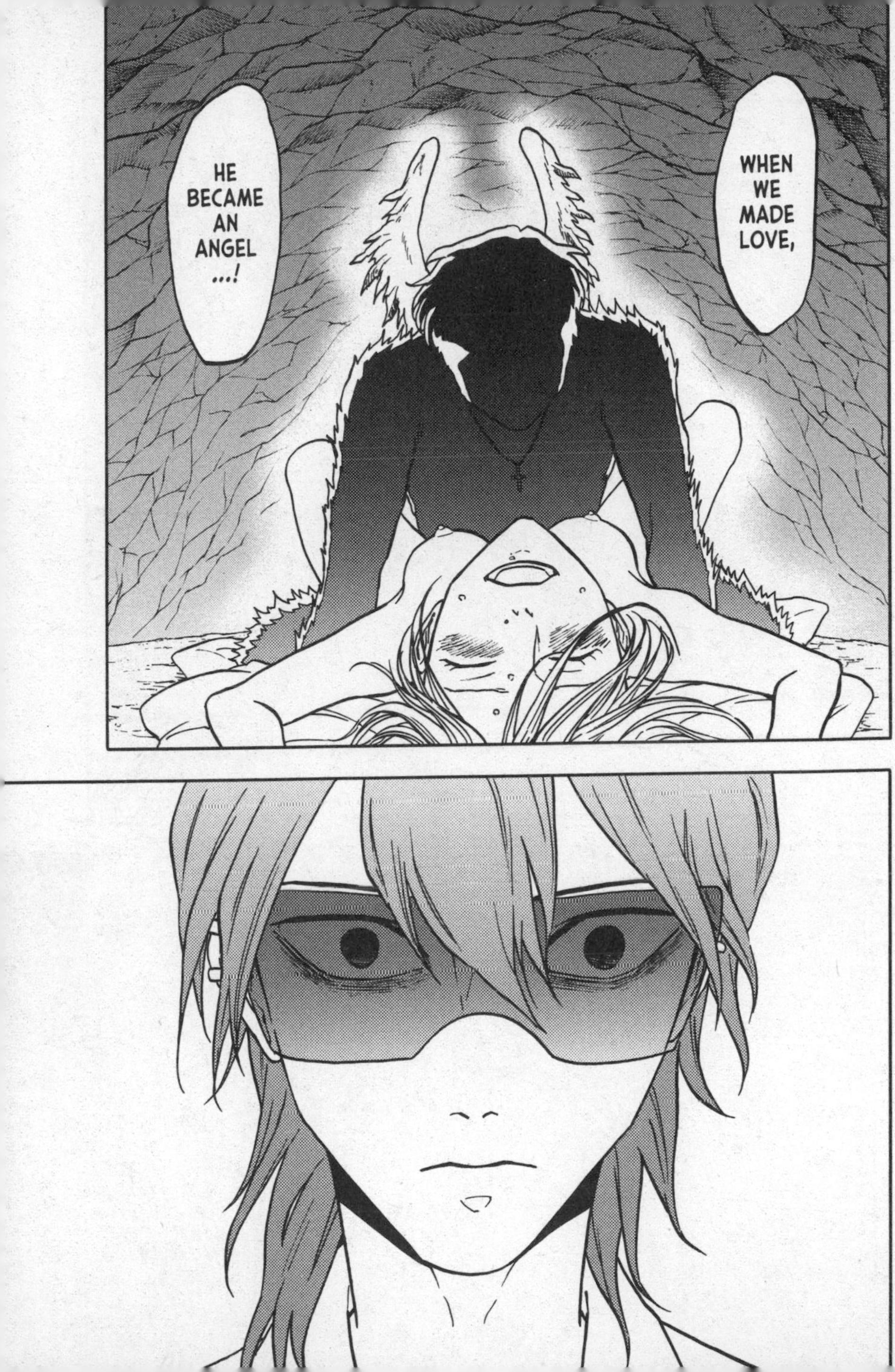
WHEN WE MADE LOVE,
HE BECAME AN ANGEL ...!

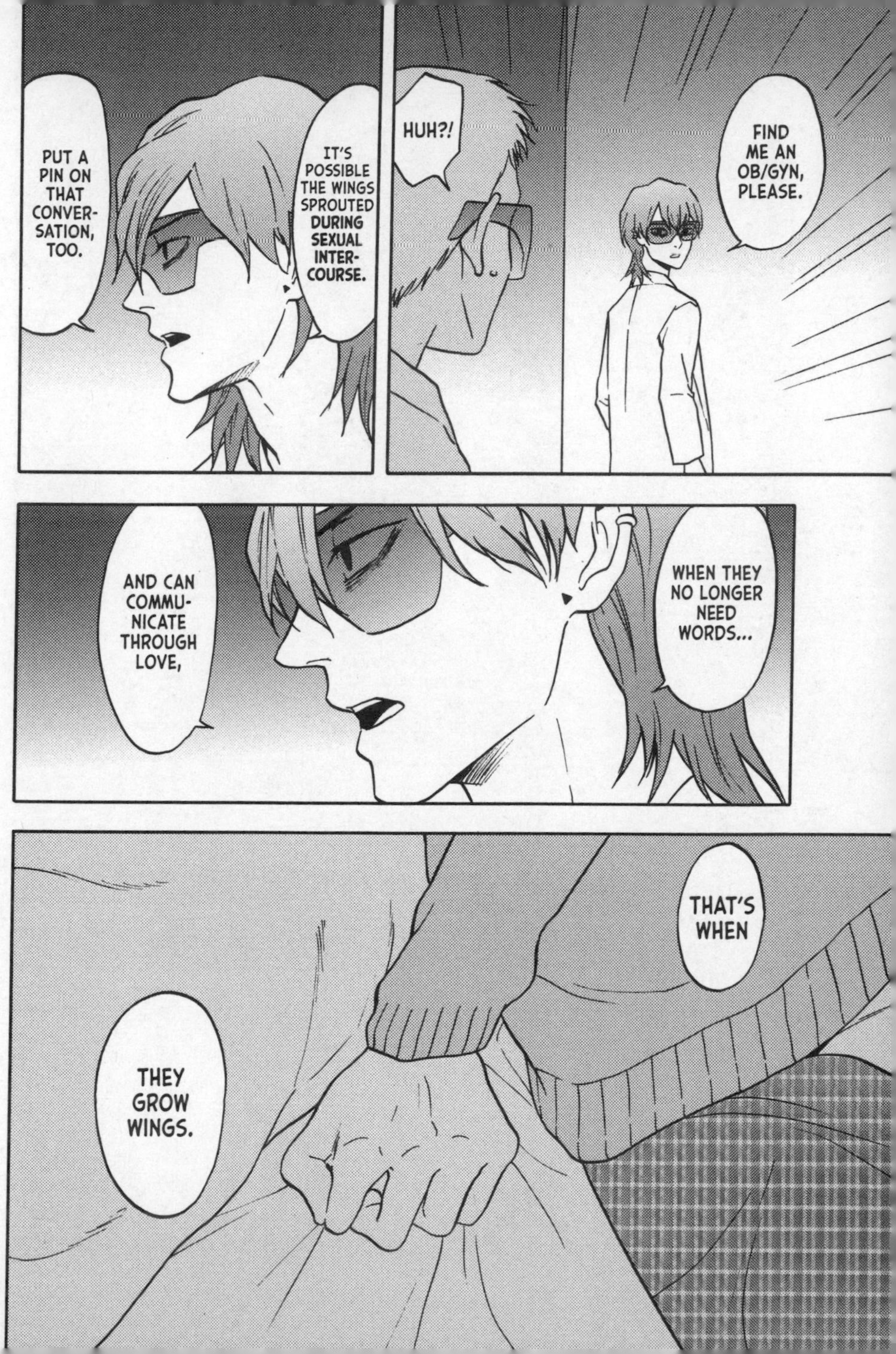
FIND ME AN OB/GYN, PLEASE.
HUH?!
IT'S POSSIBLE THE WINGS SPROUTED DURING SEXUAL INTER-COURSE.
PUT A PIN ON THAT CONVER-SATION, TOO.
WHEN THEY NO LONGER NEED WORDS...
AND CAN COMMU-NICATE THROUGH LOVE,
THAT'S WHEN
THEY GROW WINGS.

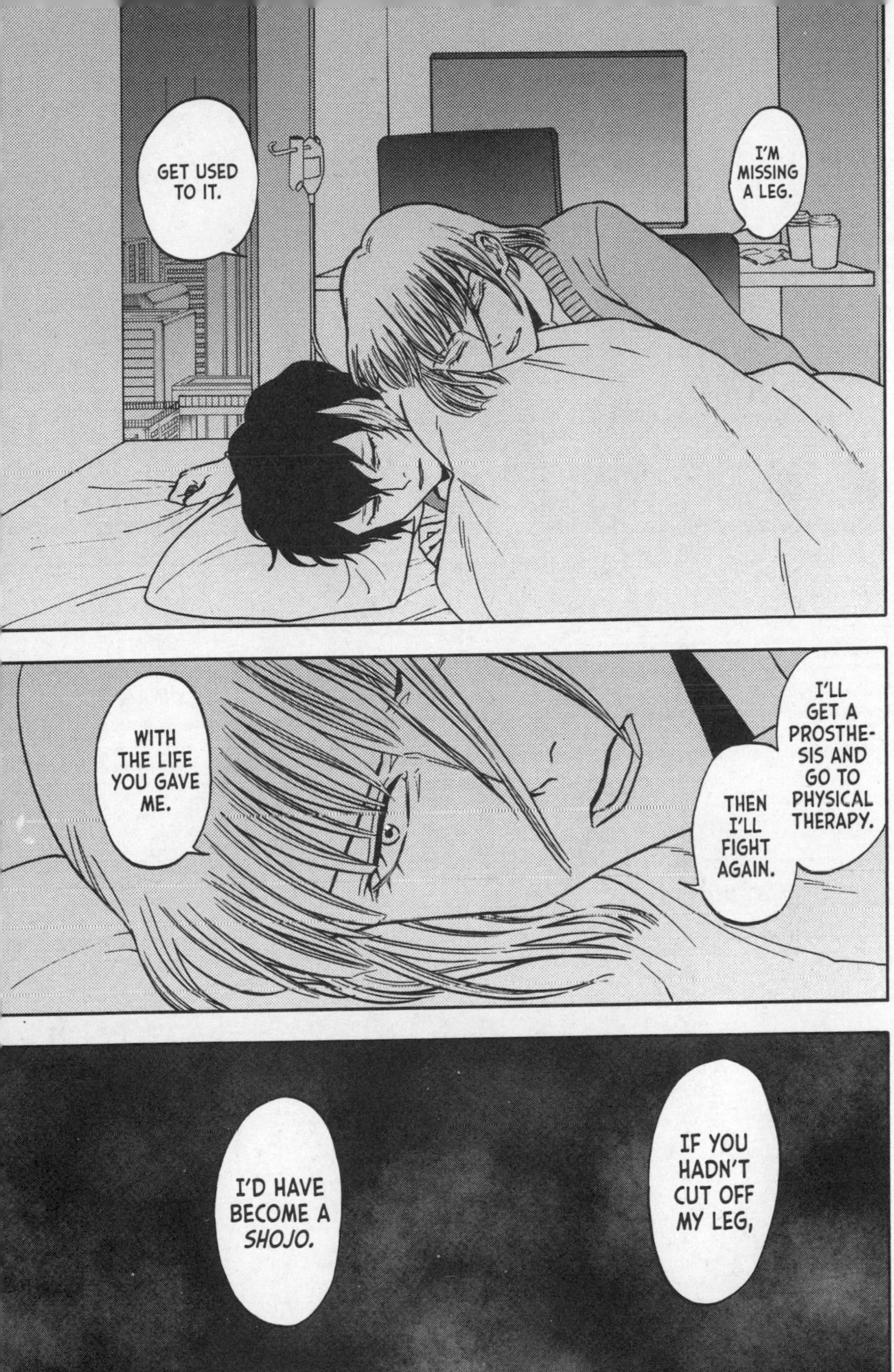
I'M MISSING A LEG.
GET USED TO IT.
I'LL GET A PROSTHESIS AND GO TO PHYSICAL THERAPY.
THEN I'LL FIGHT AGAIN.
WITH THE LIFE YOU GAVE ME.
IF YOU HADN'T CUT OFF MY LEG,
I'D HAVE BECOME A *SHOJO.*

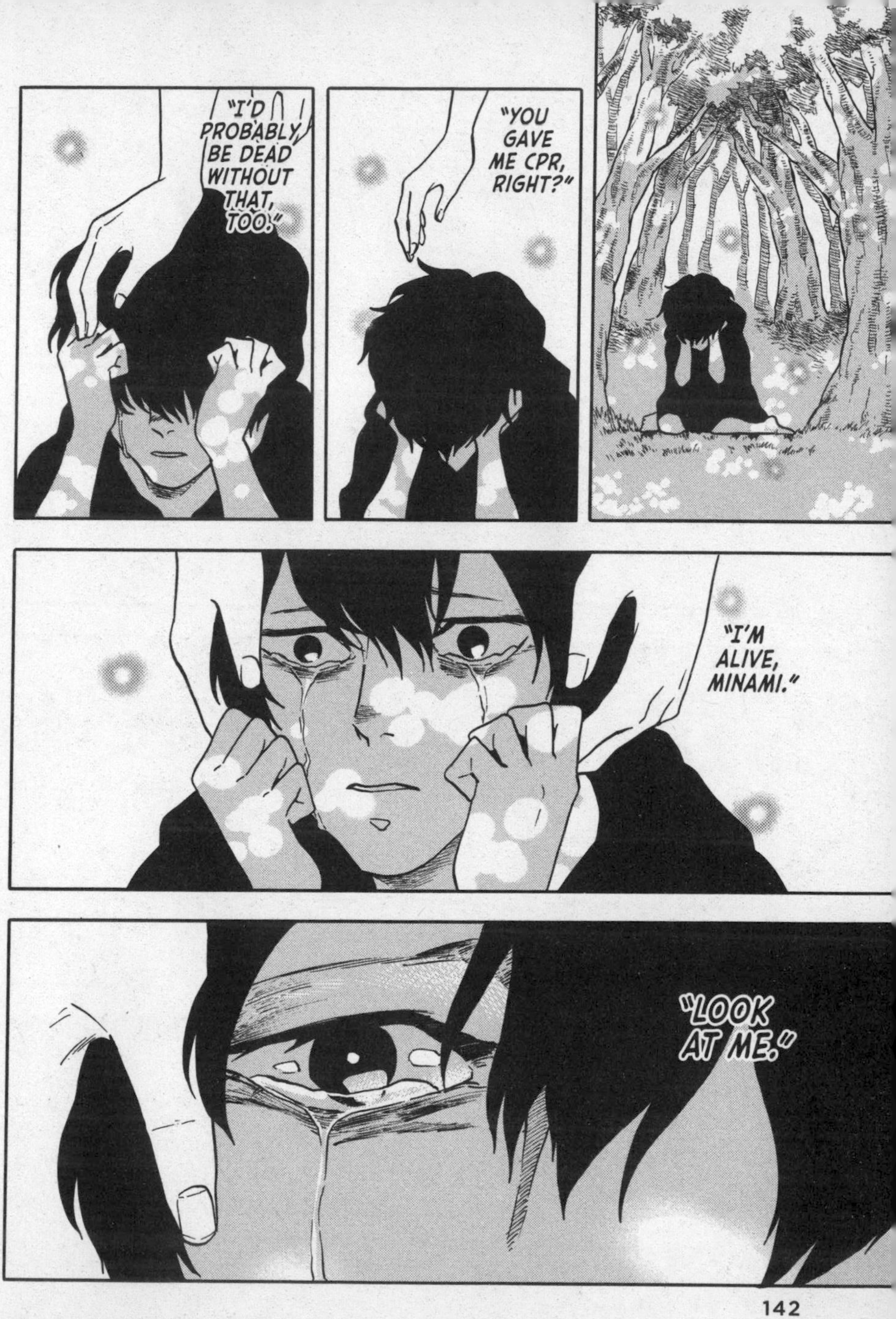
"YOU GAVE ME CPR, RIGHT?"
"I'D PROBABLY BE DEAD WITHOUT THAT, TOO."
"I'M ALIVE, MINAMI."
"LOOK AT ME."

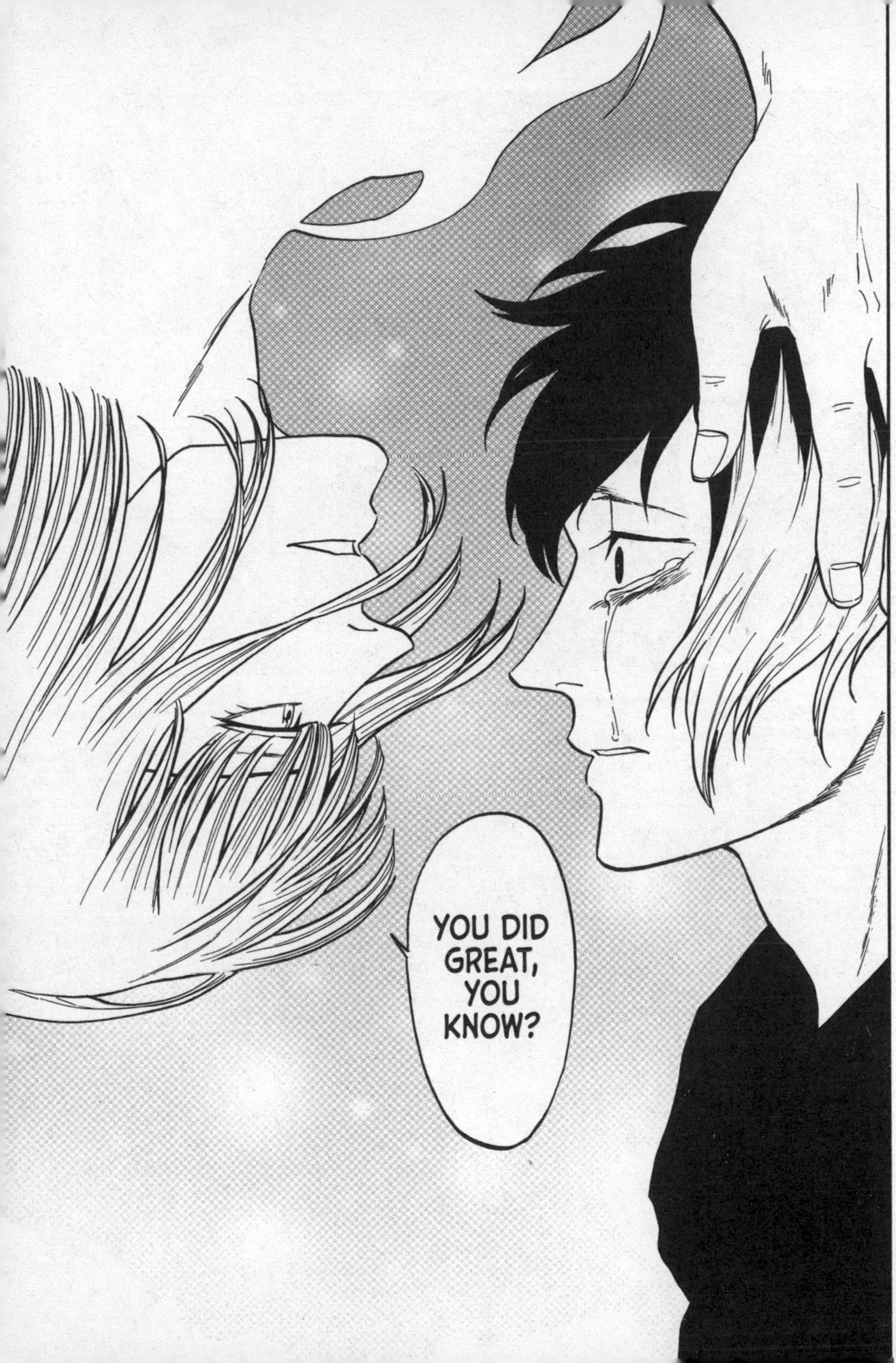
YOU DID GREAT, YOU KNOW?

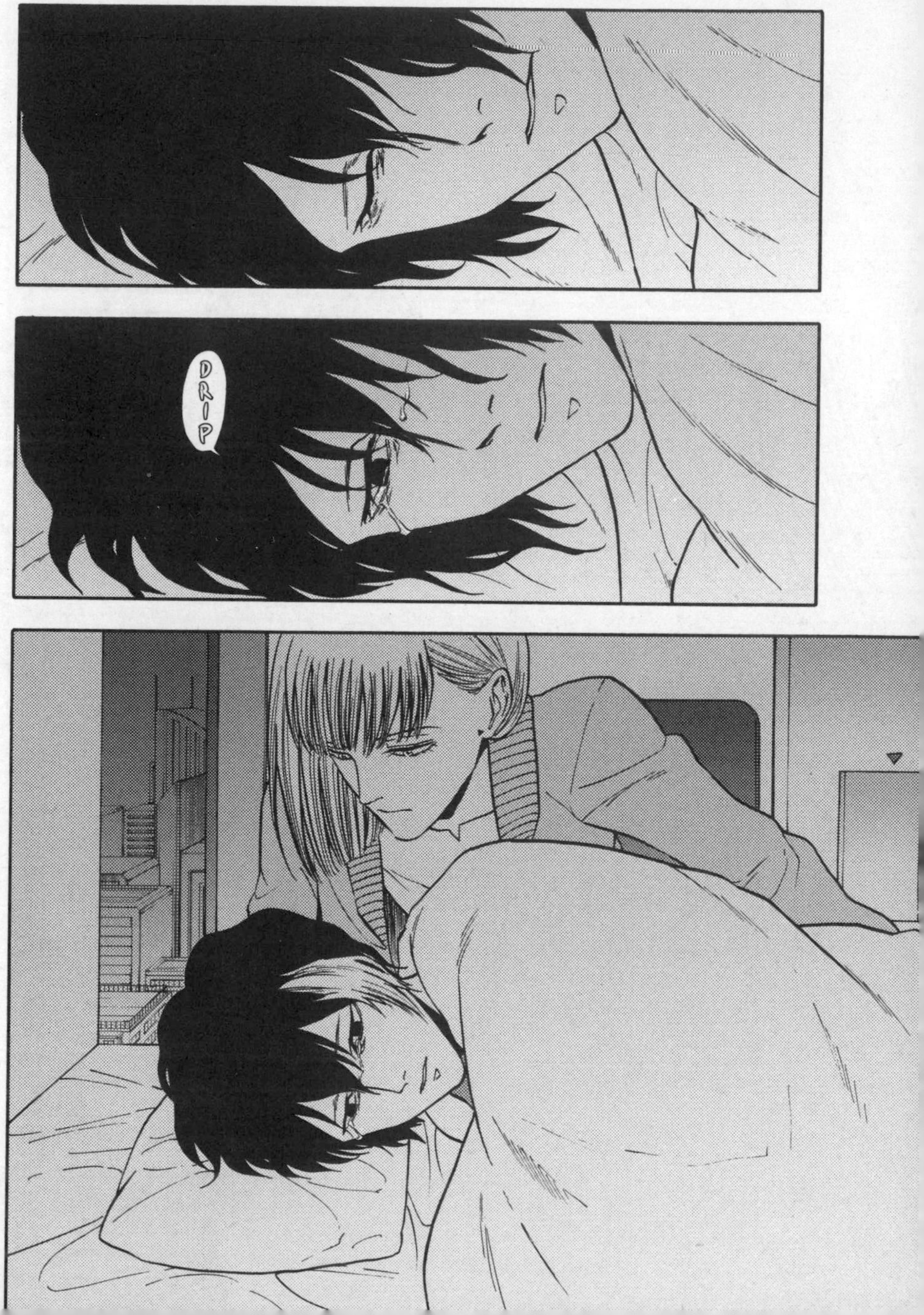
DRIP

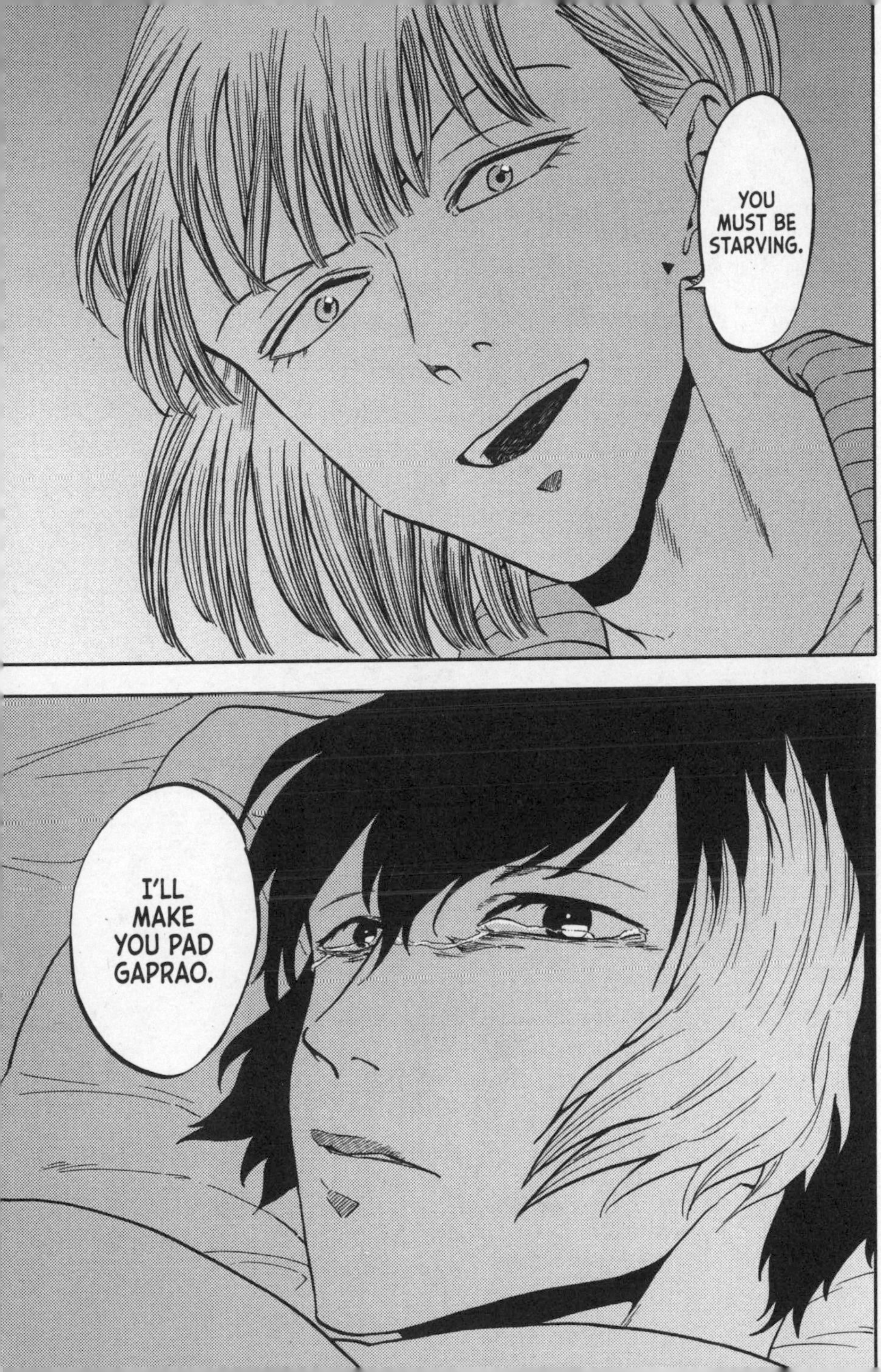
YOU MUST BE STARVING.
I'LL MAKE YOU PAD GAPRAO.

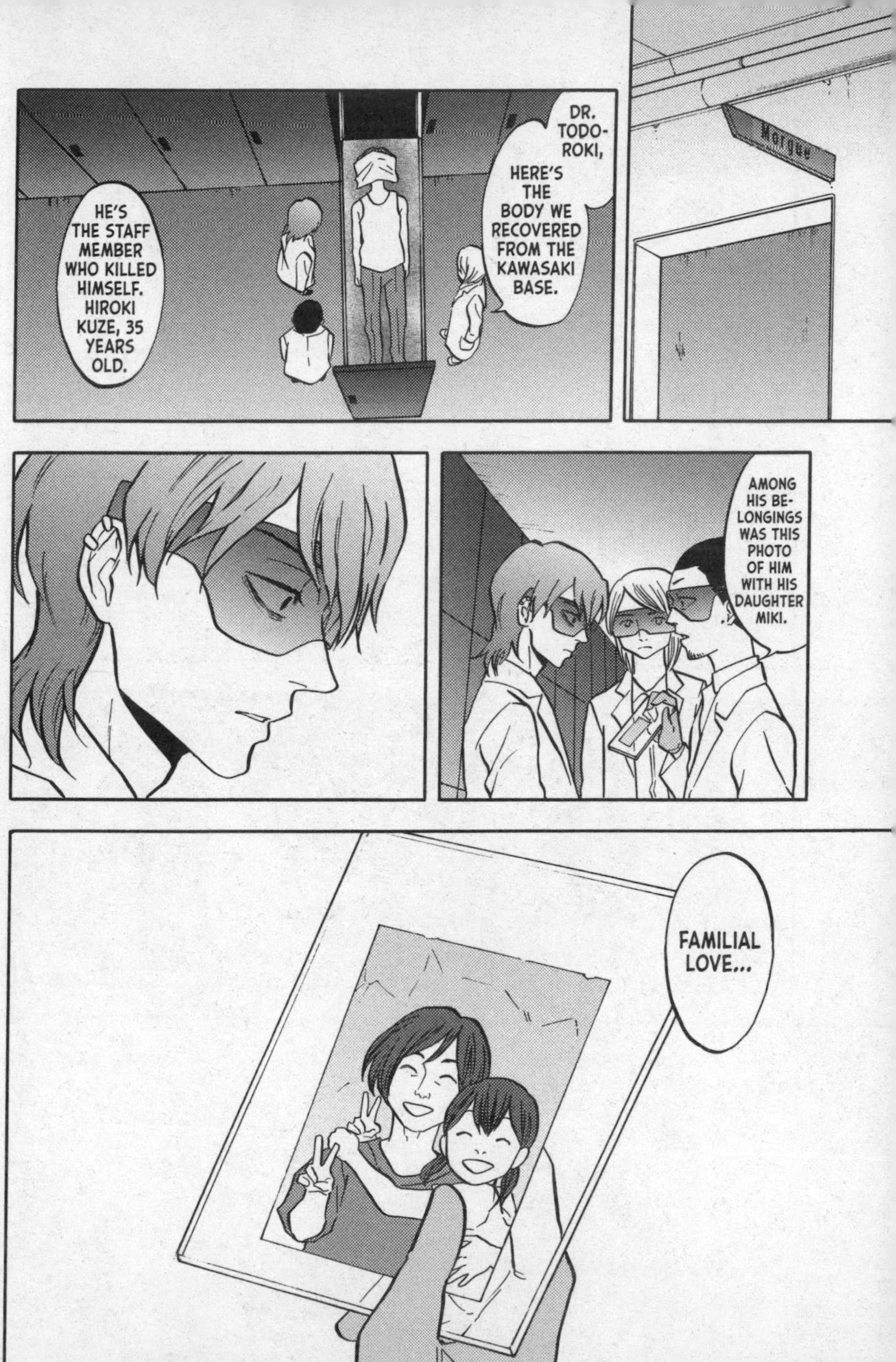
Morgue
DR. TODOROKI, HERE'S THE BODY WE RECOVERED FROM THE KAWASAKI BASE.
HE'S THE STAFF MEMBER WHO KILLED HIMSELF. HIROKI KUZE, 35 YEARS OLD.
AMONG HIS BELONGINGS WAS THIS PHOTO OF HIM WITH HIS DAUGHTER MIKI.
FAMILIAL LOVE...

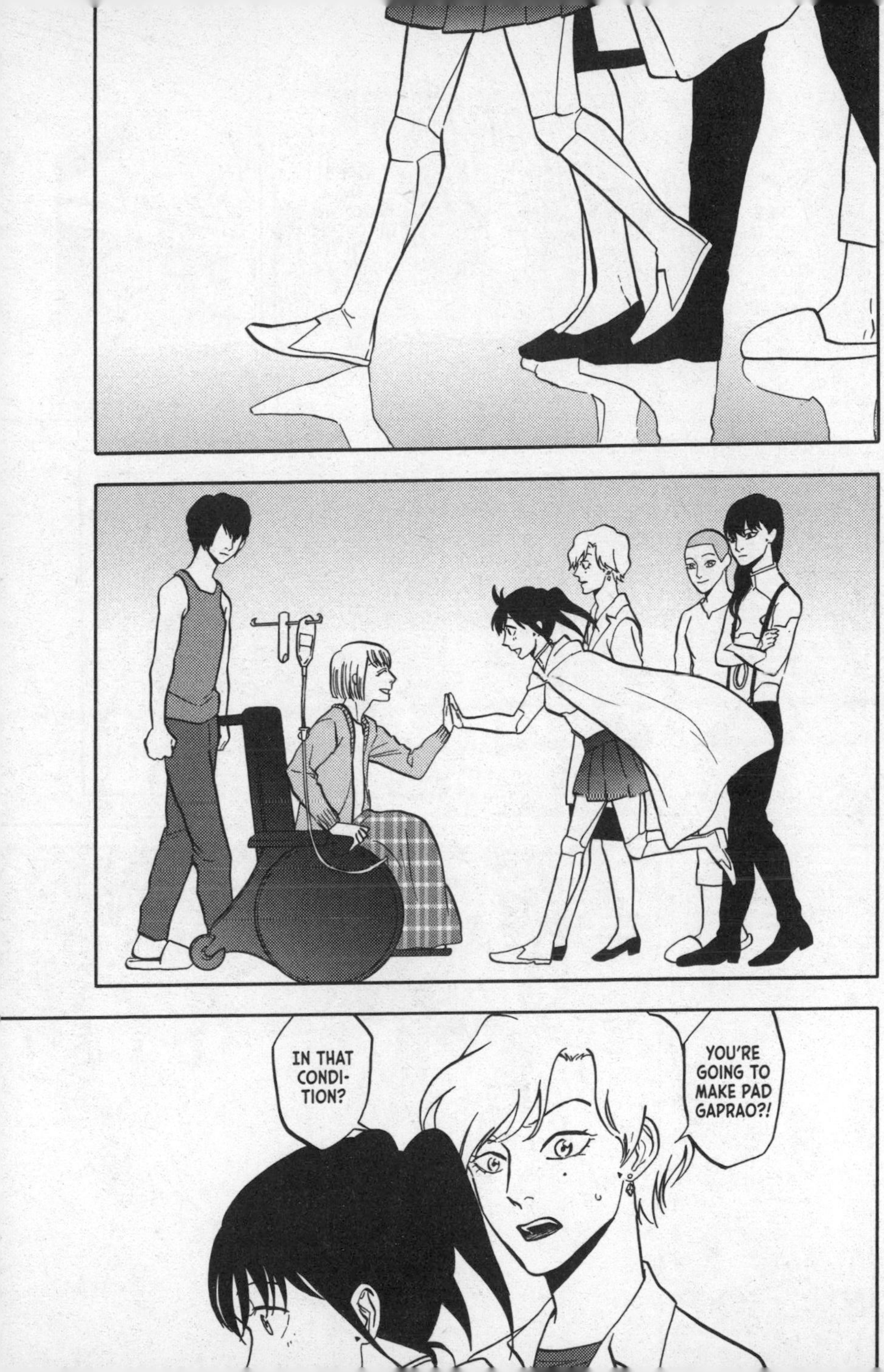
YOU'RE GOING TO MAKE PAD GAPRAO?!
IN THAT CONDI-TION?

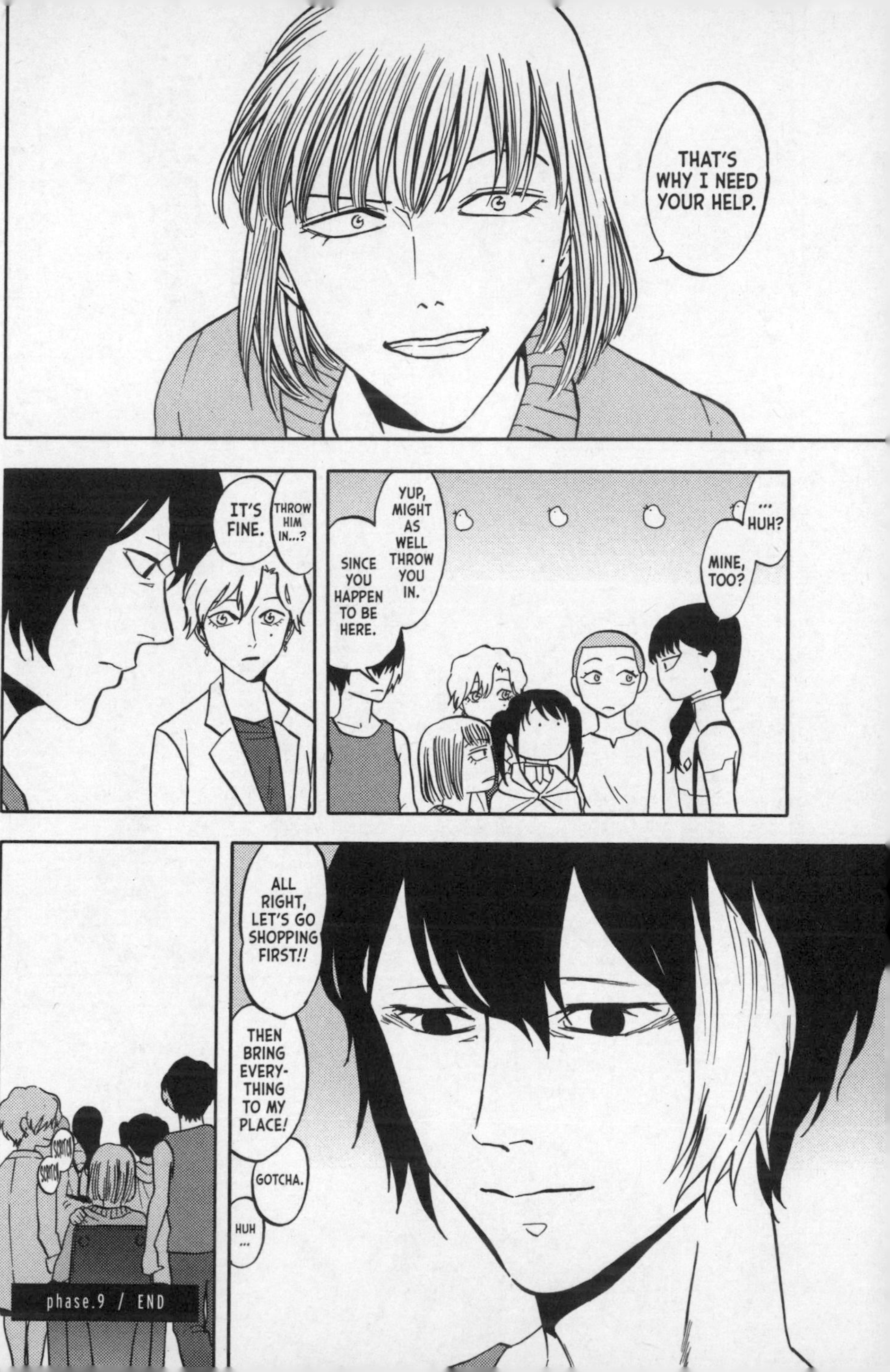
THAT'S WHY I NEED YOUR HELP.
... HUH?
MINE, TOO?
YUP, MIGHT AS WELL THROW YOU IN.
SINCE YOU HAPPEN TO BE HERE.
THROW HIM IN...?
IT'S FINE.
ALL RIGHT, LET'S GO SHOPPING FIRST!!
THEN BRING EVERY-THING TO MY PLACE!
GOTCHA.
HUH ...
phase.9 / END

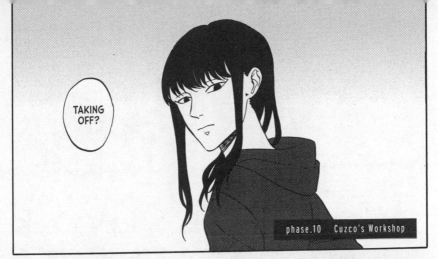

TAKING OFF?
phase.10 Cuzco's Workshop
YES.
I'M WORKING TOMORROW.
THE PAD GAPRAO CAME OUT PRETTY GOOD, RIGHT?
IT WASN'T EASY HOLDING YOU UP.
THAT WORKED BETTER THAN I THOUGHT.
DON'T ASK ME TO DO IT AGAIN.
I'LL BE GOING, TOO. THANKS FOR DINNER.
SAME WITH ME.
THAT WAS DELICIOUS.
SEE YOU.

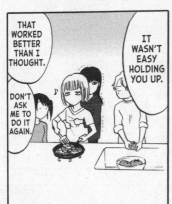

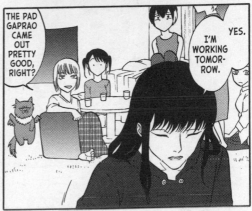

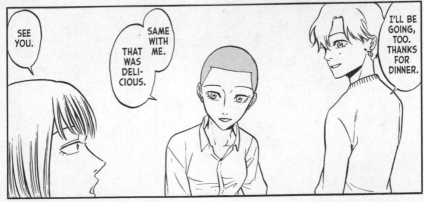

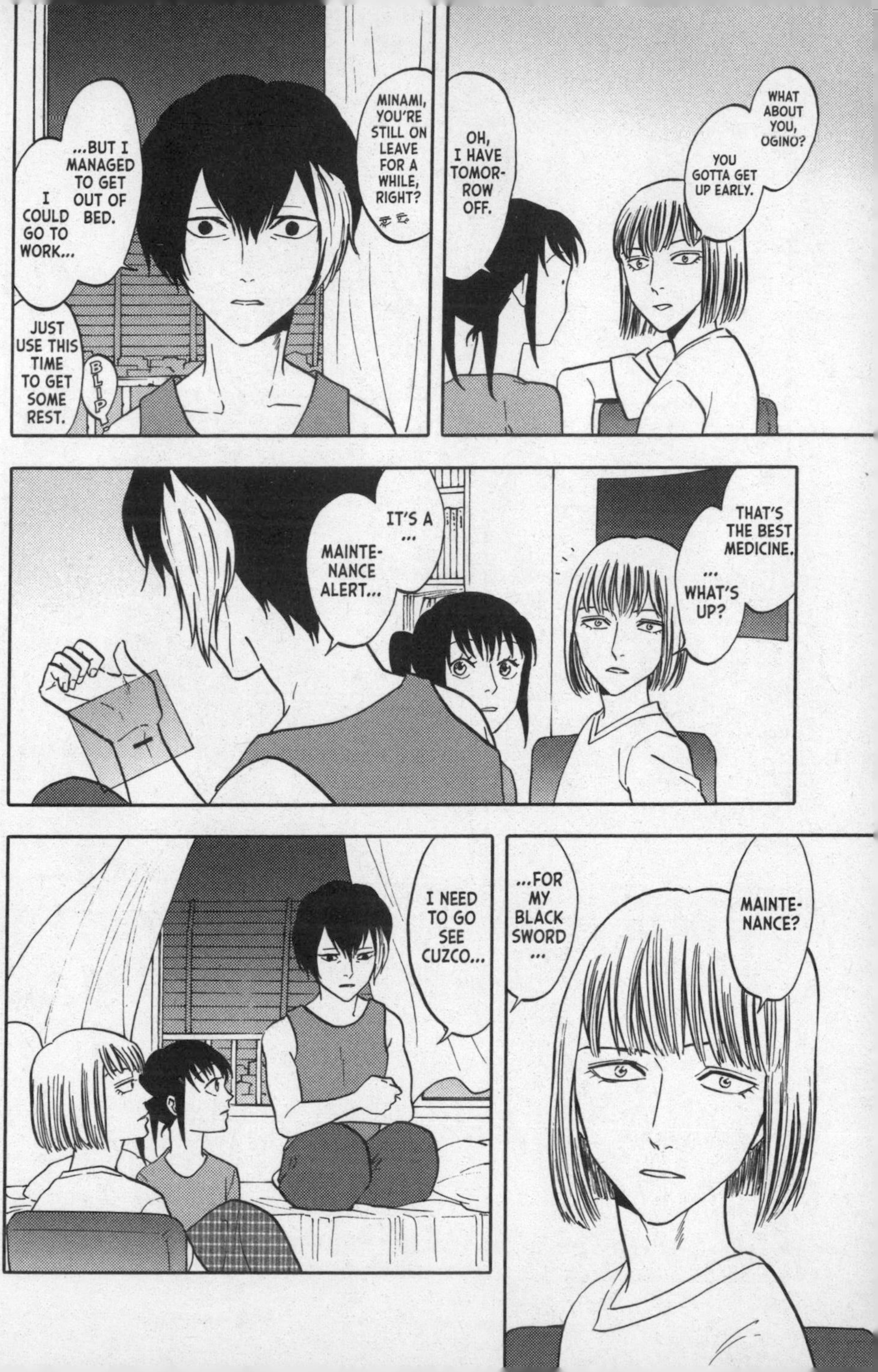
WHAT ABOUT YOU, OGINO?
YOU GOTTA GET UP EARLY.
OH, I HAVE TOMORROW OFF.
MINAMI, YOU'RE STILL ON LEAVE FOR A WHILE, RIGHT?
...BUT I MANAGED TO GET OUT OF BED.
I COULD GO TO WORK...
JUST USE THIS TIME TO GET SOME REST.
BLIP
THAT'S THE BEST MEDICINE.
... WHAT'S UP?
IT'S A ... MAINTENANCE ALERT...
MAINTENANCE?
...FOR MY BLACK SWORD ...
I NEED TO GO SEE CUZCO...

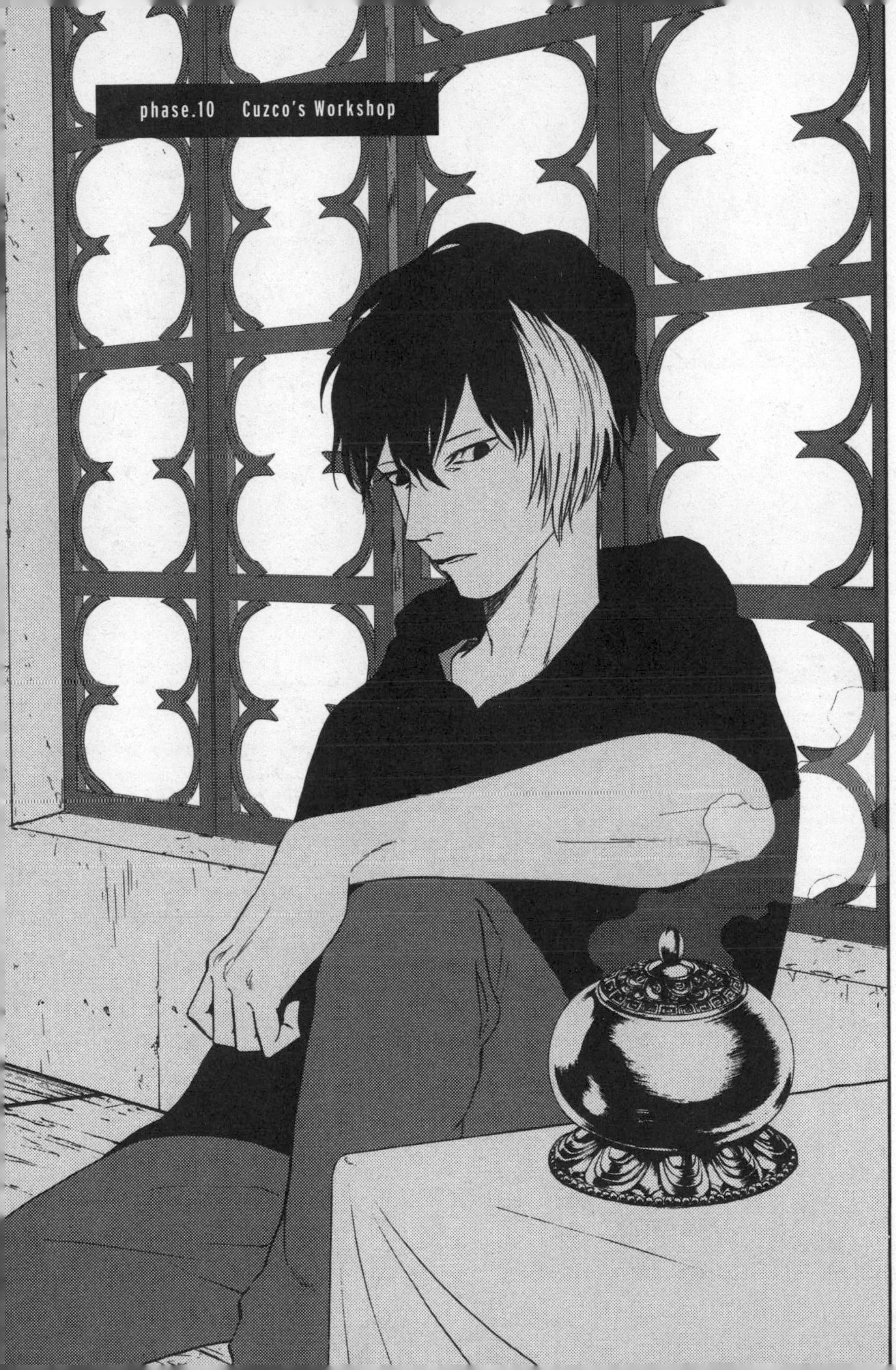
phase.10 Cuzco's Workshop

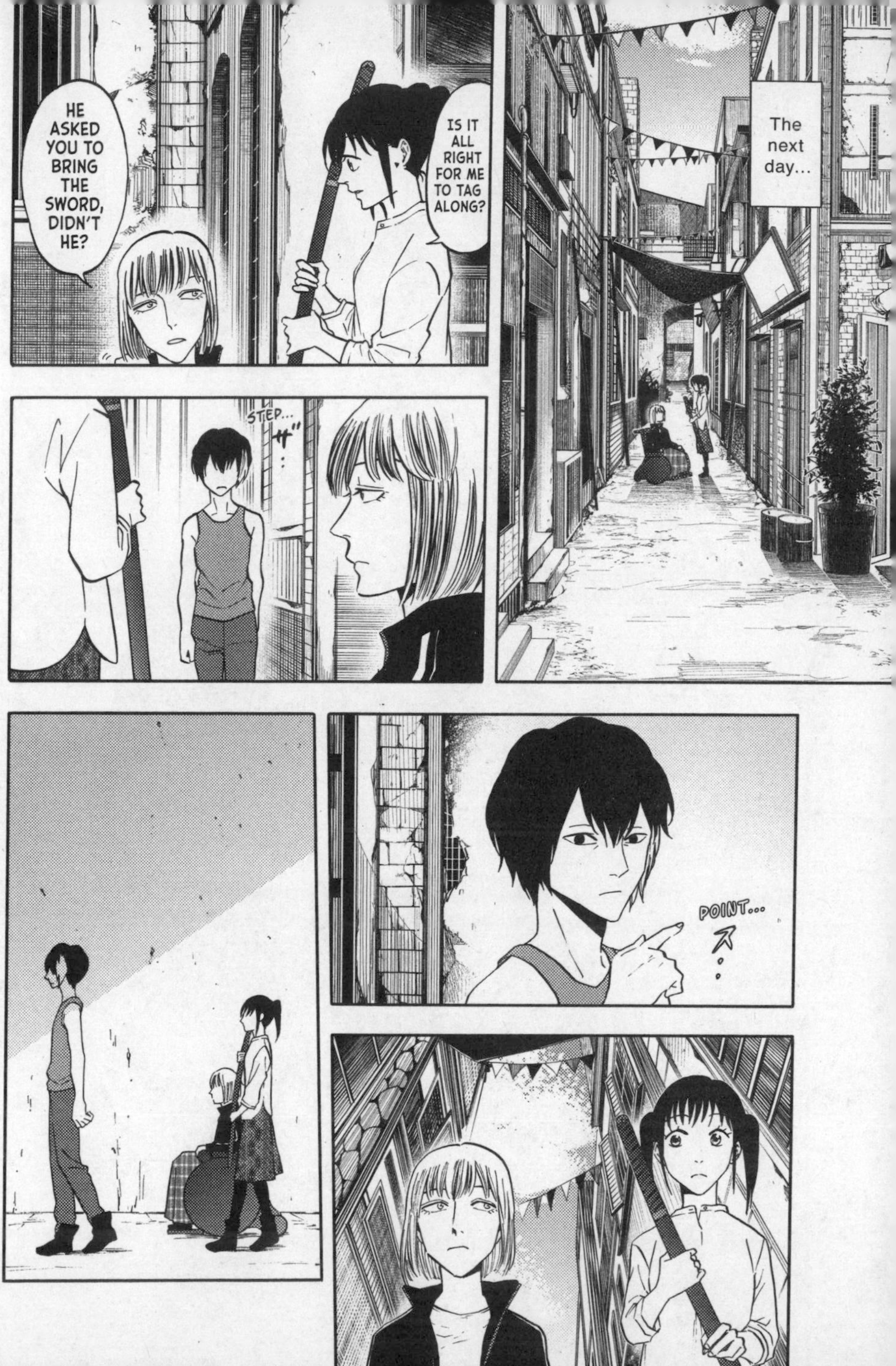
The next day...
IS IT ALL RIGHT FOR ME TO TAG ALONG?
HE ASKED YOU TO BRING THE SWORD, DIDN'T HE?
STEP...
POINT...

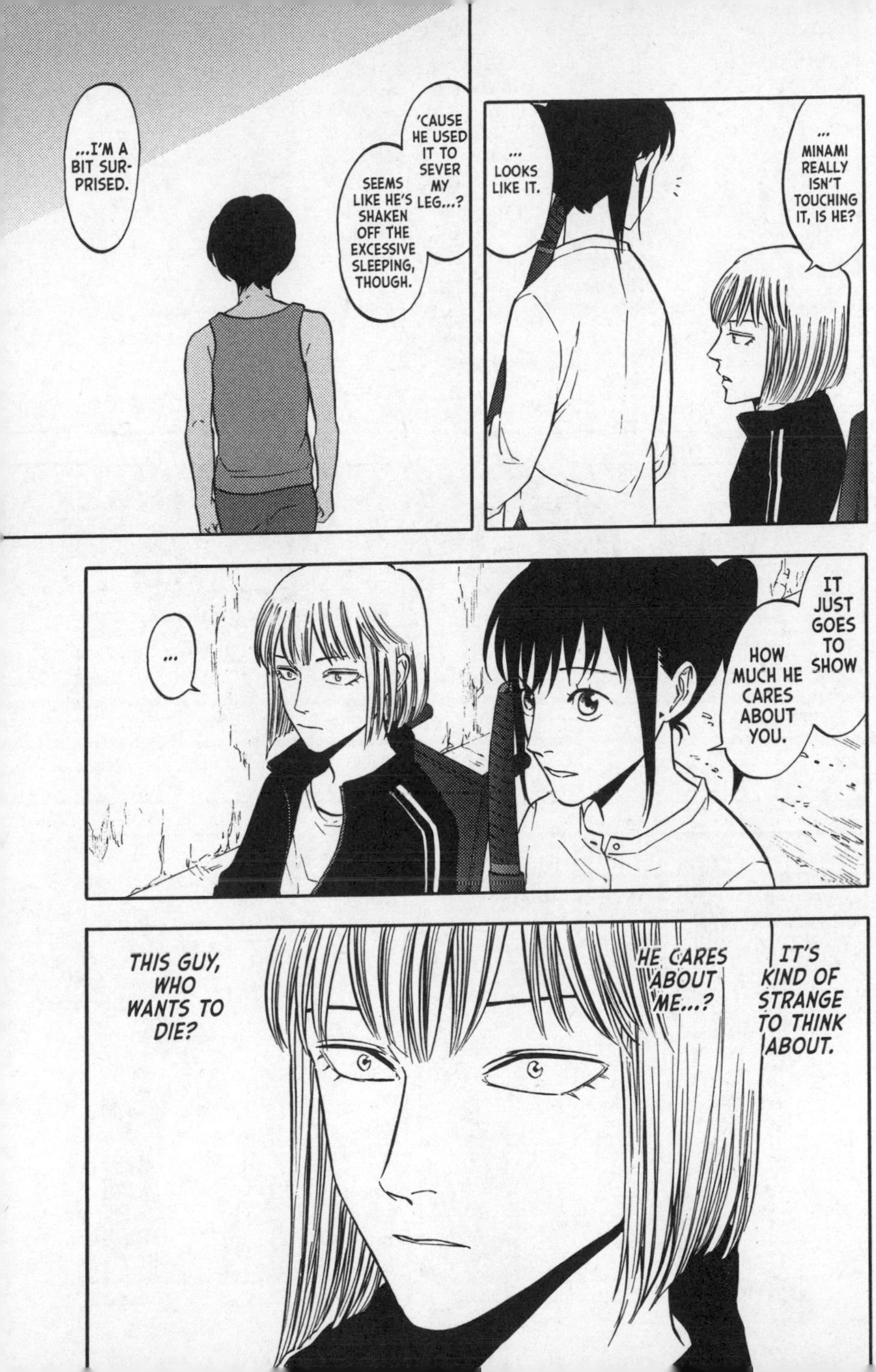
...MINAMI REALLY ISN'T TOUCHING IT, IS HE?
...LOOKS LIKE IT.
'CAUSE HE USED IT TO SEVER MY LEG...?
SEEMS LIKE HE'S SHAKEN OFF THE EXCESSIVE SLEEPING, THOUGH.
...I'M A BIT SURPRISED.
IT JUST GOES TO SHOW
HOW MUCH HE CARES ABOUT YOU.
...
IT'S KIND OF STRANGE TO THINK ABOUT.
HE CARES ABOUT ME...?
THIS GUY, WHO WANTS TO DIE?

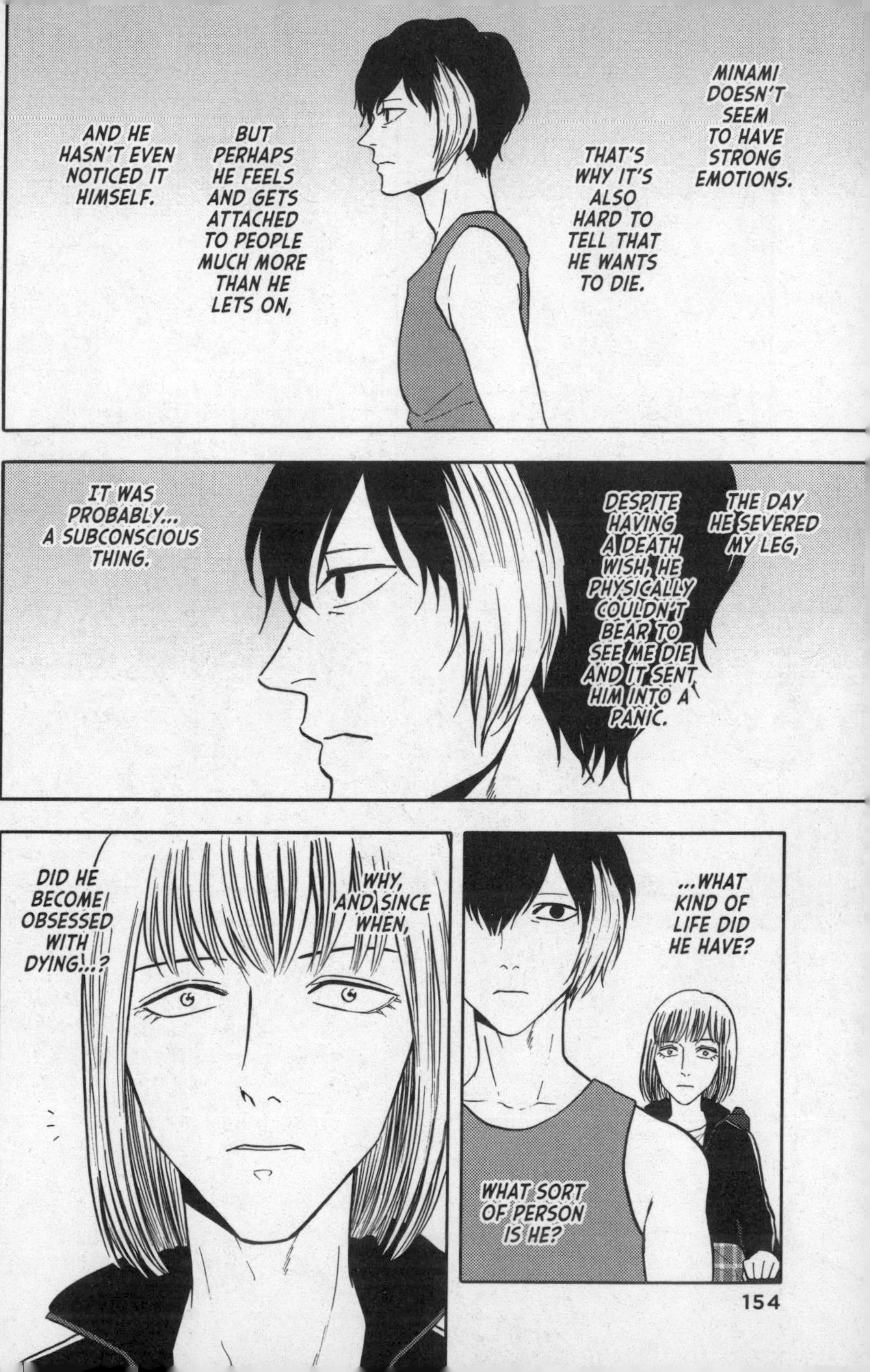
MINAMI DOESN'T SEEM TO HAVE STRONG EMOTIONS.
THAT'S WHY IT'S ALSO HARD TO TELL THAT HE WANTS TO DIE.
BUT PERHAPS HE FEELS AND GETS ATTACHED TO PEOPLE MUCH MORE THAN HE LETS ON,
AND HE HASN'T EVEN NOTICED IT HIMSELF.
THE DAY HE SEVERED MY LEG,
DESPITE HAVING A DEATH WISH, HE PHYSICALLY COULDN'T BEAR TO SEE ME DIE AND IT SENT HIM INTO A PANIC.
IT WAS PROBABLY... A SUBCONSCIOUS THING.
...WHAT KIND OF LIFE DID HE HAVE?
WHAT SORT OF PERSON IS HE?
WHY, AND SINCE WHEN,
DID HE BECOME OBSESSED WITH DYING...?

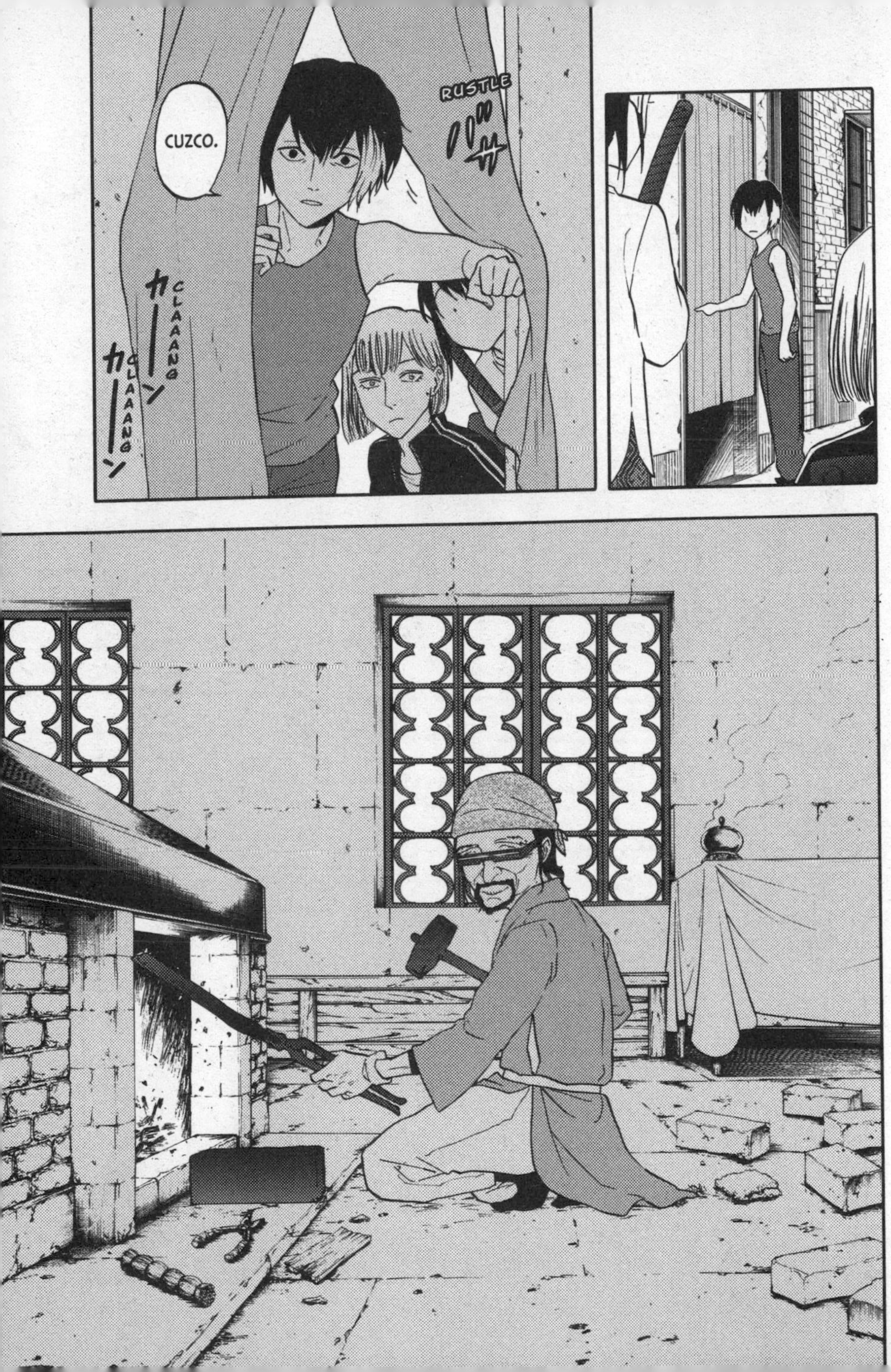
CUZCO.
RUSTLE
カーン
CLAAANG
カーン
CLAAANG

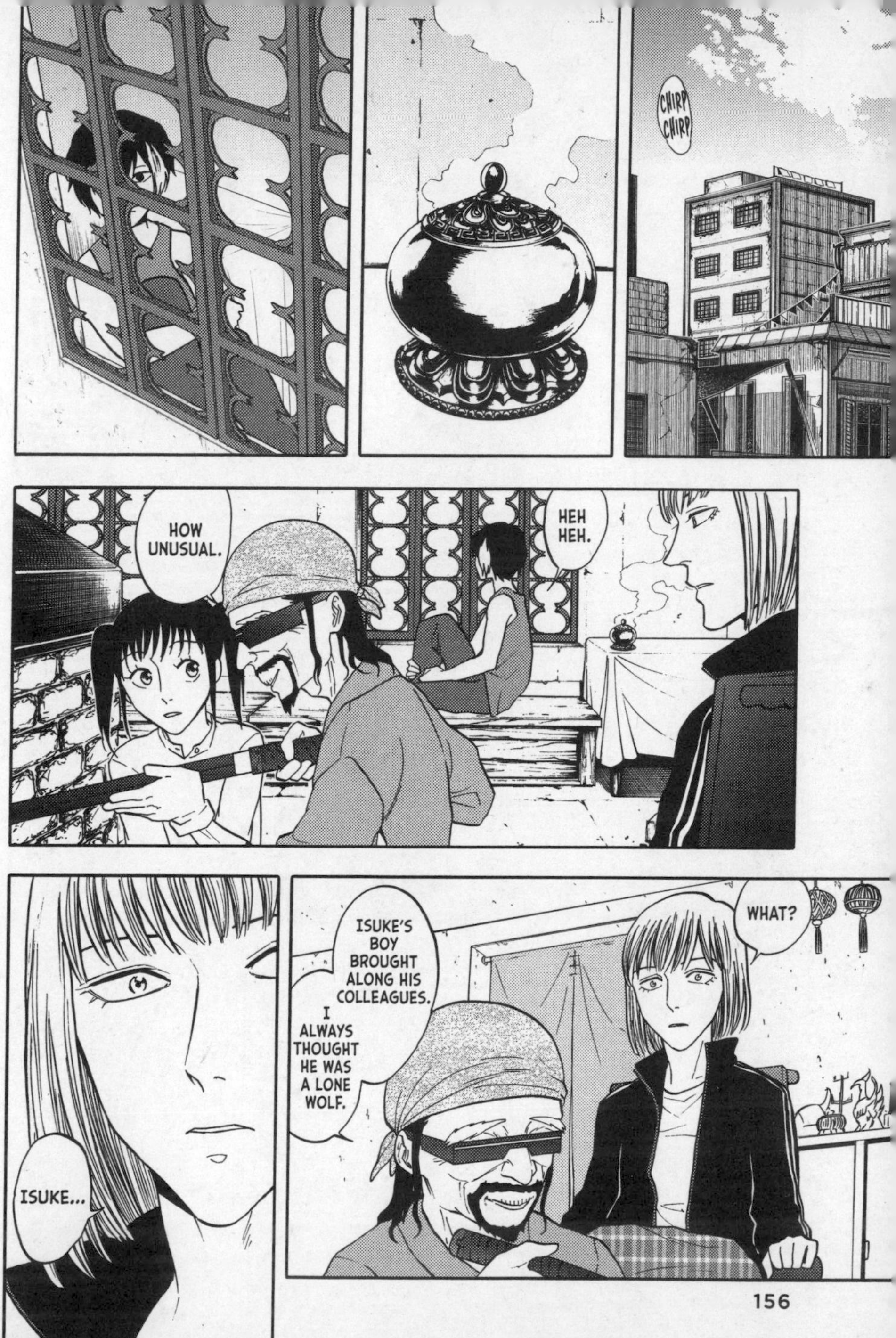
CHIRP CHIRP
HEH HEH.
HOW UNUSUAL.
WHAT?
ISUKE'S BOY BROUGHT ALONG HIS COLLEAGUES.
I ALWAYS THOUGHT HE WAS A LONE WOLF.
ISUKE...

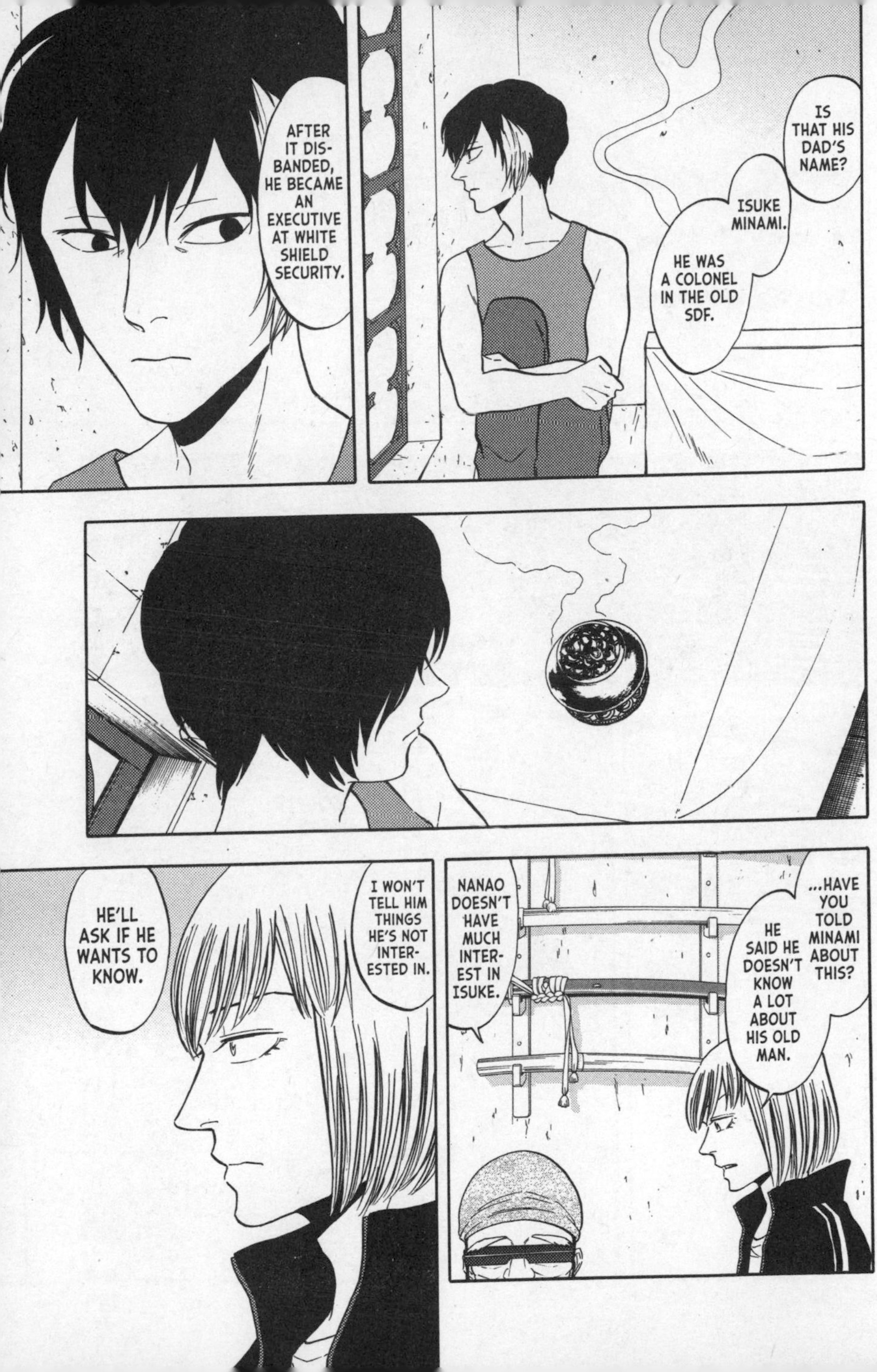
IS THAT HIS DAD'S NAME?
ISUKE MINAMI.
HE WAS A COLONEL IN THE OLD SDF.
AFTER IT DIS-BANDED, HE BECAME AN EXECUTIVE AT WHITE SHIELD SECURITY.
...HAVE YOU TOLD MINAMI ABOUT THIS?
HE SAID HE DOESN'T KNOW A LOT ABOUT HIS OLD MAN.
NANAO DOESN'T HAVE MUCH INTEREST IN ISUKE.
I WON'T TELL HIM THINGS HE'S NOT INTER-ESTED IN.
HE'LL ASK IF HE WANTS TO KNOW.

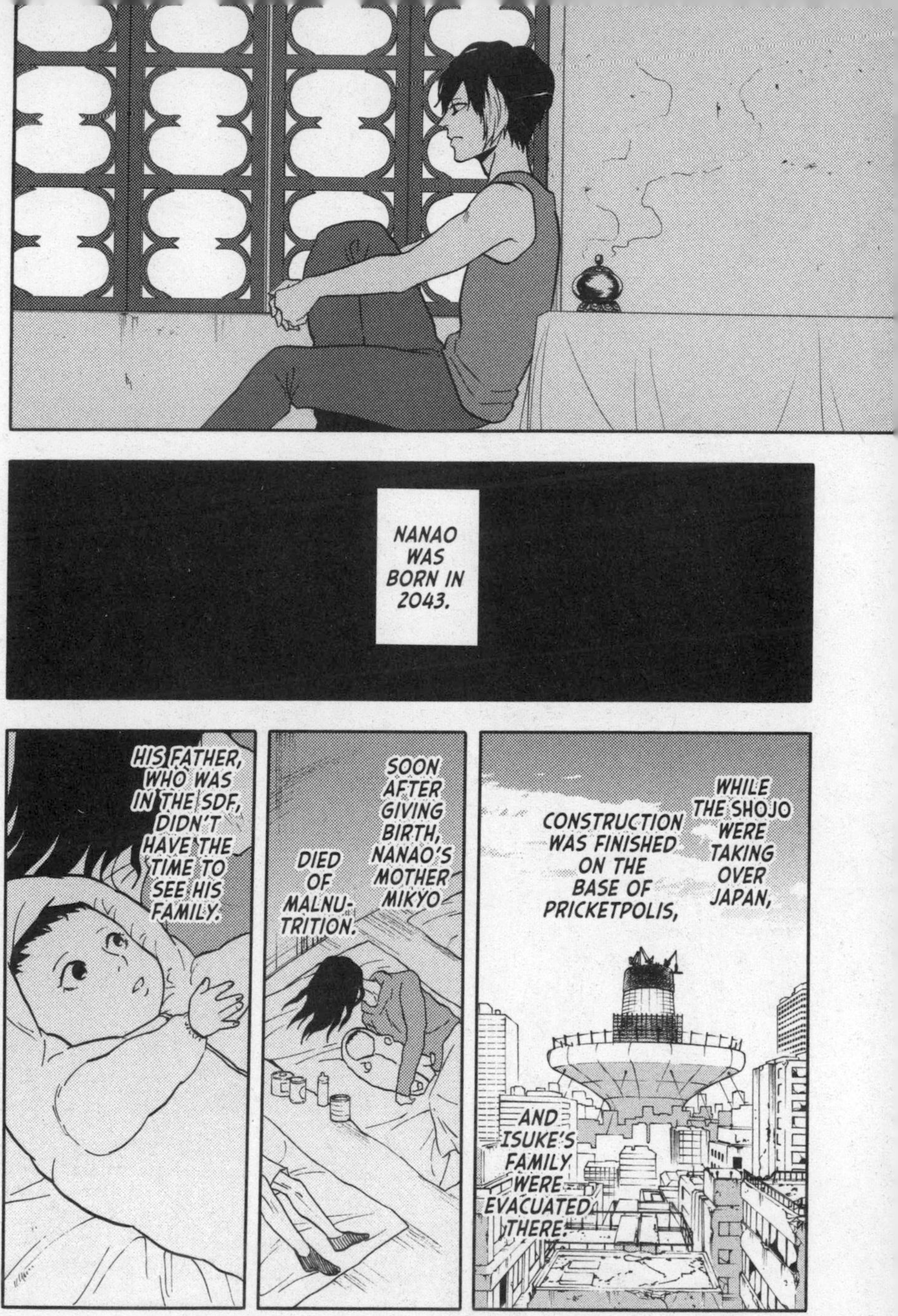
NANAO WAS BORN IN 2043.
WHILE THE SHOJO WERE TAKING OVER JAPAN,
CONSTRUCTION WAS FINISHED ON THE BASE OF PRICKETPOLIS,
AND ISUKE'S FAMILY WERE EVACUATED THERE.
SOON AFTER GIVING BIRTH, NANAO'S MOTHER MIKYO
DIED OF MALNU-TRITION.
HIS FATHER, WHO WAS IN THE SDF, DIDN'T HAVE THE TIME TO SEE HIS FAMILY.

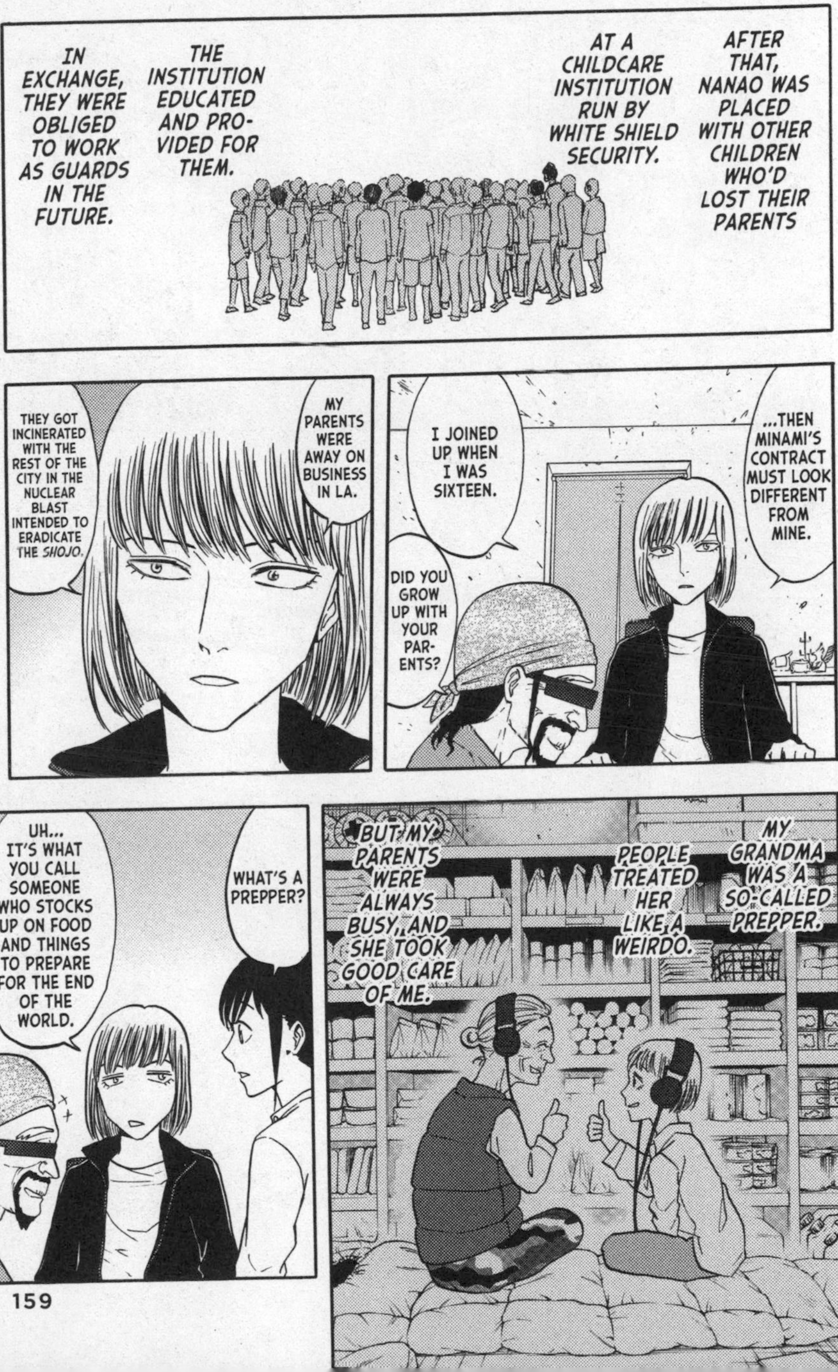
AFTER THAT, NANAO WAS PLACED WITH OTHER CHILDREN WHO'D LOST THEIR PARENTS
AT A CHILDCARE INSTITUTION RUN BY WHITE SHIELD SECURITY.
THE INSTITUTION EDUCATED AND PRO-VIDED FOR THEM.
IN EXCHANGE, THEY WERE OBLIGED TO WORK AS GUARDS IN THE FUTURE.
...THEN MINAMI'S CONTRACT MUST LOOK DIFFERENT FROM MINE.
I JOINED UP WHEN I WAS SIXTEEN.
DID YOU GROW UP WITH YOUR PAR-ENTS?
MY PARENTS WERE AWAY ON BUSINESS IN LA.
THEY GOT INCINERATED WITH THE REST OF THE CITY IN THE NUCLEAR BLAST INTENDED TO ERADICATE THE *SHOJO*.
MY GRANDMA WAS A SO-CALLED PREPPER.
PEOPLE TREATED HER LIKE A WEIRDO.
BUT MY PARENTS WERE ALWAYS BUSY, AND SHE TOOK GOOD CARE OF ME.
WHAT'S A PREPPER?
UH... IT'S WHAT YOU CALL SOMEONE WHO STOCKS UP ON FOOD AND THINGS TO PREPARE FOR THE END OF THE WORLD.

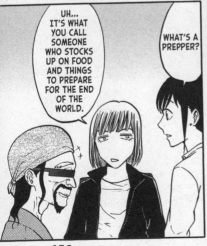

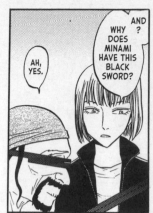

THANKS TO THAT, I DIDN'T HAVE TO LIVE IN A SHELTER.
THE END OF THE WORLD ACTUALLY FELT LIKE SOME KIND OF ADVENTURE, TOO.
HA HA HA! THAT'S THE WAY TO DO IT.
AND WHY DOES MINAMI HAVE THIS BLACK SWORD?
AH, YES.
WHEN WHITE SHIELD STARTED DEPLOYING GUARDS,
THEY WERE DEVELOPING ALL SORTS OF WEAPONS TO KILL THE *SHOJO.*
ISUKE SAID HE WANTED TO BE ON THE FRONT LINE, ARMED IN EVERY WAY POSSIBLE.
HE USED TO PRACTICE IAI,*
AND HE ASKED ME TO MAKE HIM A JAPANESE KATANA FROM THE STRONGEST POSSIBLE MATERIAL.
WHICH WOULD BE THE BLACK SWORD.
IT WASN'T EVERY DAY THAT EXECUTIVES WENT OUT TO THE BATTLEFIELD.
BUT THAT'S THE SORT OF PERSON ISUKE WAS.

* A traditional Japanese martial art that focuses on the drawing of the katana.

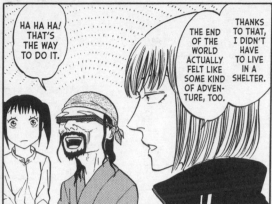

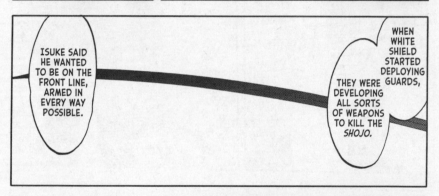

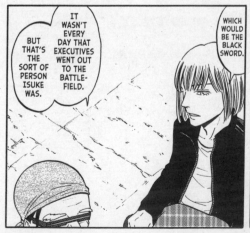

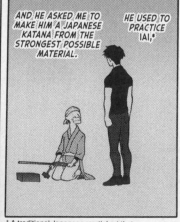

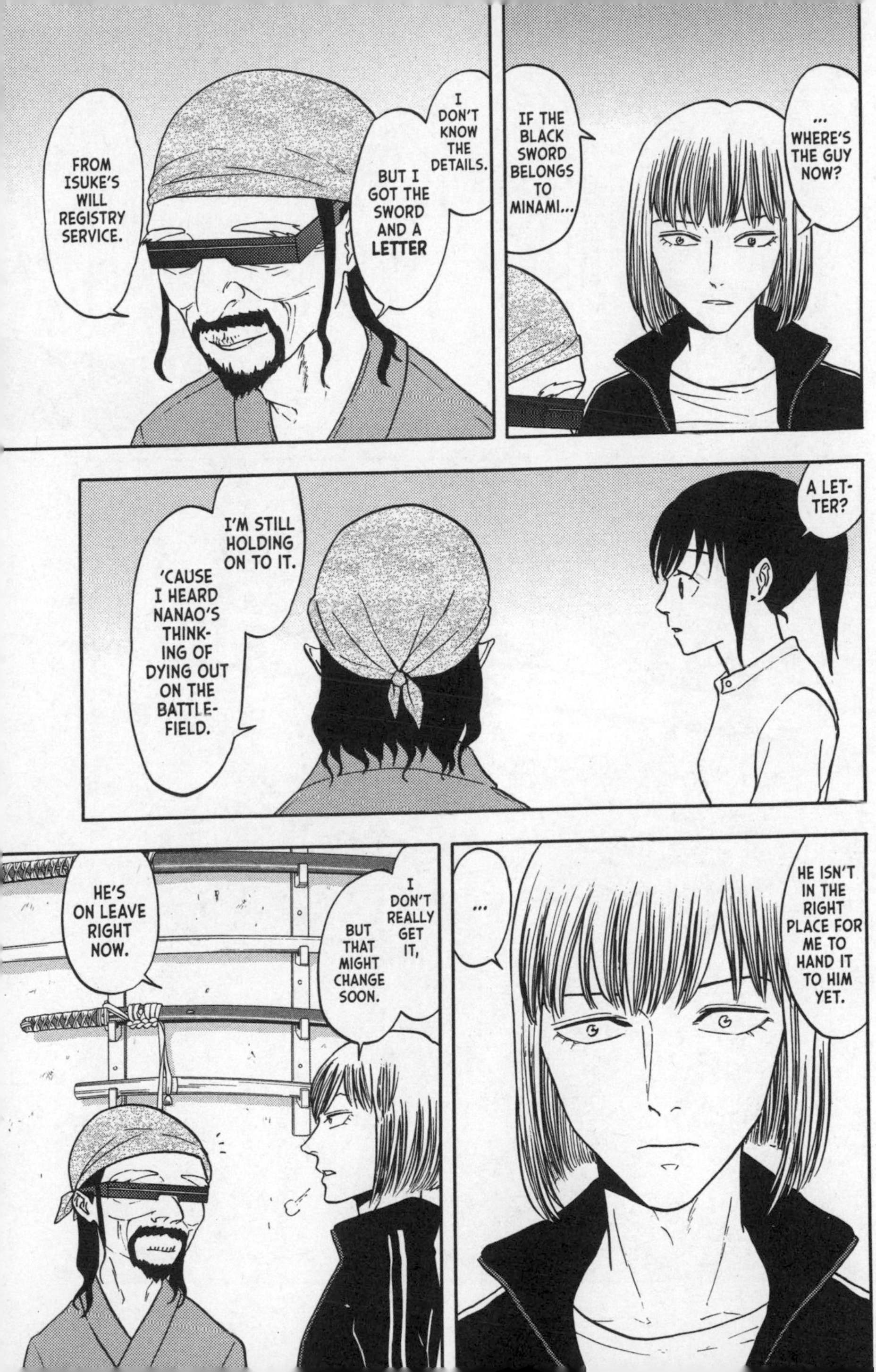
...WHERE'S THE GUY NOW?
IF THE BLACK SWORD BELONGS TO MINAMI...
I DON'T KNOW THE DETAILS.
BUT I GOT THE SWORD AND A **LETTER**
FROM ISUKE'S WILL REGISTRY SERVICE.
A LET-TER?
I'M STILL HOLDING ON TO IT.
'CAUSE I HEARD NANAO'S THINK-ING OF DYING OUT ON THE BATTLE-FIELD.
HE ISN'T IN THE RIGHT PLACE FOR ME TO HAND IT TO HIM YET.
...
I DON'T REALLY GET IT,
BUT THAT MIGHT CHANGE SOON.
HE'S ON LEAVE RIGHT NOW.

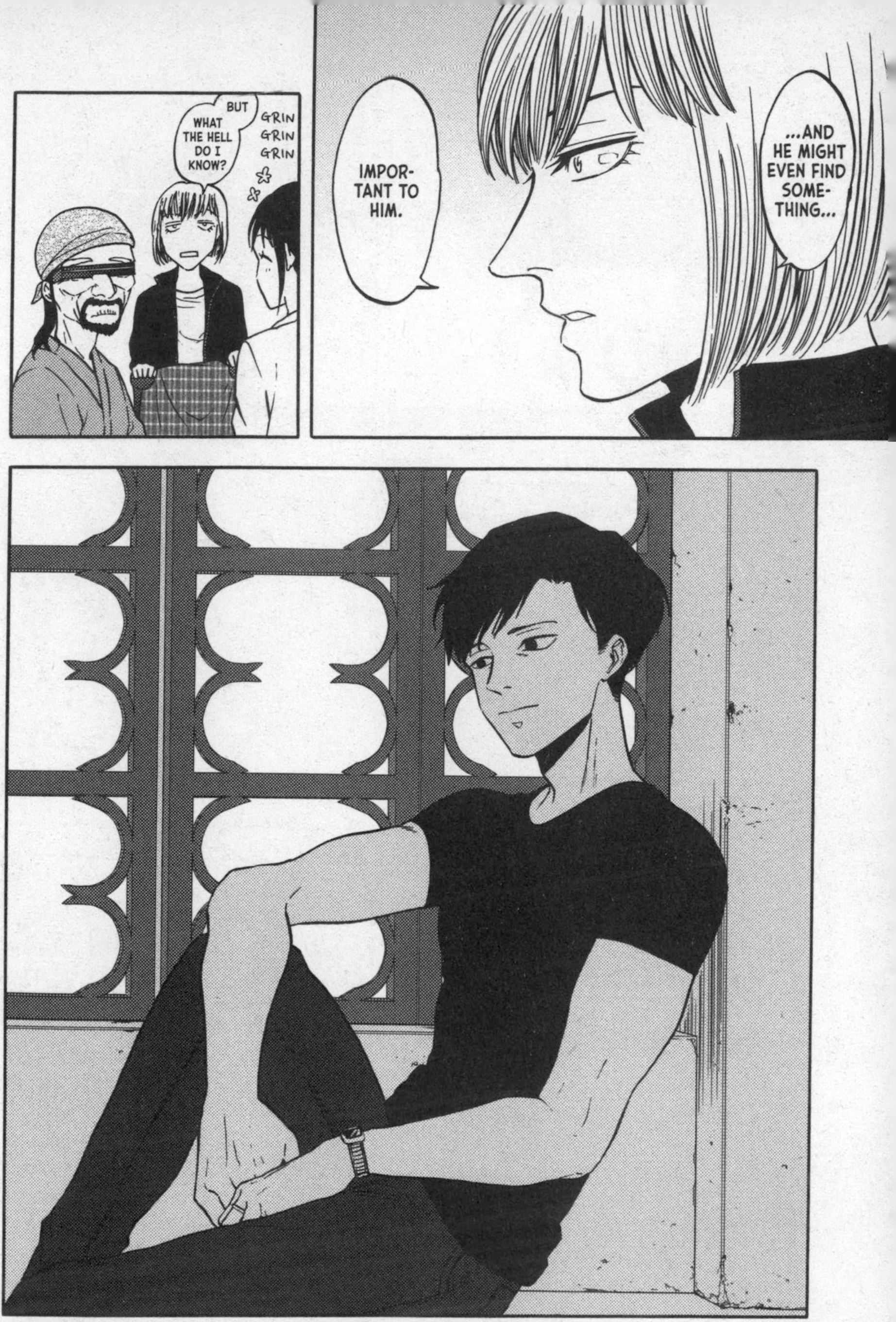
...AND HE MIGHT EVEN FIND SOME-THING...
IMPOR-TANT TO HIM.
GRIN GRIN GRIN
BUT WHAT THE HELL DO I KNOW?

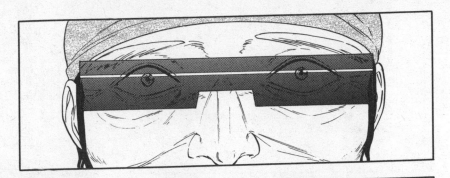

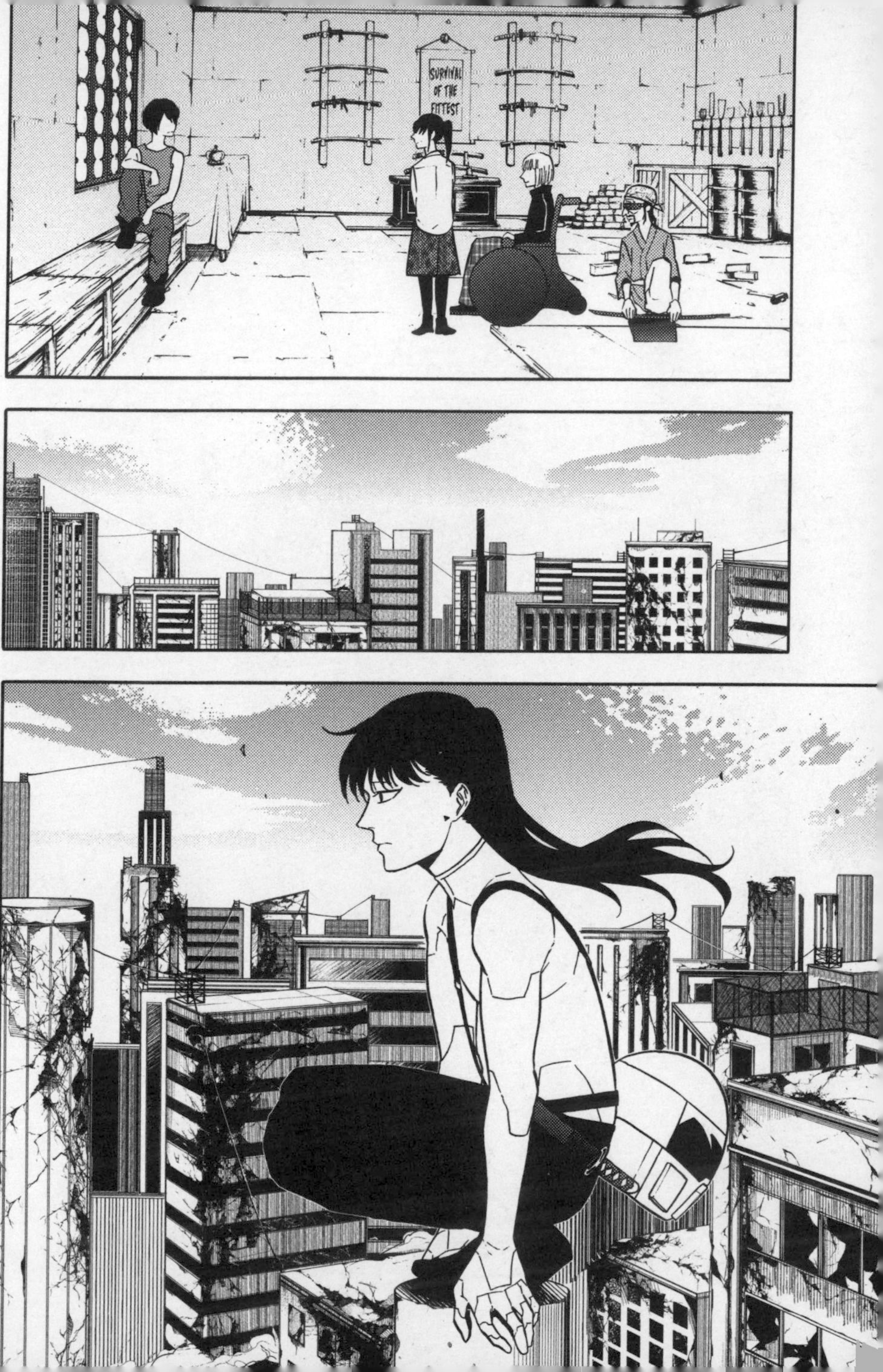
SURVIVAL OF THE FITTEST

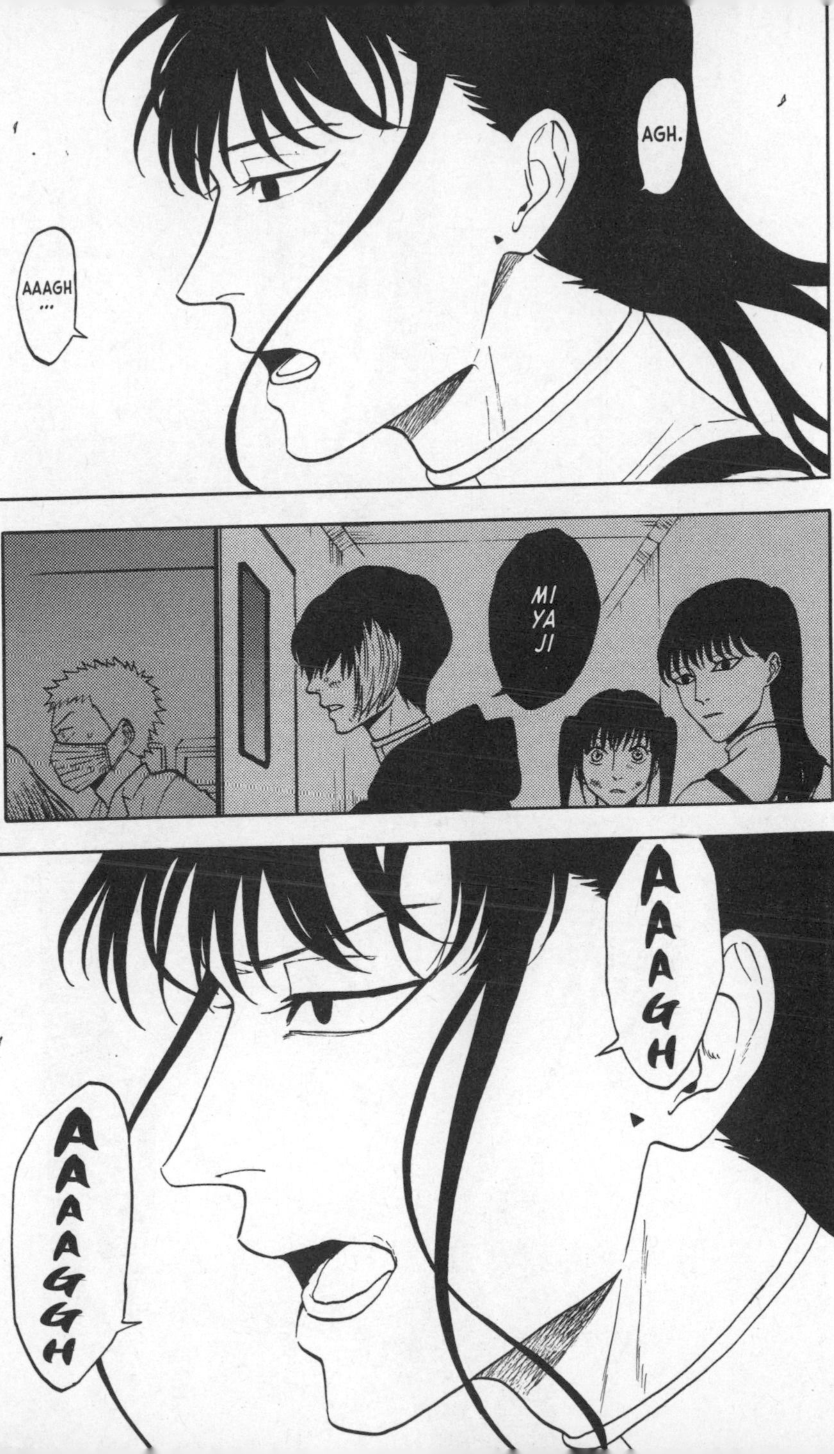
AGH.
AAAGH ...
MI YA JI
AAAGH
AAAAAGGH

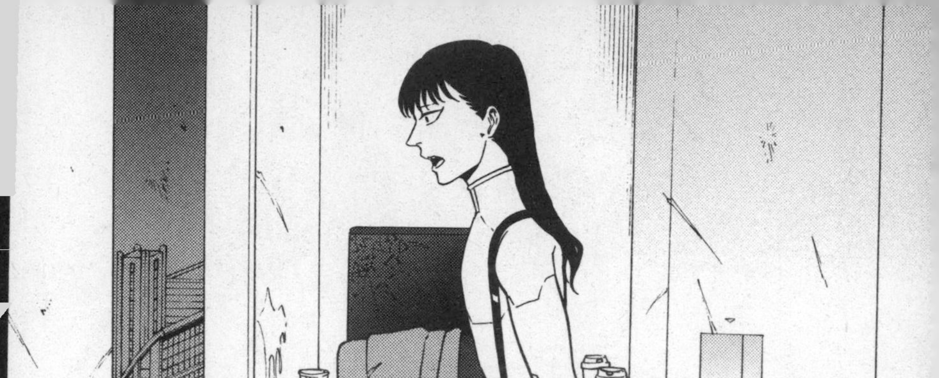
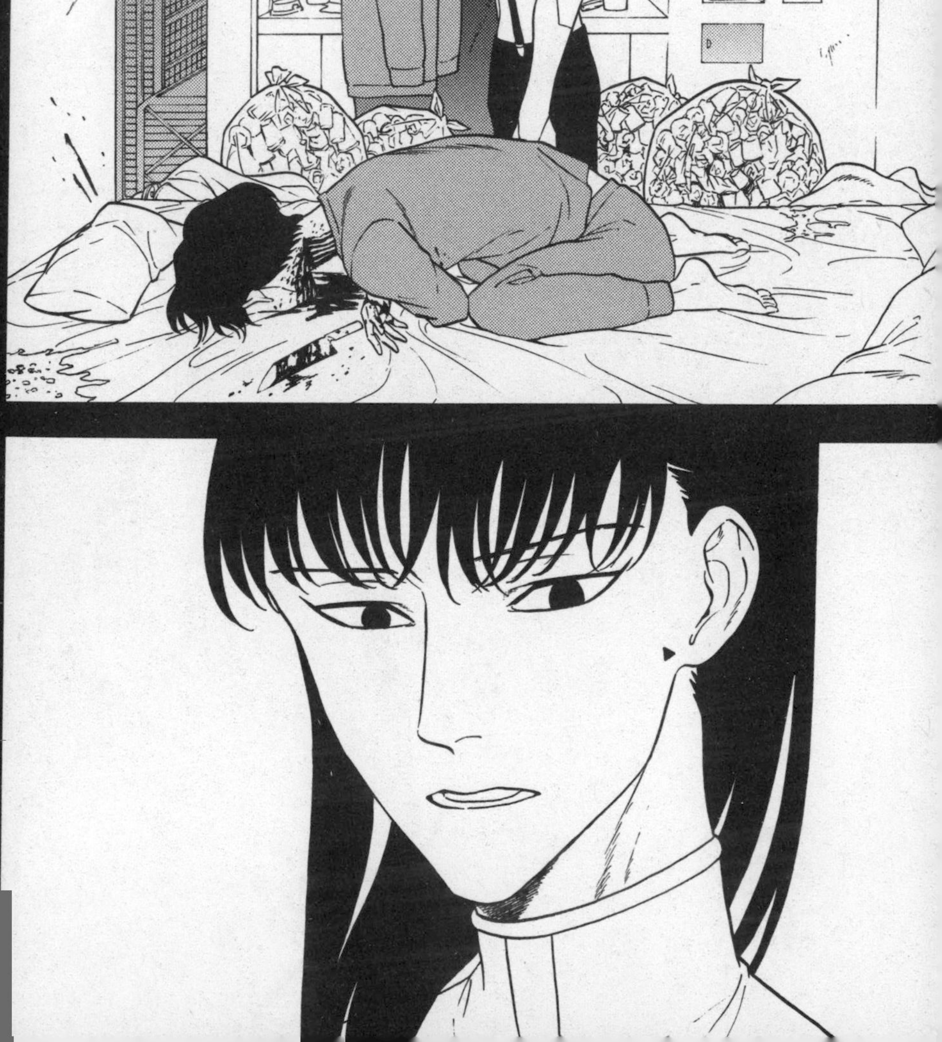

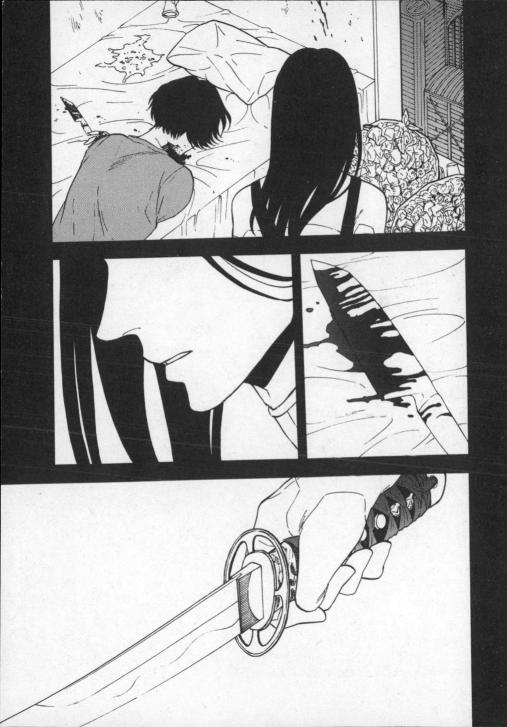

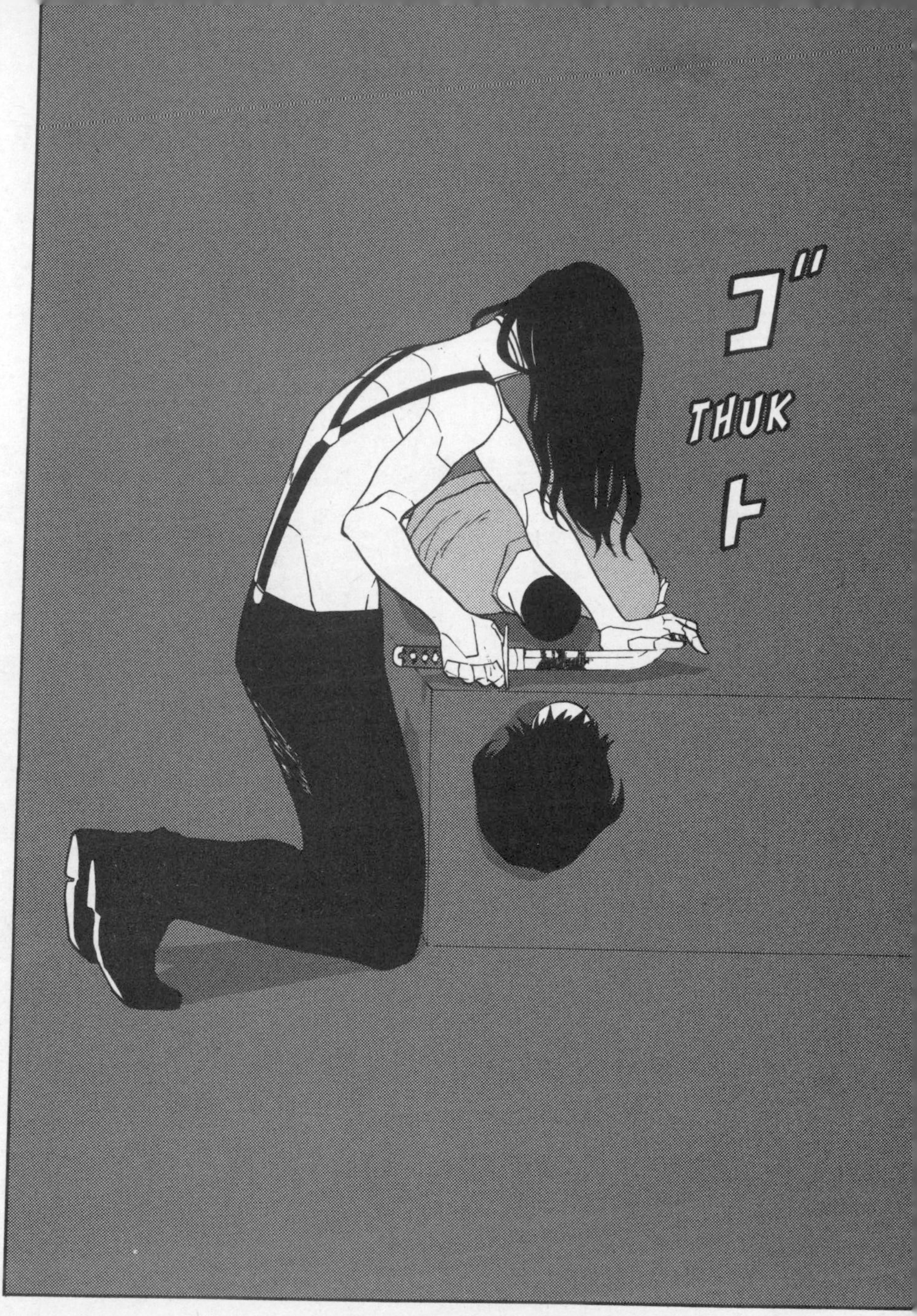
ゴ
THUK
ト

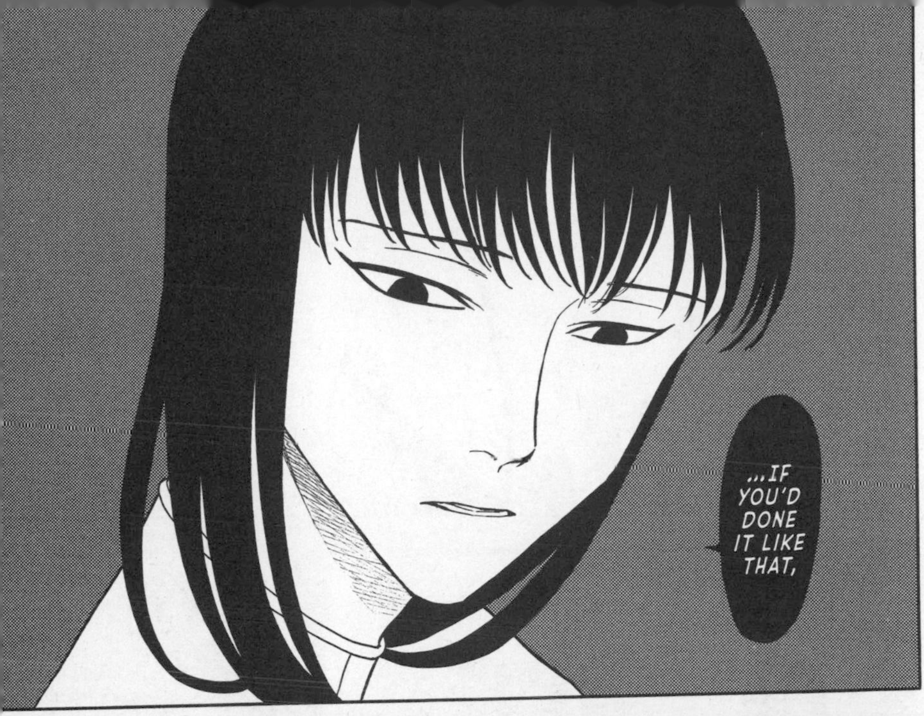
...IF YOU'D DONE IT LIKE THAT,
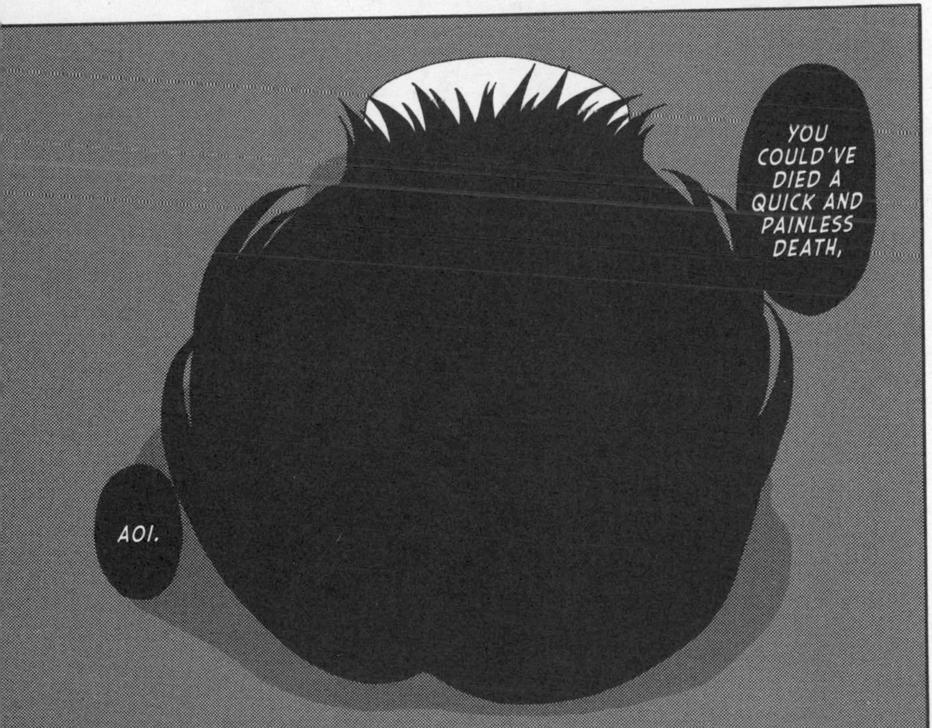
YOU COULD'VE DIED A QUICK AND PAINLESS DEATH,
AOI.

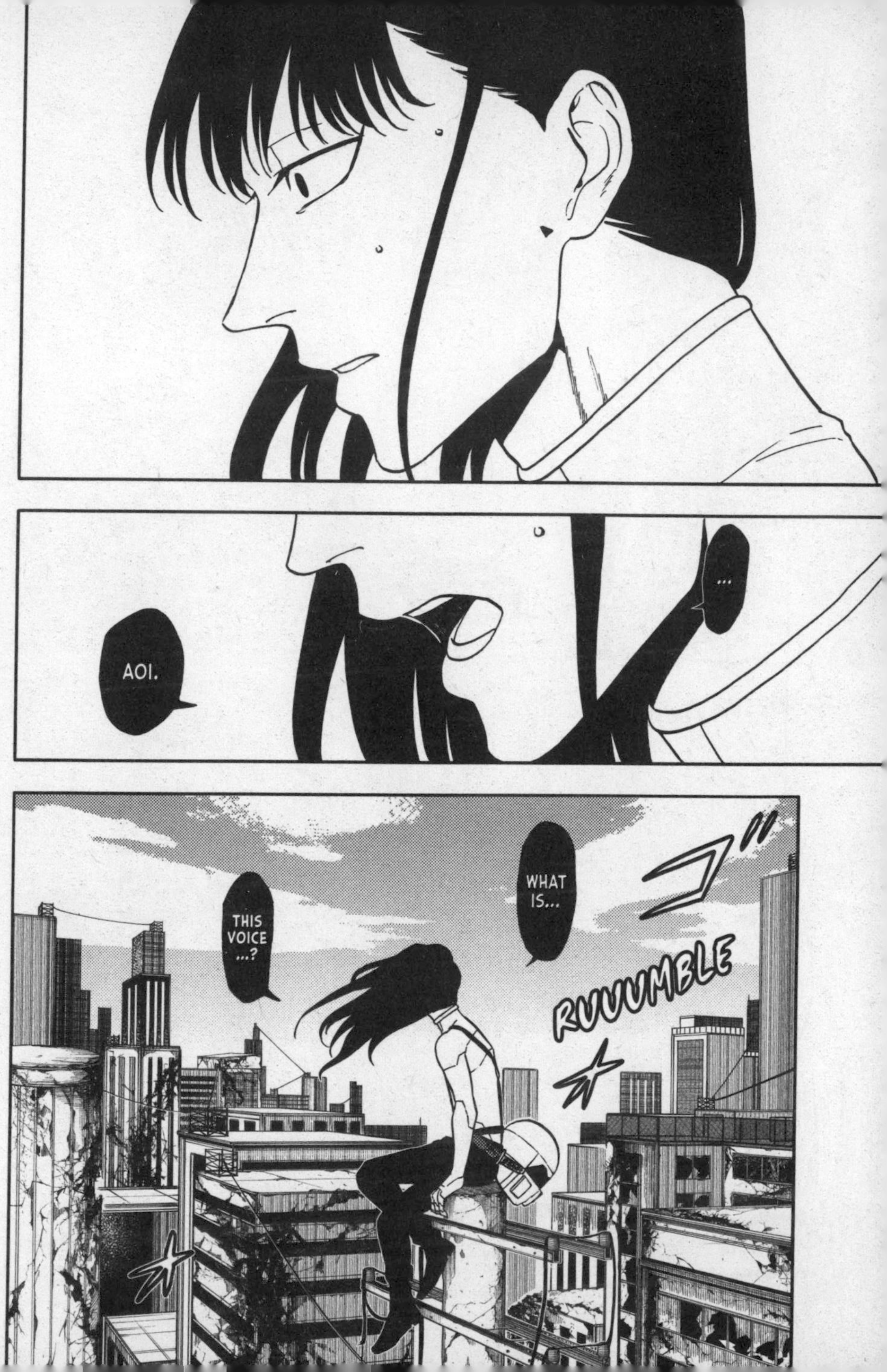
...
AOI.
WHAT IS...
THIS VOICE ...?
RUUUMBLE

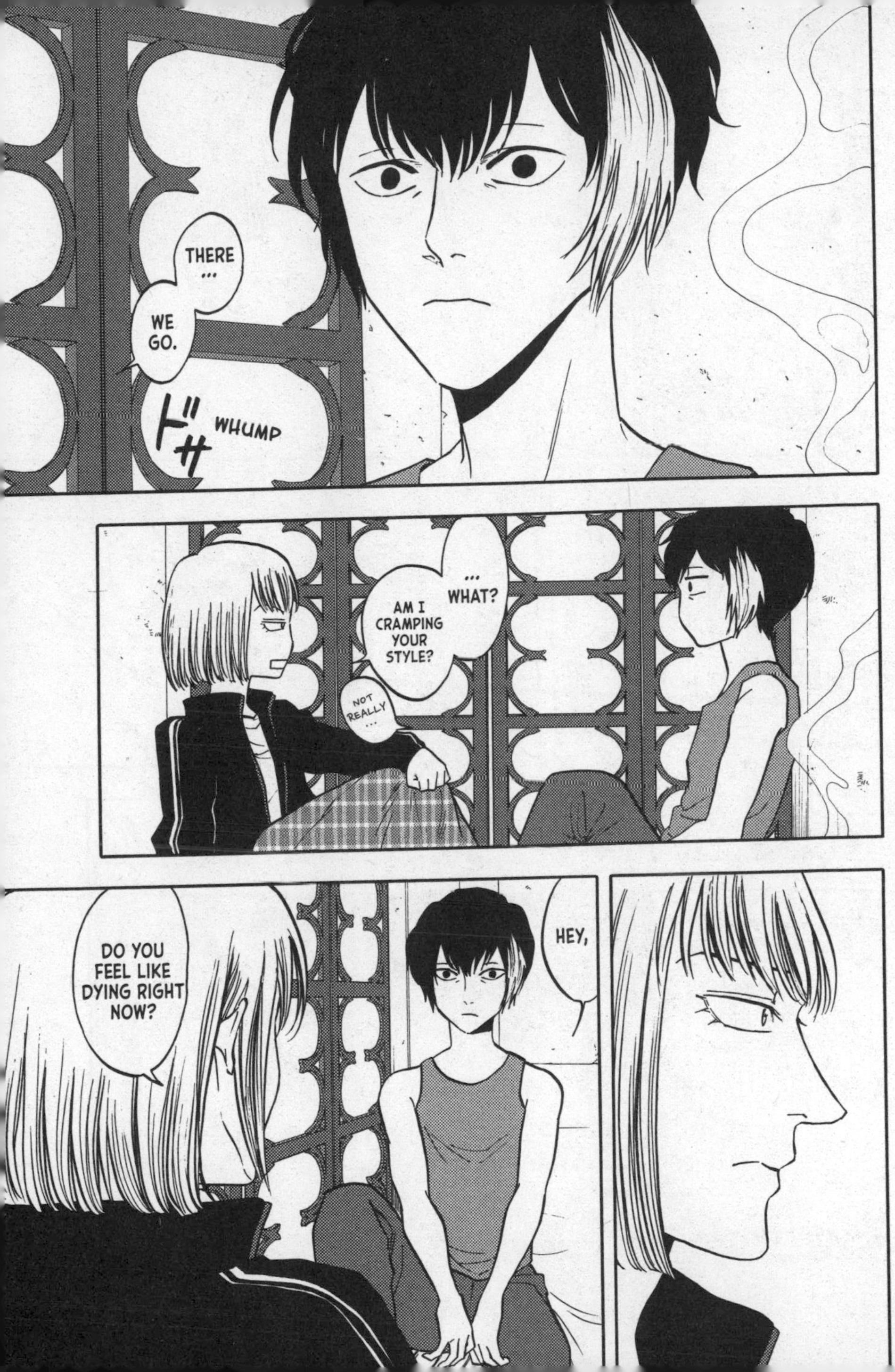
THERE ...
WE GO.
ドサ
WHUMP
... WHAT?
AM I CRAMPING YOUR STYLE?
NOT REALLY ...
HEY,
DO YOU FEEL LIKE DYING RIGHT NOW?

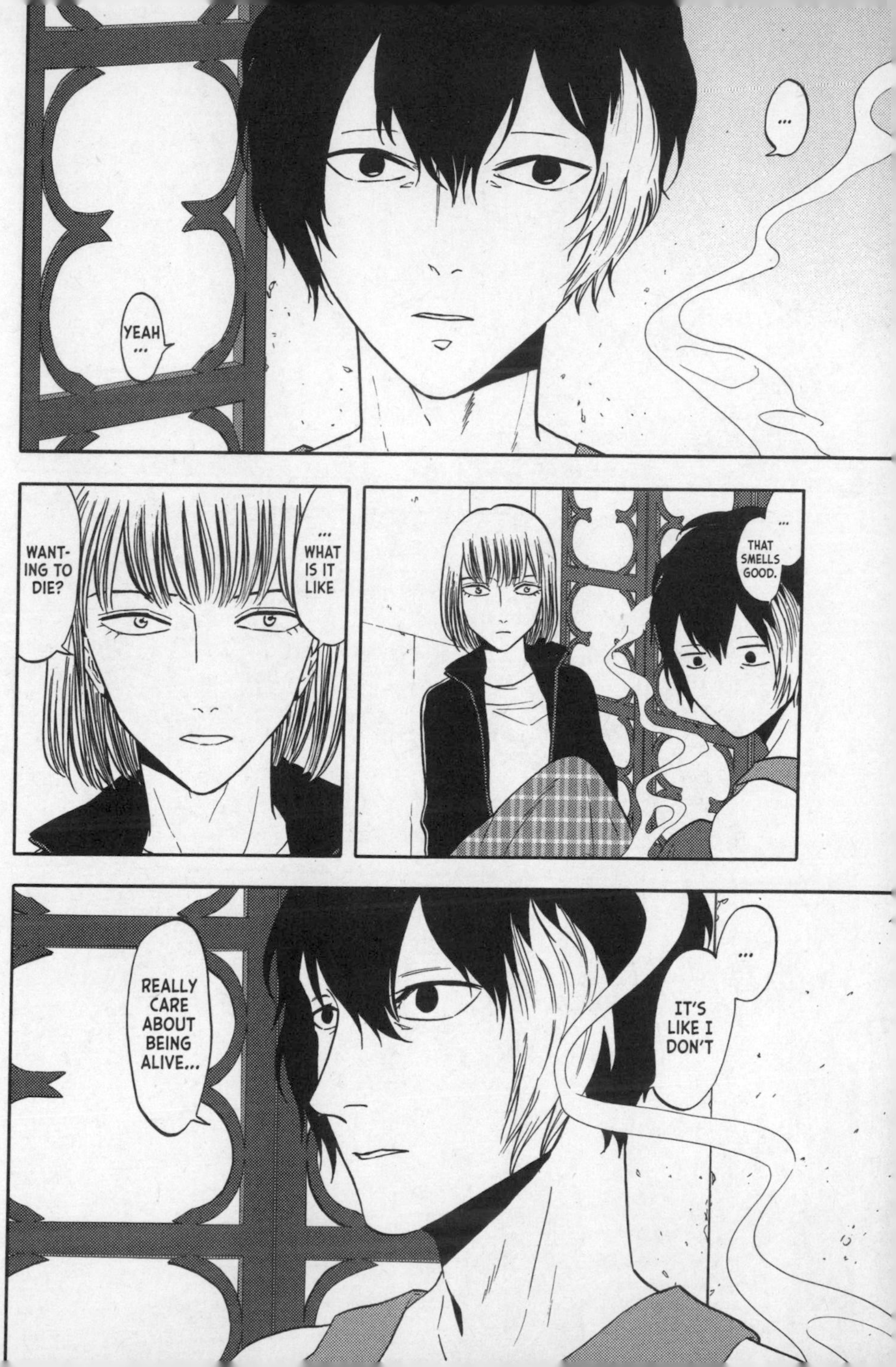
...
YEAH ...
... THAT SMELLS GOOD.
... WHAT IS IT LIKE
WANT-ING TO DIE?
... IT'S LIKE I DON'T
REALLY CARE ABOUT BEING ALIVE...

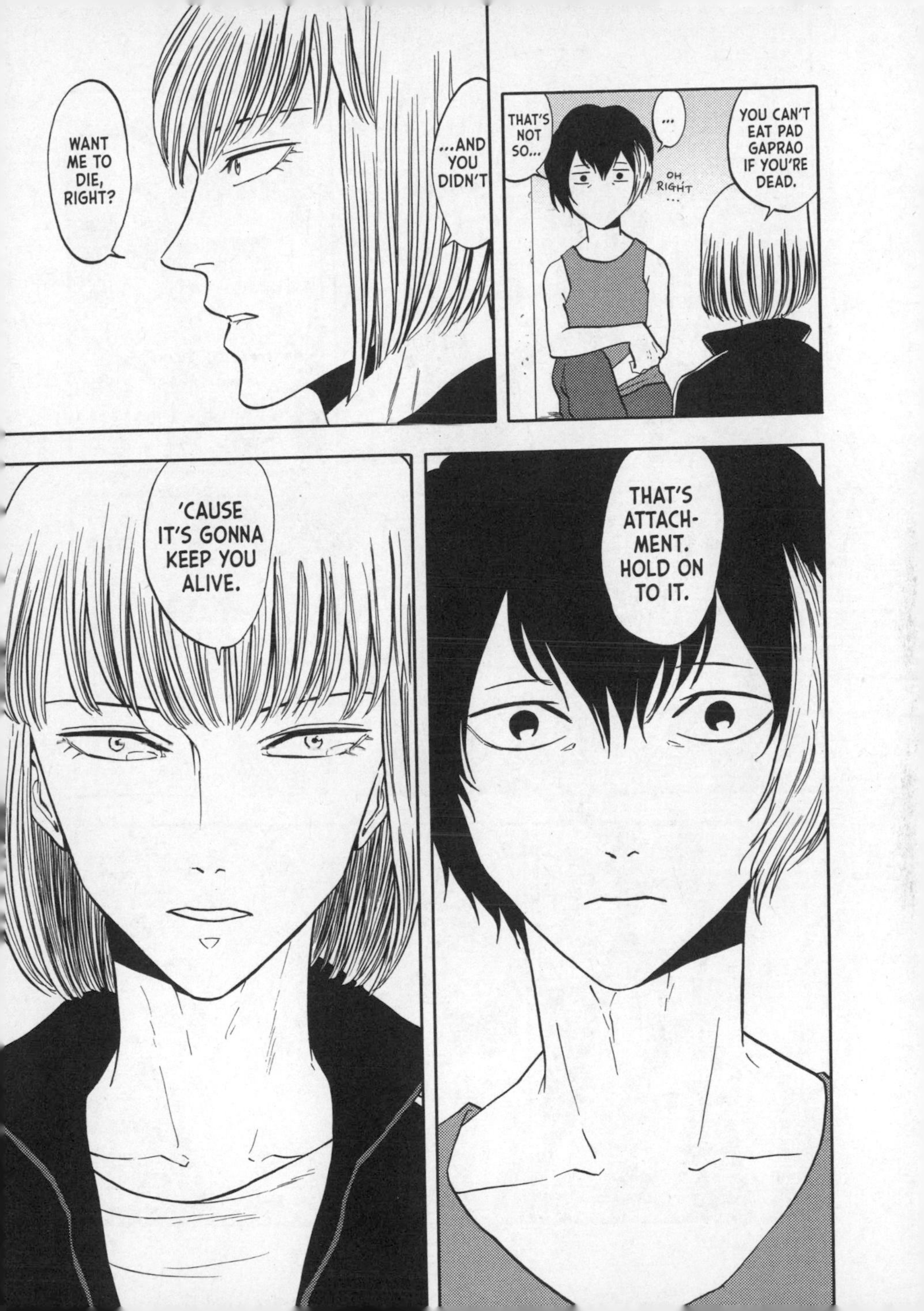
YOU CAN'T EAT PAD GAPRAO IF YOU'RE DEAD.
...
OH RIGHT ...
THAT'S NOT SO...
...AND YOU DIDN'T
WANT ME TO DIE, RIGHT?
THAT'S ATTACHMENT. HOLD ON TO IT.
'CAUSE IT'S GONNA KEEP YOU ALIVE.

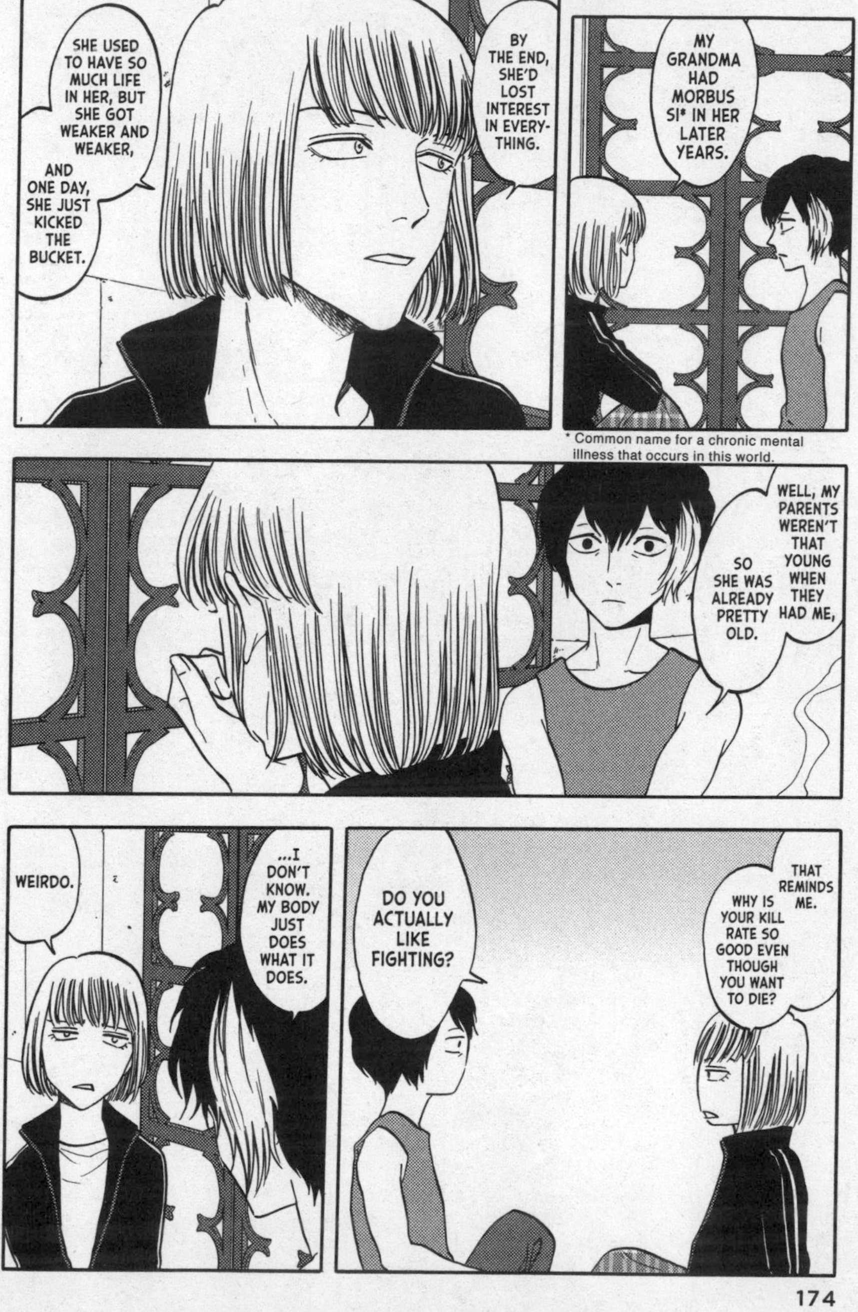
MY GRANDMA HAD MORBUS SI* IN HER LATER YEARS.
BY THE END, SHE'D LOST INTEREST IN EVERY-THING.
SHE USED TO HAVE SO MUCH LIFE IN HER, BUT SHE GOT WEAKER AND WEAKER,
AND ONE DAY, SHE JUST KICKED THE BUCKET.
WELL, MY PARENTS WEREN'T THAT YOUNG WHEN THEY HAD ME,
SO SHE WAS ALREADY PRETTY OLD.
THAT REMINDS ME.
WHY IS YOUR KILL RATE SO GOOD EVEN THOUGH YOU WANT TO DIE?
DO YOU ACTUALLY LIKE FIGHTING?
...I DON'T KNOW. MY BODY JUST DOES WHAT IT DOES.
WEIRDO.

* Common name for a chronic mental illness that occurs in this world.

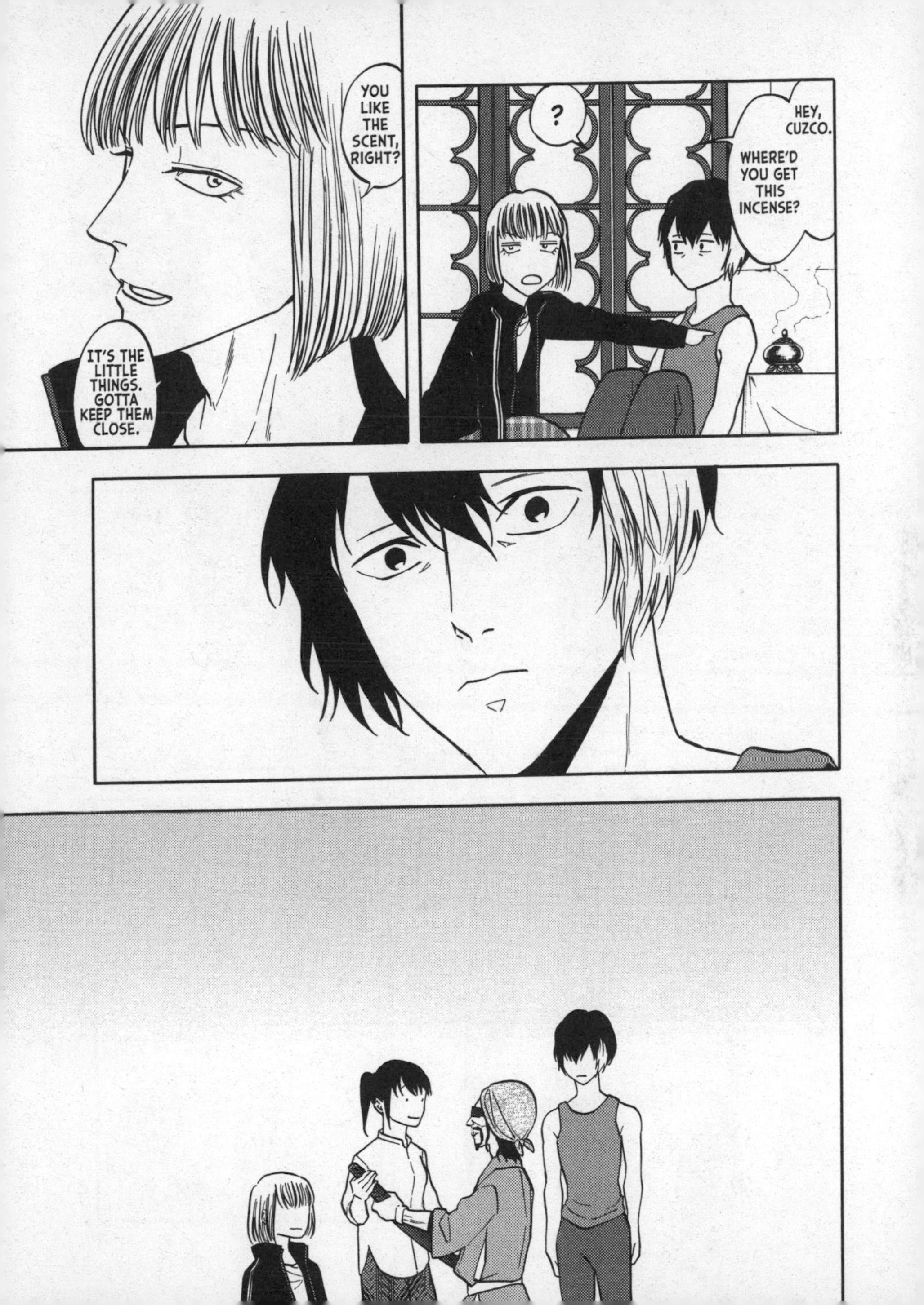
HEY, CUZCO.
WHERE'D YOU GET THIS INCENSE?
?
YOU LIKE THE SCENT, RIGHT?
IT'S THE LITTLE THINGS. GOTTA KEEP THEM CLOSE.

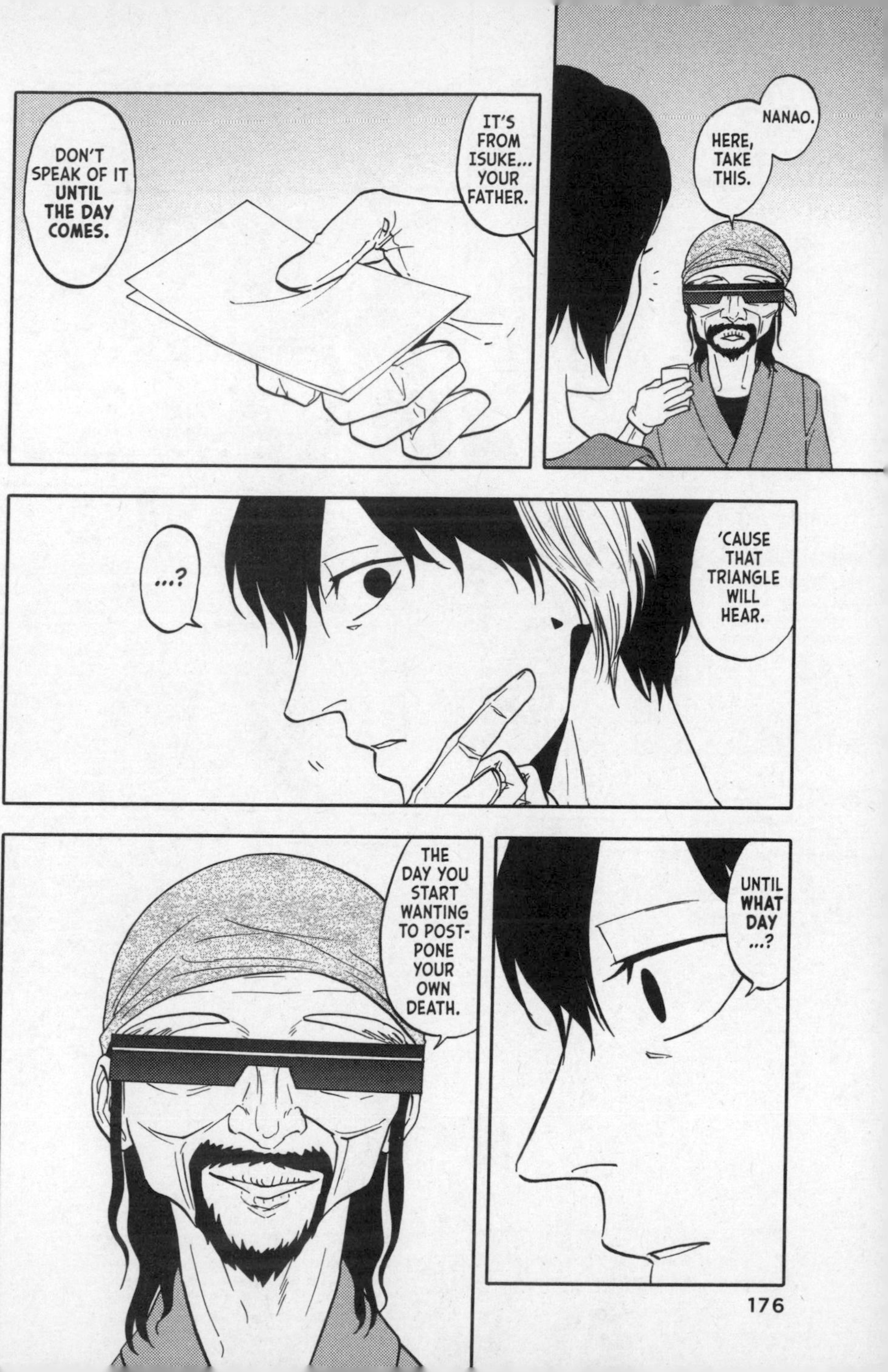
NANAO.
HERE, TAKE THIS.
IT'S FROM ISUKE... YOUR FATHER.
DON'T SPEAK OF IT UNTIL THE DAY COMES.
'CAUSE THAT TRIANGLE WILL HEAR.
...?
UNTIL WHAT DAY ...?
THE DAY YOU START WANTING TO POST-PONE YOUR OWN DEATH.

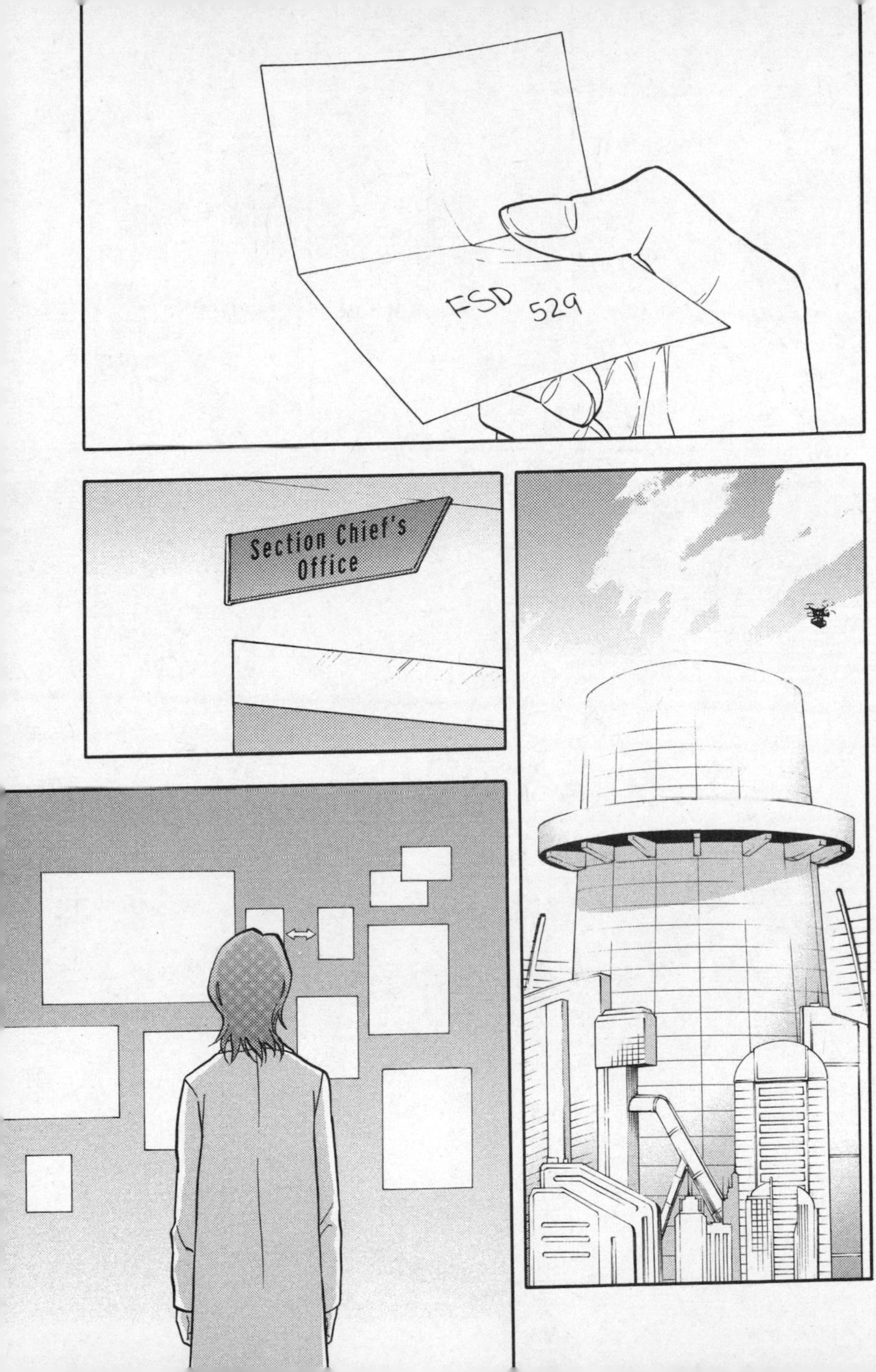
FSD 529
Section Chief's Office

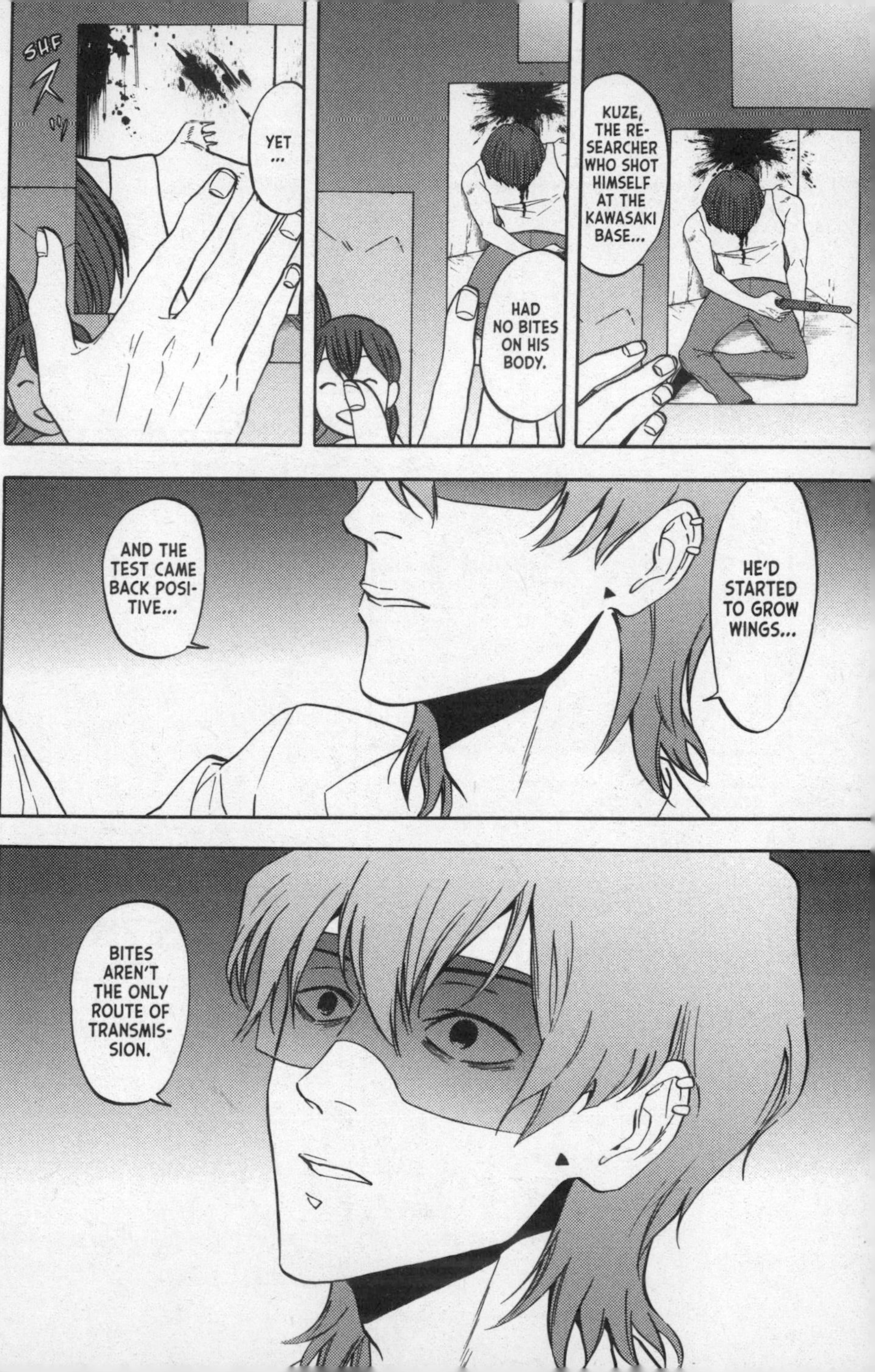
KUZE, THE RE-SEARCHER WHO SHOT HIMSELF AT THE KAWASAKI BASE...
HAD NO BITES ON HIS BODY.
SHF
スッ
YET ...
HE'D STARTED TO GROW WINGS...
AND THE TEST CAME BACK POSI-TIVE...
BITES AREN'T THE ONLY ROUTE OF TRANSMIS-SION.

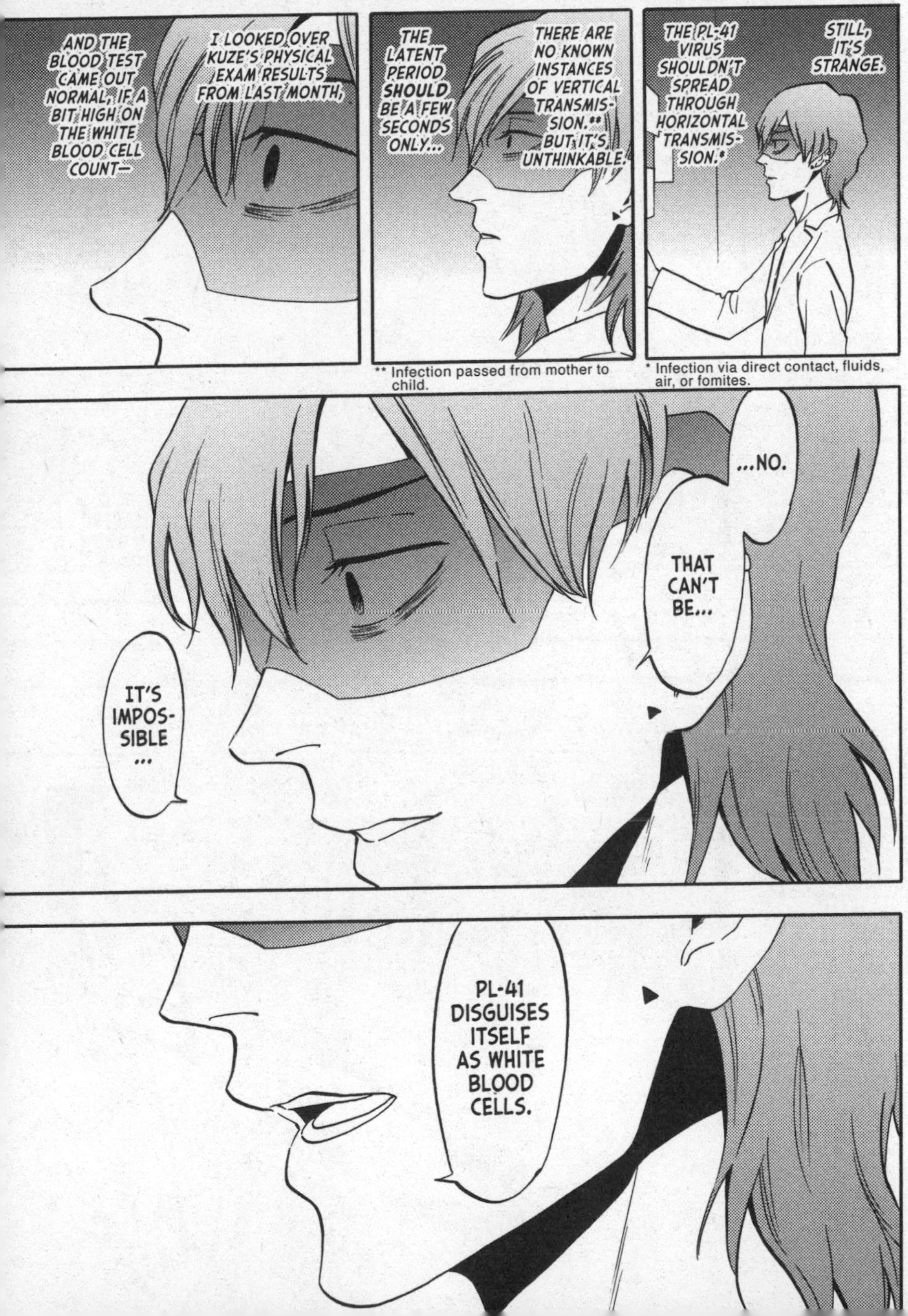
STILL, IT'S STRANGE.
THE PL-41 VIRUS SHOULDN'T SPREAD THROUGH HORIZONTAL TRANSMISSION.*
THERE ARE NO KNOWN INSTANCES OF VERTICAL TRANSMISSION.** BUT IT'S UNTHINKABLE.
THE LATENT PERIOD **SHOULD** BE A FEW SECONDS ONLY...
I LOOKED OVER KUZE'S PHYSICAL EXAM RESULTS FROM LAST MONTH,
AND THE BLOOD TEST CAME OUT NORMAL, IF A BIT HIGH ON THE WHITE BLOOD CELL COUNT—
...NO.
THAT CAN'T BE...
IT'S IMPOSSIBLE...
PL-41 DISGUISES ITSELF AS WHITE BLOOD CELLS.

* Infection via direct contact, fluids, air, or fomites.

** Infection passed from mother to child.

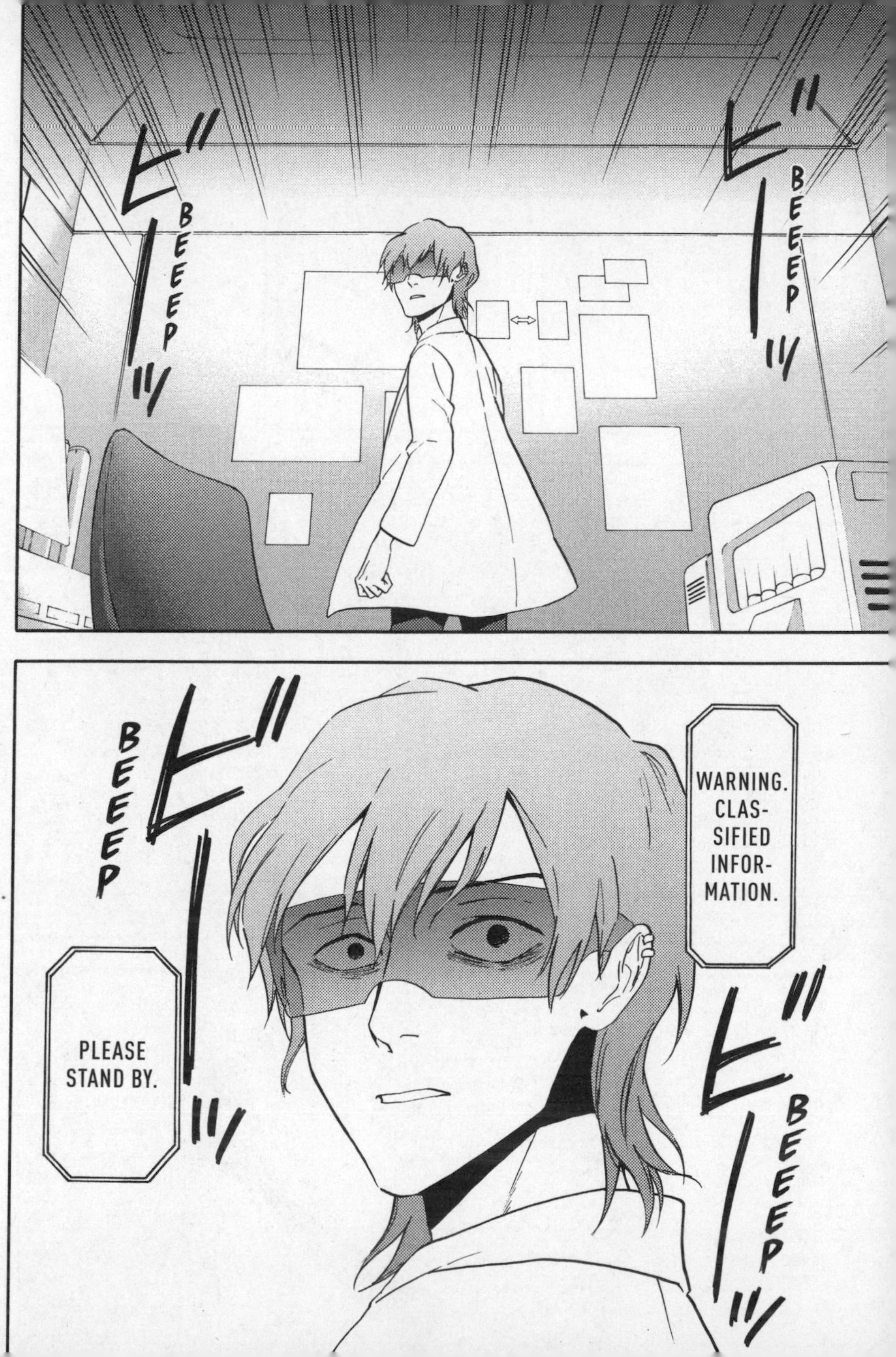
BEEEP
BEEEP
BEEEP
WARNING. CLAS-SIFIED INFOR-MATION.
BEEEP
PLEASE STAND BY.

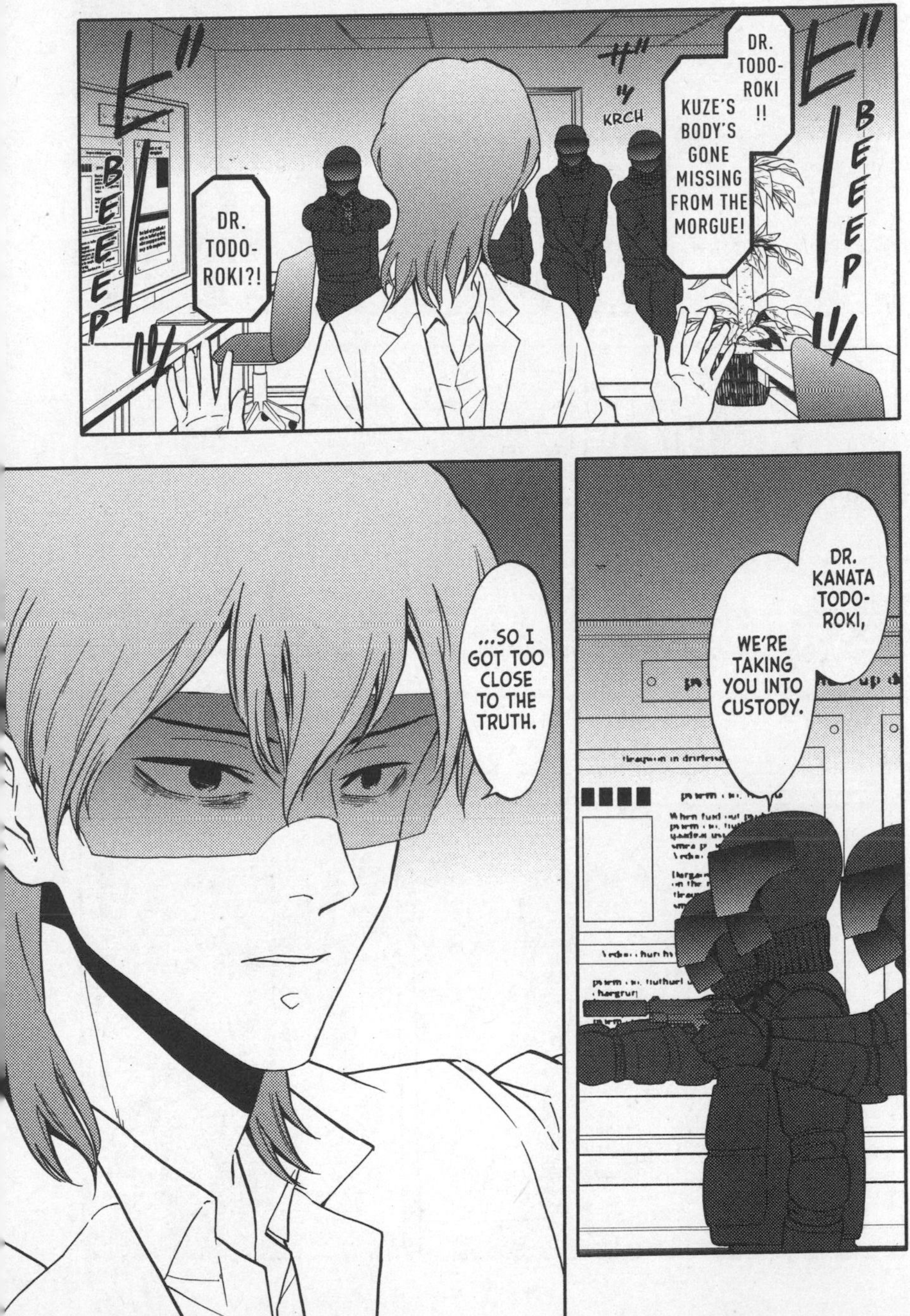
BEEEEP!!
DR. TODO-ROKI !!
KUZE'S BODY'S GONE MISSING FROM THE MORGUE!
KRCH
DR. TODO-ROKI?!
BEEEEP!!
DR. KANATA TODO-ROKI,
WE'RE TAKING YOU INTO CUSTODY.
...SO I GOT TOO CLOSE TO THE TRUTH.

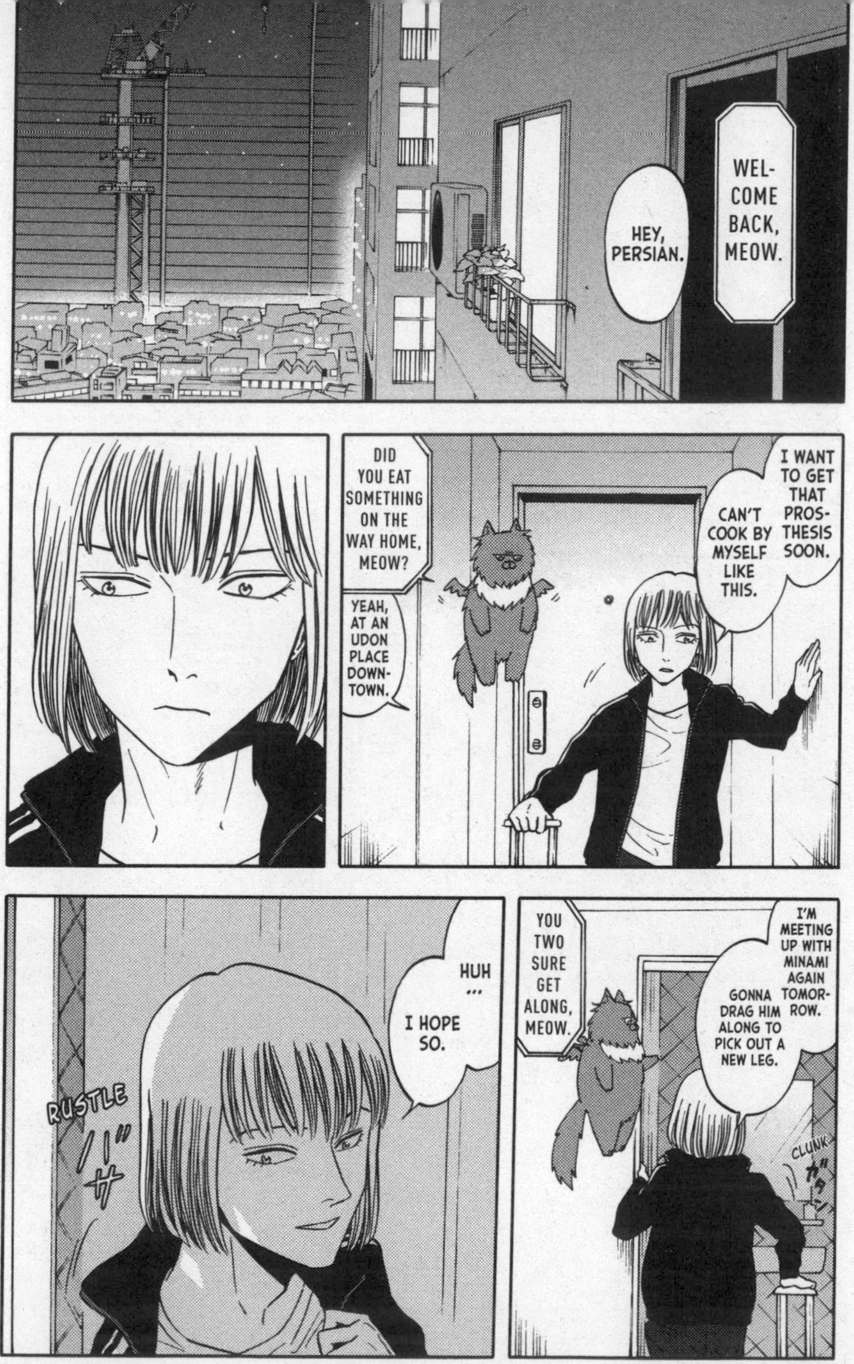
WEL-COME BACK, MEOW.
HEY, PERSIAN.
I WANT TO GET THAT PROS-THESIS SOON.
CAN'T COOK BY MYSELF LIKE THIS.
DID YOU EAT SOMETHING ON THE WAY HOME, MEOW?
YEAH, AT AN UDON PLACE DOWN-TOWN.
I'M MEETING UP WITH MINAMI AGAIN TOMOR-ROW.
GONNA DRAG HIM ALONG TO PICK OUT A NEW LEG.
YOU TWO SURE GET ALONG, MEOW.
CLUNK
HUH ...
I HOPE SO.
RUSTLE

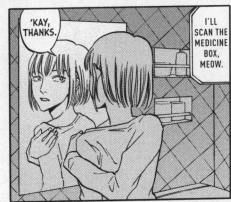

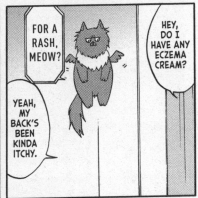

HEY, DO I HAVE ANY ECZEMA CREAM?
FOR A RASH, MEOW?
YEAH, MY BACK'S BEEN KINDA ITCHY.
I'LL SCAN THE MEDICINE BOX, MEOW.
'KAY, THANKS.

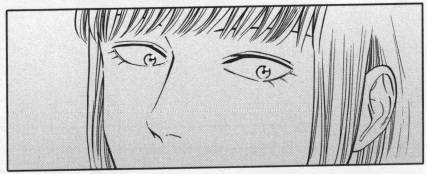

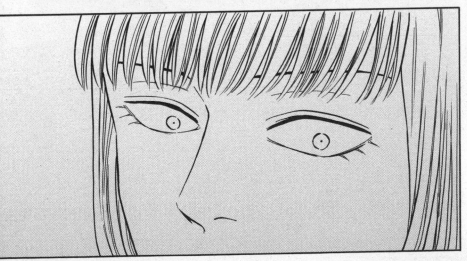

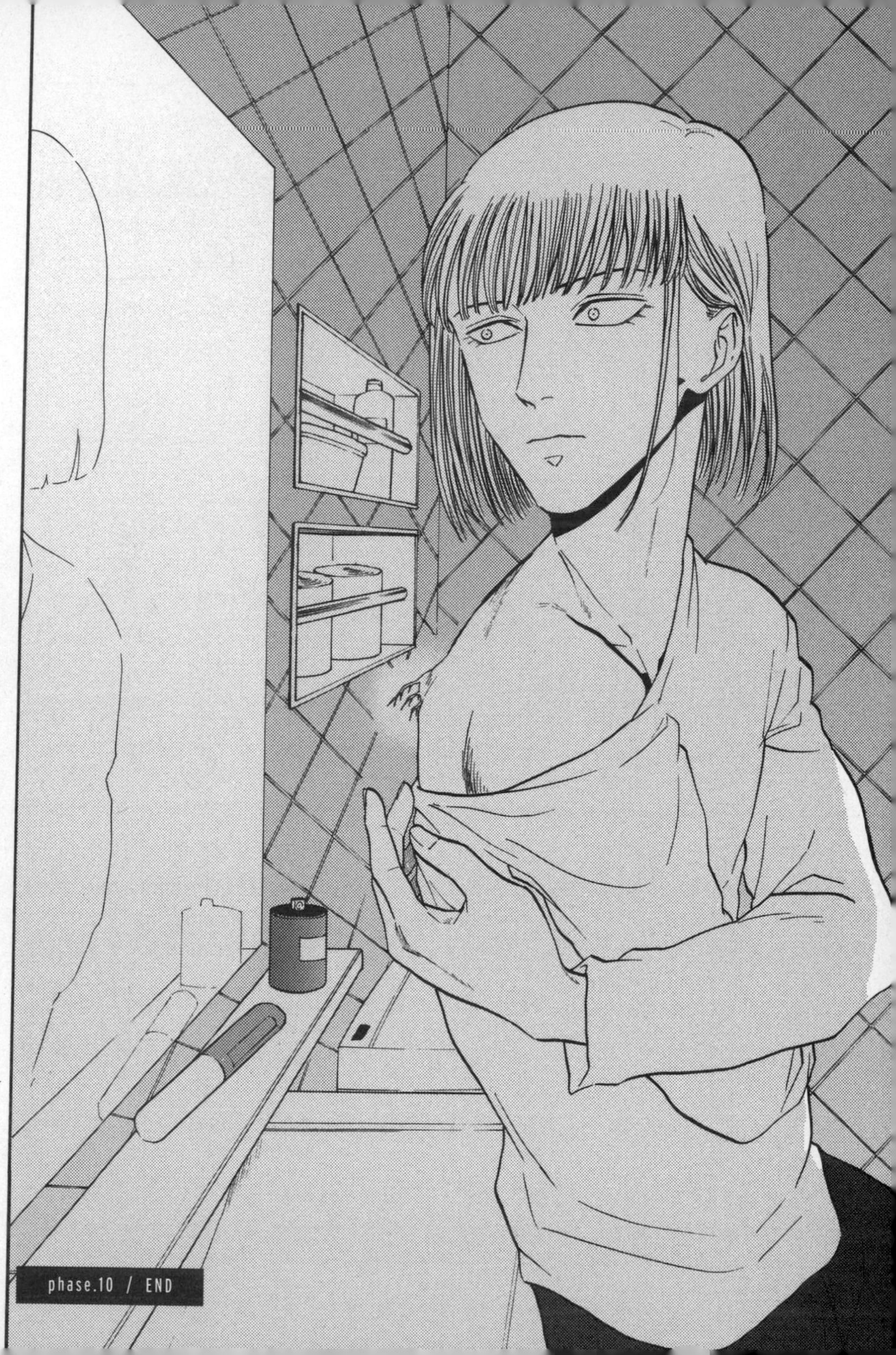
phase.10 / END

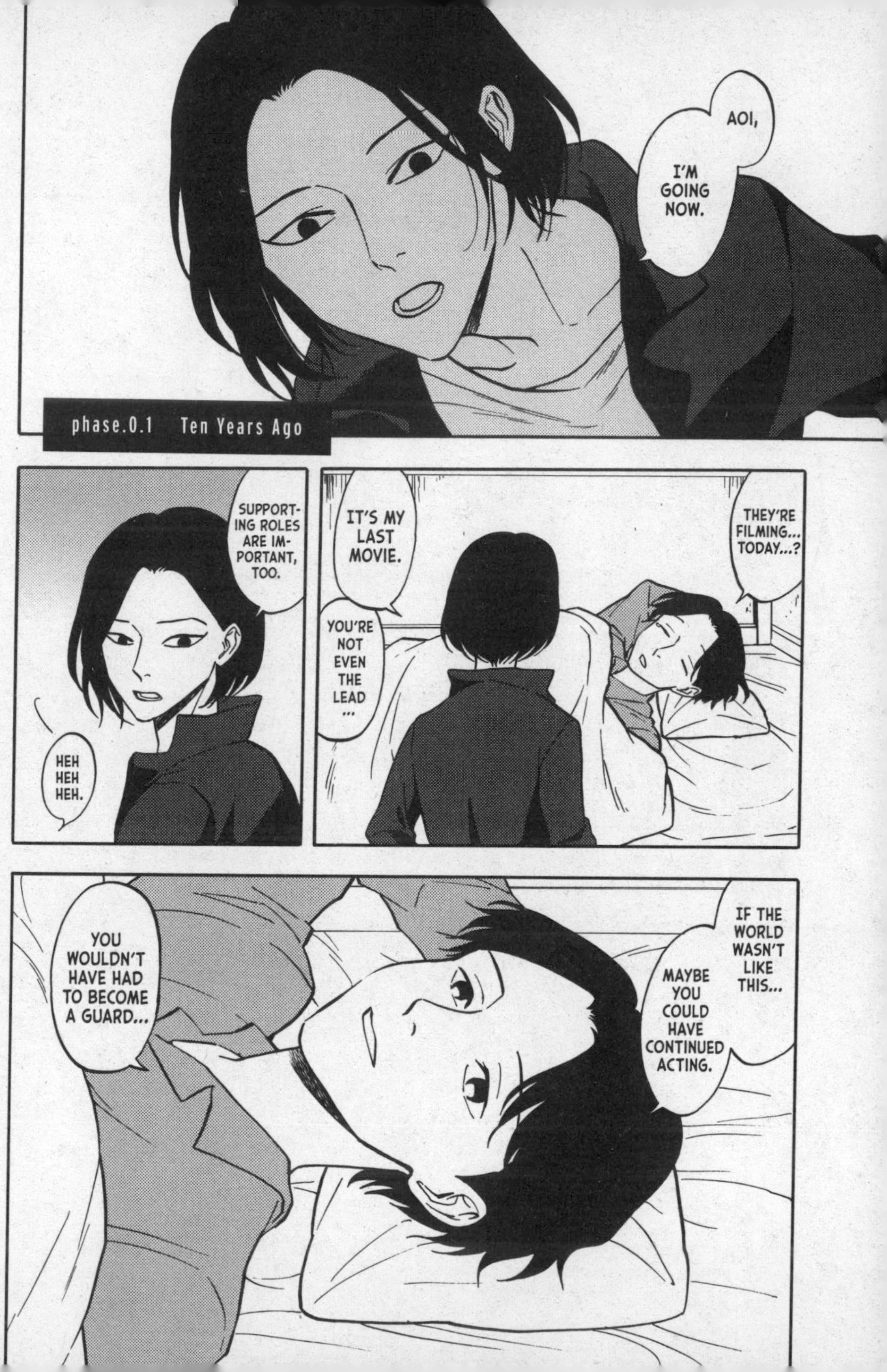
AOI,
I'M GOING NOW.
phase.0.1 Ten Years Ago
THEY'RE FILMING... TODAY...?
IT'S MY LAST MOVIE.
YOU'RE NOT EVEN THE LEAD...
SUPPORTING ROLES ARE IMPORTANT, TOO.
HEH HEH HEH.
IF THE WORLD WASN'T LIKE THIS...
MAYBE YOU COULD HAVE CONTINUED ACTING.
YOU WOULDN'T HAVE HAD TO BECOME A GUARD...

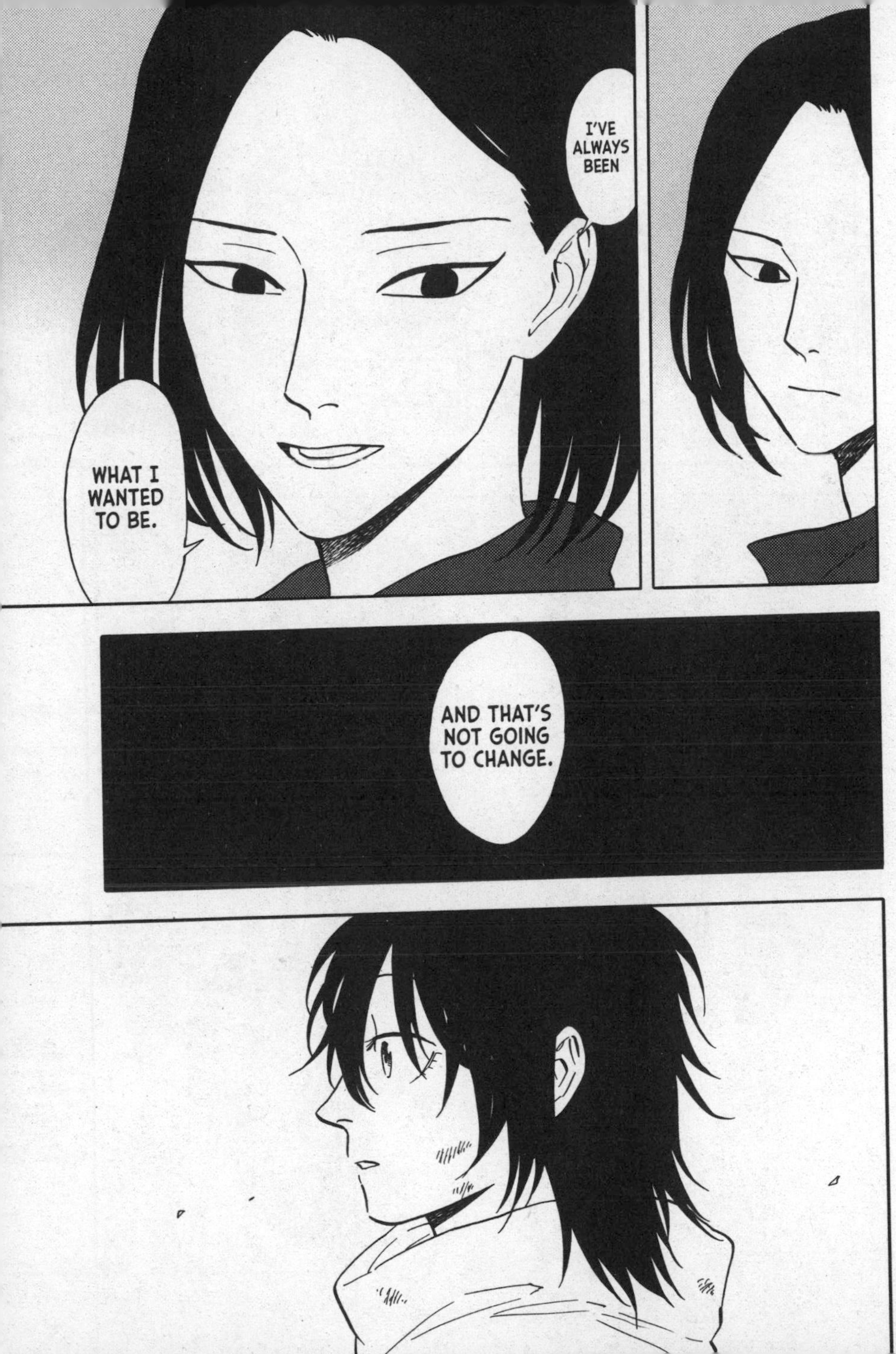
I'VE ALWAYS BEEN
WHAT I WANTED TO BE.
AND THAT'S NOT GOING TO CHANGE.

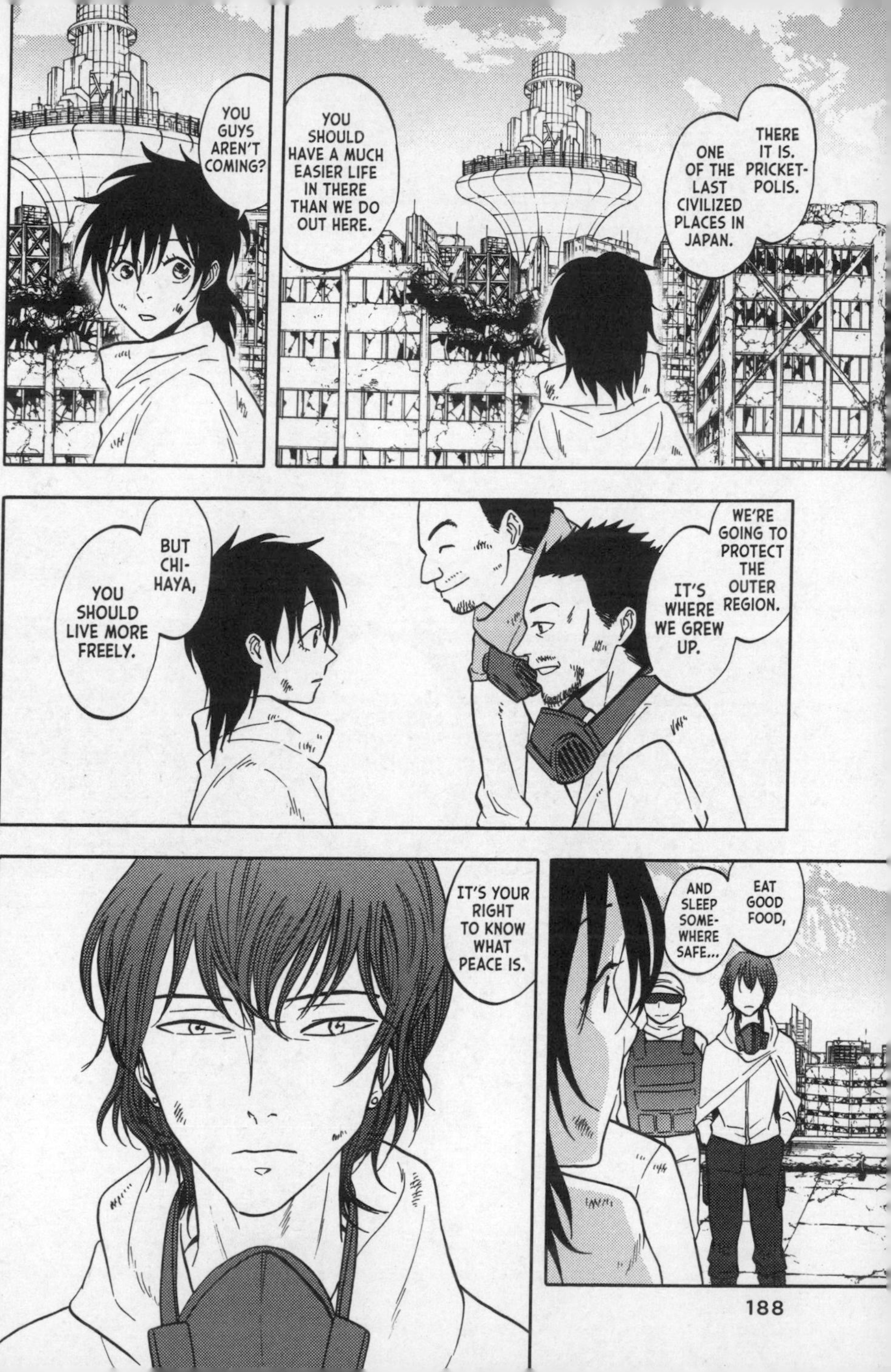
THERE IT IS. PRICKET-POLIS.
ONE OF THE LAST CIVILIZED PLACES IN JAPAN.
YOU SHOULD HAVE A MUCH EASIER LIFE IN THERE THAN WE DO OUT HERE.
YOU GUYS AREN'T COMING?
WE'RE GOING TO PROTECT THE OUTER REGION.
IT'S WHERE WE GREW UP.
BUT CHI-HAYA,
YOU SHOULD LIVE MORE FREELY.
EAT GOOD FOOD,
AND SLEEP SOME-WHERE SAFE...
IT'S YOUR RIGHT TO KNOW WHAT PEACE IS.

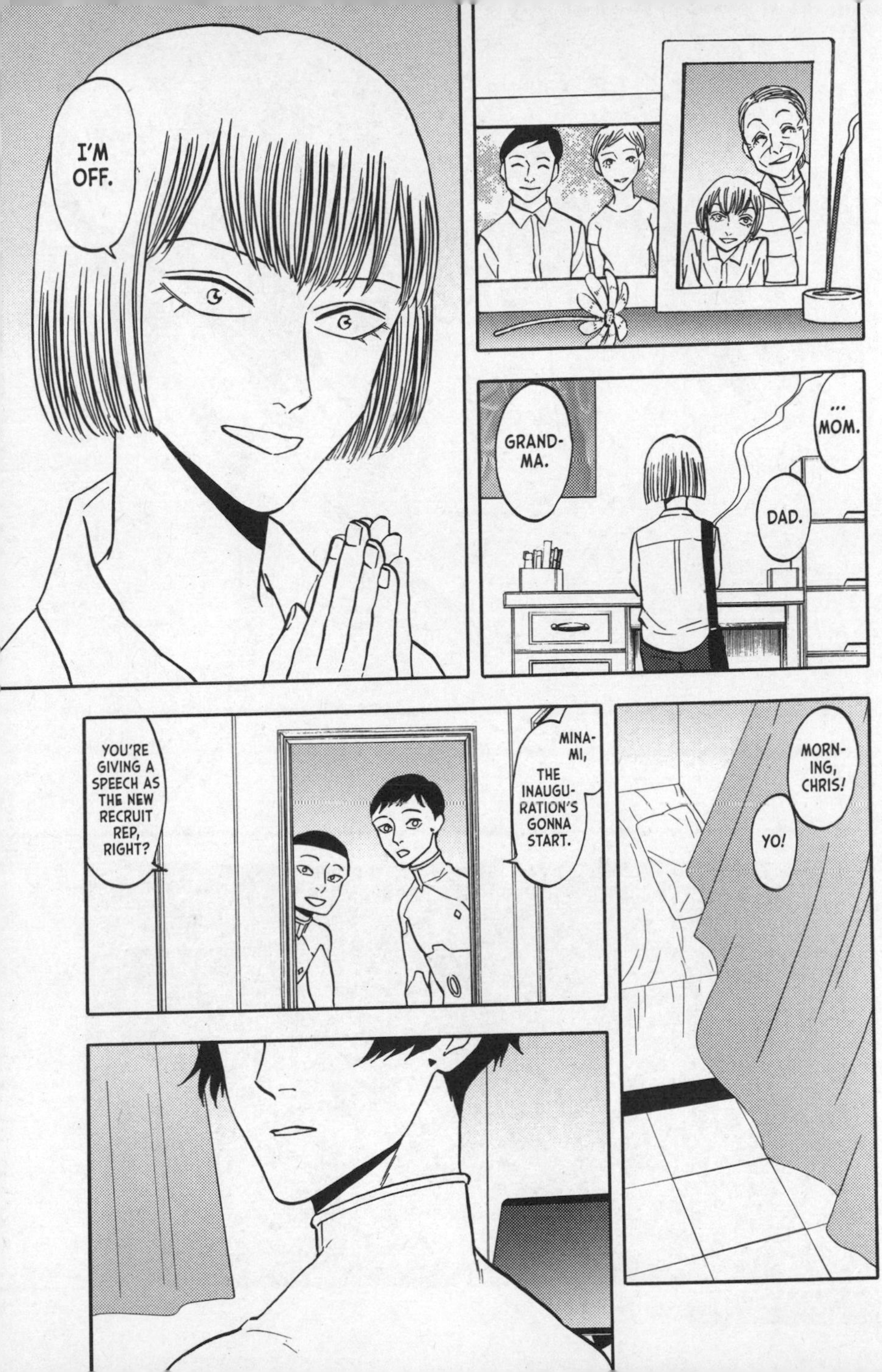
... MOM.
DAD.
GRAND-MA.
I'M OFF.
MORN-ING, CHRIS!
YO!
MINA-MI, THE INAUGU-RATION'S GONNA START.
YOU'RE GIVING A SPEECH AS THE NEW RECRUIT REP, RIGHT?

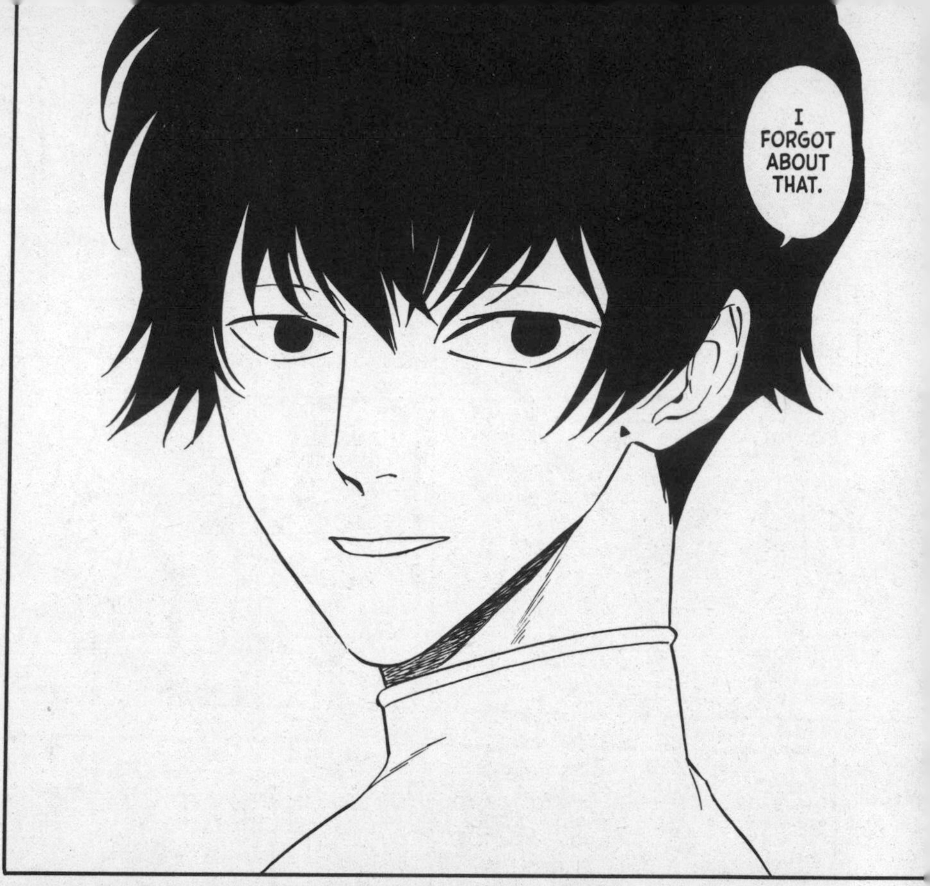
I FORGOT ABOUT THAT.

(Design)
Tadashi Hisamochi
(hive)

(Collaboration)
Nippon Shokubai Co., Ltd.

(Managing Editor)
J-Ko
S-Hara
N-Yama

(Assistants)
Chiguro Tsukishima
Yoko
Tani-H
Kazuyo Haraguchi
Yukie Saito
Shurin
Yui Tatami

(Special Thanks To)
You, dear reader

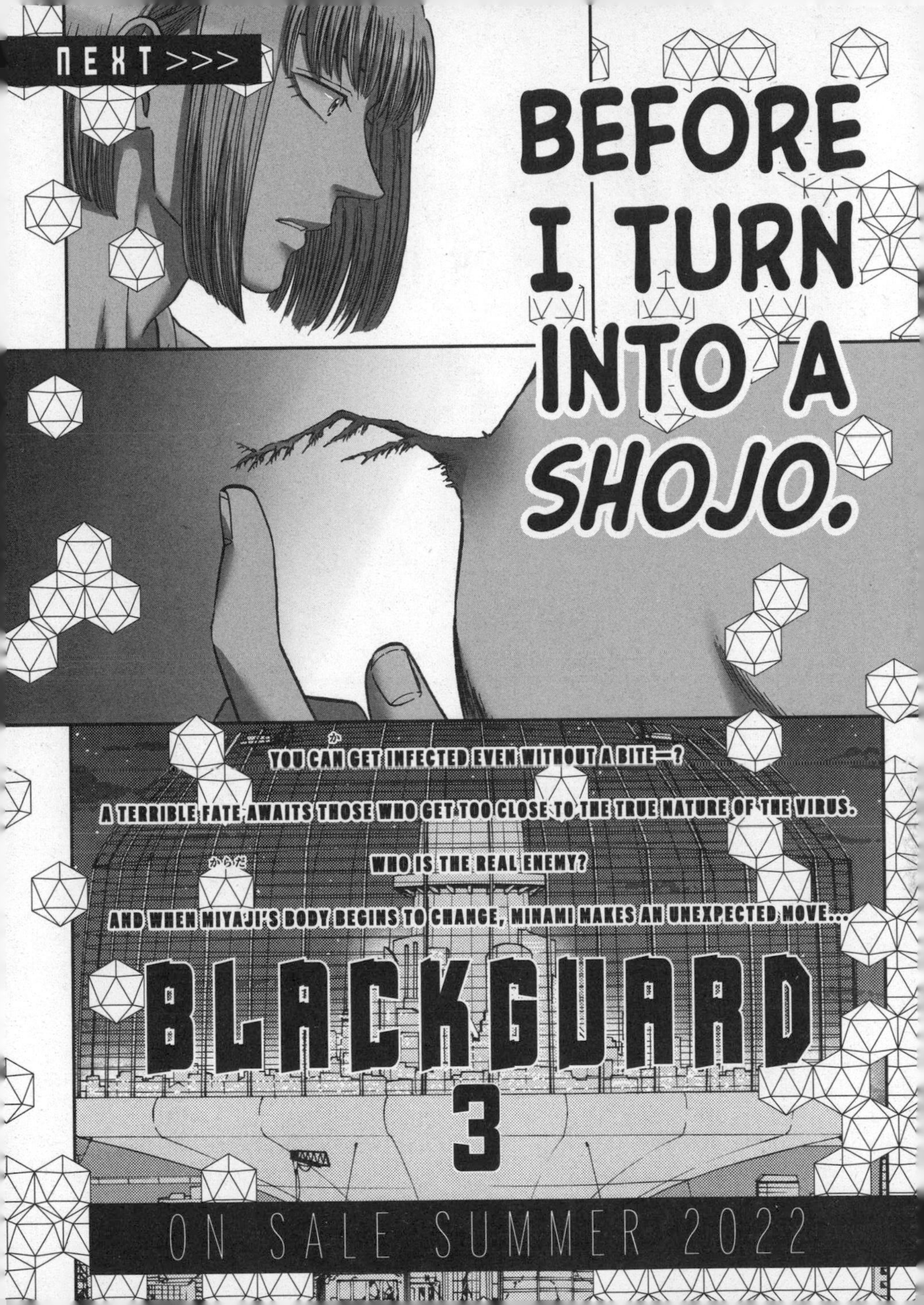
NEXT>>>
BEFORE I TURN INTO A SHOJO.
YOU CAN GET INFECTED EVEN WITHOUT A BITE—?
A TERRIBLE FATE AWAITS THOSE WHO GET TOO CLOSE TO THE TRUE NATURE OF THE VIRUS.
WHO IS THE REAL ENEMY?
AND WHEN MIYAJI'S BODY BEGINS TO CHANGE, MINAMI MAKES AN UNEXPECTED MOVE...
BLACKGUARD
3
ON SALE SUMMER 2022

BLACKGUARD

RYO HANADA

2

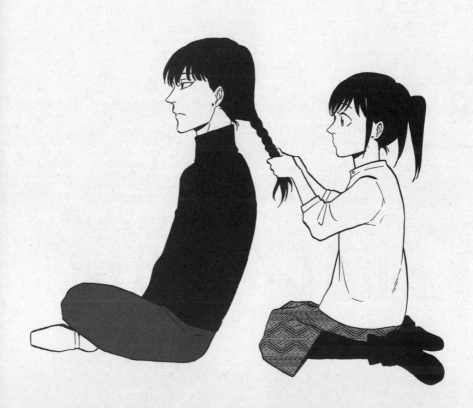

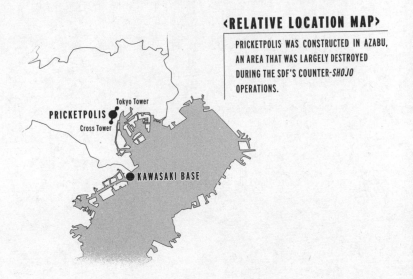

<RELATIVE LOCATION MAP>

PRICKETPOLIS WAS CONSTRUCTED IN AZABU, AN AREA THAT WAS LARGELY DESTROYED DURING THE SDF'S COUNTER-*SHOJO* OPERATIONS.

Tokyo Tower
PRICKETPOLIS
Cross Tower
KAWASAKI BASE

<LOGO OF WHITE SHIELD SECURITY, INC.>

AFTER THE DISSOLUTION OF THE SDF, THE COMPANY WAS ESTABLISHED UNDER GOVERNMENT LEADERSHIP, THEN LATER PRIVATIZED. FIELD PERSONNEL IN THE SECURITY DEPARTMENT ARE ONLY PERMITTED TO CARRY AND USE THEIR REGISTERED WEAPONS WHILE ON DUTY.

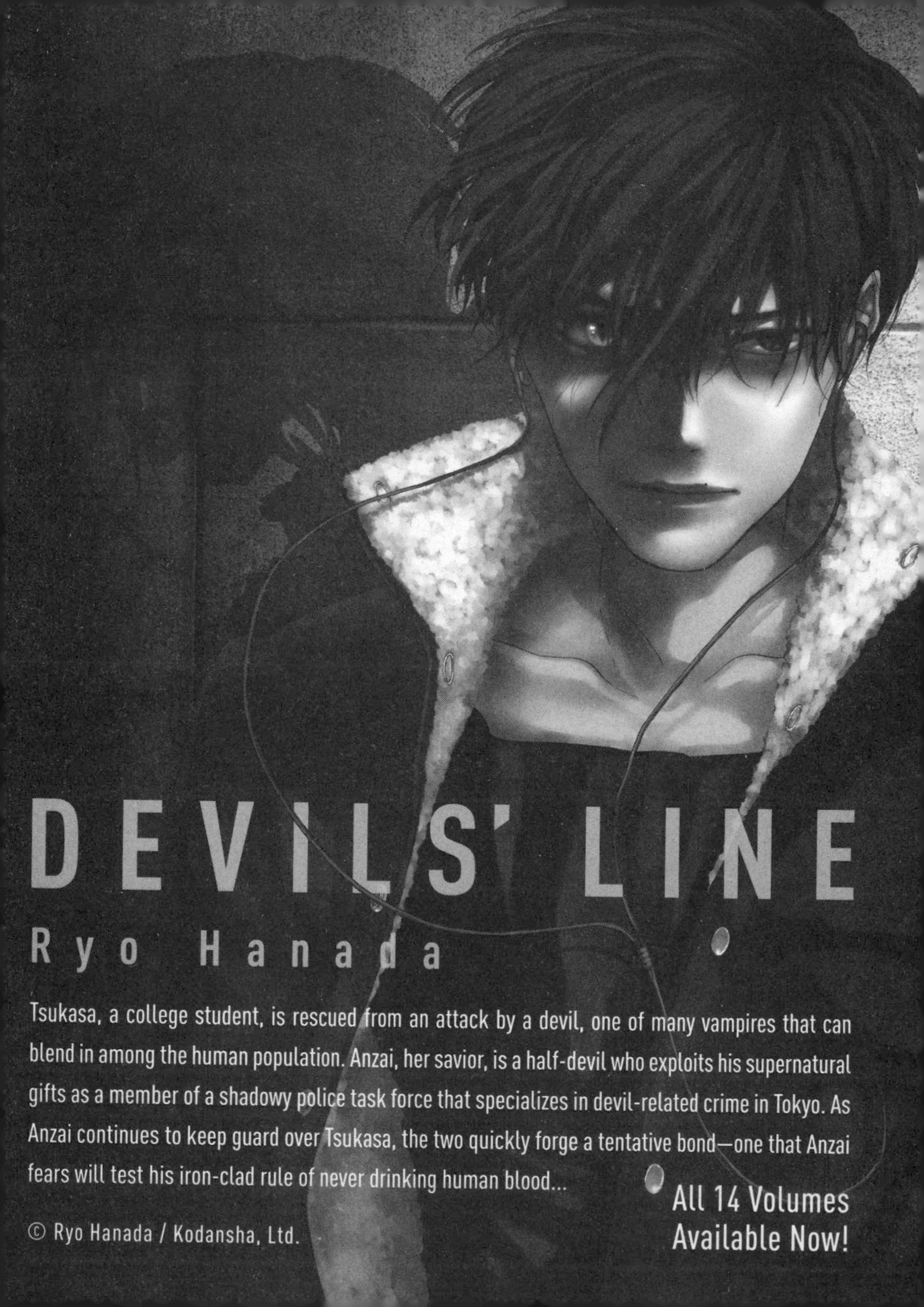
DEVILS' LINE
Ryo Hanada
Tsukasa, a college student, is rescued from an attack by a devil, one of many vampires that can blend in among the human population. Anzai, her savior, is a half-devil who exploits his supernatural gifts as a member of a shadowy police task force that specializes in devil-related crime in Tokyo. As Anzai continues to keep guard over Tsukasa, the two quickly forge a tentative bond—one that Anzai fears will test his iron-clad rule of never drinking human blood...
All 14 Volumes Available Now!
© Ryo Hanada / Kodansha, Ltd.

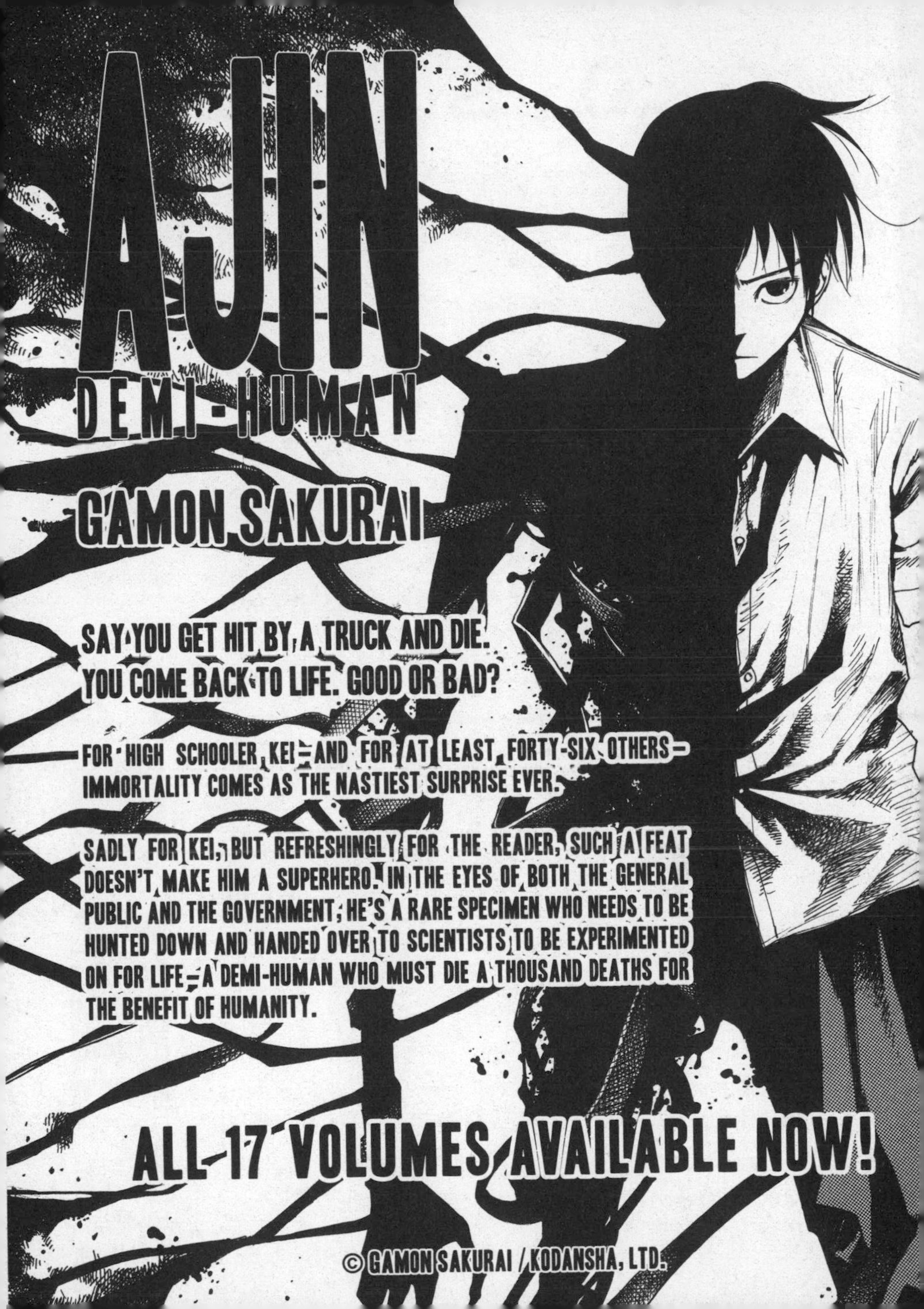
AJIN
DEMI-HUMAN
GAMON SAKURAI
SAY YOU GET HIT BY A TRUCK AND DIE.
YOU COME BACK TO LIFE. GOOD OR BAD?
FOR HIGH SCHOOLER KEI—AND FOR AT LEAST FORTY-SIX OTHERS—IMMORTALITY COMES AS THE NASTIEST SURPRISE EVER.
SADLY FOR KEI, BUT REFRESHINGLY FOR THE READER, SUCH A FEAT DOESN'T MAKE HIM A SUPERHERO. IN THE EYES OF BOTH THE GENERAL PUBLIC AND THE GOVERNMENT, HE'S A RARE SPECIMEN WHO NEEDS TO BE HUNTED DOWN AND HANDED OVER TO SCIENTISTS TO BE EXPERIMENTED ON FOR LIFE—A DEMI-HUMAN WHO MUST DIE A THOUSAND DEATHS FOR THE BENEFIT OF HUMANITY.
ALL 17 VOLUMES AVAILABLE NOW!
© GAMON SAKURAI / KODANSHA, LTD.

A P O S I M Z

**VOLUMES 1-8
AVAILABLE NOW!**

**T S U T O M U
N I H E I**

On a frigid, massive artificial planet known as Aposimz...

Eo, Biko, and Etherow, residents of the White Diamond Beam, are in the middle of combat training when suddenly a girl appears, Rebedoan Empire soldiers in hot pursuit. The girl asks for their help in keeping safe a "code" and seven mysterious "bullets." This chance encounter marks a major shift in the fate of the entire planet...

The curtain rises on a grand new adventure from Tsutomu Nihei, the author of *BLAME!* and *Knights of Sidonia*.

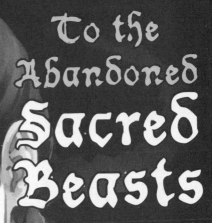

To the Abandoned Sacred Beasts

Presented by
MAYBE

During a protracted civil war that pitted the North against the South, the outnumbered Northerners used dark magical arts to create monstrous super-soldiers—Incarnates. Now that the war has ended, those Sacred Beasts must learn how to make their way in a peaceful society, or face death at the hands of a Beast Hunter.

Nancy Schaal Bancroft, the daughter of an Incarnate soldier who met an untimely end at the hands of one such Beast Hunter, turns to hunting the hunter. But once she catches up with her quarry, she discovers hard truths about the lives of the Incarnates...

VOLUMES 1-12 AVAILABLE NOW!

Blackguard 2

A VERTICAL Book

Editor: Michelle Lin
Translation: Melissa Tanaka
Production: Risa Cho
               Shirley Fang
               Lorina Mapa
Proofreading: Micah Q. Allen

First published in Japan in 2020 by Kodansha, Ltd., Tokyo
Publication for this English edition arranged through Kodansha, Ltd., Tokyo
English language version produced by Kodansha USA Publishing, LLC, 2022

Originally published in Japanese as *Burakkugarudo 2* by Kodansha, Ltd.
Burakkugarudo first serialized in *Gekkan Morning Two*, Kodansha, Ltd., 2019-2021

This is a work of fiction.

ISBN: 978-1-64729-116-7

Printed in the United States of America

First Edition

Kodansha USA Publishing, LLC
451 Park Avenue South
7th Floor
New York, NY 10016
www.kodansha.us

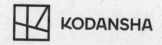

KODANSHA